**W9-BDU-224**

# The Gloria Anzaldúa Reader

A book in the series

LATIN AMERICA OTHERWISE: LANGUAGES, EMPIRES, NATIONS

Series editors:

Walter D. Mignolo, Duke University

Irene Silverblatt, Duke University

Sonia Saldívar-Hull, University of Texas, San Antonio

GLORIA E. ANZALDÚA

# The Gloria Anzaldúa Reader

AnaLouise Keating, editor

DUKE UNIVERSITY PRESS
DURHAM AND LONDON
2009

© 2009 The Gloria E. Anzaldúa Literary Trust
and AnaLouise Keating
All rights reserved
Printed in the United States of America
on acid-free paper ⊛
Designed by C. H. Westmoreland
Typeset in Quadraat
by Tseng Information Systems, Inc.
Library of Congress Cataloging-in-Publication
Data appear on the last printed page of
this book.

"Haciendo caras, una entrada." From
*Making Face, Making Soul/Haciendo caras.*
© 1990 by Gloria Anzaldúa. Reprinted by
permission of Aunt Lute Books.

"Metaphors in the Tradition of the Shaman."
From *Conversant Essays: Contemporary Poets
on Poetry,* edited by James McCorkle. © 1990
Wayne State University Press. Reprinted by
permission of Wayne State University Press.

"(Un)natural bridges, (Un)safe spaces."
From *this bridge we call home: radical visions for
transformation.* © 2002 by Gloria E. Anzaldúa.
Reprinted by permission of Routledge
Publishers.

frontispiece: photograph of Gloria Anzaldúa
by Victoria G. Alvarado

Para almas afines,
for everyone working to create
El Mundo Zurdo

# Contents

# Editor's Acknowledgments

> The act of writing is the act of making soul, alchemy. It is the quest for the self, for the center of the self, which we women of color have come to think of as "other"—the dark, the feminine. Didn't we start writing to reconcile this other within us? We knew we were different, set apart, exiled from what is considered "normal," white-right. And as we internalized this exile, we came to see the alien within us and too often, as a result, we split apart from ourselves and each other. Forever after we have been in search of that self, that "other," and each other.—GLORIA ANZALDÚA, "Speaking in Tongues"

Where to begin? With Gloria Anzaldúa, of course. Perhaps it goes without saying, but my biggest debt and greatest thanks is to Gloria herself. Gloria, the alchemist. Gloria, the nepantlera. Thank you, comadre, for your relentless acts of making soul, for your tireless quest for the self, for your other—which resonates so deeply with so many others, with our selves. Plunging so deeply into your work—sacrificing so much in the process—you give us lifelines enabling us to find ourselves and each other. Your words build community. Their intimacy reverberates with me, as with so many others, assisting us as we heal our own internal splits and self-alienation, assisting us as we transform ourselves and the world. Thank you for your writing, Gloria. And, on a more personal note, thank you for your friendship, mentorship, and support.

Many other people played roles in bringing this collection to print. Kit Quan, executor of Gloria's estate and co-trustee of the Gloria E. Anzaldúa Literary Trust, has been instrumental. Without Kit's tireless work over the past few years, without her wise advice, deep knowledge of Gloria, and steady counsel, this book would not be in print. Thanks to Hilda Anzaldúa for her ongoing support, faith in the power of Gloria's words, and rescue of Gloria's early writings. Thanks to Irene Reti for her friendship, wisdom, staunch support, and work on behalf of Gloria's writings and archives. Thanks to Sonia Saldívar-Hull, whose frequent encouragement, insights, advice, and other forms of support have been invaluable. Thanks to the anonymous readers of earlier versions of this manuscript whose suggestions greatly improved the finished product. Thanks to Christian Kelleher and the staff at the Nettie Lee Benson Latin American Collection for sending me copies of manuscripts, letters, and other archival material. Thanks to Gail Orlando, whose assistance saved me (literally!) hundreds of hours, and thanks to Colleen Moore for making all those index cards. Thanks to Glenda Lehrmann, the Faculty Information and Research Support Team librarian at Texas Woman's University, for assistance with reference material.

I am deeply grateful for the expertise of professors María Herrera Sobek and Francisco Lomelí, who took time out of their busy schedules to thoroughly proofread the manuscript and offer vital feedback on the Spanish, Náhuatl, and English; thank you, Professor Herrera Sobek, for agreeing to do this work and for enlisting Professor Lomelí's assistance. The folks at Duke University Press have been a joy to work with. I greatly appreciate Reynolds Smith's excitement about this project, as well as his ongoing encouragement and advice; Sharon Torian, Anil Aktaran, and Molly Balikov have been terrific. I thank Renae Bredin, Norma Cantú, Gloria González-López, Irene Lara, and Chela Sandoval, who have offered many forms of friendship, feedback, and support. I appreciate Liliana Wilson's generosity in sharing her work and memories of Gloria. Carrie McMaster (first student, now friend) has offered wise advice at key moments in the editorial process. Thanks to Claire L. Sahlin, for suggesting that I teach a graduate seminar on Gloria Anzaldúa, for supporting my research and Anzaldúa-focused teaching, and for being a great colleague, program director, and friend.

For the past several years, students in my graduate seminars on Anzaldúa have been inspirational; their excitement about Anzaldúa and great insights into her work have often sustained me, and I'm grateful. I especially thank those in my 2007 seminar (Tara Conley, Allison Davis, Giovanni Dortch, Rachel Duhon, Aleda Reyes, Lisa Thomas-McNew, Pamela White, and Dana Wilson) and my 2008 seminar (Tonya Bruton, Ellen Chenoweth, Rozyln Johnson, Deborah Loe, Nona McCaleb, Karin Recer, and Donna Souder). Special thanks to Allison and Pamela for requesting and encouraging me to *teach* this seminar; to Dana for recommending that I include a glossary in this book; and to Nona for catching a variety of typos in the draft.

I thank my family, Eddy Lynton and Jamitrice KreChelle Keating-Lynton, for their patience, understanding, encouragement, generosity, and all-around support. I'm a very lucky person! Over the years, Gloria has been a constant presence in our lives, and you have had to share me—first with Gloria, my friend, the flesh-and-blood person, and now with her writings and writing projects. In my obsession to finish this project (and so many others), I've been an absent presence, at times. You have bolstered my spirits and energized me, and I lack the words to truly express my gratitude. And finally, as always, I thank the spirits, orishas, and ancestors.

# Introduction

*Reading Gloria Anzaldúa, Reading Ourselves . . .*
*Complex Intimacies, Intricate Connections*

> It's not on paper that you create but in your innards, in the gut and out
> of living tissue—*organic writing* I call it. . . . The meaning and worth of
> my writing is measured by how much I put myself on the line and how
> much nakedness I achieve. —GLORIA ANZALDÚA,
> "Speaking in Tongues: A Letter to Third World Women Writers" (1981)

Whenever I listen to my students or other readers as they engage with
Gloria Anzaldúa's writings, whether they're discussing her poetry, fiction, or prose, I am struck by the profound ways that her words resonate
with so many different types of people—not with everyone, of course, but
with a surprisingly wide range, including many who do not self-identify
as Chicana, Latina, feminist, lesbian, and/or queer. They are shocked by
the intimacy of Anzaldúa's insights; they feel like she's speaking directly
to them, like she's describing their own deeply buried secrets and beliefs.
They acknowledge the many differences between their embodied locations
and Anzaldúa's–differences including but not limited to her campesino[1]
upbringing in South Texas; the specific forms of alienation and oppression she experienced due to her health, color, culture, gender, economic
status, and sexuality; and/or her complex relationship to language. But
when they read Anzaldúa they feel a sense of familiarity more intense than
that experienced with most other authors.

I attribute Anzaldúa's ability to generate such complex intimacies at
least partially to her willingness to risk the personal,[2] to put herself "on
the line" and strive for an extreme degree of "nakedness," as she asserts in
"Speaking in Tongues," quoted in the epigraph to this chapter. Anzaldúa
performs radical acts of self-excavation; stripping away social masks and
conventions, she bares herself in her writings. By plunging so deeply into
the depths of her own experiences, no matter how painful those experiences might be, and by exposing herself—raw and bleeding—she ex-
ternalizes her inner struggles and opens possible connections with her
readers.

1

The oldest child of sixth-generation mexicanos from the Río Grande Valley of south Texas,[3] Anzaldúa interacted with people and ideas from a number of divergent worlds yet refused to be contained within any single group, belief system, or geographical/political/psychic location. Thus in her early autohistoria,[4] "La Prieta," she defiantly maintains multiple allegiances and locates herself, simultaneously, in multiple worlds:

> "Your allegiance is to La Raza, the Chicano movement," say the members of my race. "Your allegiance is to the Third World," say my Black and Asian friends. "Your allegiance is to your gender, to women," say the feminists. Then there's my allegiance to the Gay movement, to the socialist revolution, to the New Age, to magic and the occult. And there's my affinity to literature, to the world of the artist. What am I? *A third world lesbian feminist with Marxist and mystic leanings.* They would chop me up into little fragments and tag each piece with a label.[5]

Although each group makes membership contingent on its own often exclusionary set of rules and demands, Anzaldúa refuses all such terms without rejecting the people or groups themselves. Instead, she moves within, between, and among these diverse, sometimes conflicting, worlds. She positions herself on the thresholds—simultaneously inside and outside—and establishes points of connection with people of diverse backgrounds:

> You say my name is ambivalence? Think of me as Shiva, a many-armed and -legged body with one foot on brown soil, one on white, one in straight society, one in the gay world, the man's world, the women's, one limb in the literary world, another in the working class, the socialist, and the occult worlds. A sort of spider woman hanging by one thin strand of web.
>
> Who, me, confused? Ambivalent? Not so. Only your labels split me.

Anzaldúa's bold assertion illustrates her personal integrity, holistic politics, and provocative challenges to conventional thinking. Whereas many progressive social-justice activists and theorists in the late 1970s and early 1980s were banding together into identity-specific groups, Anzaldúa was not. She rejected the demands for monolithic identities and exclusive, single-issue alliances and invented new forms of relational, inclusionary identities based on affinity rather than social categories.[6] As she explains in one of her final essays, "(Un)natural bridges, (Un)safe spaces," "Many of us identify with groups and social positions not limited to our ethnic, racial, religious, class, gender, or national classifications. Though most people self-define by what they exclude, we define who we are by what we include—what I call the new tribalism."[7] In this passage, as in much of her work, Anzaldúa models a flexible process for personal and collective identity formation, ethical action, and alliance building.[8] I want to underscore the radical implications of Anzaldúa's approach. Generally, identification functions through exclusion: we define who and what we are by defining who and what we are not. By shifting the focus from *exclusion* to *inclusion*, Anzaldúa invites us to reconfigure identity in open-ended, potentially transformative ways.

> Shortest bio GEA: Feminist visionary spiritual activist poet-philosopher fiction writer—GLORIA ANZALDÚA, Journal (2002)

Although generally defined by others as a "Chicana lesbian-feminist" author, Anzaldúa described herself more broadly. As the above ultra-short biographical statement indicates, she viewed herself in extremely expansive terms. Rather than emphasize her racial/cultural identity, sexuality, gender, or class, she foregrounds her thinking and writing, her spirit-inflected politics and texts. As I will explain in more detail later, this collection builds on and showcases Anzaldúa's complex, unconventional self-definition.

A versatile, award-winning writer,[9] Anzaldúa published poetry, theoretical essays, short stories, innovative autobiographical narratives (or what she calls *autohistorias* and *autohistoria-teorías*),[10] interviews, children's books, and multigenre anthologies. She is best known for *Borderlands/La Frontera: The New Mestiza* (1987), a hybrid combination of poetry and prose, which was named one of the 100 Best Books of the Century by both *Hungry Mind Review* and the *Utne Reader*.[11] Anzaldúa's published works also include a number of essays and several short stories, a handful of poems, as well as the following books: *This Bridge Called My Back: Writings by Radical Women of Color* (1981), a groundbreaking collection of essays, poetry, and letters coedited with Cherríe Moraga and widely recognized by scholars as a premiere feminist text; *Making Face, Making Soul/Haciendo Caras: Creative and Critical Perspectives by Feminists-of-Color* (1990), a multigenre edited collection of feminist theorizing by self-identified women of colors;[12] two bilingual children's books: *Friends from the Other Side/Amigos del otro lado* (1993) and *Prietita and the Ghost Woman/Prietita y La Llorona* (1995); *Interviews/Entrevistas* (2000), a memoir-like volume of her interviews; and *this bridge we call home: radical visions for transformation* (2002), a multigenre transcultural collection (which she co-edited with me) that calls for and enacts new modes of feminist/womanist theorizing, social-justice movements, and spiritual activism.

Anzaldúa was a prolific, full-time author, and these diverse publications represent only a small fraction of her extensive work. For the last twenty-seven years of her life, she made writing her primary focus. When she moved from Texas to California in 1977, she resolved to dedicate herself entirely to the writing, and for the rest of her life she did so, refusing to take full-time jobs or to do anything else that might detract from what she called "la musa bruja" and her work. She paid a large price for this commitment, sacrificing her health, her family, and her friends whenever this "witch-muse" called.[13] At the time of her passing, Anzaldúa had completed or was nearing completion on many projects, including (but not limited to!) a variety of essays, several collections of short stories and books of poetry; a novel-in-stories; a writing manual; a book of daily meditations; a young-adult novel; a play in poetic verse; a book-length exploration of imagination, creative writing, and social change; and a co-edited multi-genre collection. A number of these manuscripts are complete and had been thoroughly revised. While I cannot know for sure why Gloria did not publish more of her work, I believe that her chronic illness,[14] coupled with her perfectionist sensibilities and issues related to racism and betrayal, made her extremely cautious.

This collection contains a representative sampling of Anzaldúa's work covering a thirty-year span of her career. My selection process was guided by three primary interrelated goals. First, I wanted the book to be useful for a wide variety of readers, ranging from those who are entirely unfamiliar with Anzaldúa and her writings to scholars who have studied her works for years. Second, I wanted to showcase Anzaldúa's diversity in topics, genres, and approaches so that even the most "expert" readers might be startled by her range and gain insights into the diverse, intertwined layers of her work. And third, I wanted to respect and remain true to Anzaldúa's carefully considered aesthetics, stylistic preferences, complex self-definition, and holistic vision.

These goals shaped the volume in significant ways. In addition to a wide range of Anzaldúa's published and previously unpublished work, a detailed index, and brief introductions to each piece, the *Reader* contains several appendices: a glossary of common Anzaldúan theories and terms, a timeline with some highlights from Anzaldúa's life, and a bibliography of primary and secondary publications. I have included many of Anzaldúa's best-known published writings, as well as some frequently overlooked publications. Originally, I had hoped to reprint two very different chapters from *Borderlands*: "La conciencia de la mestiza/Towards a Mestiza Consciousness" and "La herencia de Coatlicue/The Coatlicue State."[15] While the former is one of Anzaldúa's most frequently quoted, discussed, and reprinted pieces, the latter is rarely excerpted in anthologies or examined in Anzaldúan scholarship. Given its provocative linkages between spirituality, sexuality, revisionary myth, and psychic experience, it's not surprising that scholars rarely examine "La herencia de Coatlicue."[16] However, these issues were crucial to Anzaldúa herself and represent some of the most innovative, visionary dimensions of her work.

I also include pieces designed to highlight Anzaldúa's interests in the visual arts and education, as well as her role in the genesis of queer theory. As a child, Anzaldúa painted, drew, and did other forms of art. As she explains in *Interviews/Entrevistas*, she seriously considered a career in the visual arts before deciding to focus on literature. In this volume, "Border Arte: Nepantla, El Lugar de la Frontera," "Bearing Witness: Their Eyes Anticipate the Healing," and Anzaldúa's own drawings (in the gallery of images) reflect her intense interest in this area. Throughout her life, Anzaldúa explored education-related issues; she had her teaching certificate and taught a wide variety of students, ranging from prekindergarten to doctoral.[17] Two previously unpublished pieces, "The New Mestiza Nation" and "Transforming American Studies," as well as the interview with Linda Smuckler, illustrate some of her pedagogical interests. I selected "La Prieta," "To(o) Queer the Writer," and "El paisano is a bird of good omen," as well as previously unpublished poems like "The Occupant" and "The coming of el mundo surdo," to emphasize Anzaldúa's formative role in developing queer theory, a role that theorists generally overlook. Why have theorists so often ignored Anzaldúa's groundbreaking contributions to queer theory? I don't know. Do many heterosexually identified scholars fear being censured or labeled as gay? Do they simply not see the provocative, transgressive elements in her work? Are most queer theorists so Eurocentric or masculinist in their text selections that they have entirely ignored *This Bridge Called My Back*, where Anzaldúa's queer theorizing first occurs in print?

Many readers also overlook or seem to be unaware of Anzaldúa's lifelong struggles with her health. Due to a rare hormonal imbalance, Anzaldúa began menstruating while still an infant and went through puberty when only six years old (she had a hysterectomy in 1980). Throughout her childhood, she was marked by this physical difference in ways that profoundly shaped her work, giving her an expansive, nuanced understanding of difference as well as tremendous compassion for those who are marked as outside the norm.[18] These health-related issues were central to Anzaldúa herself; readers interested in exploring this aspect of her life and her work might find the previously unpublished "Disability & Identity: An Email Exchange & a Few Additional Thoughts" especially useful. This piece, which began as an email exchange between Gloria, my students, and me, was one of Anzaldúa's final writings. (She was revising it into an essay during the last year of her life.)

Over half of the material in this volume has not been previously published, and many of the previously published pieces are currently out of print. As I sorted through the enormous amount of unpublished writings, trying to decide what to include, I was guided by my desires to introduce readers to additional aspects of Anzaldúa and her work and to trace her theoretical and aesthetic development. Thus, for example, I selected the interview with Linda Smuckler because it offers a complex, multifaceted view of Anzaldúa, focusing on the relationship between spirituality, sexuality, and her work. Drawn from two very different points in Anzaldúa's career (1982 and 1998), this interview also enables us to chart important shifts and continuities in Anzaldúa's thought. Other pieces, like "Creativity and Shifting Modes of Consciousness," "On the Process of Writing *Borderlands/La Frontera*," "Dream of the Double-Faced Woman," "Memoir— My Calling; or, Notes for 'How Prieta Came to Write,'" "How to," and "When I write I hover" offer fascinating insights into Anzaldúa's writing process, *Borderlands'* origins, and other writing-related issues.

Because many readers view Anzaldúa almost exclusively as a prose writer, it seemed especially important that this collection also highlight her poetry, fiction, and experimental autohistorias.[19] From the early 1970s until the end of her life, Anzaldúa defined herself as a poet and fiction writer and spent much of her energy in these genres. At the time of her death, she had written over forty stories, including *La Prieta/The Dark One*, a novel-in-stories, which she viewed as one of the highlights of her career. As she explains in her writing notas,[20] *La Prieta* is

> about transformation and metamorphosis, about the relation between nature and culture, between humans and animals. The stories interweave the surreal, unconscious subreality of the inner world of thought, fantasy, and dream and the world of the spirit with the everyday life. All converge at the liminal space I call nepantla, the interface space between all the worlds.

Prieta experiences a sense of self that is and is not tied to time, space, or society. She experiences unusual events—a shamanistic event which awakens her, or a paranormal event where different realities converge. She undergoes a radical shift in her way of seeing the world, a coming-to-consciousness which changes her identity.

As this description indicates, Anzaldúa interwove many of her own theories and philosophical concerns into her fiction. Indeed, she viewed her fiction as central to her entire creative process and a major catalyst for her thinking. In addition to including one of the stories from La Prieta, I have included two previously published short stories: "El paisano is a bird of good omen" and "Ghost Trap." These stories are fascinating on many levels, including (but not limited to) gender relations, sexuality, social conventions, and paranormal perception.

> I write because it's my calling, my task to do in the world. I write. It is a ritual, a habit, a propensity bred in my bones. It is what I do. I write because I like to think on paper. I write because I like to think, and to track my thoughts. I write because I want to leave a discernable mark on the world. —GLORIA ANZALDÚA, "When I write I hover" (1997)

I first met Gloria Anzaldúa back in 1991 and began working closely with her a few years later when, through a series of serendipitous events, I edited a volume of her interviews. After this collection, Interviews/Entrevistas, was accepted for publication, we began collaborating on several more projects. Working so intimately with Gloria gave me many insights into her intense writing and revision process. As she indicates in the preceding epigraph, writing was her vocation, her mission in life, her "task to do in the world." Perhaps not surprisingly, then, Anzaldúa approached her writing like a ritual or a prayer. Her creative process was thoughtful, recursive, and communal, involving extensive research, multiple, heavily revised drafts, and peer critiques with her "writing comadres" and others. Seeking precisely the exact word or term which could most effectively convey her meaning to a specific audience, she carefully examined and revised each metaphor and analogy, every sentence, paragraph, line of poetry, and stanza.[21] She could happily devote an entire day to revising a handful of pages; she could spend weeks, months, or even years revising her work. Especially during the last phase of her career, Gloria did not want to release a manuscript for publication until she felt that it was ready— "ready" as she defined the term, not as others might. In fact, the publication of our co-edited book, *this bridge we call home*, was delayed by an entire year because she absolutely refused to stop revising her essay "now let us shift."[22] Similarly, she was very reluctant to publish "Let us be the healing of the wounds: the Coyolxauhqui imperative—la sombra y el sueño" (included in this volume) because she wanted to revise it further. Only the impassioned pleas of the book's editors, combined with encouragement from her writing comadres, compelled her to permit the essay's publication.

I describe Anzaldúa's meticulous, spirit-inflected approach to her art as "shaman aesthetics" to underscore her faith in language and imagination, her belief in writing's potentially transformative power. Anzaldúa posited an intimate interrelationship between image, metaphor, and change. Thus in "Metaphors in the Tradition of the Shaman" she maintains that writers' words enter into and transform their readers: "Like the shaman, we transmit information from our consciousness to the physical body of another." Throughout her work, Anzaldúa attempts to enact this transformation. Her careful, deliberate writing process relies on rigorous self-excavation, multiple revisions, and extraordinary, painstaking attention to image, metaphor, and individual word choice. Flesh becomes text as she intensely self-reflects and strives for words that can move through the body, transforming herself and her readers on multiple levels.

Anzaldúa's two most influential works (thus far) are the multigenre co-edited collection *This Bridge Called My Back: Writings by Radical Women of Color* (1981) and her single-authored text *Borderlands/La Frontera: The New Mestiza* (1987). Widely regarded as a feminist classic, *This Bridge Called My Back* broke new ground. Bringing together U.S. women-of-color feminists from diverse ethnic/racial, economic, sexual, and national backgrounds, *This Bridge* offered a crucial challenge to conventional feminist theorizing and the mainstream women's movement in the United States.[23] Although some scholars describe *This Bridge* as women of colors's entry into the feminist movement, I see the book somewhat differently, as a crucial reminder that feminism was not and never had been a "white"-raced women's movement with a single-issue, middle-class agenda. Anzaldúa and the other contributors self-identified as feminists, and most had done so for many years before *This Bridge*'s publication. In *This Bridge Called My Back*, they remind readers that feminism, defined broadly and flexibly, offers crucial points of connection for social-justice workers of diverse backgrounds. Although they critique the racism, classism, and white supremacism within certain strands of feminism, they do not describe feminism itself as "white" or as belonging primarily to "white"-raced women.

Instead, they call for new kinds of feminist communities and practices; they simultaneously invite women of colors to develop new alliances and challenge "white" middle-class feminists to recognize and rectify their racism, classism, and other biases. Consisting of poetry, letters, analytical essays, interviews, and prose narratives, *This Bridge* also demonstrated the transformative possibilities that arise when we theorize in multiple genres and modes.

While *This Bridge* brought Anzaldúa important attention from feminists and led to numerous speaking engagements in the early 1980s, she is best-known for *Borderlands/La Frontera* (1987), an innovative blend of personal experience with history and social protest with poetry and myth. Although *Borderlands* resists easy classification, scholars often describe it as a complex cultural autobiography that builds on and expands previous uses of the genre. Anzaldúa herself describes this text as "autohistoria-teoría," a term she coined to describe women-of-color interventions into and transformations of traditional western autobiographical forms. Autohistoria-teoría includes both life-story and self-reflection on this story. Writers of autohistoria-teoría blend their cultural and personal biographies with memoir, history, storytelling, myth, and other forms of theorizing. By so doing, they create interwoven individual and collective identities. Frequently anthologized and often cited, *Borderlands* has challenged and expanded previous views in a number of academic fields, including (but not limited to) American studies, border studies, Chicano/a studies, composition studies, cultural studies, ethnic studies, feminism, literary studies, critical pedagogy, women's studies, and queer theory. As Sonia Saldívar-Hull notes, *Borderlands* is a "transfrontera, transdisciplinary text" that has "traveled between" many disciplines.[24]

Focusing especially on Anzaldúa's theories of the "Borderlands," the "new mestiza," and "mestiza consciousness," scholars have critiqued and revised their disciplinary paradigms and contemporary identity-based issues. *Borderlands* has also significantly impacted the ways we think about Chicano/a studies, border issues, the concept of the Borderlands, ethnic/gender/sexual identities, code-switching,[25] and conventional literary forms. Anzaldúa uses the term "Borderlands" in two complex, overlapping yet distinct ways. First, she builds on previous views of the borderlands as a specific geographical location: the Southwest border between Mexico and Texas. Second, she redefines and expands this concept to encompass psychic, sexual, and spiritual Borderlands as well. For Anzaldúa, the Borderlands—in both its geographical and metaphoric meanings—

represent painful yet also potentially transformational spaces where opposites converge, conflict, and transmute.

Anzaldúa's theory of the "new mestiza" has been equally influential and represents an innovative expansion of previous biologically based definitions of mestizaje. For Anzaldúa, "new mestizas" are people who inhabit multiple worlds because of their gender, sexuality, color, class, body, personality, spiritual beliefs, and/or other life experiences. This theory offers a new concept of personhood that synergistically combines apparently contradictory Euro-American and indigenous traditions. Anzaldúa further develops her theory of the new mestiza into an epistemology and ethics she calls "mestiza consciousness": holistic, relational modes of thinking and acting or, as she explains in "La conciencia de la mestiza," "a more whole perspective, one that includes rather than excludes."

As this *Reader* demonstrates, Anzaldúa's post-*Borderlands* writings expand these concepts and others in provocative ways. Thus, for example, her later theories transform the Borderlands into nepantla, new mestizas into nepantleras and nos/otras, and mestiza consciousness into conocimiento.[26] Perhaps because scholars, publishers, students, and others have focused so much of their attention on *Borderlands*, these theories have not yet received the attention they deserve. I hope that this volume will encourage readers to explore Anzaldúa's later writings in more detail and recognize the important developments she made in the years following the publication of *Borderlands*.

In editing this volume, I have tried to respect Anzaldúa's wishes and follow her intentions as closely as possible. Thanks to the years we spent working together, I developed a solid understanding of her literary expectations and aesthetics, her beliefs about what constitutes good writing, and her personal standards as an author. Because she was such a perfectionist, I seriously debated including a few pieces, like "Creativity and Switching Modes of Consciousness" and "On the Process of Writing *Borderlands*," which are not as polished as Gloria might prefer. However, I decided that these essays give us such valuable insights into her work that they should be available to a broad readership. Although Anzaldúa sometimes (often!) continued revising her work after publishing it, I usually included the earliest published versions rather than the later revisions because we anticipate publishing the revised versions at a later date.[27] I did stray from this practice in two ways: First, and in keeping with Gloria's strongly expressed preference, I chose not to italicize Spanish, Náhuatl, or other non-English words. As Gloria often explained, such italics have a denormalizing, stigmatizing function and make the italicized words seem like deviations from the (English/"white") norm. Second, in instances when the published versions had typographical errors and in instances when there was a lack of clarity (probably generated by the publishing process itself), I went back to the manuscripts in order to ascertain Anzaldúa's intentions. For those pieces which were previously unpublished, I generally used the most recent versions. Throughout this volume, the footnotes are my own, designed to provided additional information that might be helpful to readers. The endnotes are Anzaldúa's original notes. Editorial additions to these notes are placed in square brackets.

I have arranged the selections chronologically, divided into three periods marked by specific points in Anzaldúa's publication history: The "early writings" cover her work up to and including the second edition of *This Bridge Called My Back* (1983); the "middle writings" include work shortly before and after *Borderlands* (1987); and the "late writings" include her work from the mid-to-late 1990s until her death in 2004. I made these divisions somewhat arbitrarily (one decade per "period") and for my own convenience the first time I taught a graduate seminar on Anzaldúa. However, as my students and I made our way through the writings, I realized that these divisions can reflect distinct periods in Anzaldúa's career: a spiraling yet cyclical movement, a contraction followed by an expansion of sorts. More specifically, Anzaldúa's writings from the early and late periods are broadly inclusive, at times positing a global citizenship of sorts, while some of her work from the middle period is less inclusionary, more focused on rigid identity labels and categories, and (therefore) more restrictive.[28]

Indeed, some of my students have reacted quite strongly to a few of Anzaldúa's pieces from this middle period, insisting that Anzaldúa seems to rely on stereotypes and monolithic categories; this reliance leads to broad generalizations that entirely reject those labeled "white," male, and/or members of the dominating culture. In short, these student readers, when focusing solely on some of Anzaldúa's work from this middle period, feel as if they have been reduced to a false stereotype and actively excluded from her theories. I caution against such assumptions. As I've explained to my students, we need to read each piece in (at least) two contexts: first, the original audience and historical period, keeping in mind Anzaldúa's experiences at that time; and second, the full trajectory of Anzaldúa's work, a trajectory energized by her attempts to forge inclusionary, community-building theories and endeavors. Moreover, even during her more exclusionary moments, Anzaldúa enacts inclusionary gestures. (See, for instance, "The New Mestiza Nation," where she writes, "Progressive whites who have friends from different worlds and who study different cultures become intellectual mestizas. They may not be emotional mestizas and certainly are not biological mestizas. But there can be empathy between people of color and progressive, sensitive, politically aware whites.")

> I believe in free dialogue & abhor academic censorship of any kind, especially that which seeks to "protect" me or "my" image. . . . Any of you estudiantes, please feel free to unravel these concepts (or any other of "my" concepts)—once they go out into the world they cease to "belong" to me.—GLORIA ANZALDÚA,
> "Identity & Disability" (2003)

This statement, written only seven months before her death, illustrates Anzaldúa's generous attitude toward her literary reputation and her work. Once she had released her words "into the world," she tried to detach her ego from them. They were not her personal, private words but "belonged" to anyone who read them. Gloria was not possessive about her theories and ideas—except in those instances when others tried to police the meanings, circumscribe the definitions in narrow terms, and/or appropriate her ideas and pass them off as their own.[29] She was fascinated by the various ways people interpreted her work, and she often wove their interpretations into her later writings.[30] She did not believe that any particular person or group—not Chicanas, not queers, not women, not tejanas, not mexicanas, not personal friends or colleagues—had an exclusive, superior, insider perspective into her theories and her writings. Anzaldúa's inclusionary vision, coupled with her ability to create expansive new categories and interconnections, makes her work vital to contemporary social actors, thinkers, and scholars.

And so, I close with an invitation, from Anzaldúa herself, to build on and "unravel" Anzaldúa's words, to remember and enact her bold insights and holistic, relational vision.

## Notes

Thanks to Pamela White for reading and commenting on this introduction.

1. In keeping with Anzaldúa's own preference, I do not italicize Spanish, Náhuatl, or other non-English words. Italicizing non-English words denormalizes them.

2. I describe this radical self-reflective process as *risking the personal* to underscore the dangers involved. For more on this topic, see my introduction to Anzaldúa's *Interviews/Entrevistas*. Keating, "Risking the Personal: An Introduction."

3. For extensive biographical information, see the timeline located in the second appendix.

4. "Autohistoria" is a term Anzaldúa coined to describe a specific type of self-writing. For more information, see the glossary in the first appendix.

5. All Anzaldúa quotations, except those from her journals, are drawn from pieces included in this volume.

6. In her later writings Anzaldúa explores these affinity-driven identities in her theory of "new tribalism." See also her theories of El Mundo Zurdo and nepantleras.

7. Anzaldúa, "(Un)natural bridges, (Un)safe spaces," 3.

8. Unlike conventional forms of "tribalism," which generally rely on very specific forms of kinship-based identity and belonging, Anzaldúa's new tribalism relies on an open-ended process of personal affinities, self-selection, and political commitments.

9. Anzaldúa won numerous awards, including the Before Columbus Foundation American Book Award, the Lamda Lesbian Small Book Press Award, an NEA Fiction Award, the Lesbian Rights Award, the Sappho Award of Distinction, and the American Studies Association Lifetime Achievement Award.

10. Anzaldúa coined these terms to describe the innovative forms of autobiographical writings that she and some other contemporary writers, especially women-of-color authors, employ. For more on these topics, see the glossary.

11. I mention these accolades by *Hungry Mind Review* and the *Utne Reader* because they were so important to Anzaldúa herself. I think that she valued the fact that *Borderlands* had an audience beyond the academy.

12. I use the phrase "women of colors" rather than "women of color" to underscore our complex diversity.

13. For more on Anzaldúa's determination to focus her life on her writing, see her "On the Process of Writing *Borderlands/La Frontera*" and "Memoir—My Calling," included in this volume.

14. In 1992 Anzaldúa was diagnosed with Type 1 diabetes, but even before this she had endured a number of chronic physical conditions throughout her life, including a hormonal imbalance that led to childhood menstruation and a hysterectomy in 1980.

15. Unfortunately, due to the stipulations and concerns of *Borderlands*' publisher, I was unable to include any material from *Borderlands* in this reader; however, several pieces in part 2 serve a similar representative function and reflect Anzaldúa's thinking during this period. See especially "Encountering the Medusa," "Del Otro Lado," "Creativity and Switching Modes of Consciousness," "On the Process of Writing *Borderlands / La Frontera*," and "The New Mestiza Nation: A Multicultural Movement." Everyone interested in Anzaldúa should read *Borderlands* in its entirety.

16. Anzaldúa made a similar point: "The 'safe' elements in *Borderlands* are pro-created and used, and the 'unsafe' elements are not talked about. One of the things that doesn't get talked about is the connection between body, mind, and spirit—anything that has to do with the sacred, anything that has to do with the spirit. As long as it's theoretical, if it's about history or about borders, that's fine, that's something [scholars and other readers] want; talking about borders is a concern that everybody has. But if you start talking about nepantla—this border between the spirit, the psyche, and the mind—they resist." For exceptions to this resistance, see María Lugones's work and my *Women Reading Women Writing*.

17. From 1969 to 1973, Anzaldúa was employed as a teacher and taught a range of classes, preschool through high school; in 1972 she obtained her M.A. in English and education; and during 1973–74 she served as the liaison between the Indiana public school system and migrant farm workers' children. For the remainder of her life she periodically taught writing workshops, as well as occasional literature and creative writing courses at various universities. For a description of Anzaldúa's teaching style, see Caren Neile's "The 1,000-Piece Nights of Gloria Anzaldúa," which offers a first-person account of a graduate course Anzaldúa taught in 2001.

18. For more on Anzaldúa's health, see her *Interviews/Entrevistas* and my "Working towards Wholeness."

19. Thanks to one of the anonymous readers for encouraging me to include a wide variety of genres. For important exceptions to scholars' focus on Anzaldúa's prose, see Linda Garber's work on Anzaldúa's poetry, Mary Loving Blanchard's exploration of Anzaldúa's short story, and Edith Vásquez's analysis of Anzaldúa's children's books.

20. I borrow the term *writing notas* from Anzaldúa herself, who used it to describe the hundreds of pages of notes she made as part of her writing process. These notas can be found in her archives at the Nettie Benson Library, University of Texas, Austin.

21. For Anzaldúa's own words on her writing and revision process, see "How to" and "Memoir—My Calling," both included in this volume.

22. Gloria wrote over thirty drafts of this essay. The drafts can be found at her archives, located at the Benson Library.

23. For discussions of *Bridge*'s influence, see Norma Alarcón, "The Theoretical Subject(s) of *This Bridge Called My Back* and Anglo-American Feminism"; Rebecca Aanerud, "Thinking Again"; Cynthia Franklin, *Writing Women's Communities*; and my "Charting Pathways."

24. Saldívar-Hull, "Introduction to the Second Edition," 12–13.

25. At its most general, "code-switching" refers to shifting among various languages or dialects within a single language. For Anzaldúa, code-switching entailed transitions from standard to working-class English to Chicano Spanish to Spanglish to Náhuatl-Aztec. At the time *Borderlands* was first published, scholars generally viewed such code-switching in highly negative terms.

26. For more on these Anzaldúan theories, see the glossary and index. For a

discussion of the ways Anzaldúa built on her *Borderlands* theories, see also my introduction to *EntreMundos/AmongWorlds*.

27. I am referring specifically to "To(o) Queer the Writer," "Border Arte," and the foreword to *The Encyclopedia of Queer Myth, Symbol and Spirit*.

28. For examples of Anzaldúa's inclusionary phases, see "La Prieta" and "Let us be the healing of the wound"; for examples of her less inclusive phase, see "Haciendo caras, una entrada," "Border Arte," and "Bridge, Drawbridge, Sandbar or Island." For an example of Anzaldúa's transition from exclusionary to inclusionary, see her "The New Mestiza Nation."

29. See Anzaldúa's interview with Debbie Blake and Carmen Abrego in her *Interviews/Entrevistas*.

30. Anzaldúa's theory of new tribalism is one of the most obvious examples of this interweaving. As she explains in "now let us shift," she borrowed the term from a scholar who used it to criticize her work.

# Part One

## "Early" Writings

I am a wind-swayed bridge, a crossroads inhabited by whirlwinds. Gloria, the facilitator, Gloria, the mediator, straddling the walls between abysses. "Your allegiance is to La Raza, the Chicano movement," say the members of my race. "Your allegiance is to the Third World," say my Black and Asian friends. "Your allegiance is to your gender, to women," say the feminists. Then there's my allegiance to the Gay movement, to the socialist revolution, to the New Age, to magic and the occult. And there's my affinity to literature, to the world of the artist. What am I? *A third world lesbian feminist with Marxist and mystic leanings.* They would chop me up into little fragments and tag each piece with a label.

You say my name is ambivalence? Think of me as Shiva, a many-armed and -legged body with one foot on brown soil, one on white, one in straight society, one in the gay world, the man's world, the women's, one limb in the literary world, another in the working class, the socialist, and the occult worlds. A sort of spider woman hanging by one thin strand of web.

Who, me, confused? Ambivalent? Not so. Only your labels split me.

—From "La Prieta"

This poem, written in 1974 and published in 1976 in *Tejidos*, a literary journal, was Anzaldúa's first publication. Adopting the voice of an Aztec ceremonial knife, Anzaldúa explores issues that recur throughout her work. Significantly, Anzaldúa included this poem in her poetry manuscript version of *Borderlands* (1985) and titled the manuscript's first section "Tihueque / Now let us go."

## TIHUEQUE[1]

One year in a distant century during Teoteco,
The 12th month of the solar year Five Rabbit,
in the reign of the Four-Water Sun,
I carved 12,000 hearts in honor
of Huitziltopochtli, God of War,
who made the sun rise each morning.

In each succeeding year thereafter
ceremonial drunkenness robbed me
as many hearts embraced the furnace sacrifice.
Only the hearts of the finest Náhuatl braves
and luckiest prisoners and warriors
ate the sacred flesh.

Today I lie in a musty museum
and register 5.5 on Mohs scale.
But my origin, volcanic obsidian,
hard as granite
comes in good stead.

In my childhood I was a mirror.
I threw a vitreous luster, dark-green.
But now the iron oxide running in my veins
dulls my edge
and the air bubbles trapped in me
reflect my age.
        Time passes.
        I rest and await the flesh.

1. Náhuatl word meaning "Now let us go."

In this poem, written in 1974 and never before published, Anzaldúa draws from and reflects on her experiences teaching in the south Texas public school system.

## To Delia, Who Failed on Principles

Because of four lousy points
Delia, a senior, repeating
A sophomore course
      Failed.

Short of hair, cow-eyed, humble-proud
From cooking class brought me cookies
From Oregon, an apple. But I stuck to
      My principles.

In arbitrary tests the high score
Of momentarily memorized words and facts
I passed, but you
      Didn't graduate.

I stuck to my principles
And for a week couldn't sleep
The following year
I passed all repeaters who tried
      On principle.

Written in 1974, this previously unpublished poem resonates strongly with sections of *Borderlands/La Frontera* and "The New Mestiza Nation," indicating that even in the early 1970s, Anzaldúa defined herself in terms of multiplicity and transformation.

# Reincarnation

*for Julie*

I

slithered shedding

my  self

on the path

then

looked back and

contemplated

the husk

and wondered

which me

I had discarded

and was it the second

or the two thousand and

thirty-second

and how many me's

would I slough off

before voiding

the core

if ever

June 20, 1974
South Bend, IN

Anzaldúa often included this never before published poem, written in the mid-1970s, in her poetry readings during the early 1980s. Titled in earlier drafts "One of Us" and "Possession," this short poem illustrates Anzaldúa's challenges to conventional concepts of identity and relationships.

## The Occupant

I wake one morning
to his body filling mine
I watch him crowd my
entrails out through my navel
His head's too snug in mine
the pressure's making my skull plate flap
like the cover of a boiling kettle
A cock's growing out of my cunt
I'm getting hair on my chest
I'm for sharing
but this is absurd

One of us has got to go

One of us is going to
occupy the other to death
One of us is going to emerge sobbing
with sorrow from the bloody
remnant of the other.

This previously unpublished poem, written in 1974, was one that Anzaldúa sometimes read at poetry readings during the late 1970s and early 1980s. In its expression of a desire to be radically transformed and inspired, the poem offers interesting insights into her aesthetics. (Note the connections with "Speaking in Tongues," also included in part 1.)

## I Want To Be
## Shocked Shitless

I'm afraid, I told them,
that you will open no gates for me,
that neither one of you will floor me.

I fear that the hooks
in your words will not grip me
that I will vanish
into that inner terrain
where none follow.
I fear you will bore me.

I know you will call me
on the awkward line,
the hollow word.
But the truths I don't uncover,
the visions I don't aim toward,
don't reach, will you——

I don't want to be told
what to write
I can excavate my own content
I want to be pushed into
digging deep wells
in unheard of lands.
I want you to give me eyes in
in the back of my head.
Be a thunder clap
and rouse me.
Be an earthquake
make me tremble
Be a river raging rampant
in my veins.
Shock me shitless.

This previously unpublished poem, written in the mid-1970s, offers insight into Anzaldúa's poetics and her beliefs about language, inspiration, and poets' roles in society. "The New Speakers" also seems to hint at some of Anzaldúa's own writerly desires.

## The New Speakers

(For Frieda)

Words are our trade
we speak them soft
we speak them hard
we do not push the hand
that writes, the times do that.
We are our age's mouthpiece.

There is no need for words
to fester in our minds
they germinate in the open
mouth of the barefoot child,
in the midst of restive crowds.
They wither in ivory towers
and are dissected in college classes.

Words. Some come trippingly
on the palate. Some come laboriously.
Some are quickened by friends,
some prompted by passersby.

Critics label the speakers: male, female.
They assign genitals to our words
but we're not just penises or vaginas
nor are our words easy to classify

Some of us are still hung-
up on the art-for-art trip
and feel that the poet
is forever alone.
Separate.
More sensitive.
An outcast.

That suffering is a way of life,
that suffering is a virtue
that suffering is the price
we pay for seeing the future.

Some of us are still hung up
substituting words for relationships
substituting writing for living.

But what we want
—what we presume to want—
is to see our words engraved
on the people's faces,
feel our words catalyze
emotions in their lives.
What we want is to become
part of the common consumption
like coffee with morning paper.

We don't want to be
Stars but parts
of constellations.

This epistolary essay, which Anzaldúa began drafting in 1979, was published in *This Bridge Called My Back: Writings by Radical Women of Color* (1981). Here Anzaldúa offers one of her most sustained discussions of writing and illustrates her career-long belief in the power of the written word.

## Speaking in Tongues

A Letter to Third World Women Writers[1]

21 mayo 80

Dear mujeres de color, companions in writing—
I sit here naked in the sun, typewriter against my knee, trying to visualize you. Black woman huddles over a desk in the fifth floor of some New York tenement. Sitting on a porch in south Texas, a Chicana fanning away mosquitos and the hot air, trying to arouse the smouldering embers of writing. Indian woman walking to school or work, lamenting the lack of time to weave writing into your life. Asian American, lesbian, single mother, tugged in all directions by children, lover, or ex-husband, and the writing.

It is not easy writing this letter. It began as a poem, a long poem. I tried to turn it into an essay but the result was wooden, cold. I have not yet unlearned the esoteric bullshit and pseudo-intellectualizing that school brainwashed into my writing.

How to begin again. How to approximate the intimacy and immediacy I want. What form? A letter, of course.

My dear hermanas, the dangers we face as women writers of color are not the same as those of white women, though we have many in common. We don't have as much to lose—we never had any privileges. I wanted to call the dangers "obstacles," but that would be a kind of lying. We can't *transcend* the dangers, can't rise above them. We must go through them and hope we won't have to repeat the performance.

Unlikely to be friends of people in high literary places, the beginning woman of color is invisible both in the white male mainstream world and in the white women's feminist world, though in the latter this is gradually changing. The *lesbian* of color is not only invisible, she doesn't even exist. Our speech, too, is inaudible. We speak in tongues like the outcast and the insane.

Because white eyes do not want to know us, they do not bother to learn our language, the language which reflects us, our culture, our spirit. The

26

schools we attended or didn't attend did not give us the skills for writing nor the confidence that we were correct in using our class and ethnic languages. I, for one, became adept at, and majored in, English to spite, to show up, the arrogant racist teachers who thought all Chicano children were dumb and dirty. And Spanish was not taught in grade school. And Spanish was not required in high school. And though now I write my poems in Spanish as well as English I feel the rip-off of my native tongue.

> I lack imagination you say
>
> No. I lack language.
> The language to clarify
> my resistance to the literate.
> Words are a war to me.
> They threaten my family.
>
> To gain the word
> to describe the loss
> I risk losing everything.
> I may create a monster
> the word's length and body
> swelling up colorful and thrilling
> looming over my mother, characterized.
> Her voice in the distance
> unintelligible illiterate.
> These are the monster's words.
> —CHERRÍE MORAGA[2]

Who gave us permission to perform the act of writing? Why does writing seem so unnatural for me? I'll do anything to postpone it—empty the trash, answer the telephone. The voice recurs in me: *Who am I, a poor Chicanita from the sticks, to think I could write?* How dare I even considered becoming a writer as I stooped over the tomato fields bending, bending under the hot sun, hands broadened and calloused, not fit to hold the quill, numbed into an animal stupor by the heat.

How hard it is for us to *think* we can choose to become writers, much less *feel* and *believe* that we can. What have we to contribute, to give? Our own expectations condition us. Does not our class, our culture as well as the white man tell us writing is not for women such as us?

The white man speaks: *Perhaps if you scrape the dark off of your face. Maybe if you bleach your bones. Stop speaking in tongues, stop writing left-handed. Don't cultivate your colored skins nor tongues of fire if you want to make it in a right-handed world.*

> "Man, like all the other animals, fears and is repelled by that
> which he does not understand, and mere difference is apt to connote
> something malign."—ALICE WALKER[3]

I think, yes, perhaps if we go to the university. Perhaps if we become male-women or as middleclass as we can. Perhaps if we give up loving women, we will be worthy of having something to say worth saying. They convince us that we must cultivate art for art's sake. Bow down to the sacred bull, form. Put frames and metaframes around the writing. Achieve distance in order to win the coveted title "literary writer" or "professional writer." Above all do not be simple, direct, nor immediate.

Why do they fight us? Because they think we are dangerous beasts? Why *are* we dangerous beasts? Because we shake and often break the whites' comfortable stereotypic images they have of us: the Black domestic, the lumbering nanny with twelve babies sucking her tits, the-slant-eyed Chinese with her expert hand—"They know how to treat a man in bed," the flat-faced Chicana or Indian, passively lying on her back, being fucked by the Man a la La Chingada.

The Third World woman revolts: *We revoke, we erase your white male imprint. When you come knocking on our doors with your rubber stamps to brand our faces with* DUMB, HYSTERICAL, PASSIVE PUTA, PERVERT, *when you come with your branding irons to burn* MY PROPERTY *on our buttocks, we will vomit the guilt, self-denial, and race-hatred you have force-fed into us right back into your mouth. We are done being cushions for your projected fears. We are tired of being your sacrificial lambs and scapegoats.*

I can write this, and yet I realize that many of us women of color who have strung degrees, credentials, and published books around our necks like pearls that we hang onto for dear life are in danger of contributing to the invisibility of our sister-writers. "La Vendida," the sell-out.

*The danger of selling out one's own ideologies.* For the Third World woman who has, at best, one foot in the feminist literary world, the temptation is great to adopt the current feeling fads and theory fads, the latest half truths in political thought, the half-digested new age psychological axioms that are preached by the white feminist establishment. Its followers are notorious for "adopting" women of color as their "cause" while still expecting us to adapt to their expectations and their language.

How dare we get out of our colored faces. How dare we reveal the human flesh underneath and bleed red blood like the white folks. It takes tremendous energy and courage not to acquiesce, not to capitulate to a definition of feminism that still renders most of us invisible. Even as I write this I am disturbed that I am the only Third World woman writer in this handbook. Over and over I have found myself to be the only Third World woman at readings, workshops, and meetings.

*We cannot allow ourselves to be tokenized. We must make our own writing and that of Third World women the first priority.* We cannot educate white women and take them by the hand. Most of us are willing to help, but we can't do the white woman's homework for her. That's an energy drain. More times than she cares to remember, Nellie Wong, Asian American feminist writer, has been called by white women wanting a list of Asian American women who can give readings or workshops. We are in danger of being reduced to purveyors of resource lists.

*Coming face to face with one's limitations. There are only so many things I can do in one day.* Luisah Teish, addressing a group of predominantly white feminist writers, had this to say of Third World women's experience:

> If you are not caught in the maze that [we] are in, it's very difficult to explain to you the hours in the day we do not have. And the hours that we do not have are hours that are translated into survival skills and money. And when one of those hours is taken away it means an hour that we don't have to lie back and stare at the ceiling or an hour that we don't have to talk to a friend. For me it's a loaf of bread.

> Understand.
> My family is poor.
> Poor. I can't afford
> a new ribbon. The risk
> of this one is enough
> to keep me moving
> through it, accountable.
> The repetition like my mother's
> stories retold, *each* time
> reveals more particulars
> gains more familiarity.

> You can't get me in your car so fast.
> —CHERRÍE MORAGA[4]

"Complacency is a far more dangerous attitude than outrage."
—NAOMI LITTLEBEAR[5]

Why am I compelled to write? Because the writing saves me from this complacency I fear. Because I have no choice. Because I must keep the spirit of my revolt and myself alive. Because the world I create in the writing compensates for what the real world does not give me. By writing I put order in the world, give it a handle so I can grasp it. I write because life does not appease my appetites and hunger. I write to record what others erase when I speak, to rewrite the stories others have miswritten about me, about you. To become more intimate with myself and you. To discover myself, to preserve myself, to make myself, to achieve self-autonomy. To dispel the myths that I am a mad prophet or a poor suffering soul. To convince myself that I am worthy and that what I have to say is not a pile of shit. To show that I *can* and that I *will* write, never mind their admonitions to the contrary. And I will write about the unmentionables, never mind the outraged gasp of the censor and the audience. Finally, I write because I'm scared of writing but I'm more scared of not writing.

*Why should I try to justify why I write? Do I need to justify being Chicana, being woman? You might as well ask me to try to justify why I'm alive.*

The act of writing is the act of making soul, alchemy. It is the quest for the self, for the center of the self, which we women of color have come to think of as "other"—the dark, the feminine. Didn't we start writing to reconcile this other within us? We knew we were different, set apart, exiled from what is considered "normal," white-right. And as we internalized this exile, we came to see the alien within us and too often, as a result, we split apart from ourselves and each other. Forever after we have been in search of that self, that "other," and each other. And we return, in widening spirals and never to the same childhood place where it happened, first in our families, with our mothers, with our fathers. The writing is a tool for piercing that mystery but it also shields us, gives a margin of distance, helps us survive. And those that don't survive? The waste of ourselves: so much meat thrown at the feet of madness or fate or the state.

24 mayo 80

It is dark and damp and has been raining all day. I love days like this. As I lie in bed I am able to delve inward. Perhaps today I will write from that deep core. As I grope for words and a voice to speak of writing, I stare at my brown hand clenching the pen and think of you thousands of miles away clutching your pen. You are not alone.

> Pen, I feel right at home in your ink doing a pirouette, stirring the cobwebs, leaving my signature on the window panes. Pen, how could I ever have feared you. You're quite house-broken, but it's your wildness I am in love with. I'll have to get rid of you when you start being predictable, when you stop chasing dustdevils. The more you outwit me the more I love you. It's when I'm tired or have had too much caffeine or wine that you get past my defenses and you say more than what I had intended. You surprise me, shock me into knowing some part of me I'd kept secret even from myself. —Journal entry*

In the kitchen María's and Cherríe's voices falling on these pages. I can see Cherríe going about in her terrycloth wrap, barefoot, washing the dishes, shaking out the tablecloth, vacuuming. Deriving a certain pleasure watching her perform those simple tasks, I am thinking *they lied, there is no separation between life and writing.*

The danger in writing is not fusing our personal experience and world view with the social reality we live in, with our inner life, our history, our economics, and our vision. What validates us as human beings validates us as writers. What matters to us is the relationships that are important to us whether with our self or with others. We must use what is important to us to get to the writing. *No topic is too trivial.* The danger is in being too universal and humanitarian and invoking the eternal to the sacrifice of the particular and the feminine and the specific historical moment.

The problem is to focus, to concentrate. The body distracts, sabotages with a hundred ruses, a cup of coffee, pencils to sharpen. The solution is to anchor the body to a cigarette or some other ritual. And who has time or energy to write after nurturing husband or lover, children, and often an outside job? The problems seem insurmountable and they are, but they cease being insurmountable once we make up our mind that whether married or childrened or working outside jobs we are going to make time for the writing.

Forget the room of one's own—write in the kitchen, lock yourself up in the bathroom. Write on the bus or the welfare line, on the job or during meals, between sleeping or waking. I write while sitting on the john. No

---

* Anzaldúa was a prolific journal writer. Her journals, sealed until 2024, are held in her archives in the Nettie Lee Benson Latin American Collection, University of Texas, Austin.

long stretches at the typewriter unless you're wealthy or have a patron—you may not even own a typewriter. While you wash the floor or clothes listen to the words chanting in your body. When you're depressed, angry, hurt, when compassion and love possess you. When you cannot help but write.

*Distractions* all—that I spring on myself when I'm so deep into the writing, when I'm almost at that place, that dark cellar where some 'thing' is liable to jump up and pounce on me. The ways I subvert the writing are many. The way I don't tap the well nor learn how to make the windmill turn.

Eating is my main distraction. Getting up to eat an apple danish. That I've been off sugar for three years is not a deterrent nor that I have to put on a coat, find the keys, and go out into the San Francisco fog to get it. Getting up to light incense, to put a record on, to go for a walk—anything just to put off the writing.

Returning after I've stuffed myself. Writing paragraphs on pieces of paper, adding to the puzzle on the floor, to the confusion on my desk, making completion far away and perfection impossible.

26 mayo 80

Dear mujeres de color, I feel heavy and tired and there is a buzz in my head—too many beers last night. But I must finish this letter. My bribe: to take myself out to pizza. So I cut and paste and line the floor with my bits of paper. My life strewn on the floor in bits and pieces and I try to make some order out of it working against time, psyching myself up with decaffeinated coffee, trying to fill in the gaps.

Leslie, my housemate, comes in, gets on hands and knees to read my fragments on the floor and says, "It's good, Gloria." And I think: *I don't have to go back to Texas, to my family of land, mesquites, cactus, rattlesnakes, and roadrunners. My family, this community of writers. How could I have lived and survived so long without it. And I remember the isolation, re-live the pain again.*

"To assess the damage is a dangerous act,"[6] writes Cherríe Moraga. To stop there is even more dangerous.

It's too easy, blaming it all on the white man or white feminists or society or our parents. What we say and what we do ultimately come back to us, so let us own our responsibility, place it in our own hands and carry it with dignity and strength. No one's going to do my shitwork, I pick up after myself.

It makes perfect sense to me now how I resisted the act of writing, the commitment to writing. To write is to confront one's demons, look them in the face and live to write about them. Fear acts like a magnet; it draws the demons out of the closet and into the ink in our pens.

The tiger riding our backs (writing) never lets us alone. *Why aren't you writing, writing, writing?* It asks constantly till we begin to feel we're vampires sucking the blood out of too fresh an experience; that we are sucking life's blood to feed the pen. Writing is the most daring thing I have ever done and the most dangerous. Nellie Wong calls writing "the three-eyed demon shrieking the truth."[7]

Writing is dangerous because we are afraid of what the writing reveals: the fears, the angers, the strengths of a woman under a triple or quadruple oppression. Yet in that very act lies our survival because a woman who writes has power. And a woman with power is feared.

> What did it mean for a black woman to be an artist in our grandmother's time? It is a question with an answer cruel enough to stop the blood.
> —ALICE WALKER[8]

I have never seen so much power in the ability to move and transform others as from that of the writing of women of color.

In the San Francisco area, where I now live, none can stir the audience with their craft and truthsaying as do Cherríe Moraga (Chicana), Genny Lim (Asian American), and Luisah Teish (Black). With women like these, the loneliness of writing and the sense of powerlessness can be dispelled. We can walk among each other talking of our writing, reading to each other. And more and more when I'm alone, though still in communion with each other, the writing possesses me and propels me to leap into a timeless, spaceless no-place where I forget myself and feel I am the universe. This is power.

It's not on paper that you create but in your innards, in the gut and out of living tissue—*organic writing* I call it. A poem works for me *not* when it says what I want it to say and *not* when it evokes what I want it to. It works when the subject I started out with metamorphoses alchemically into a different one, one that has been discovered, or uncovered, by the poem. It works when it surprises me, when it says something I have repressed or pretended not to know. The meaning and worth of my writing is measured by how much I put myself on the line and how much nakedness I achieve.

> Audre said we need to speak up. Speak loud, speak unsettling things and
> be dangerous and just fuck, hell, let it out and let everybody hear whether
> they want to or not. —KATHY KENDALL[9]

I say mujer mágica, empty yourself. Shock yourself into new ways of
perceiving the world, shock your readers into the same. Stop the chatter
inside their heads.

Your skin must be sensitive enough for the lightest kiss and thick enough
to ward off the sneers. If you are going to spit in the eye of the world, make
sure your back is to the wind. Write of what most links us with life, the
sensation of the body, the images seen by the eye, the expansion of the
psyche in tranquility: moments of high intensity, its movement, sounds,
thoughts. *Even though we go hungry we are not impoverished of experiences.*

> I think many of us have been fooled by the mass media, by society's con-
> ditioning that our lives must be lived in great explosions, by "falling in
> love," by being "swept off our feet," and by the sorcery of magic genies that
> will fulfill our every wish, our every childhood longing. Wishes, dreams,
> and fantasies are important parts of our creative lives. They are the steps a
> writer integrates into her craft. They are the spectrum of resources to reach
> the truth, the heart of things, the immediacy and the impact of human
> conflict. —NELLIE WONG[10]

Many have a way with words. They label themselves seers, but they will
not see. Many have the gift of tongue but nothing to say. Do not listen to
them. Many who have words and tongue have no ear; they cannot listen
and they will not hear.

There is no need for words to fester in our minds. They germinate in
the open mouth of the barefoot child in the midst of restive crowds. They
wither in ivory towers and in college classrooms.

Throw away abstraction and the academic learning, the rules, the map
and compass. Feel your way without blinders. To touch more people, the
personal realities and the social must be evoked—not through rhetoric
but through blood and pus and sweat.

*Write with your eyes like painters, with your ears like musicians, with your feet like
dancers. You are the truthsayer with quill and torch. Write with your tongues of fire.
Don't let the pen banish you from yourself. Don't let the ink coagulate in your pens.
Don't let the censor snuff out the spark, nor the gags muffle your voice. Put your shit
on the paper.*

We are not reconciled to the oppressors who whet their howl on our
grief. We are not reconciled.

Find the muse within you. The voice that lies buried under you, dig it up. Do not fake it, try to sell it for a handclap or your name in print.

Love,
Gloria

## Notes

1. Originally written for *Words In Our Pockets* (Bootlegger: San Francisco), the Feminist Writer's Guild Handbook.

2. Cherríe Moraga's poem, "It's the Poverty," from *Loving in the War Years*, an unpublished book of poems. [Moraga's book was later published as *Loving in the War Years: Lo que nunca pasó por sus labios* (Boston: South End, 1983).]

3. Alice Walker, ed., "What White Publishers Won't Publish," *I Love Myself When I Am Laughing—A Zora Neale Hurston Reader* (New York: Feminist Press, 1979), 169.

4. Moraga, "It's the Poverty."

5. Naomi Littlebear, *The Dark of the Moon* (Portland: Olive Press, 1977), 36.

6. Cherríe Moraga's essay, see "La Güera" [in *This Bridge Called My Back*].

7. Nellie Wong, "Flows from the Dark of Monsters and Demons: Notes on Writing," *Radical Woman Pamphlet* (San Francisco, 1979).

8. Alice Walker, "In Search of Our Mother's Gardens: The Creativity of Black Women in the South," *Ms.* [*Magazine*], May 1974, 60.

9. Letter from Kathy Kendall, March 10, 1980, concerning a writer's workshop given by Audre Lorde, Adrienne Rich, and Meridel LeSeur.

10. Nellie Wong, "Flows from the Dark of Monsters and Demons."

This previously unpublished poem, written in 1977, contains one of Anzaldúa's earliest ex-pressions of her theory of el mundo surdo (the "left-handed world"), a theory she continued developing throughout her career in works like *This Bridge Called My Back*, "La Prieta," and "now let us shift . . . the path of conocimiento . . . inner work, public acts." For Anzaldúa, the left-handed world represents a visionary form of community building where people from diverse backgrounds with diverse needs and concerns coexist and work together to bring about revolutionary change. El mundo zurdo offers a methodology of relational difference and posits communities based on commonalities rather than sameness.

## The coming of el mundo surdo*

(For Joya Santanlla)

"This is not Pharoh's Egypt and we are not his slaves."
— *The Passover Plot*

I walk among you
I see sad things in my head
not being free is being dead

This is the year
the people of peace
break out of bondage

Together we will walk
through walls    by the lunar
light see our
left-handedness
with our third eye

I am the temple

I am the unmoving center
Within my skin all races
sexes    all trees    grasses
cows and snails    implode

* Although "surdo" is typically spelled with a z and pronounced like a z, Anzaldúa intentionally altered the spelling in order to honor the soft s sound of south Texas pro-nunciation. (For more on this spelling choice, see the glossary.)

spirals    lining    thought
to feeling

The day of I am is    now
I discard the wings
and claws I wear to
disguise my humanness
A collective of wo/men
and androgynes will proclaim    me
One will prepare the way
Love is the doctrine

I am becoming-being
the questor    the questing    the quest
You and I have already met
We are meeting we will meet

The real unknown is feeling
The real unknown is love
do not be afraid
to touch each other
We go naked here.

This is not the year of revenge
Give it up    give up that hatred
of yourself rise    up    reach
Come to me my sister-brother
We will share the moment
We are the awakening feminine presence
We are the earth
                We are the second coming

Anzaldúa began working on "La Prieta" in 1979 and hurried to finish it in time for the publication of *This Bridge Called My Back* in 1981. This essay, or autohistoria, includes important autobiographical information about Anzaldúa: her early menstruation and her subsequent sense of alienation from family and friends, her mugging in 1974, and her hysterectomy and near-death experience in 1980. Like the piece that follows, with its blurring of conventional gender roles and critique of heterosexuality, "La Prieta" also points to Anzaldúa's formative role in queer theory, her challenge to conventional views of reality, and an early version of her spiritual activism.

## La Prieta

When I was born, Mamagrande Locha inspected my buttocks looking for the dark blotch, the sign of indio, or worse, of mulatto blood. My grandmother (Spanish, part German, the hint of royalty lying just beneath the surface of her fair skin, blue eyes, and the coils of her once blond hair) would brag that her family was one of the first to settle in the range country of south Texas.

Too bad mi'jita* was morena, muy prieta, so dark and different from her own fair-skinned children. But she loved mi'jita anyway. What I lacked in whiteness, I had in smartness. But it was too bad I was dark like an Indian.

"Don't go out in the sun," my mother would tell me when I wanted to play outside. "If you get any darker, they'll mistake you for an Indian. And don't get dirt on your clothes. You don't want people to say you're a dirty Mexican." It never dawned on her that, though sixth-generation American, we were still Mexican and that all Mexicans are part Indian. I passed my adolescence combatting her incessant orders to bathe my body, scrub the floors and cupboards, clean the windows and the walls.

And as we'd get into the back of the "patrón's" truck that would take us to the fields, she'd ask, "Where's your gorra (sunbonnet)?" La gorra—rim held firm by slats of cardboard, neck flounce flowing over my shoulders— made me feel like a horse with blinders, a member of the French Foreign Legion, or a nun bowed down by her wimple. One day in the middle of the cotton field, I threw the gorra away and donned a sombrero. Though it didn't keep out the Texas 110 degree sun as well as the bonnet, I could now see in all directions, feel the breeze, dry the sweat on my neck.

When I began writing this essay, nearly two years ago, the wind I was

* Shortened form of "mi hijita."

accustomed to suddenly turned into a hurricane. It opened the door to the old images that haunt me, the old ghosts and all the old wounds. Each image a sword that cuts through me, each word a test. Terrified, I shelved the rough draft of this essay for a year.

I was terrified because in this writing I must be hard on people of color who are the oppressed victims. I am still afraid because I will have to call us on a lot of shit like our own racism, our fear of women and sexuality. One of my biggest fears is that of betraying myself, of consuming myself with self-castigation, of not being able to unseat the guilt that has ridden on my back for years.

> These my two hands
> quick to slap my face
> before others could slap it[1]

But above all, I am terrified of making my mother the villain in my life rather than showing how she has been a victim. Will I be betraying her in this essay for her early disloyalty to me?

With terror as my companion, I dip into my life and begin work on myself. Where did it begin, the pain, the images that haunt me?

Images That Haunt Me

When I was three months old tiny pink spots began appearing on my diaper. "She's a throwback to the Eskimo," the doctor told my mother. "Eskimo girl children get their periods early." At seven I had budding breasts. My mother would wrap them in tight cotton girdles so the kids at school would not think them strange beside their own flat brown mole nipples. My mother would pin onto my panties a folded piece of rag. "Keep your legs shut, Prieta." This, the deep dark secret between us, her punishment for having fucked before the wedding ceremony, my punishment for being born. And when she got mad at me she would yell, "He batallado más contigo que con todos los demás y no lo agradeces!" (I've taken more care with you than I have with all the others and you're not even grateful.) My sister started suspecting our secret—that there was something "wrong" with me. How much can you hide from a sister you've slept with in the same bed since infancy?[†]

---

[†] Anzaldúa refers here to a hormonal imbalance which caused her to menstruate from infancy, threw her into adolescence in early childhood, and triggered horrendously painful periods each month. See her *Interviews/Entrevistas* for more on this topic.

What my mother wanted in return for having birthed me and for nurturing me was that I submit to her without rebellion. Was this a survival skill she was trying to teach me? She objected not so much to my disobedience but to my questioning her right to demand obedience from me. Mixed with this power struggle was her guilt at having borne a child who was marked "con la seña," thinking she had made me a victim of her sin. In her eyes and in the eyes of others I saw myself reflected as "strange," "abnormal," "QUEER." I saw no other reflection. Helpless to change that image, I retreated into books and solitude and kept away from others.

The whole time growing up I felt that I was not of this earth. An alien from another planet—I'd been dropped on my mother's lap. But for what purpose? One day when I was about seven or eight, my father dropped on my lap a 25¢ pocket western, the only type of book he could pick up at a drugstore. The act of reading forever changed me. In the westerns I read, the house servants, the villains, and the cantineras (prostitutes) were all Mexicans. But I knew that the first cowboys (vaqueros) were Mexicans, that in Texas we outnumbered the Anglos, that my grandmother's ranch lands had been ripped off by the greedy Anglo. Yet in the pages of these books, the Mexican and Indian were vermin. The racism I would later recognize in my school teachers and never be able to ignore again I found in that first western I read.

My father dying, his aorta bursting while he was driving, the truck turning over, his body thrown out, the truck falling on his face. Blood on the pavement. His death occurred just as I entered puberty. It irrevocably shattered the myth that there existed a male figure to look after me. How could my strong, good, beautiful, god-like father be killed? How stupid and careless of god. What if chance and circumstance and accident ruled? I lost my father, god, and my innocence all in one bloody blow.

Every 24 days, raging fevers cooked my brain. Full flowing periods accompanied cramps, tonsillitis, and 105° fevers. Every month a trip to the doctors. "It's all in your head," they would say. "When you get older and get married and have children the pain will stop." A monotonous litany from the men in white all through my teens.

The bloodshed on the highway had robbed my adolescence from me like the blood on my diaper had robbed childhood from me. And into my hands unknowingly I took the transformation of my own being.

> Nobody's going to save you.
> No one's going to cut you down

cut the thorns around you.
No one's going to storm
the castle walls nor
kiss awake your birth,
climb down your hair,
nor mount you
onto the white steed.

There is no one who
will feed the yearning.
Face it. You will have
to do, do it yourself.[2]

My father dead, my mother and I turned to each other. Hadn't we grown together? We were like sisters—she was 16 when she gave birth to me.

Though she loved me she would only show it covertly—in the tone of her voice, in a look. Not so with my brothers—there it was visible for all the world to see. They were male and surrogate husbands, legitimate receivers of her power. Her allegiance was and is to her male children, not to the female.

Seeing my mother turn to my brothers for protection, for guidance—a mock act. She and I both knew she wouldn't be getting any from them. Like most men they didn't have it to give, instead needed to get it from women. I resented the fact that it was OK for my brothers to touch and kiss and flirt with her, but not for my sister and me. Resenting the fact that physical intimacy between women was taboo, dirty.

Yet she could not discount me. "Machona-india ladina" (masculine-wild Indian), she would call me because I did not act like a nice little Chicanita is supposed to act: later, in the same breath she would praise and blame me, often for the same thing—being a tomboy and wearing boots, being unafraid of snakes or knives, showing my contempt for women's roles, leaving home to go to college, not settling down and getting married, being a politica, siding with the Farmworkers. Yet while she would try to correct my more aggressive moods, my mother was secretly proud of my "waywardness." (Something she will never admit.) Proud that I'd worked myself through school. Secretly proud of my paintings, of my writing, though all the while complaining because I made no money out of it.

Vergüenza (Shame)

. . . being afraid that my friends would see my momma, would know that she was loud—her voice penetrated every corner. Always when we came into a room everyone looked up. I didn't want my friends to hear her brag about her children. I was afraid she would blurt out some secret, would criticize me in public. She always embarrassed me by telling everyone that I liked to lie in bed reading and wouldn't help her with the housework.

. . . eating at school out of sacks, hiding our "lonches"‡ papas con chorizo behind cupped hands and bowed heads, gobbling them up before the other kids could see. Guilt lay folded in the tortilla. The Anglo kids laughing—calling us "tortilleros," the Mexican kids taking up the word and using it as a club with which to hit each other. My brothers, sister, and I started bringing white bread sandwiches to school. After a while we stopped taking our lunch altogether.

There is no beauty in poverty, in my mother being able to give only one of her children lunch money. (We all agreed it should go to Nune, he was growing fast and was always hungry.) It was not very romantic for my sister and me to wear the dresses and panties my mother made us out of flour sacks because she couldn't afford store-bought ones like the other mothers.

> Well, I'm not ashamed of you anymore, Momma.
>
> My heart, once bent and cracked, once
> ashamed of your China ways.
> Ma, hear me now, tell me your story
> again and again.
> —NELLIE WONG, "From a Heart of Rice Straw,"
> *Dreams of Harrison Railroad Park*

It was not my mother's fault that we were poor, and yet so much of my pain and shame has been with our both betraying each other. But my mother has always been there for me in spite of our differences and emotional gulfs. She has never stopped fighting; she is a survivor. Even now I can hear her arguing with my father over how to raise us, insisting that all decisions be made by both of them. I can hear her crying over the body of

‡ For the English word "lunches."

my dead father. She was 28, had had little schooling, was unskilled, yet her strength was greater than most men's, raising us single-handed.

After my father died, I worked in the fields every weekend and every summer, even when I was a student in college. (We only migrated once when I was seven, journeyed in the back of my father's red truck with two other families to the cotton fields of west Texas. When I missed a few weeks of school, my father decided this should not happen again.)

. . . the planes swooping down on us, the fifty or a hundred of us falling onto the ground, the cloud of insecticide lacerating our eyes, clogging our nostrils. Nor did the corporate farm owners care that there were no toilets in the wide open fields, no bushes to hide behind.

Over the years, the confines of farm and ranch life began to chafe. The traditional role of la mujer was a saddle I did not want to wear. The concepts "passive" and "dutiful" raked my skin like spurs, and "marriage" and "children" set me to bucking faster than rattlesnakes or coyotes. I took to wearing boots and men's jeans and walking about with my head full of visions, hungry for more words and more words. Slowly I unbowed my head, refused my estate, and began to challenge the way things were. But it's taken over thirty years to unlearn the belief instilled in me that white is better than brown — something that some people of color never will unlearn. And it is only now that the hatred of myself, which I spent the greater part of my adolescence cultivating, is turning to love.

La Muerte, the Frozen Snow Queen

*I dig a grave, bury my first love, a German Shepherd. Bury the second, third, and fourth dog. The last one retching in the backyard, going into convulsions from insecticide poisoning. I buried him beside the others, five mounds in a row crowned with crosses I'd fashioned from twigs.*

*No more pets, no more loves — I court death now.*

. . . Two years ago on a fine November day in Yosemite Park, I fall on the floor with cramps, severe chills and shaking that go into spasms and near convulsions, then fevers so high my eyes feel like eggs frying. Twelve hours of this. I tell everyone, "It's nothing, don't worry, I'm alright." The first four gynecologists advise a hysterectomy. The fifth, a woman, says wait.

. . . Last March my fibroids conspired with an intestinal tract infection and spawned watermelons in my uterus. The doctor played with his knife. La Chingada ripped open, raped with the white man's wand. My soul in one corner of the hospital ceiling, getting thinner and thinner, telling me to clean up my shit, to release the fears and garbage from the past that are hanging me up. So I take La Muerte's scythe and cut away my arrogance and pride, the emotional depressions I indulge in, the head trips I do on myself and other people. With her scythe I cut the umbilical cord shackling me to the past and to friends and attitudes that drag me down. Strip away—all the way to the bone. Make myself utterly vulnerable.

. . . I can't sleep nights. The mugger said he would come and get me. There was a break in the county jail and I *just know* he is broken out and is coming to get me because I picked up a big rock and chased him, because I got help and caught him. How *dare* he drag me over rocks and twigs, the skin on my knees peeling, how *dare* he lay his hands on my throat, how *dare* he try to choke me to death, how *dare* he try to push me off the bridge to splatter my blood and bones on the rocks twenty feet below. His breath on my face, our eyes only inches apart, our bodies rolling on the ground in an embrace so intimate we could have been mistaken for lovers.

That night terror found me curled up in my bed. I couldn't stop trembling. For months terror came to me at night and never left me. And even now, seven years later, when I'm out in the street after dark and I hear running footsteps behind me, terror finds me again and again.

*No more pets, no more loves.*

. . . one of my lovers saying I was frigid when he couldn't bring me to orgasm.

. . . bringing home my Peruvian boyfriend and my mother saying she did not want her "Prieta" to have a "mojado" (wetback) for a lover.

. . . my mother and brothers calling me puta when I told them I had lost my virginity and that I'd done it on purpose. My mother and brothers calling me jota (queer) when I told them my friends were gay men and lesbians.

. . . Randy saying, "It's time you stopped being a nun, an ice queen afraid of living." But I did not want to be a snow queen regal with icy smiles and fingernails that ripped her prey ruthlessly. And yet, I knew my being distant, remote, a mountain sleeping under the snow, is what attracted him.

> A woman lies buried under me,
> interred for centuries, presumed dead.
>
> A woman lies buried under me.
> I hear her soft whisper

the rasp of her parchment skin
fighting the folds of her shroud.
Her eyes are pierced by needles
her eyelids, two fluttering moths.[3]

I am always surprised by the image that my white and non-Chicano friends have of me, surprised at how much they *do not* know me, at how I do not allow them to know me. They have substituted the negative picture the white culture has painted of my race with a highly romanticized, idealized image. "You're strong," my friends said, "a mountain of strength."

Though the power may be real, the mythic qualities attached to it keep others from dealing with me as a person and rob me of being able to act out my other selves. Having this "power" doesn't exempt me from being prey in the streets nor does it make my scrambling to survive, to feed myself, easier. To cope with hurt and control my fears, I grew a thick skin. Oh, the many names of power — pride, arrogance, control. I am not the frozen snow queen but a flesh and blood woman with perhaps too loving a heart, one easily hurt.

*I'm not invincible, I tell you. My skin's as fragile as a baby's. I'm brittle bones and human, I tell you. I'm a broken arm.*

*You're a razor's edge, you tell me. Shock them shitless. Be the holocaust. Be the black Kali. Spit in their eye and never cry. Oh broken angel, throw away your cast, mend your wing. Be not a rock but a razor's edge and burn with falling.* —Journal Entry, Summer Solstice, 1978.


Who Are My People

I am a wind-swayed bridge, a crossroads inhabited by whirlwinds. Gloria, the facilitator, Gloria, the mediator, straddling the walls between abysses. "Your allegiance is to La Raza, the Chicano movement," say the members of my race. "Your allegiance is to the Third World," say my Black and Asian friends. "Your allegiance is to your gender, to women," say the feminists. Then there's my allegiance to the Gay movement, to the socialist revolution, to the New Age, to magic and the occult. And there's my affinity to literature, to the world of the artist. What am I? *A third world lesbian feminist with Marxist and mystic leanings.* They would chop me up into little fragments and tag each piece with a label.

You say my name is ambivalence? Think of me as Shiva, a many-armed and -legged body with one foot on brown soil, one on white, one in straight society, one in the gay world, the man's world, the women's, one limb in the literary world, another in the working class, the socialist, and the occult worlds. A sort of spider woman hanging by one thin strand of web.

Who, me, confused? Ambivalent? Not so. Only your labels split me.

Years ago, a roommate of mine fighting for gay rights told MAYO, a Chicano organization, that she and the president were gay. They were ostracized. When they left, MAYO fell apart. They, too, being forced to choose between the priorities of race, sexual preference, or gender.

In the streets of this gay mecca, San Francisco, a Black man at a bus stop yells "Hey Faggots, come suck my cock." Randy yells back "You goddamn nigger, I worked in the Civil Rights movement ten years so you could call me names." Guilt gagging in his throat with the word, nigger. . . . a white woman waiting for the J-Church streetcar sees Randy and David kissing and says "You should be ashamed of yourselves. Two grown men—disgusting."

. . . Randy and David running into the house. The hair on the back of my neck rises, something in their voices triggers fear in me. Three Latino men in a car had chased them as they were walking home from work. "Gay boys, faggots," they yelled, throwing a beer bottle. Getting out of their car, knife blades reflect the full moon. . . . Randy and David hitting each other in the hall. Thuds on the wall—the heavy animal sounds.

. . . Randy pounding on my door, one corner of his mouth bleeding, his glasses broken, blind without them, he crying "I'm going to kill him, I'm going to kill the son of a bitch."

*The violence against us, the violence within us*, aroused like a rabid dog. Adrenaline-filled bodies, we bring home the anger and the violence we meet on the street and turn it against each other. We sic the rabid dog on each other and on ourselves. The black moods of alienation descend, the bridges we've extended out to each other crumble. We put the walls back up between us.

Once again it's faggot-hunting and queer-baiting time in the city. "And on your first anniversary of loving each other," I say to Randy, "and they had to be Latinos," feeling guilt when I look at David. Who is my brother's keeper, I wonder—knowing I have to be, we all have to be. We are all responsible. But who exactly are my people?

> *I identify as a woman. Whatever insults women insults me.*
> *I identify as gay. Whoever insults gays insults me.*
> *I identify as feminist. Whoever slurs feminism slurs me.*

That which is insulted I take as part of me, but there is something too simple about this kind of thinking. Part of the dialectic is missing. What about what I do not identify as?

I have been terrified of writing this essay because I will have to own up to the fact that I do not exclude whites from the list of people I love; two of them happen to be gay males. For the politically correct stance we let color, class, and gender separate us from those who would be kindred spirits. So the walls grow higher, the gulfs between us wider, the silences more profound. There is an enormous contradiction in being a bridge.

Dance To the Beat of Radical Colored Chic

This task—to be a bridge, to be a fucking crossroads for goddess' sake.

During my stint in the Feminist Writers' Guild many white members would ask me why Third World women do not come to FWG meetings and readings. I should have answered, "Because their skins are not as thick as mine, because their fear of encountering racism is greater than mine. They don't enjoy being put down, ignored, not engaged in equal dialogue, being tokens. And, neither do I." Oh, I know, women of color are hot right now and hip. Our afro-rhythms and latin salsas, the beat of our drums is in. White women flock to our parties, dance to the beat of radical colored chic. They come to our readings, take up our cause. I have no objections to this. What I mind is the pseudo-liberal ones who suffer from the white women's burden. Like the monkey in the Sufi story, who upon seeing a fish in the water rushes to rescue it from drowning by carrying it up into the branches of a tree. She takes a missionary role. She attempts to talk for us—what a presumption! This act is a rape of our tongue, and our acquiescence is a complicity to that rape. We women of color have to stop being modern medusas—throats cut, silenced into a mere hissing.

Where Do We Hang The Blame?

*The pull between what is and what should be.*

Does the root of the sickness lie within ourselves or within our patriarchal institutions? Did our institutions birth and propagate themselves and are we merely their pawns? Do ideas originate in human minds or do they exist in a "no-osphere," a limbo space where ideas originate without our help? Where do we hang the blame for the sickness we see around us—

around our own heads or around the throat of "capitalism," "socialism," "men," "white culture"?

If we do not create these institutions, we certainly perpetuate them through our inadvertent support. What lessons do we learn from the mugger?

Certainly racism is not just a white phenomenon. Whites are the top dogs and they shit on the rest of us every day of our lives. But casting stones is not the solution. Do we hand the oppressor/thug the rocks he throws at us? How often do we people of color place our necks on the chopping block? What are the ways we hold out our wrists to be shackled? Do we gag our own mouths with our "dios lo manda" resignation? How many times before the cock crows do we deny ourselves, shake off our dreams, and trample them into the sand? How many times do we fail to help one another up from the bottom of the stairs? How many times have we let someone else carry our crosses? How still do we stand to be crucified?

It is difficult for me to break free of the Chicano cultural bias into which I was born and raised, and the cultural bias of the Anglo culture that I was brainwashed into adopting. It is easier to repeat the racial patterns and attitudes, especially those of fear and prejudice, that we have inherited than to resist them.

Like a favorite old shoe that no longer fits, we do not let go of our comfortable old selves so that the new self can be worn. We fear our power, fear our feminine selves, fear the strong woman within, especially the black Kali aspect, dark and awesome. Thus we pay homage not to the power inside us but to the power outside us, masculine power, external power.

I see Third World peoples and women not as oppressors but as accomplices to oppression by unwittingly passing on to our children and our friends the oppressor's ideologies. I cannot discount the role I play as accomplice, that we all play as accomplices, for we are not screaming loud enough in protest.

The disease of powerlessness thrives in my body, not just out there in society. And just as the use of gloves, masks, and disinfectants fails to kill this disease, government grants, equal rights opportunity programs, welfare, and food stamps fail to uproot racism, sexism, and homophobia. And tokenism is not the answer. Sharing the pie is not going to work. I had a bite of it once and it almost poisoned me. With mutations of the virus such as these, one cannot isolate the virus and treat it. The whole organism is poisoned.

I stand behind whatever threatens our oppression. I stand behind whatever breaks us out of our bonds, short of killing and maiming. I stand with whatever and whoever breaks us out of our limited views and awakens our atrophied potentials.

How to turn away from the hellish journey that the disease has put me through, the alchemical nights of the soul. Torn limb from limb, knifed, mugged, beaten. My tongue (Spanish) ripped from my mouth, left voiceless. My name stolen from me. My bowels fucked with a surgeon's knife, uterus and ovaries pitched into the trash. Castrated. Set apart from my own kind, isolated. My life-blood sucked out of me by my role as woman nurturer—the last form of cannibalism.

## El Mundo Zurdo (the Left-handed World)[4]

*The pull between what is and what should be.* I believe that by changing ourselves we change the world, that traveling El Mundo Zurdo path is the path of a two-way movement—a going deep into the self and an expanding out into the world, a simultaneous recreation of the self and a reconstruction of society. And yet, I am confused as to how to accomplish this.

I can't discount the fact of the thousands that go to bed hungry every night. The thousands that do numbing shitwork eight hours a day each day of their lives. The thousands that get beaten and killed every day. The millions of women who have been burned at the stake, the millions who have been raped. Where is the justice to this?

I can't reconcile the sight of a battered child with the belief that we choose what happens to us, that we create our own world. I cannot resolve this in myself. I don't know. I can only speculate, try to integrate the experiences that I've had or have been witness to and try to make some sense of why we do violence to each other. In short, I'm trying to create a religion not out there somewhere, but in my gut. I am trying to make peace between what has happened to me, what the world is, and what it should be.

*"Growing up I felt that I was an alien from another planet dropped on my mother's lap. But for what purpose?"*

The mixture of bloods and affinities, rather than confusing or unbalancing me, has forced me to achieve a kind of equilibrium. Both cultures deny me a place in *their* universe. Between them and among others, I build my own universe, El Mundo Zurdo. I belong to myself and not to any one people.

I walk the tightrope with ease and grace. I span abysses. Blindfolded in the blue air. The sword between my thighs, the blade warm with my flesh. I walk the rope—an acrobat in equipoise, expert at the Balancing Act.

The rational, the patriarchal, and the heterosexual have held sway and legal tender for too long. Third World women, lesbians, feminists, and feminist-oriented men of all colors are banding and bonding together to right that balance. Only *together* can we be a force. I see us as a network of kindred spirits, a kind of family.

We are the queer groups, the people that don't belong anywhere, not in the dominant world nor completely within our own respective cultures. Combined we cover so many oppressions. But the overwhelming oppression is the collective fact that we do not fit, and because we do not fit *we are a threat*. Not all of us have the same oppressions, but we empathize and identify with each other's oppressions. We do not have the same ideology, nor do we derive similar solutions. Some of us are leftists, some of us practitioners of magic. Some of us are both. But these different affinities are not opposed to each other. In El Mundo Zurdo I with my own affinities and my people with theirs can live together and transform the planet.

## Notes

1. From my poem, "The Woman Who Lived Forever." All subsequent unacknowledged poems will be from my own writings. [This poem has not been published but can be found in manuscript form in Anzaldúa's archives in the Nettie Lee Benson Latin American Collection, University of Texas, Austin.]

2. From "Letting Go." [A later version of this poem appears in *Borderlands / La Frontera*, 186–88.]

3. From "A Woman Lies Buried Under Me." [This poem has not been published but can be found in manuscript form in Anzaldúa's archives in the Nettie Lee Benson Latin American Collection.]

4. This section consists of notes "Toward a Construction of El Mundo Zurdo," an essay in progress. [This essay has not been published but can be found in Anzaldúa's archives in the Nettie Lee Benson Latin American Collection.]

Originally titled "La Boda" (The Wedding), this story went through many drafts. Anzaldúa began working on "La Boda," which she conceptualized as a story "about a wedding of the 1940s or '50s," in September 1974. She was inspired to write it while reading Flaubert's *Madame Bovary*; as she explains in a journal entry from 30 September 1974, her goal was to "fuse the objective and subjective more tightly together than Flaubert did." During the 1980s, Anzaldúa viewed this story as part of a novel which she referred to as "*Andrea*"; this novel's protagonist was Andrea de la Cruz. As you will see, the protagonist in this story enacts Anzaldúa's holistic, participatory epistemology and her definition of queer, a definition that includes but goes far beyond sexual identity. Versions of this story were published in *Conditions* in 1982 and a year later in *Cuentos: Stories by Latinas*, edited by Alma Gómez, Cherríe Moraga, and Mariana Romo-Carmona.

## El paisano is a bird of good omen

Andrea straddles the mesquite post of the corral. Balanced on the top of it, she watches the white sky dwarf the chaparral, the cattle and horses, the house, and the portal with the guests moving under it. The sun

dominates the land. Always. La tierra. Everywhere, punctuated here and there with mesquite thickets and clumps of prickly pear. Under the quickening hum of the guests' conversation and the clinking of knives on plates, she hears the cackle of the hens clucking over their finds, a fat earthworm or dry grass seeds. On the highest branch of The Mesquite a mockingbird imitates another bird's trill. Under her, the hard roundness of the mesquite post seems an appendage of herself, a fifth limb, one that's also part of the corral, the corral that's part

of the land. The corral is a series of thick posts sunk side by side into the ground with just enough space between them to accommodate, horizontally, half a dozen logs alternating one on top of the other. The logs lock into each other between the paired posts, like people who try pairing, then stacking to accommodate each other. If the tops of the posts aren't flush with the average height their heads are either lopped off to make a tidy corral or they are cast out as deficient, unsuitable. She feels her body flowing from

one post to another until it, too, encircles what the corral encircles. But the gates are wide open, the circle will be incomplete until dusk when the newly calved cows are rounded in for the night. No, not complete until her new house is finished. Anda en la garra—on the rag. During her menses she feels fragile, expansive, the limits of her body stretched beyond her skin, she flows out like a sheet, encompassing, covering trees, people, everything around her. There is still time.

There is still time to change her mind. She shifts her bottom, the post is now on the left side of her cunt. Gently, she sways back and forth. If she does it just right she can bring herself to orgasm. Not as good as during a fast run, the wind whipping the mare's mane, her own hair across her mouth, no one hears her. She wonders: what encircles, what excludes, what sets apart.

"Andrea." Her mother is walking towards her. She's dressed in a pin-striped two-piece suit, white blouse, black hat veiled at the back, white open-toed pumps. Her mother made it a point to dress better than the other women.

"Sí, Amá,* ¿Qué quieres?" she asks, jumping down.

"What's the matter with you?"

"Everything. Why? What do you care?"

"You look hollow-eyed, hot. I don't want you embarrassing me today."

"The feeling, Amá. It's come back."

"No seas tonta, mi'jita. You must mingle with the guests. And get out of those man's pants. I find it totally incomprehensible why you moon out here like a lost calf and why Zenobio keeps himself hidden all afternoon in the house with your sisters draping themselves around him like a harem."

"And what's the harm in that? Why can't he just do what he wants?"

All day he keeps away from her, waiting for her to act, watching her from the corner of his eye (*Therefore shall a man leave his father and his mother.*) expecting a word from her: But if he's not around to remind her she may never say it.

"Go and change, greñuda, muchacha chiflada. And comb the mesquite leaves out of your hair—go! Chase your sisters out of the house. Tell them to bring out more tortillas de masa y la carne."

* Shortened form of "Mamá."

"No."

Her mother opens her mouth then closes it. Then more gently, Andrea says, "Why don't *you* go and do that and talk to Doña Inés. Todos la hacen menos." Both turn and look at Doña Inés, Zenobio's mother. She stands alone in the middle of the portal, wringing a pair of black gloves. Under a crownless parachute hat her face is emaciated and passive. Her beige jacket hangs loose from her thin shoulders, her black wide hemmed skirt drags on the dirt.

"All she talks about is how well her 'baby' can cook. I suppose if he wanted to she would let him take up sewing," says Andrea's mother.

"If he enjoys cooking, why shouldn't he cook," says Andrea turning away, at once regretting her habit of contradicting her mother, her habit of heaping all her griefs, from infancy to womanhood, on her mother's back. She knows that on top of the stored-up grievances, she will lay future ones. But the thought is an old one, too familiar to explore, and almost at once she forgets her mother.

The land. She never tires of looking at the land. She could never leave the land. The house faces east. It is an oasis in the middle of the brushland. To its right, on the gnarled limbs of The Mesquite, her brothers have roofed a shelter for guests and tables of food. The portal, erected with corrugated aluminum of different lengths and cedar branches that still distill their piney fragrance, looks unnatural. The Mesquite reigns over the portal, the house, the yard. Only The Windmill rivals its height. Perhaps its fifty- or sixty-foot-deep roots tap the same underground water source as The Windmill. She wants to tap that deep place, too. Maybe if she stayed still long enough her feet would worm roots into the moist core. Her two things: The Papalote, The Windmill, that she built with her brothers' help and The Mesquite she claimed as soon as she could climb it. Both connected . . . somehow. The trunk—a black wrung-out piece of cloth whose whorls and twists point toward some

revelation. She studies the gnarls and tries to unravel them. The Mesquite looks like an ancient ballet dancer doing a one-legged twirl, arms and head appealing to the sky. The trunk oozes a black gummy secretion from a lipless vagina mouth. If only she knew how to listen to the tree she would know what the mouth is screaming. She could once. She remembers gazing up at the tree and talking to it in its own language when she was about three. What is it that Tío Efraín is always platitudinizing? "Beautiful women and trees are more apt to be embrujadas." Bewitched. She climbs the corral again to see The Mesquite better. As the wind stirs the tree's limbs, Andrea sways

like The Papalote. Andrea sways, her hair becomes ruffled leaves. The tree is a tree. But is it just a tree? ("*Ego jungo ves in matrimonium.*") To the right of the portal, the partially finished house, looking like the gutted side of a cow, two walls up, a skeleton roof, the floor strewn with pieces of lumber and buckets of nails resembling the rotting entrails of the animal. Laughter erupts from a group of men sitting on two thick cedar logs and half a dozen bales of sorghum that lie sprawled in a semi-circle under the portal. She is not part of this half

circle. She is outside of it. (*The priest sprinkles water over their bowed heads.*) Directly west of the house are the corrals. Next to them, towering over the ranch house and corrals, is The Windmill, a permanent silver sunflower. She twists around. The Windmill, the beacon that guides the hands home from a sea of brush and cactus, is moving. The wind has turned the vane. The vane, an arrow shaft, points toward the south. On the vane, the words DE LA CRUZ shine bright in the afternoon sun. Hay algo en al aire. Something is in

the wind. The Windmill's sails rotate faster and faster as the south wind surges louder and louder. Though she sits motionless, Andrea too rotates with the sails. She doesn't have to sit up there, she *is* up there. She feels the guests' sly glances brush over her wild henna hair. She can hear their heads repeating over and over, "strange, too willful and impulsive." They would like to throw a saddle on her, dig their spurs deep into her sides, pull hard on the bridle until her mouth runs red, loses its adamancy. Or, tie her to a post like a wild heifer, tail between her legs, head caught in the trough and

milk her. Sand down her dentata to a

toothless grin. Well, she's not going to laugh at their jokes and snide remarks nor smile. Already her mouth hurts from not smiling. She touches her throat, touches

pearls. The string of pearls she didn't wear. She will not wear. Her hands smooth the silk of her dress, the dress she does not wear. She will not wear dresses here. Not here—maybe in another place. No, no, no. Sweat drenches the hair in her armpits. She takes a deep breath. Another. After a while the no's become quiet like baby chicks under the mother hen. She weans her attention away from The Windmill and waits for the everyday-ness to fold its wings around her again. Warm and safe. Home.

A handful of steers drink at the edge of the waterhole beyond The Wind-mill. Half a mile beyond the waterhole is the dark green of the lagoon. Andrea blinks and half of her moves to the lagoon's edge. The greedy land slowly sucks at the meager rains it trapped in its hold during January and February. Insidious roots slither silently toward its edge and swell like thin sponges. Low dark clouds crowd the horizon. If only the wind would turn. Huisache and prickly pear fringe the lagoon. The yellow-orange flowers of the cactus and the pale gold of the huisache, the sole colors in the brown and barren land. It is April: the semidesert is in bloom. The huisache's tiny pompom blossoms move gently, dispersing their delicate perfume in the hot wind. Andrea feels the leaves' feathery softness on her face, soft like the heads of newly hatched chicks, crests still wet and yielding. A thorn scratches her cheek dispatching her other half

back. Instantly, the lagoon and huisache are far away. The men's voices grow louder . . . "Las mujeres, they're more susceptible to it. Their fury is more unbridled than ours. They can't temper their . . . well, their tempers. And they're fickle by nature."

"What do you know about females? The closest you've been to one is that cow you keep in your kitchen."

"You mean his wife?" There is a roar of laughter.

"No, no," interrupts another, "it gets in their blood, there they boil vile vapors. When they belch they infect everyone near them."

"Yes," says another, "if a pregnant woman comes near them she'll mis-carry and lose the child." Andrea pushes

their voices away. Her grandmother was one. And now she is too. And what else can she do that others can't, besides remembering events be-fore they happen? She jumps off the corral. Walks to The Windmill. As she climbs up, the rough wooden tiles under her hands and feet feel im-mensely thick and deep. They can plumb the center of the world. Now she's on the platform under the blade and must be wary of wind change—it wouldn't do to get rapped on the head by the sails, by anything. She has to—no, not think, just allow the quiet to seep into her body and wait for the flash to strike, — 'the knowing.' Today. Zenobio. Her land. Her people. The people not as much hers as the land. Beyond

the lagoon is the monte where the cattle shelter, nibbling mesquite pods or what grass they can find. ("*You will go through this ceremony, cabezona.*") The dark clouds are looming nearer. North of the house, to the right, are three lone dark green cedars. Quiet sentinels watching over the land. Always watching. Half a dozen vehicles are parked under them. Some of the guests disembark from old Fords and Chryslers. A Willys jeep, a relic from the war that has just ended, had earlier emptied a large family from tiny tots to aged grandparents. It looked like a tree at first light vacating chickens that have roosted there all night. A few guests had arrived on horseback. ("*You have to go through with it. You don't want to end up a solterona like your aunt Ramona?*") Don Efraín had driven his '41 Lincoln Continental Coupe. He gives more care to it than he does his to family. He is seen spitting on it then shining out the spots of dirt with the shirt tail under his forearm. He is heard whispering love words to it. The platform

trembles. Andrea blinks. Expands. The other Andrea flows down, down. The men are talking of something else now. "No one can imagine. It was so long ago. That kind of quake, thrown to the ground. The earth became a crazy dancer. It was as if a dissident orchestra had mutinied and each musician had played a different song. So long ago, when the Indians were free." Back. Looking

down she sees it's only her Uncle Efraín scaling up. His arm muscles taut. Her own muscles taut. The fingers grasping the ladder become her fingers. She is beside her uncle. "You shouldn't pretend to be younger and stronger than you are," she tells him, stretching out her hand to help him.

"You're not supposed to know that," he says ignoring her hand. He gives a little hop and lands his scrawny buttocks on the platform. "Saying truths is not the thing to do, hija. People won't stand for it and men will always try to impress you, you know that."

"Why do they have to always prove themselves?" she asks.

"Sepa Dios. ¿Qué te pasa? Your mamá said you were being difficult."

"Difficult is the only way I *can* be with her. It's all this fuss and bother. I can't decide." Andrea remains silent for a while.

"There's nothing to decide, it's all been decided for you. Like it was for me. I wouldn't go through with it a second time, though. Not for all the land in The Valley. Why in my time . . ." Andrea stops listening. The land, people married for it.

"It's peaceful here, like being in another world," says Andrea. "Or another self."

"You're right, hija. It's a tiny island floating above everything."

"That was a nice gift you brought us, tío. It must have taken you weeks to carve it."

"It took me months. Yes, that paisano was a long time coming. But how I loved working on it! Couldn't get it right until I got the idea of carving a base for it. For balance. Had to send my boys out into the brush. They came back with enough cowhorns to make a dozen roadrunners and enough bones for m'ija to paint on for months." His daughter had presented Andrea with a cow pelvic bone with a small hole and a thin strip of cowhide with which to hang it around her neck. On the bone carved and painted: The Mesquite with The Windmill in the background. Andrea puts her hand between her breasts. The bone is warm.

"You've got that look in your eye, my girl. What you need is some cerveza." They climb down.

Andrea takes her beer which she isn't supposed to be drinking, the frown on her aunts' faces and the male guests' eyes tell her.

Andrea takes her beer to the corral and places it on a post.

Andrea is not anywhere near the corral or a post.

Andrea places her beer on the post where it rocks a bit but doesn't topple. She looks at the women. Andrea does not look

at the women. The bridesmaids, wide pink skirts (they wear identical dresses) swirling around their calves, cast coquettish looks at one muchacho or another as they traffic among the tables, ladling out chunks of carne asada, arroz con pollo, and papas con frijoles, serving beer or lemonade or chocolate. Not much to say for their lot until they learn to say no. (*Andrea's bouquet sails into the sun over the heads of the shrieking bridesmaids. Sweat pours down their faces. The flowers hit one girl in the face. Clutching them, she scrambles away laughing. The men will get hit in the face too. Later. "Así son las cosas, mi'jita," her mother would say every time Andrea complained of the restrictions marriage imposes on people.*) She hasn't eaten since yesterday noon, but that's not why it

happens. That López girl has nice tits and her . . . Andrea blinks. Andrea leaves

herself—the self that sits atop the corral. The men sit on the bales of hay in their stiff dark cotton suits eating, their felt stetsons on the ground beside them or hanging from the mesquite branches. Some are rolling or smoking their Buglar and drinking, discussing the drought. Now one talks of the quarantine of his cattle by the government, another cuts in with the movidas del compadre Juan. One signals to her but she pretends not to see—feeling angry at the pretense, wanting to hit him in the face. It's only when they're bunched up in herds; alone, not one of them would dare look her in the eye. Zenobio brings her a plate of food and leaves before she can say anything. She doesn't touch it—she's no longer there. The músicos are feeding their music with whiskey, fueling the songs' fire before the dance begins, their instruments beside them on the ground like crippled birds. As she picks up her beer her hands start to tingle. The flow of liquid down her throat feels like a wind

milling down her middle. Her hands are fluid. Where does the edge of the glass end and her mouth begin? Then she tries to define the "feeling" but can't and becomes afraid. She smiles. Yes, when she wants to be *gone*, to be *that*, all she has to do is look carefully, focus steadily on something and she takes leave of

herself. The women sit taking turns talking about what their hijos do, what their maridos say. They seem to rush through their words in a desperate attempt to make up for the usual isolation of their lives. Funerals and weddings, the only events that bring them together. Their men and children. Andrea wants to run away. She wants to run to her grandmother and, kneeling before her, bury her face in her ample thighs, smell the smell. (*Because the fourth finger of the left hand is the least active finger of the hand least used.*) Her grandmother is sitting on the Windsor chair that Andrea has taken out of the house for her. She sits near but not with the women. Andrea feels removed from the women, from everyone. It seems that she inhabits a space that is not there, impervious to the bodies milling around her, to the food and laughter. There. But not there. Here. But not here. Hearing, yet deaf to the chortles that follow the jokes, the tittering of the young in the backyard. Motionless, feeling nothing, thinking nothing, rooted to the post, not even seeming to breathe. (*But señorita, you must find your certificate of baptism. I never was baptised because I never was born. Mamagrande gave birth to me in her kettle. Mamá's baby was born dead. I was put in its place so she wouldn't grieve its death. Stop it, Andrea. Don't listen to her, Father, she likes to make jokes.*) A world lay in that smell. She would not cook for the man, nor bear his dark moods and snotty children. She would not bolster his spirits when the cattle died off like flies, nor his balls when he dried up. Zenobio is not like the others, he would accept this. Another world lies out there. Perhaps she could be her

self out there. "Fue un escándalo," she had overheard. "Sleeping naked with la serpiente. A huge rattler. A diamond back, the most vicious killer of them all. Her henna hair wild over her body, her body glistening, the serpent entwined around her middle, its head peering from her pubic patch, its dry scaly tail rubbing the silk of her. She lavishes on her pet the warmth she cannot lavish on a man." Rubbing the depression on each side of its

snout, between eye and nostril. Víbora loved that. She would take its tail between her hands and study its hollow, ring-like bulbs at the tail entering the biggest ring and the other rings gradually diminishing in size, each opening to its neighbor. Several times a year, it would shed its skin. A new one would form beneath the old one. Then the old one would be sloughed off. But not completely. It would retain something of the old skin. The old tail sheath would remain loosely fitting over the new one. With each molting another joint would be added. Some would wear away with time. If only she could shed her old skin and grow a new one as easily. She loved to feel the rapid vibrations of the tail. She'd had it since it was a baby, no more than a foot long and thin as a tapeworm. Now it was over eight feet long and as thick as her thigh. Now she had to keep it outside in the nopal thicket—everyone in the house was terrified of it. That she had such a pet in her family the neighbors could accept more readily than the fact that the snake always returned after its nightly excursions. Even after weeks of absence. The people could stomach

her taming wild bulls and mad dogs

but not a snake. On one of the tables a head of a steer, pit barbecued, is spiraling steam out of its dull gaping eyes toward the branches of The Mesquite. She smells the rich odor, too rich. It's as if her nose were buried in the head. Revulsion pinches her gut. Surely it's not one of her favorites. The wild ones sometimes get caught, too. Her mother had gotten up at three in the morning, spicing the head, wrapping it in burlap, burying it in the ground, and covering it with live coals. It has slowly simmered for ten hours. Don Sebastian, it was told, had taken the entrails of one of his dead cows into his kitchen and laying the bowels over a gridiron had lighted the stove murmuring, "That will make the bruja real hot." Hombre. Why does he fear us. The more female we are the more he fears us. Is it our strength or our

tenderness he fears? The only way not to alarm him is to acquiesce and allow him to lock us up in a room. A will indifferent to his own he cannot abide. How dare we have wills. He wants us to mother him, give him pleasure, grant all his wishes and ask for nothing. Someone puts

a hand on her shoulder. (*God made them male and female.*) Without looking she knows it's Zenobio. What Zenobio fears is her power to evoke in him the naked helplessness of his being. The power to make him aware that he has no control over that feeling. That to him is betrayal. But she never takes advantage of him when he is the most exposed. He knows I never will, Andrea thinks, yet . . . Zenobio grins, puts a pomegranate in her hand then

disappears. She blinks. The pink, blue, and white frosted cake lies on the middle of the center table. Looking at the stiff figures of the novia y novio smiling inanely on top, she already feels herself becoming stiff. She touches her arm to reassure herself. Pan de polvo, empanadas de calabaza, and pitchers of hot chocolate lie by the cake awaiting la merienda. (*She stands at Zenobio's right hand. The madrinas and padrinos stand behind.*) Tall glass vases with huge red and white roses from her grandmother's jardín flank each end of the table. The stain,

the chocolate stain disfigures the white lace tablecloth.

Hearing a burst of laughter, Andrea looks down the length of the corral.

Hearing laughter, Andrea refuses to look up.

Andrea looks up. The younger men congregate at one end of the corral. Astride posts, legs dangling, bottoms squirming, they pummel each others' arms as they trade witty nonsenses. She might as well be sitting right

next to them. Secretive whispers, boasts of prowess at roping, at riding, at fucking the cantineras. They ogle the girls, most often the López girl. A few eye the horses in their beautiful sleek flesh snorting water from the trough or standing stiff-legged, tails swishing off flies. (*As is required, I will instruct you in the doctrine. Now, the nature of marriage is obedience . . .*) This marriage will save us from having to marry, she thinks. She hears the thud of knives that a couple of adolescent boys are throwing at a tree stump out of sight in the backyard. José Manuel had better not come around smirking. The "bullseye" from one of the boys drowns out the laughter of the guests. A young boy tears across the backyard, chased by an enraged tom turkey. The boy runs into the rope that some girls are jumping and sprawls amid skirts and squeals and slaps. Soft bodies and soft hands slap

Andrea. She ducks, then turns around furtively to see if anyone is look-ing. She'll have to burn prickly pear and mesquite pods to feed the cattle this summer if the rains don't come. Everyone will be upset, not so much at her doing a man's work but for doing it better. A group of screeching children surround a boy in a yellow shirt dangling a horned toad over a heap of swarming red ants. The horned toad squirms, body convulsing. The piercing pain in

her arms and hands almost shock her into crying out. She rolls up her sleeves. The red spots on her arms were made from climbing the windmill, from the splinters. And those on the back of her hands? Finally a boy in a purple shirt scatters the children and releases the horned toad. The toad scuttles out of sight under some nopales. (*The two altar boys carry the vessel of holy water to the altar, the sprinkler, and the little basin that will hold the ring. The priest walks behind them.*)

"¡Hijita! Get off of there. A fine hostess you are." Andrea looks down. Her mother again, arms crossed, a scowl on her face.

"I want to be alone, Amá."

"Andrea de la Cruz, get down and go greet la familia Flores." The pearls around her neck bubble up and down. "They've just arrived—late as usual."

"They shouldn't have bothered."

"Pórtate bien, Andrea. You must stop this bickering with your cousin."

"All right, but I didn't start it, he did, and if he makes a wrong move I'm going to flatten him." Andrea leaps off, raising a little cloud of dust from which her mother backs off, the scowl, a permanent feature now.

"It's not good for women to quarrel with men, especially about . . . well, it's just not good."

"You mean it's not good for women to have opinions on anything. In fact it's not good for women to do anything."

The Flores approach and she greets them, but turns away from José Manuel's smirk and outstretched arms.

"Here's your wedding gift. I'm sure Zenobio will like it," he says, smiling. She remains silent. He holds the cage out to her, then drops it at her feet, almost on her toes. "The paisano will bring you good fortune," he says, a weasel in his smile.

"I've already received my good fortune," she says. What had ever possessed Zenobio. It's not like José Manuel is the only one around. There's Pete and Mando. (*I hereby proclaim the coming nuptials of Andrea de la Cruz and Zenobio Ríos. Those who wish to bring to light any obstacles that stand in the way of this union, let them come forward. This prenuptial announcement will also be made during the next two misas as befits canon law.*)

"No one can have too much of a good thing," says José Manuel, weasel mustache twitching. "Fried paisano is a remedio for the itch, or so they say." Someone snickers.

"A caged thing never brings anyone luck, least of all the one who captures it," says Andrea.

"How do you like that for thanks," says José Manuel, ears flattening against his skull as he surveys the guests that have bunched up around them. All avoid his beady eyes. It is to Andrea that they always come when they're short of money or water or feed for their cattle. At other times, when their cows go dry, they whisper behind her back, say that fulano saw her cast a stone over her left shoulder toward the west. Or that once she made midnight of high noon. Andrea looks men full in the face. Andrea looks

fully at him, her eyes absorb the hostility emanating from him. Her body full of it. And he knows. He and Zenobio. Innocent, trusting Zenobio. Then "the betrayal" as Zenobio dramatically called it when he told her about it. And she even more stupid—she should have warned Zenobio. Poor Zenobio, duped, seduced, betrayed. She would never forget his pain. Andrea blinks and says, "You are not welcome here," She is herself again.

"I'm always welcome at the house of my aunt."

"Make any trouble and I'll boot you off of my land."

"Your land? You're a woman—or are you? Women don't inherit."

"Va 'ber[†] pedo. A fight, a fight," the boy in the yellow shirt chants. José Manuel pushes her once. Twice. As he tries to push her a third time she takes a knife out of her jeans and his hand

runs into it. Shocked, he backs off staring at the blood dripping from his hand. Don Efraín pushes his way through the group. "Now, now, now," he says putting his arm around Andrea and turning her around. Complete silence, all eyes riveted on the blood dripping.

"Consider Zenobio," Don Efraín whispers, moving her away while at the same time José Manuel's brother takes José Manuel's arm and pulls him toward the portal. José Manuel muttering, "Should have given her the yerba—would of cured the chingadera out of her." . . . He swallows the last words, hand on his throat, gagging. He turns to find her standing very still, her eyes wide, her gaze aimed directly at his throat. The saliva in his mouth turns to rust, the weasel in his eyes wild with fear. In the future I will not need a knife, she thinks. She stands

holding the cage at eye level with both hands. The paisano cocks its head to one side, then the other, looking at her through first one eye then the other. Killer of rattlers. Killer of alacranes and tarántulas. The bird blinks its fierce eye, film clouding and unclouding it. The bare patch of vivid blue and red skin behind the eye fascinates her. The bird blinks again, the eye clears then films. Clear then clouded, unclouded then filmed, over and over and over. The *feeling*, and a tingling in her hands. The boy in the purple shirt watches her. She opens

the cage door. A beautiful cage made of bleached dry twigs and grass stems. It doesn't move. Just the eye. Clouding and unclouding. The paisano takes off down the back road in a streak so fast it seems to be skimming the ground, long legs churning, tail flat. The road forks out to the

---

[†] Shortened form of "Va a haber."

right and another branch to the left. Andrea silently urges the paisano to cross the right road from left to right. Squatting, she looks at the track, two toes pointing forward, two toes pointing backward—to mislead the evil spirits, people say. (*Cállate el hocico, Zenobio. You've asked me what time it is a hundred times in the last five minutes. Cállate, she'll be here on time.*) She looks toward the north, clenches her fist and concentrates. Lightning flashes in the north. She counts slowly and when she gets to seven there is a low rumble. She begins to count again and at seven the wind comes sweeping over the rancho. Andrea turns to find the boy in the purple shirt looking at her. "Will you teach me how to do that?" he asks. Both smile. Andrea looks for Zenobio. He's not in the house. He's not with José Manuel. He's with his mother on one of the benches that have been set up to accommodate the Flores. The benches, she notices, close off

the circle. He's standing by the wedding cake, laughing at something Don Efraín is saying. They stand close together. Don Efraín never should have married. It's not too late, she thinks. Not too late. Not

too late. "Oh, there you are, corazón," says Don Efrain, putting his arm over Andrea's shoulder. "Oye, paisana, I was just telling your hombre here how lucky you are."

"Ya lo sé." She doesn't want to hear anymore about 'luck.' "I'm bailing him out. And myself. We're rescuing each other, for now anyway."

"What nonsense you talk sometimes, hijita. You sound more and more like your mamagrande everyday. Be careful. People do not tolerate what's different." Zenobio doesn't seem put out by their conversation, she thinks, annoyed with herself and everyone. She's never seen him flustered or even self-conscious. He always looks beautiful. She looks at Don Efraín and studies the sombrero in his hand. The small holes around the crown form a pattern of inverted squares inside of which more holes bisect their angles to form a

cross. Sun wrinkles spread outward around the eyes gazing at her. Why, he's chuckling at our situation. And pitying it, she realizes. A lizard scurries out from

between her legs. She is partial to lizards. (*La cagamos, the ring doesn't fit, says Zenobio. You didn't think it would, did you. It's not supposed to fit. Nothing is supposed to fit so don't start expecting things to, she tells him.*) "Some more mescal, Tío?"

"Yes, but I'll get it. I know you want to be alone to fight with your 'novio,'" he says, accentuating the novio. The music starts. The men begin moving all the tables to make room for the dancing. Everyone turns to look at Andrea and Zenobio. Don Efraín is there beside them, urging them to the center of the portal, saying, "The bride and groom always start the first dance."

"I don't want to dance with him. Nothing personal, Zeno."

"Cagada, let's get it over with," says Zenobio, putting his arm around her. They stand motionless, freeze a smile for the photographer. They are waltzing smoothly. Her hands on his thin shoulders, his bony hands on her waist. (*For the wife does not rule over her own body, but the husband does; likewise the husband does not rule over his own body* . . .) She is a substanceless body doing the courting being courted. He is a substanceless body doing the courting being courted.

"Why are you looking at me that way?"

"I feel like not going through with it," she says.

"'Tás loca.[‡] It's the night before."

"I don't see the point of it. Just why are we doing this? Pa'no casarnos deveras. So we won't have to go through a 'real' marriage? We're being hooked into it. Into doing what's 'done.'" She looks around. Others are dancing. The waltz becomes a polka, a foot-tapping, dust-raising Texas Mexican polka full of ajúas; Andrea walks away, Zenobio follows. They stand on the sidelines watching the dancers. Everyone, old and young, is dancing. The girls left without partners are trying to cajole their young brothers into dancing with them. Two seven-year-old girls dance with each other. Andrea walks up to the López girl who's been turning down man after man, all bunched up around her like cattle around a salt lick, tongues falling out.

"Ven. Baila conmigo." The López girl smiles, her teeth gleam as Andrea takes her into her arms and whirls her around the circle. Andrea's head is full of the music. The strings of the guitar twang inside her skull. The beat becomes her heartbeat, opening her, widening her diaphragm, her hips expanding. Only the tune exists and Belinda López. Throbbing. Her pelvis makes circles around Belinda's navel. She shakes her head and blinks, lips

[‡] Shortened form of "Estás loca."

glisten, jaw falls slack. Her spine is undulating. Gradually, she notices that most of the dancing couples have taken root right in the middle of the portal and are staring at the two women, lips thinned and whitening.

"Stop, let go," says Belinda López, teeth whiter than ever.

"Aw come on, you like it."

"Yes. But we're not supposed to."

"I'm tired of the millions of things we're not supposed to do," says Andrea.

"Well, you're the only one that can get away with doing things we're not supposed to do."

"Ay chulita, I'll tell you my secret. I just do them."

"But you're different. They're scared of you. Andrea la Bruja, they call you behind your back, making the sign of the cross when they say your name," she says. She breaks from Andrea's hold, running out of the circle of petrified eyes. Her palpitating breasts affront the men and bring a look of envy to the women's eyes.

Andrea walks back to Zenobio. "¿Qué pendejada fue ésa, Andrea?"

"I did it because I wanted to—just like you want to dance with the boy in the purple shirt staring at you," she says.

"What I want and what I do are two different things."

"Oh yeah? What about José Manuel?" says Andrea. "Oh let's stop squabbling. We're beginning to sound like we're married already."

"OK, I know what you're thinking. You want to run off and leave me," he says. "But we need each other, Andrea. We understand each other. No one else does. We have to stay together." And when she makes no reply, he says, "Take me with you." They put their arms around each other. The image of a tumbleweed wrapped around a post with the wind whirling past is in her mind. But who is the tumbleweed and who the post? Over Zenobio's shoulder appears the frowning face

of her mother. Andrea feels a vague sense of guilt, a diffused disloyalty. The warmth and affection and love that is her mother's due she lavishes on her grandmother, on Zenobio, on Víbora, on the land.

"I wish we hadn't started building our own home yet," she tells him.

"It'll be finished in a month, then we'll have some privacy."

"You don't know my mother."

"Querida, it won't matter. We can put up with her for a month. And she with us."

"Or, we can skip out. It's not just her, Zeno, it's me. And it's you. We don't fit here. So maybe we won't fit anywhere else, but maybe we will. Maybe there's a place for people like us somewhere."

"You mean in the gavacho[§] world?"

"I don't know. Zenobio, don't look like that."

"I want you to stop talking like this. You're scaring me. Besides, I'm hungry. Let's go eat."

"You go, I'm not hungry. I'm going to talk to Mamagrande."

Her grandmother is sitting on a bench under The Windmill, arms on her lap, quietly rocking.

"I was waiting for you, mi'jita." They remain silent. Silence—their way of talking. Finally her grandmother says, "It's a closeness, a connection."

"Yes," says Andrea, "with people and things. But only with certain people and certain things at certain times. It's frightening."

"Only because it's new and unfamiliar. Soon it will become comfortable and in time indispensable."

"I don't mean that. I mean others' fear of it and my fear of their fear. Why do I seem evil to them?"

"Because you are wholly yourself. That terrifies people who are prisoners of others' upbringing, who are molded by others," says her grandmother.

"I don't know what to believe. It's terrible! I don't want it. It means being alone."

"Which? ¿Tu poder o tu querer?"

§ Tejano spelling for "gabacho."

"Both," she says, surprised that her grandmother knows about su "querer." Yet nothing her grandmother knows really surprises her. "Don't the two go together, Mamagrande?" asks Andrea.

Andrea walks back toward the portal, then turns to go back to the corral. A small group has gathered around José Manuel. He playfully puts a pair of pants over a heifer's head, one of the ladinas. He opens the gate and hits her sharply on the shanks. Blinded, she whirls around and around trying to shake off the cloth over her eyes. Frightened and enraged she runs straight toward Andrea. From the guests—an audible sucking in of air. The heifer is almost on top of Andrea. Andrea jerks the pants off her horns. The animal stops dead in her tracks, wild-eyed, spewing rivulets of saliva. Andrea whispers to her and walks into the corral. The wild heifer follows her meekly. Andrea turns and locks the gate. The circle is complete. She ignores the remarks addressed to her, repeating to herself *It is not a sickness, nor is it evil.*

Another melody attaches to the first—I must do it I must do it. An incantation to ward off . . . A white glare

lays over everything like a fine dust. Another world, a different one, superimposed over the normal one. The land, the people, everything takes on a fused quality. Like figures carved out of the same white rock. What was it like before? Where's the Andrea that left her bed that morning? What was the dream about that woke her up?

She is standing on the banks of a river holding a bucket. She fishes by dropping it into the water and scooping it up. At first she catches a big beautiful paisano. She knows it's a rare one. She throws it back into the river. It metamorphoses into Víbora, her pet snake. Víbora stands on the water flicking her tongue, then with a rattle of her tail, turns and swims for the shore. Once on land, she crawls toward the west. Andrea wakes up saying to herself, a dream about my future.

She hurries back to the portal and sits down beside Zenobio (*And the two shall become one. And they shall be one flesh.*) who has multiplied, and his several selves fan out around him like cards held in a hand. The physical Zenobio draws the others. (*I pronounce you man and . . .*) These others are Zenobios that she's never met. She feels a tightness in her head and a great wind in her bones.

"¿Pa' dónde vas?" Zenobio asks when she starts to leave.

"Away from here."

She finds herself once more on top of The Windmill. She doesn't re-member climbing up.

The world gradually settles down around her, forming a different rock-bed. There is nothing that she can compare the feeling with—except maybe dreams. She puts her hands on her temples and presses hard. It must all be part of what could have been or what is, she thinks. The vane now points toward the west. I am that I am. The paisano is a bird of good omen. She descends

from The Windmill and walks slowly to the portal. She dips a broom sprig in water. A fine rain begins to fall. The feathers of an eagle consume all other feathers if they're mixed together. Leaning against the gnarled Mesquite, hair touching some of its leaves, she begins to bid the guests goodbye.

This short piece is the sixth chapter of Anzaldúa's unpublished book-length autohistoria, *La Serpiente Que Se Come Su Cola: The Death and Rebirth Rites-of-Passage of a Chicana Lesbian*. During her New York City years, Anzaldúa focused much of her writing energy on this project, completing three drafts with various subtitles. I have included this chapter because it so effectively indicates some of the philosophical issues that she developed in her later writings. The metaphor of a double-faced woman was extremely important to Anzaldúa during this period. She referred to it in interviews and even titled one of her journals from 1982 "Dream of the Doubled Faced Woman."

# Dream of the Double-Faced Woman

*En Carne Viva*

> All psychic processes are material. There is not a single process that does not require the expenditure of a certain substance corresponding to it . . . —OUSPENSKY, In Search of the Miraculous, 198

She attributed most of her ills to the separation of the flesh from the spirit: A separation of the economics of the physical life with the economics of the spirit. A poverty suffered on one level is a poverty suffered on the other. And as a woman from a people deprived of many material necessities, who have no avenues of enriching their physical lives or satisfying their physical needs turn those unused energies to enriching what they can. Faith and hope cost much but not in cents and dollars. These she and the other poor could cultivate.

As for the spiritual/political split in the woman's movement, in the world—this was acted out in her body. Spirit is spirit only if it lives in mass, in flesh, in bones or astral energy fields. The bone too has its own oscillating pulse, of cells and their dance of nuclei and its positive and negative electrons.

She had found that she could not divorce her body from her spirit. The followers of Christ did this, elevating the spirit and denigrating the body. The indigenous people had (some still have) a fine balance between the body and the spirit. The Aztecs lost it in thinking that to maintain that balance they had to sacrifice the body to the spirit. And her people, the offspring of La Chingada, the india, must achieve that balance again, must acknowledge the existence of the two on the same plane. El espíritu es carne viva. Carne viva es el espíritu. That's why they were here–in the flesh on earth.

She did not have a language nor a vocabulary to talk about the body, about making love. The clit, her serpent's tongue, her sexual tongue had been silenced. Or because of disuse, she had forgotten to speak its language, how to move its tongue.

She was not allowed, nor had she allowed herself, to express who she was sexually. She had abnegated the responsibility to *be* who she was, to act out who she really was.

The body-split. She knew absolutely nothing about her body. Her clothes estranged her from it. The tight jacket, the tight pants, the cramped waist. Only when her body manufactured a sore throat or a stomach virus to tell her something was wrong with the way she was living life, only when illness scared her did she deign to listen to the body. It is then that she measured the beat of its burp, fart, sigh. And what an incredible song she heard. The flesh sings. The bones, that old workhorse, whispers: oh mujer, minha amor, what flor and what canto of flesh touching flesh, teeth teeth, fingers holes. There was no dead rhetoric, no boring abstractions in the sound of that bass drum heart, in the dance of hand strumming flesh. Oh, you body-mujer overcoming the tradition of muteness. Let me hear you sing. And her heart sang: transform your relation to another's body. And she nodded inwardly to herself and thought, "you can take that one step further: there can be no political liberation without a sexual liberation first. That is the liberation of women."

For if she changed her relationship to her body and that in turn changed her relationship to another's body then she would change her relationship to the world. And when *that* happened she would *change* the world.

When Persephone Press, the first publisher of *This Bridge Called My Back: Writings by Radical Women of Color* (1981), went bankrupt, Moraga and Anzaldúa arranged to have the collection published by Kitchen Table Press, and each of them wrote a new foreword for the second edition. In this short piece, we see Anzaldúa's spiritual activism in its earlier stages. Note also her unconventional use of italics to single out the English, rather than the Spanish.

## Foreword to the Second Edition

¿Qué hacer de aquí y cómo?
(*What to do from here and how?*)

Perhaps like me you are tired of suffering and talking about suffering, estás hasta el pescuezo de sufrimiento, de contar las lluvias de sangre pero no las lluvias de flores (*up to your neck with suffering, of counting the rains of blood but not the rains of flowers*). Like me you may be tired of making a tragedy of our lives. A abandonar ese autocanibalismo: coraje, tristeza, miedo (*let's abandon this autocannibalism: rage, sadness, fear*). Basta de gritar contra el viento—toda palabra es ruido si no está acompañada de acción (*enough of shouting against the wind—all words are noise if not accompanied with action*). Dejemos de hablar hasta que hagamos la palabra luminosa y activa (*let's work not talk, let's say nothing until we've made the word luminous and active*). Basta de pasividad y de pasatiempo mientras esperamos al novio, a la novia, a la Diosa, o a la Revolución (*enough of passivity and passing time while waiting for the boy friend, the girl friend, the Goddess, or the Revolution*). No nos podemos quedar paradas con los brazos cruzados en medio del puente (*we can't afford to stop in the middle of the bridge with arms crossed*).

And yet to act is not enough. Many of us are learning to sit perfectly still, to sense the presence of the Soul and commune with Her. We are beginning to realize that we are not wholly at the mercy of circumstance, nor are our lives completely out of our hands. That if we posture as victims we will be victims, that hopelessness is suicide, that self-attacks stop us in our tracks. We are slowly moving past the resistance within, leaving behind the defeated images. We have come to realize that we are not alone in our struggles nor separate nor autonomous but that we—white black straight queer female male—are connected and interdependent. We are each accountable for what is happening down the street, south of the border or across the sea. And those of us who have more of anything: brains, physical strength, political power, spiritual energies, are learning to share them with those that don't have. We are learning to depend more and more on our own sources for survival, learning not to let the weight of this burden, the bridge, break our backs. Haven't we always borne jugs of water, children, poverty? Why not learn to bear baskets of hope, love, self-nourishment and to step lightly?

With *This Bridge* . . . hemos comenzado a salir de las sombras; hemos comenzado a reventar rutina y costumbres opresivas y a aventar los tabes; hemos comenzado a acarrear con orgullo la tarea de deshelar corazones y cambiar conciencias (*we have begun to come out of the shadows; we have begun to break with routines and oppressive customs and to discard taboos; we have commenced to carry with pride the task of thawing hearts and changing consciousness*). Mujeres, a no dejar que el peligro del viaje y la inmensidad del territorio nos asuste—a mirar hacia adelante y a abrir paso en el monte (*Women, let's not let the danger of the journey and the vastness of the territory scare us—let's look forward and open paths in these woods*). Caminante, no hay puentes, se hacen puentes al andar (*Voyager, there are no bridges, one builds them as one walks*).

Contigo,
Gloria Anzaldúa

This interview with Linda Smuckler took place on November 5, 1983. During the early 1980s, Smuckler and Anzaldúa were friends and for a time lived in the same house in San Francisco. According to Anzaldúa's journals, this interview focused on "spirituality—how it affects my work" and "sexuality," and indeed, Anzaldúa explores both topics with great honesty. Anzaldúa used this interview transcript as she worked on the prose section of *Borderlands / La Frontera*. The interview is preceded by a brief exchange between Gloria and myself, which took place in 1998 and focuses on this 1983 interview. Gloria and I had planned to include this Smuckler interview in *Interviews/Entrevistas*; however, because of space limitations we were forced to remove it.

## Spirituality, Sexuality, and the Body

*An Interview with Linda Smuckler*

1998 Interview

AnaLouise Keating: In this interview you discuss feeling an intense inter-connectedness with people and things. Do you still have this sense of interconnectedness?

Gloria E. Anzaldúa: Yes. Sometimes I'll bump into a chair and I'll say "Excuse me." I'll go for a walk and I'll stare at a tree, the way it's silhouetted, and I feel such a connection to it, as though its roots grow out of my feet and its branches are my arms rising to the sky. Other times, when I'm so into the tasks I need to do, I lose that connection. Then when I walk I become oblivious to the sky, the trees, the sea otters, the whales, and whatever is out there in the sea. I have to bring myself back, and as soon as I put my attention on a little leaf or on the way the waves are coming in, I again feel that deep connection. This society doesn't encourage that kind of thing. Because we live in an accelerated age, we have so much thrown at us that there's no time to just look at the sky. Many people will schedule their walks, but instead of just walking and observing, they'll have their walkman on or they'll walk with a friend and be so busy talking that they won't even see the sky or Monterrey Bay. It's a constant struggle for me to bring myself back to connecting with things.

ALK: The connections are there, but you need to be in a certain frame of mind in order to recognize them.

GEA: The connections are there, the signs I read in the environment—if a snake crosses my path when I'm walking across Lighthouse Field, it means something to me. I'll look at that tree silhouetted by the sun, and its design says something to me, to my soul, which I then have to decipher. We get these messages from nature, from the creative consciousness or whatever you want to call the intelligence of the universe. It's constantly speaking to us but we don't listen, we don't look. At this point in my life it's hard for me to listen and look because there are so many things demanded of me. I need to simplify my life and slow it down so that I have these moments of connection. The same thing happens when I relate to people: If I'm talking to you but not really listening or observing your body language and I'm not really empathic with you, I don't really hear or see you. It's a multi-level kind of listening—not just to inanimate objects or animals, but to people. You listen with both outer ear and inner ear. This is the spiritual dimension of "la mano zurda," which combines activism with inner, subjective listening. It's a different way of being in tune with people and the environment.

ALK: Your statement now is quite different from the interview, where you talk about putting up a wall inside yourself so that you don't get overwhelmed by the interconnectedness. But here you talk about the necessity to become *more aware* of the interconnectedness.

GEA: Well, it goes both ways. At this time in my life, I need a lot of solitude. I live in my imagination, in my inner world. There has to be a balance: I need a community of people, I need to go out into the world, I need that connection. So it's either extreme. When I find myself being too much out in the world I have to put shields around myself so that I can come home, recuperate, recharge, and reconnect. But if I'm in my little womb of a house (for me, the house is always a symbol of the self), if I'm too protective, too much of a hermit, I have to take those shields off and let people in. That's why I like doing gigs: It allows me a way of earning a living and opens me up to different communities.

1983 Interview

*Origins of Spiritual Development*

Linda Smuckler: I want this interview's focus to be on spirituality—its effect on your life now and its involvement in your writing. I really want to talk about what you're doing and the larger sense of your work. Could you begin by tracing the origins and some of the history of your spiritual involvement? Was there a time when you didn't feel so connected?

GEA: My awareness of a spiritual dimension started when I began differentiating between who I was as a little kid and who my mother was, what the table was, what the wall was. When I was about three years old,

I was sitting on the floor and above me, on the table, were some oranges I wanted but couldn't reach. I remember reaching for the oranges; I could feel my arms getting really long. I really wanted those oranges, and suddenly there were three bodies, like I was three of me. (Like an ear of corn, which has all these coverings on it like sheaths: There was me and then from my center there were these three ears of corn and they were like my bodies, but they all came from one place.) I don't remember if I really got the oranges or not. Right after that experience I began to feel apart, separate from others. Before this point, I couldn't differentiate between myself and other things. I'd feel like I was part of the wall.

My spiritual awareness may have been triggered by my family's stories about the other world. Weird stuff, especially from my grandmother, Mama Ramona. I would listen to my father tell my mother about the phantom dogs that followed him sometimes when he drove around the fields and patrolled the ranch land, checking on the cattle. As he drove he'd see this big black dog on his left. He'd put his foot on the pedal and go faster and faster—and the dog would keep abreast. This happened to him repeatedly. He wasn't prone to fears or anything. He was very practical, but he always saw this big black dog. Sometimes there'd be two or three demon dogs.

My awareness of the spirit world also had to do with death. My brothers and my father were hunters. You had to be if you lived on the ranch. My people supported themselves and hunted to eat. They didn't go out and shoot like hunters do, during season, but if we needed something to eat they'd just go out and get it. I remember learning to hold a gun, my brother killing birds. My father had gotten BB guns for my brothers, later we got twenty-two caliber guns.

I was a pretty good shot. But I didn't like to kill anything; I just liked to shoot tin cans. I remember there was this cow that died and there were all these vultures eating the cow. In those days there were a lot of wild animals and they'd get run over by cars. You'd see rabbits, snakes, big birds, and deer dead by the side of the road. (All of that is gone now.) Very much like when it rains and you see a lot of frogs by the side of the road and they get run over by cars. It was real strange because here were these things that had gone to another place and that other place was inaccessible to me. It was scary because I couldn't see it.

LS: Did it have a lot to do with the land?

GEA: I think it had a lot to do with the environment. It made a very strong impression on me, and I was this little kid who was wide open. I was like a sponge; everything came in. I had no defenses, no way of keeping anything out, so I was constantly bombarded with everything. For example, once when I was in Prospect Park in Brooklyn for a picnic everyone was smoking cigarettes and putting them out in the grass. My whole body reacted: I could feel the pain of the grass. These people were turning their live cigarettes on it.

LS: Do you remember anyone in your family who was an ally or did you feel alone in this?

GEA: My brother Nune understood a little, but sometimes he used that understanding against me. I was most vulnerable to him because he was the one who got in the most and so could hurt me. (He still knows me pretty well.) But, no, I didn't feel that I had an ally. The land was my ally, but I also felt the dangers there. The physical and psychic energies there could also harm me. I'd hear people say that evil spirits (mal aigre [aire]) rode the wind, and that when a person got sick it was because the bad air had gotten in. When I grew up I scoffed at these ideas, but now that I'm older I know it's true. Bad vibrations come in the air; when someone is thinking bad about you—feeling envy, jealousy, or whatever and directing it at you—you get the evil eye; people really get sick. Mexicans heal the evil eye with an egg. We let the egg absorb the jealousy, envy, whatever emotion another person is directing at you. But I found that out later. You can be in a really horrible mood and I can be on top of the world and, if we're sitting here, after a while I start to absorb your stuff. Well, what happened with me was not only this type of one-to-one influence, but sometimes I'd feel depressed. I was grieving—not from anything that had to do with me or with anyone around me. I was grieving for the world. It was so strange. Sometimes I'd be walking around a neighborhood and feel everything going on in the block; a lot of times I don't want to go out. New York City has such tragedy and poverty and people selling drugs on the street. I saw a forty-five-year-old woman with severed neck muscles and a big hump on her back who couldn't hold her head up. I was thinking, "Here's this woman who for the rest of her life has to look at the ground; she can never look up." I came home and felt a lot of despair. But then I thought, "Well, this woman is probably coping really well. Maybe, because she looks at the ground all the time, she has unique insights. Her particular weakness, her illness, gives her access to certain kinds of things that we don't have." When I was little I didn't have that insight.

LS: It also sounds as if you had a feeling of becoming one with everything happening around you. It sounds like this still happens to you now.

GEA: Yes, it comes and goes: At times, I feel a real unification with people, real identification with someone or something—like the grass. It's so painful that I have to cut the connection. But I can't cut the connection, so instead of putting a shield between myself and you and your pain, I put a wall inside, between myself and my feelings. For a long, long time I had a really hard time getting in touch with what I was feeling—especially around pain because I had very severe menstrual periods. Instead of walling people out, I'd censor my feelings within my body. So the origin of my belief that there's something greater than myself came both from that empathy and identification I had with things and from the isolation when I didn't have it. When I had too much identification, I couldn't process the feelings; it was too painful. I'd be sitting here and I'd be feeling the subway, the birds, you, what you were feeling, the people below. I was like a tape recorder, picking up everything. You and I are listening to each other and you're focusing on what I'm saying and the other sounds fade, but with me it was different; everything came in at the same volume.

LS: Did you go through a process of protecting yourself?

GEA: Yes. I needed a lot of time by myself. I was a very studious little kid and used books as my refuge, a little cave I could enter—a cave with a door through which I could go into other worlds. I also had my imagination and a very strong imaginative life. When I was a kid, I'd make up stories at night for my sister, fantastic stories about the coyotes, this little girl named Prietita (which was my nickname), dogs, and horses. We were way old when I was still telling her stories. Last year was the very first time I'd gone home for Christmas in years. At one point during the two or three weeks I was there, I got up and started walking into the dining room and my sister grabbed my arm and said, "Tell me a story." Then she realized what she'd said and walked on. It was something out of the past: We were these two little kids and she was wanting a story. She was really embarrassed by it. She wanted to be nurtured, she wanted comfort, and she didn't know how to ask for it.

So I had those two retreats: the books and the knowledge. I could sit for hours and do all kinds of stuff. I could be the heroine. You know when you're a little kid, school is so unbearable; that's the only way I made it through school, by daydreaming and books. Under my English book, I'd be reading *Jane Eyre* or *Robinson Crusoe*.

## Education

LS: What happened when you reached adolescence? Did you put a lot of it away?

GEA: Oh yeah. I denied a whole lot of my sense of connection as I got to be an adolescent: All that stuff was superstition—the stories about demon dogs, La Llorona, and La Jila—all the tales that people of my culture tell. I was going through that "putting down my culture" thing. It was all connected to race. It was better to say I was Latin American or Spanish. In Texas and the Southwest, if you said you were Mexican, you were nothing. It's changed somewhat in the last few years, but when I was young it was like you had leprosy if you were a Mexican. I don't know how to explain it to you. Well, you know how it is because of the way people sometimes treat you if they know you're a lesbian. That's the way we were treated, but all the time because we were visibly Mexican. School educated Mexican kids to believe that their culture and spiritual stuff were no good. When I was a teenager, I tried to fit in, so I became very sophisticated. I had all this book knowledge; I read philosophy and psychology, and viewed mal de ojo, susto, and other Indian and Mexican indigenous beliefs about the spirit as "superstitious."

## Family Religion/Spirituality

LS: Let's back track for a second. Did you go to church? Was your family religious, in the formal sense?

GEA: No, my family was spiritual but not religious. They were brought up Catholic, but not Orthodox or Roman Catholic. It's a blend of indigenous, pagan religion with Catholicism. La Virgen de Guadalupe is an Indian equivalent of Mary. There was a Catholic church in Hargill, but none of us went to church. We kids were forced to make first communion. Most kids make their first communion when they're about seven; it's a pre-puberty rite of some sort: You dressed in white and everything. All four of us made the first communion at the same time. Only my little brother was seven. The church felt very alien to me.

LS: Was the priest white?

GEA: He was Spanish, from Spain; the Catholic Church had trouble getting Americans to be priests. Even after the masses all over the United States started to be in English, ours were still in Latin. I'd go for the music and for the incense.

LS: What was the church like?

GEA: Typically it was about as wide as this apartment; it was stone and had an A-shaped roof. The pews were wooden; there was a huge wooden cross on the altar, a statue of Jesus nailed to the cross, and on the right side a statue of the Virgen of Guadalupe with all these little votive candles around it. It was pretty bare and plain. Behind the altar were small cubicles where the priest dressed and where the altar things were kept. The women in the town took turns sweeping and washing the linen, and around the time we were making the first communion—which was before my father died—it was my mother's turn. She'd take us along, and we'd clean the altar and put flowers up. We'd go into the little room where the priest dressed, and I'd look at the things, the books, and his wine. It was like a sacred place—not because it was a church but because it dealt with the spirit. (I also feel that my room is a sacred place. Wherever there's incense and candles and people meditate or pray becomes a sacred place.)

The only times I went to church were for la doctrina (when you were being taught in the faith), the first communion, when my father died, and a couple of times when I was in Austin at the university. I went then to see what these modern Catholics were doing because they were celebrating mass with guitar music. That's about the extent of my going to church.

My grandmother Ramona was very spiritual. Almost everyone in my family had an altar for la Virgen de Guadalupe. I don't believe in personalized deities. The only reason I have la Virgen de Guadalupe is because Elva gave her to me. I also have Ganesh, the Indian goddess of fortune, Kali, Coatlicue, Tlazoltéotl, and my serpents. But I didn't believe most of the Catholic church's doctrine.

*University and Teaching*

LS: How long did the period last when you tried to put all of the spiritual life you had grown up with away?

GEA: Through high school and the early part of college—a seven- or eight-year period. But I couldn't really keep the spiritual down because I was always reading about mythology and religion. Then in college I took two courses: The Life of Christ and The Bible as Literature. I'd read religion, but I just didn't believe what Protestantism and Catholicism were doing to the spirit. This was around the time when the Chicano movement developed in the late 60's and I started reading Chicano poets and working in the movement. I was in a Chicano youth organization, MAYO (Mexican American Youth Organization), which met in the church I described.

LS: This was when you were in college?

GEA: Yes.

LS: Were you in college close to home?

GEA: I wanted to get away. At home, I could be a part but not all of myself. In *Home Girls* Barbara Smith says that at home she can be herself, but I couldn't be myself at home. I went as far away as I could: twelve hours north on the bus, eight hundred miles to Texas Woman's University in Denton. I went there the first year on scholarship and I worked, but the only help I received from my family was five dollars from my mother. I couldn't afford it, so I quit for two years and worked. When I started up again I went to Pan American, which was nearby and my mother would drive me. I went to school at night and worked days. When I was a sophomore, I bought my own car. Because I was going to become a teacher they made the payments small; the payments increased when I became a teacher. I was paying about $30 a month for the car. The third year, I worked as a teacher's aide and went to school full time and worked in the fields on weekends. I don't know how I did it. I was getting about two hours sleep a night. The fourth year, I did my student teaching, took nineteen hours, and worked a full-time job.

I graduated in December and started work the following week. I taught bilingual pre-school, working with five-year-olds. The second year I taught emotionally disturbed, mentally retarded kids. I couldn't teach in the high schools because Mexicans are only "good enough" to teach elementary. For three years they wouldn't let me teach high school.

When I taught high school I had to get up at 5:30 in the morning and drive forty miles, do bus duty at 7:30 in the morning, and then teach five classes in a row with forty kids in each class. I was a shy teacher, but it was either failing to be a teacher and not commanding respect, or doing it. And I did it. I taught Freshman, Sophomore, Junior, and Senior English and Literature and one Art class. (Because I was the new teacher, I had a lot of different preparations to make.) They had CVEA— Co-ordinated Vocational Academic—for migrant Chicanos who worked and weren't in school full time. They also had regular English and elevated sections. They'd give me a "plus" class (the geniuses), and a class with real trouble makers, hardened kids who were older than I was. For the first two weeks the "bad kids" gave me hell: They peed in the paper basket, smeared the walls with shit, and refused to do their work. They'd get up while I was talking and walk out the door without permission; they'd come in late—all kinds of shit. The other teachers sent them to the principal or the counselors, but I wouldn't. I talked to them and taught them. One day at the end of the first two weeks I walked into the room: Everyone was in their seats doing their work; the walls were clean, there was no piss in the wastebasket, no tacks on my seat; there was a little vase of flowers on my desk and about thirty apples. (Each kid had brought an apple.) When I walked in, nobody was talking. I couldn't believe it! I said, "What's wrong with you?" And one kid said, "Well we decided you were the best teacher around. You're really trying to help us. You're not bullshitting, so we're going to treat you good because you're the only one who has treated us with any kind of respect." So I was happy.

*Chicano Movement and Spiritual Roots*

LS: Can you say more about your involvement with the Chicano movement?

GEA: I started realizing that the stuff about the indigenous culture—ethnic spiritual beliefs—were not all superstition. I read *I am Joaquín*, by Corky Gonzales. It takes the Chicanos back to our roots: We weren't these alien people. We weren't white so the whites didn't want us, and we weren't Mexican so the Mexicans didn't want us. We were no longer second-class people, strangers in their own land. That's how we felt and how we were treated. César Chávez, Corky Gonzales, and La Raza Unida (a Chicano political party that began in the 60's), all made me want to go back and revise my view. I was reading Aztec mythology, Mayan history, Chicano literature, and I was teaching my kids. I started teaching them stories written by Chicanos even though the principal objected and threatened to fire me because Chicano literature wasn't "American literature." Also, I started working with the migrants; I went to Indiana and started supervising the migrant program.

But it all had to do with going back into my roots spiritually. When I started working on my master's I had one teacher, Dr. Sledd, who was a heretic and encouraged me to explore my roots in my writing. He was the first white person in college to encourage me. With him, being Mexi-

can was a positive thing, not a liability. In Indiana when I was working with the migrant program I felt very isolated. You know how when
you're alone a lot your fears rise up: You feel like there's somebody at the
window, or if your body gurgles a certain way and it scares you? All your
worst fears—you confront them when you're alone because there's no
energy going out to anybody else. I didn't have a lover. I had very few ac-
quaintances. I traveled throughout the whole state and was never in one
place for long. I lived in motels and had an apartment in South Bend. On
my days off, I'd just stay in the apartment. Things from another world
were all around me, but they were very amorphous; I couldn't concre-
tize them and say it was this shape or that shape. I just felt presences
around me.

When I went to Austin to work on my Ph.D., I started having really
weird experiences. In my apartment I started noticing that behind and
slightly above my left shoulder was this tall person I thought was a man.
This person would be saying to my head the things I was writing—like
somebody dictating to me. It was my own writing, my own stories and
ideas, but it was like somebody telling me. But it was a benign presence, not like in Indiana. I didn't feel threatened; I felt very comfortable. Sometimes when I'd walk to school it would follow me for two or
three blocks. This continued for a few semesters and one day my friend
Randy saw it. He described this person exactly as I pictured it. At the
time I thought it was a spiritual aspect of Julio Cortázar, my favorite
writer. Randy thought it was my father, but the person was real tall and
very skinny, and my father was not that tall. Later I thought it was just
a spirit I clothed in male garb but could have been female; it could have
been my father; it could have been anything. But to me, it was this long,
tall, thin man who was Cortázar. I moved and it didn't come with me. I
don't know what happened to it. It disappeared.

LS: Were you writing at this time?

GEA: Yes. I started writing in 1974 when I was in Indiana. The first thing
I wrote was a poem about a sacrificial knife. The second thing I wrote
was a short story, about sixty pages, called "The Private Gesture."* It's
about a man who commits suicide by cutting his heart out. Then I took
a class with a woman, Elaine Hemley who was teaching at IU. She loved
my writing and said "Oh, you should send this to a good quality literary

* This unpublished manuscript can be found in Anzaldúa's archives in the Nettie Lee
Benson Latin American Collection, University of Texas, Austin.

magazine. You've got to come to this conference and you've got to take my class next semester." It was a class on writing novels. So yes, I was writing and I was writing about these things too.

*Spirituality, Sexuality, and the Body*

LS: So by the time you got involved with your own work, your spiritual involvements had expanded?

GEA: Yes. One reason I kept the spirituality down is because it was so connected to the sexual, to the physical. I had this body that was a freak: I went into puberty and started bleeding when I was three months old; I had tremendous hot flashes; my breasts started growing when I was six. I was totally alien. Also, I was this wide open little kid who was picking up people's feelings, thoughts, and words and taking them all very seriously. It was very very painful. My childhood was a nightmare. I started shutting down where the pain was, in my body, and became nothing but reason, head, mind. When I started opening up to the body, the spiritual thing came out too because it was really connected with the body and sexuality.

LS: What were the experiences that helped you become more open in the acceptance of your body?

GEA: Well, fucking for the first time. The women in my school were already fucking in the seventh grade; by high school they were pregnant. They were working class, and sometimes the only way they could survive was to sell their bodies. Or the white employers would take advantage of them and make them their mistresses or whatever. When I was in the sixth or seventh grade, I had a friend named Lupe who worked with me in the fields. One day I was looking for her in the fields. (I liked to go with her because she sang and I liked listening to her songs; it was like having a radio while we worked.) I saw her in the irrigation ditch with a white patrón fucking her. She was about thirteen. That same afternoon in another ditch, he was fucking Aurora, her sister. Aurora got pregnant. I don't know if they fucked because they wanted to, because it was the only way they could keep their jobs, or because the guy was white and powerful. I don't know why. All my friends were like that, but I wasn't. My family wasn't. We were different. And within my family, I was different from the other family members. So when I had this boyfriend, the first time I had sexual intercourse with a man, I felt like I was normal. I was like all the other girls. Finally I was fucking someone, and I was already in my late twenties. I had already started teaching. I was dressing up, wearing heels. I was feeling really pretty and I weighed about 102 pounds. I looked really good, and I had all these men—and some girls too—chasing after me. So it felt like I had been led back into the flock, into the fold.

LS: You felt you had accomplished something that made you a person in the world?

GEA: I felt that I was no longer this stray sheep.

LS: How do you define the relationship between sexuality and spirituality?

GEA: I feel I'm connected to something greater than myself like during orgasm: I disappear and am just this great pleasurable wave, like I'm uniting with myself in a way I have not been. In this union with the other person I lose my boundaries, my sense of self. Even if it's just for a second, there's a connection between my body and this other's body, to her soul or spirit. At the moment of connection, there is no differentiation. And I feel that with spirituality. How can I say this without sounding like a book? Let me back up. When I'm there being sexual, sensual, erotic, it's like all the Glorias are there; none are absent. They've all been gathered to this one point. In spirituality I feel the same way. When I'm meditating or doing any kind of spiritual thing, there's a connection with the source. Then all the Glorias are connected: Gloria who's compassionate, Gloria who's jealous, Gloria who's a freak, Gloria who's lazy. It's ok to be me. In both the sexual and the spiritual act, all the "you's" are there, and it's a tremendous amount of energy.

LS: Do you ever feel that all these different "you's" conflict with each other, in the sexual or the spiritual experience?

GEA: Yes. It has to do with concentration. Instead of being with the event itself, I think about what I'm feeling, what the other person is feeling, where my head should be, or what I should do with my mouth. In the spiritual experience I wonder "When am I going to be enlightened? When is this energy going to flow into me?" Or I think about what I have to do during the day, instead of keeping my attention on the soul's presence. It's the same kind of distraction. The trick is to get to the place where I don't think about things, where I just act. That's difficult for someone with seven air signs! I always want to control everything, which means I have to supervise and plan everything. I'm either in the future or the past and never in the present.

*Writing and the Other*

LS: Do you find this happens in the writing too?

GEA: Yes, it's all part of the same thing. Last May, I realized that what I do in meditation is no different than washing my face or typing on the typewriter. I was doing a meditation when the soul appeared to me in the form of a woman. (I even wrote a poem about it.) It changed my whole life around. Now, everything I do is with this soul awareness, this spirit, in the back of my mind. If I'm sitting with you doing this interview or talking with Mirtha, I no longer think about the other things I have to do. In the past, only certain acts had my total dedication. I felt that writing and teaching were my work on this planet and that nothing else mattered: I wasn't attentive to people; eating was a chore; sweeping the floor had no meaning. But now everything has meaning and is sacred—the people, the trees, you. There aren't some people who are more important than others, even though I love some people more. Being a writer isn't more important than being a ditch digger. The definitions, categories, and restrictions society has put on these activities are wrong, not the activities themselves. A person assimilates society's definitions. The ditch digger probably feels like the lowest person in the social scale, while the writer, the artist, feels elevated in stature—not economically, but in their own self-righteous thinking—feels like somebody special.

Some days I feel totally competent, like I can do everything, but other days I don't. The other day Mirtha moved into the building and the movers couldn't get the desk through the door. Nobody could figure it out, and I went down there and said, "Let's think about this." I looked at it, figured out what was wrong, and suggested a way it would work. I felt so competent. Some days, though, I can't even take the wrappings off a new tape.

LS: Do you ever sabotage yourself?

GEA: Yes.

LS: Why does that happen?

GEA: Initially it takes a lot of energy to gather those forces, to concentrate to do the writing, to make love, or to meditate. Before I sit down to write, I'll sweep, mop, go for a walk—anything. It's so easy when I do it—so why don't I do it more often? Why don't I fuck more often? Why don't I write and not fight the writing? Why don't I meditate and not fight the meditation? I've been doing meditation now for seven years, a meditation every night and every morning. Why do I still fight it? You asked about the contradictory Glorias? The conscious part of myself that identifies as Gloria thinks she owns it all. She thinks that's who I am. When I had those experiences with the soul and the spirit, I was bigger than that little space or that person. My consciousness extended outside that sphere. It was a spark from the divine — if you think of the divine as this huge fire and all the people in the world as these little sparks from this huge fire; we return to that fire and we go out from it when we reincarnate. But this little spark is the conscious "I."

LS: You have an image.

GEA: Yes, the ego image that wants to be top dog. It doesn't want to have masters; it doesn't want to share with anyone. So there's the conscious I's resistance: It doesn't want anything to do with the soul or the Self because it would see itself as a little clod in a big field, and it wants to be the big field. The other resistance is fear. To a certain extent, you're happy with Linda and I'm happy with Gloria. But there are parts of Linda you probably keep down because you think that it wouldn't be admissible for those parts — especially the sexual parts, the parts religion and society don't permit — to rise up. We're afraid of the parts of us that are sub-human, that are like animals. We only know the consciousness part of ourselves because we don't want to think that there's this alien being in the middle of our psyche. For my whole life, I've felt like there's this alien being inside myself.

LS: And by tapping this place there's a fear. Do you think this is the fear you had when you spoke of being afraid of going mad?

GEA: Yes. I didn't know if I was imagining it, hallucinating it, or if it was real.

LS: Do you think that fear comes from the same place?

GEA: Yes. It's a fear of the "other." The movie *Alien* affected me greatly because I really identified with it. There was this serpent-like alien being, a parasite, in this man's chest. It exploded; the being rushed out — very much like my out-of-body experience. In the film, it seemed like they were taking all the things they fear and hate about themselves and projecting them onto the monster. Just like we did with blacks and like people do with queers — all the evils get projected. My sympathies were not with the people at all; they were with the alien. I think that's how the soul is: It's treated like an alien because we don't know it. It's like a serpent; it's slimy and bad. That's what they did with women's sexuality and with women. Men were the ones with the soul; they were supposed to be spiritual, and women carnal. All the evils get projected onto children, third world people, animals, and women. So much is projected onto women: They want to "cut a man's balls," they're the "temptress," they keep a man from achieving. The same thing happens with blacks: Blacks were animals, they had no intelligence, they raped, they killed—everything evil. And I think that's what people have done to the soul.

LS: I think we do it to ourselves too.

GEA: Yes. So for me it was a recognition of everything I hated and feared which was alien, other, incomprehensibly horrible because it was not "I." I remember looking at my dead father's face and realizing that he was on the other side now. He was this other thing, he wasn't human, he was dead and so in this realm of the other. To me spirituality, sexuality, and the body have been about taking back that alien other. According to society and according to Eastern philosophy and religion, I must suppress or kill a certain part of myself—the ego or sexuality. But I don't believe you have to slay the ego. I believe you have to leave it and incorporate all the pieces you've cut off, not give the ego such a limelight but give some of the other parts a limelight.

I need to accept all the pieces: The fucked-up Glorias go with the compassionate, loving Glorias; they're all me. To say I'm going to get rid of this Gloria or that Gloria is like chopping off an arm or leg. To accept this view, I also had to accept the fact that God is the Devil; they're the same person; good and evil are different parts of the same coin. Christianity did this horrible thing by polarizing God and the Devil.

LS: In this culture it's easy to polarize things because there's a desire to project negative things onto something that will absorb them—like creating all these monsters and saying that it's an "other" thing. To say it's part of the same thing means you have to accept it and love it in yourself, no matter what it is.

GEA: Today our scapegoats are the faggots, lesbians, and third world people, but in the future it will be people from other planets or even artificial humans—androids, people born in a test tube rather than the uterus. People will have different ways of projecting their shadows onto others. So my whole thing with spirituality has been this experience with this other alien in the body, the spirit, the writing, and the sexuality. When I was young I was one with the trees, the land, and my mother; there weren't any borders. Then I became separate, and made other people and parts of myself the other. Then I went one step beyond, into the supernatural world—the subtle world, the "other" world—and dealt with that kind of otherness. Plus the uncanny—the demon, the ghost, the evil, the apparition—become even more "other." There are different gradations of otherness. When I got so far from my feelings, my body, my soul I was—like, other other other. But then something kept snapping. I had to gather; I had to look at all these walls, divisions, gradations of being other other other, and determine where they all belonged. It was an energy of refocusing and bringing it all back together.

LS: Do you think that's why you had to write?

GEA: Exactly. Writing saved my life. It saved my sanity. I could get a handle on the things happening to me by writing them down, rearranging them, and getting a different perspective.

Oh! That's another thing I wanted to talk about, Linda: How I identify with all of these things and then separate myself from them. The same thing happens in the writing. When I'm coughing out stuff, when I'm totally identified with the emotions in what I'm writing, I even get sick. (I got sick yesterday. I was working on a poem about a crazy woman; my entire self was concentrated on it.) That happens in my good periods; most of the time only one part of myself concentrates on the writing. When I'm totally there, I sit at my desk, putting it out on the typewriter or on the paper, and I look at the clock and eight hours have gone by. I haven't even noticed. Those are the good times. They don't happen very often. Other times, I distance the material from myself: I cut the cord and separate myself, then look at it from out here, get a perspective on it, and re-arrange it. Then in rewriting and editing it I'm wholly there, experiencing it again but also detaching and getting a perspective also. It's really strange. It's like being on the inside and the outside at once: feeling what the character is feeling and at the same time judging whether you did this right or if you should change it so that the feeling will be . . .

LS: stronger or clearer?

GEA: Right. The same kind of dynamic happened in my life: When I tried to separate myself from other people, I separated myself from myself. I got so split, so divided from myself that I came close to dying. At times, the separation has been so extreme that the link almost snapped. Then I'd gather it all together again. So there's this dynamic—when I get sick, when I write, when I make love: The sense of otherness and the sense of wholeness.

LS: Since I've known you, you seem to maintain a fairly isolated type of existence. You seem to take care of your working place and your place to be Gloria.

GEA: Well, I haven't had very many lovers. My Venus is in Virgo and it's very picky. Very early I had this idealized picture of what I wanted from a relationship, and none of my relationships have come close, or I haven't been ready, or the other person hasn't been ready. There have been a couple of people . . . but maybe ten years from now. You know? Also, my body is only about three years old, so sexuality is really new. Two other things: First, I have Saturn in the seventh house which means I like my space, my liberty, and want to do things my way. Second, I obsess with people. I want to be there—total merging, but then I feel guilty, like I'm being too needy. It's been really difficult. I thrive when I live with other people, but I also meditate and need a lot of space.

LS: And no restrictions on you.

GEA: And no restrictions. So there are two different people in me. Every time I'm hooked, I get hooked on a woman, but then I start obsessing and say "I can't do that." I've been trying to work it out, but I think the isolation is over. That's another complaint of mine with the lesbian community. If you don't fuck a lot, if you're celibate or auto-erotic, you're . . .

LS: an outsider?

GEA: You said it. Even within the lesbian community, as a Chicana, as a woman who doesn't fuck enough, and as a spiritual person—I feel like an outsider. It's always the outside of the outside of the outside. I'm writing a poem about Texas called "del otro lado," "of the other side." We're also called "half and half."

LS: Half and half, what's that?

GEA: The people in Hargill, in south Texas, believed that if you were a lesbian, you were a woman for six months of the year and had periods, and for the other six months, you were a man and had a penis. My society pushes me out, and the lesbian community and feminist movement have their own little borders. You know, this side of the tracks, that side of the tracks. There's only so far you can be pushed back to the other side of the other side of the other side. It's all about worth.

LS: You mentioned that you used to be a painter. Was this when you were in school or before that? What happened to change the focus of your art, or did you ever think of painting as your career?

GEA: When I was little, I learned leathercraft. I'd make purses with lions and tigers, moccasins, belts, and wallets, and draw on them. So I got into drawing. Later, I became a seamstress and made my own designs.

I made clothes for myself, my sister, my mother, and a few cousins. People in town would come and I'd sew for them. In college I had a double major of Art and English with a minor in secondary education. I started teaching Art and became a painter, and my thing was oils. One of the first things I ever painted was Eve and the serpent in the Garden of Eden. My paintings were huge. I also sculpted and did design. Even as a child I knew I was going to be either an artist or a writer. When I was really young, I started writing in my journal. I'd write ideas for stories and poems, but I never wrote the actual pieces. In college, I couldn't afford oils; my family was poor. (Remember I told you the total contribution to my education was five dollars?) I made my own frames, got the gesso and the modeling paste; I did everything. My paintings were three-dimensional because I put modeling clay on them. My subconscious was communicating through my painting, but I wanted to articulate the ideas. I thought that writing was a better vehicle for my art, and that's when I started writing. I intend to combine writing and visual art. I also intend to do film, and I've written a play. I want to be multidimensional, but I have to get the writing together. I'm writing a book of stories called El Mundo Zurdo and Other Stories;[†] I've got about twelve stories in different draft stages. One story is about the soul, another is about borders, another is about a woman who goes through walls. I'm fictionalizing the things I believe in—all my spiritual and creative ideas. I'm writing a story called "The Woman Who Had a Penis;" it's a sexual/ spiritual fantasy I had.

## Writing/Spirituality

LS: What's your relationship between the writing and the spiritual? Is one secondary and one primary?

GEA: It's now like hand and glove, but it never used to be. Before, I obsessed about the writing: It was something different, my mission or task in life, and the spiritual was a way to manifest it. Now it's the other way around, or rather my mouth and the words from the typewriter are channels for what the soul has to manifest. I stopped obsessing about the writing. It's no longer set apart and elevated; instead, it's part of my life, like eating and drinking and taking a shit. I just walk to the typewriter and type whatever; it's not such a big deal anymore. But it

[†] The manuscript has not been published. It can be found in Anzaldúa's archives in the Nettie Lee Benson Latin American Collection.

took a long long time for me to get to that place. Sometimes I'll still fall back and obsess about the writing; then on Monday I'll say, "What did I do? Saturday and Sunday are my days off!" I was worrying about not writing and had forgotten my days off! But I think I'm getting to a point where if it's just a part of breathing and shitting and I feel like doing it on my days off, fine. I used to have a schedule: six hours per day at the typewriter. Usually I put in a fifteen-hour day. Three to six hours average on the typewriter and the rest of the time revising, reading, studying, taking notes, doing research and correspondence. But it's all writing-related so that the actual time of creativity is very small compared to the time getting it out.

*The Psychic*

GEA: A lot of my awareness of spirituality comes from the psyche, from the soul in a psychological point of view. I read Jung on the archetypes of the unconscious, Neumann on the creative unconscious and mythology, Hillman on dreams, death psychology, self-help books, how to discipline yourself, Nietzsche's *The Will to Power*. I was sort of my own shrink, and the writing was the medium. I couldn't afford to see a shrink and I was fucked up because of traumatic events and a horrendous childhood. My Uranus in Gemini is in the sixth house, the house of work which means that I want to invent new systems, new perspectives, new ways of looking at things. I study systems all the time—systems like psychology, archetypes, alchemy, all the stages of transformation, numerology, the Tarot, the I-Ching, the Sabian Symbols, and astrology. It's all for the purpose of knowing myself—knowing other people too, but especially for knowing myself. The more knowledge I have about the world, nature, psychology, philosophy, and all the different systems and belief systems of people, the better I can know myself and other people, and the better I can write.

The first book that changed my life was *The Art of Selfishness* by David Seabury. I realized it was all right for me to stay in bed, to read, study, and do the things I wanted to do—and not to feel bad about it, not to listen to my sister and mother say I was selfish because I didn't want to do housework. I preferred reading to doing the dishes or ironing my brothers' shirts. That accusation of selfishness really stayed with me because I was a sensitive kid. It's the worst internalized belief I had about myself, and it's been really hard dealing with it. Through psychology,

I realized that . . . I had gone ahead and done my own thing. I wasn't going to be what other people wanted me to be. I was going to go ahead and be what I wanted to be. If you come from where I come from, that's really radical. To leave home was radical because no one in my extended family had left home for seven generations. They'd been in the land from the beginning of time—I don't know how long, since before the Spaniards. No one had ever left home, gone to school, or wanted to expose family secrets through writing. No one was born like I was, bleeding. There were all these things I was supposed to do to be a good Chicana: Not leave home, not want to study, be satisfied with a woman's role, get married. I wasn't doing these things and I felt guilty. Reading *The Art of Selfishness* liberated me intellectually from those beliefs. Emotionally, I was still caught up with the guilt.

I started learning psychology after reading *The Art of Selfishness*, and psychology is one of my favorite fields. My master's thesis was an archetypal approach to literature using Jungian psychology. I'll be talking to other people—for example, to Christine who's going to be a psychoanalyst—I'll be asking them things about their field, and many times I'll find out that I have a wider knowledge than they do because I love the stuff. Right now I'm reading a James Hillman book, *Healing Fiction*, about fiction and how everything is a fiction. You have an experience and the way you interpret it is a fiction. I'm also reading *Echo's Subtle Body*, which is about Echo. Remember Echo and Narcissus? I love this stuff. I also read Mexican psychology and mythology and everything. I think that's the glue that brought my body and my spirit together.

## Goddesses

LS: I'm interested in Kali and the other goddesses and helping deities around you. Do you feel that these deities have different powers for you?

GEA: I'm very close to death, so I feel close to Kali, Tlazoltéotl, and Coatlicue. Also, most of them have to do with sexuality, witchcraft, and the repressed. All my life I felt those bad parts of myself punished and so ostracized that I wanted to bring them to the light. Not only personally, but collectively, like all of women's religion had been taken and pushed into the underworld. I see a resurgence of all of it. My whole struggle has very much been represented by Kali, the Hindu goddess of destruction and death but also of life, the blackness, the negativity, the alien.

There she is, so alien, and then there's Coatlicue with the face of two serpents facing each other. She has human skulls around her neck; her skirts are serpents, and her hands are eagle claws. She's so animal, so totally other, not human.

I'm concerned with why people differentiate animals from humans. To me, we're all related, even to the grass. People don't see animals . . . and they treat children the same way. I get really emotional when I think of this. Children are these little people with no rights. People aren't even aware that animals have a consciousness or souls or anything. Human is everything, and everything that's not human is a servant to mankind.

So these deities that aren't human remind me that part of myself is not human. You know how the fetus goes through different stages of evolution, the little tadpole and all that? We evolved from a one-cell animal. It's all recorded in the cells of the body. We're part animal, but people just want to be divine and angelic. They disown part of the self. People made the serpent into the most vile, obnoxious, horrible of all creatures, so I've made it a symbol of the soul. I don't think I'm just reacting—like here you have heterosexuality and so you have these real rebellious dykes and faggots and all their energy is counter-balanced by the opposition in them? I don't think that's what I'm doing. I think mine is an act of integration, but maybe it isn't. Maybe it's my ego thinking it's integrating. But I don't think so.

Sexuality was one of the aspects of myself personally that was relegated to the deepest depths because of my uterus and because of my two cultures. The Spaniards and the Indians are very sexually repressive of female sexuality. From the time I was a little girl, people tried to put strictures around what I did. I was supposed to be passive. I went through my tomboy stage when I was both the things a little girl was supposed to be and the things a little boy should be, and I got away with it. I think dykes can get away with it; I don't know about anybody else. It's pretty difficult for men to get away from the roles they're supposed to follow. We at least can wear pants and stuff. So these deities are very dykey deities. They're going against the rules. The Virgen of Guadalupe has never really appealed to me. I think I have her to please Elva.

LS: Because she gave it to you?

GEA: Yes. I should get over my prejudice against established religion. I hate Protestantism, I hate Christianity, I hate Judaism. Not the spirituality of it, but the establishment, the bureaucracy, the dogma.

# Part Two

## "Middle" Writings

My identity is always in flux; it changes as I step into and cross over many worlds each day—university, home community, job, lesbian, activist, and academic communities. It is not enough for me to say I am a Chicana. It is not enough for me to say I am an intellectual. It is not enough for me to say I am a writer. It is not enough for me to say I am from working-class origins. All of these and none of these are my primary identity. I can't say, this is the true me, or that is the true me. They are all the true me's.

—From "The New Mestiza Nation: A Multicultural Movement"

Although Anzaldúa included this poem in her all-poetry version of *Borderlands* (1985), she did not include it in the final manuscript. However, it effectively illustrates her developing aesthetics and her belief in the poet's subversive, transgressive powers.

## Enemy of the State

*for Adam Hall**

Stress level rising,
jumping in the thick of things
      trying to make sense of everything
always the questioning.

Being up against it day and night
don't have to forage
in garbage dumps
      with the rats.

Just walk down any day or street
turn over stiffening bodies
      yes, this one was poisoned–smell her breath
      that one raped, see the blood seeping.
Stress level rising, rising.

Ferreting in the dark
      psyches of a people
uncovering secrets
      taking notes.

Returning to her warren
to decipher the melody
      in the beat of the heart
the maggot's tracks
      on putrefied flesh
sniff out the alphabet
      in blood's metallic smell.

* During the 1970s and early 1980s, Adam Hall was one of Anzaldúa's favorite espionage writers.

Sitting still, pacing,
  muttering under her breath,
letting the images mold
  themselves in the dark
letting the voices divulge
  go public in the family's dirty laundry.

It's no use teaching her
  to sweep dirt under rugs
  to keep the lid on
  frequent closets filled with camouflage clothing
to censor, deny, lie.

No fading into the woodwork
  in her purple, red, fuschia.
Who'd ever think her
  a spy
betraying her country
  unmasking her country
  risking neck to chopping block.
Poet: enemy
  of the state.

This poem, which was published in revised form in Juanita Ramos's *Compañeras: Latina Lesbians*, was included in Anzaldúa's poetry manuscript of *Borderlands* (1985) but not in the 1987 published version. As its title, which translates into English as "Of/from the Other Side," might suggest, the poem explores the sense of alienation and homelessness experienced by many queers.

## Del Otro Lado

She remembers
the horror in her sister's voice
"Eres una de las otras,"
the look in her mother's face
as she says, "I am so ashamed.
I will never be able to raise
my head in this pueblo.
Me doy un tiro en la cabeza
I'll shoot myself in the head with a gun
if you tell the people of this town
that you're a jota."
The mother's words are barbs
digging into her flesh.
De las otras. Untouchable.
"But I'm me," she tells her.
"I've always been me."
"Don't bring your queer friends
into my house, my land, the planet.
Get away, don't contaminate us.
Vete a la chingada de aquí."

Away, she went away.
But every place she went to
they'd push her to the other side
and that other side pushed her to its other side
and the tracks went on forever.
Kept in the shadows of others.
No right to sing, to rage, to explode.
"You should be ashamed of yourself.
People are starving in Ethiopia,
dying in Guatemala and Nicaragua

while you talk about gay rights and orgasms."
Pushed to the end of the world
there she made her home on the edge
of towns, neighborhoods, blocks, houses.
Pushed always toward the other side.
In all lands alien, nowhere citizen.
Away, she went away
but each place she went to
pushed her to the other side,
al otro lado.

Written in 1984, this poem was included in the poetry manuscript of *Borderlands* (1985) but not in the published version. This never before published poem serves as a bridge of sorts in Anzaldúa's transition from western to indigenous myth. Note the similarities between this encounter with Medusa and Anzaldúa's encounters with Coatlicue in "La herencia de Coatlicue" of *Borderlands/La Frontera*.

## Encountering the Medusa

"Who in me says I'm ugly, makes me feel guilty;
who is it in my soul that needs you so desperately?"
—JAMES HILLMAN, *Revisioning Psychology*, 139

Regular visitor she's become
can't seem to shake her
        out of my hair
everywhere I turn she's there
        her cold piercing stare
one glimpse and I freeze.

It's no use reciting my list
when I make the slightest move
with my hand
                they hiss and writhe
                the snakes in her hair
                stop me in my tracks
                bring the sweat every time

Too familiar she's become
you'd think I'd get used to it
I look in the mirror
                see her numinous glare
                know the daemon is there
                what a nightmare

I want to take a machete
hack off her head
        slip it on
turn my enemies to stone
        deaden desire

She was a horse
moved with the speed of lightning
till something frightened her
someone laid a curse on her
                    paralyzed her

let's go, Ice Maiden, *move it*
make something, do something
                    anything
Don't just sit there
letting emptiness gnaw    your bones
            Move it.

No use, I'm stuck in her grip
            ice cold
in the mirror
            her glittering eye
she can't move forward
I can't move backwards
frozen in this borderland
            this no-man's-land
            forever inbetween
dry whisper of scales
            fill my ears

They thresh and hiss
                    the snakes in my hair
                    my cold piercing stare
                    I'll turn you to stone.

This never before published essay is a revised version of a talk Anzaldúa gave in May 1986 at Vermont College. At the time, Anzaldúa was writing the prose chapters for *Borderlands/La Frontera*. Although this piece is not as polished as some of Anzaldúa's other work, it offers important linkages with *Borderlands* and enables us to see the ways she was developing her epistemology and her theories of the imagination and reading.

## Creativity and Switching Modes of Consciousness[1]

There are many modes of consciousness: the rational, reasoning mode, which is to me connected with the external reality, with the world that we inhabit right now; and other modes of consciousness connected with the world of imagination, the world of fantasy, and the world of images. Writers, artists, and creative scientists traffic back and forth between these worlds, switching from one mode of consciousness to another. There are probably many intermediary modes of consciousness that we're not even aware of, that we tune out, because we're so focused on physical reality. The same applies when we're in our daydreaming stages, our fantasy stages, our creative stages: we don't hear the buses roaring down the street or the voices in the next apartment, we're so focused on that inner world.

I want to talk about the interfaces one crosses when switching between the upper, or external, reality and the underworld, the world of the soul and its images. One reason I'm concerned with these realities is because my last name, "Anzaldúa," is a Basque name, where "an" means above, the upper worlds, the sky, the spirit; "zal" means the underworld, the world of the soul, of images, of fantasy; and "dúa" is the bridging of the two; and the bridge, to me, is the interface.

When I was really little, I felt like the external reality was too much. I had a very thin skin, and everything came in. I guess you could say I was "sensitive." I had some physiological problems: My hormones were over-developed from the time I was about three months old until about five years ago when my ovaries were taken out in a hysterectomy. As a three-year-old, a six-year-old, an eight-year-old, I had the body and some of the feelings of an adolescent, a person going into puberty. I never had a conventional childhood; my body, my hormonal activity, made me a freak. So I felt a lot of pain when I was growing up because I was different, because I had breasts and the other little girls didn't have breasts; because I had a period, I bled, and the other muchachitas didn't bleed. And because I had a very thin skin, everything came in — people's words, people's looks, any kind of put-down. If another person was hurting, I would hurt. If my mother killed a chicken or a hog or a steer, I would feel that pain. I couldn't even kill a mosquito, and in south Texas mosquitoes were rampant before they were sterilized in the 60's. To this day I cannot kill a cockroach. Everybody thinks I am silly because I will not squash them, but squashing them is painful to me.

I had to cope with this over-sensitivity and sense of difference, and to cope I escaped from the external reality into the inner world, the world of dreams, the world of daydreams, the world of images. I became a storyteller. I'd tell my sister stories, and later I became a book junkie. The outer world was painful, but so was the inner. There were certain realizations about myself that I had to face, and when I tuned in to myself, those realizations hurt. I had a lot of faults, a lot of flaws. Because I had always expected more from myself than is humanly possible to expect from oneself, both the introspective space and the outer world were full of pain. I used reading to switch out of both worlds. I'd escape into the world of the text. I immersed myself in reading—not just the serious stuff, like philosophy, psychology, history, mythology, fiction, and poetry, but also into junk reading: westerns, mysteries, fantasies, science fiction, gothics, spy thrillers. . . . all popular genres. (Now, I'm coping much better.)

When I studied painting and writing, I discovered that I could create concrete universes. Rather, I didn't create them; I was the conductor for them, the channel. Sometimes these worlds would write or paint themselves out. But writing is not easy. (I should say, for me it's not easy to *start* writing, but once I start it's fairly easy.) All my escape modes had problems: I couldn't be in the outer world all the time because that was painful. I couldn't be in the inner world all the time because that was painful, too. I couldn't be in the artistic world—off creating through paint, or through words—because that meant confronting all my fears and all the problems in my life that I was trying to resolve and bring to order through the writing. So I became very adept at switching from one mode of consciousness to another.

Besides feeling like a freak, like I had no skin, there was also the stoop labor that I grew up doing as a farm worker. Growing up en el rancho, the only jobs available to us were picking cotton, hoeing cotton, picking cabbages, strawberries, tomatoes, watermelon, cantaloupe, carrots, and onions, or working in the bodegas—the packing sheds, which meant washing, sorting, weighing, and getting things ready for the market. That kind of labor was so horrendous, supposedly fit only for Mexicans and

Indians. We were dumb, we were lazy; all we were good for was stoop labor, and we did it from the time we got up in the morning at four or five o'clock until the sun went down at eight—as much as fifteen hours a day. After a few months, a few years, a few decades, a few centuries . . . you started feeling like an animal: You were nothing and possessed no dignity. This racial, cultural stigma was so unbearable that I would do anything to get out; and the only way I could get out was to educate myself even though my family, my relatives, the people in surrounding farms and ranches were not people who went to school. (Most didn't even get as far as the third grade; others dropped out in the sixth or seventh grade. Books were not acceptable to them.) I was so horrified at this kind of pain; I just had to get out, and so I started teaching myself. From reading books, I realized that there were other roles besides being a Mexican farm worker.

It seems like one of my functions is to go in and out of various worlds. Over there in south Texas, where I come from, there are hardly any white people. I didn't see any white people until I went to high school, and even then I didn't talk to one until I was working on my master's degree. The terrain in south Texas is different. My homeland was desert until they started irrigating and turned the desert into a subtropical paradise, a garden that grows everything from papayas, to avocados, to sugar cane, to . . . whatever . . . all in the space of my lifetime. The straight world, the gay world, the literary world, the world of academia . . . I go in and out of these worlds. I think that's why I picked this topic tonight, so that I could give you a different perspective. The function of a teacher is to give other people a different perspective.

> ii. The conqueror overcomes the old inhabitant in the body, but
> succumbs to his spirit.—JUNG [*Civilization in Transition*]

When the Spaniards conquered the Indians—gave us the Spanish language, and took over the whole of Mexico and the Southwest—perhaps they really did not "conquer" the Indians? After all, Chicanos are about 80% Indian, and almost everything in our culture is Indian. There is very little Spanish. That's history.

Anthropologists like Levi-Strauss talk about the "primitive" mode of consciousness, what they call the "participation mystic," the magical mind, the savage mind. From this perspective, "mind" is the world of imagination, the world of the soul, the world of the spirit, and these worlds are just as real as the physical reality. The white anthropologists claimed that Indians are unsophisticated, that their minds are too primitive, that they cannot think in the "highest" mode of consciousness, rationality. These anthropologists split the world of imagination from the world of the spirit from the world of the soul from waking conscious reality, defining external reality as the official reality. The alarm goes off, you get up and go to your job. You cross the street. You buy groceries and you pay bills. This reality is privileged over the others. But there is another world, and it crops up when we least expect it. . . . when we're sitting and go in and out of different states of consciousness.

When we least expect it, usually when we're tired or bored, daydreams may come. Daydreams are images or scenarios that occur in little sequential dramas; usually the daydreamer is the hero or the heroine and daydreams are about things the dreamer wants—a good lover, or a good life, a promotion in a job, a car, an award, money.

I passed a lot of my time in high school sitting in classes, open book in hand, daydreaming. It was my way of escaping the boredom and the total isolation I experienced. When I became a teacher, I'd doodle and write in my journal through endless faculty meetings.

Most people don't realize that they are switching modes or when they do switch modes. Do you notice when you go from daydream mode? Do you remember your dreams at night? Do you remember your reveries (reveries are the hypnagogic states just before sleep, between waking and sleeping)? Most people don't remember their dreams unless they make a conscious effort to remember them, to write them down and work with them. Others say that they never dream, but that's not true. Everybody dreams an average of five dreams per night.

Nothing is separate. It all filters through from one world to another, from one mode of consciousness to another.

The Function of Imagination

We are told by our culture that waking is one state of being and dreams are the other, and that never the twain shall meet. But why must these boundaries and stratifications be made? Some of us are awake while dreaming and dreaming while awake.

Whatever occurs back in the external world first occurs in the imagination. We use the imagination to rehearse what we're going to say to our friend, to our teacher, what we want five years from now (to have a college degree, a good job, a settled existence, to be physically together). We constantly act out these scenarios in our inner minds, playing them over and over again. Conversations, scenes, events that have happened—we revise what we said into what we should have said, what happened into what should have happened. We learn lessons in this manner.

Images

When I'm writing, I sketch images in order to gather and organize my thinking. For me, this sketching is better than making outlines. An image is worth a thousand words because there is a cluster of meanings associated with each image, with each thing that I sketch. There's a difference between people who use rational thought and people who use visual images, who use sensory images, to organize their thoughts. Images speak to us. They have their own meaning, and you sort of get behind the symbology and see what they are saying. Sometimes these images are very important because they connect different experiences that we have had, and give meaning to them.

Picture the ocean, then picture the shore. Let's say that the ocean represents the unconscious, the imagination, the imaginal world, the underworld. The ocean comes sweeping over the land (the land representing rationality, the reasoning mode). The water comes in and then goes out, connecting the shore with the ocean. I think of the creative person/artist as a little boat that is moored to the earth, to the shore, to the pier, but it also goes out into the ocean, the unconscious, the world of the imagination. The boat traffics back and forth between the two worlds.

Often when reading a poem or a story, before it even hits your mind, it's already plucking at your flesh, tugging at your heart. When it does that to you before it hits your mind, it has activated your imagination. You'll feel and experience things, not just visually or kinesthetically, but with your whole body and mind.

The spirit world, the underworld, and the world of imagination can be experienced as one world or as several. A person in the Santería tradition will say that stones talk to her. Somebody in the western mode will disagree and insist that stones can't talk to her, but for the Santería both are equally real. Because the various worlds are equally real, we can have the presence of the tree or the rock talking to us. The wind or the whirlwind are bringers of messages, while "Western man" would call these messages acts of imagination, of fiction. People make up stories, entirely "fictitious" stories, according to the way they've been raised.

To me, everything is real. Fiction is as true as whatever happened literally to people. (James Hillman talks about similar ideas in *Healing Fictions*.) The body does not discern between different kinds of stimuli; the body doesn't distinguish between what happens in the imagination and what happens in the material world. Every time you have a nightmare or think about meeting someone, your mental/emotional scenario makes you nervous and flustered. The body responds. The body mediates these two realities; it is in the body that they coexist. There's frustration in trying to separate the two and in making distinctions between them. We, the body, are the union, and that's part of the frustration in trying to mediate between the two. You see yourself as a body going through these things, like in a film. You're lying down and present in external reality, and you're seeing yourself as though in a movie; your dream body (your imagined body) is actually walking on the ocean, by the hillside . . . It's real. That's what I meant about fiction not being fiction, or being real. Either that or everything is fiction, but it's not one or the other. What happens in the imagination is not fiction.

I often ask my writing students to do an exercise invoking the imagination. Each pretends that she'll be getting an award for her work. She comes on stage, people applaud. She feels so proud and so full of joy and her heart beats fast. If she goes through this scenario when she's relaxed, her body goes through the experience as if she were really receiving that award. It's a kind of priming life to give her that reality; because her body has already experienced it, she is much more likely to get that award.

When you die there's an alteration of the body's chemicals and minerals. What's left over is supposed to be the soul. Some people call this the total self, the dream body that lives on after the physical body dies. But there was an earlier "alteration": The existence of the soul before it entered this plane of reality, the whole human race as it existed before it altered into flesh and blood, it materialized as body.

Some people call the body that exists in our world the dream body. According to this belief, once upon a time, we didn't exist as physical entities but instead existed as dream bodies—pure spirit or pure soul. Out of the dream body, out of the idea, emerged physical reality. Trees, frogs, sky, earth, animals, and people became concrete, took on flesh and blood. But according to this concept, we didn't leave the dream body behind, we didn't leave the soul behind. It speaks to us through daydreams, reveries, dreams, and creative acts; it speaks to us in the moments when we are least aware.

In the Christian myth about the Garden of Eden, the loss happened because Eve ate the apple; she is blamed for being tempted by and succumbing to the serpent. But there's another interpretation of that loss: The leaving of Paradise occurred 3.5 billion years ago when the first sign of any kind of sentient life began on this earth. That "alteration" changed from the idea form (the dream-body, the non-physical entity) into carnality, the idea-form becoming body. Before that idea-form, the self was free, unlimited. Because it had no body, it had no sex, it didn't have to scrounge around for food, it didn't have to protect itself. All of a sudden it changed into body and had to contend with its limitations, with having to clothe and feed and procreate itself. It became two sexes with two genders. Some believe there is a deeper spirit which encompasses the body, that there is a physical level, a dream level, an image level, a soul level, and an over soul level.

There are various ways that you can get into the threshold of creativity, the gateway to the imaginal universes, the dream world. One is via deep muscle relaxation and another is by slowing the cycle of your brain waves. The cycle that we operate in when we're wide awake and functioning is called alpha. It's between twelve to eight cycles per second. Next is beta, which is a little slower—around six cycles. You're more likely to experience images and access the dream state, the daydream state and the reveries, in the beta cycle. The hypnagogic stages come right after that, just before you fall asleep. Then comes theta, four cycles per minute, deep sleep. You can get into these states at will by doing breathing exercise. Or you can buy a machine called INNER QUEST 2 or 3 which uses sound and flickering lights to induce these states.

Have you ever been on a train, plane, or bus, and you were tired, but you couldn't sleep, yet you knew that for about thirty seconds you did go to sleep . . . isn't that a weird kind of twilight time? I believe that we all live in this world some of the time, but only a few people are aware of it. Artists cultivate entrance into this state because it gives them material to work with. We artists live half the time in the imaginary worlds and the other half in other kinds of mental worlds. I'm not sure that we live in physical reality very much at all or that physical reality can exist without being represented by the mind.

Have you ever been asleep, and you had a dream that was so real that you thought you were awake? And you think that maybe you were awake in this dream, while you were asleep? So, would you say they lied to us about saying that sleep is one state, and waking is another state, and that they're distinct and separate? Why do you think our cultures lie to us? Remember the example of being in the boat. You were a boat, and you went out to sea a little bit, and then you went out to sea a little bit more, and then you went up back to the shore. The writer/artist has access to this conduit— between waking consciousness and other states, sometimes automatically accessing altered states through deep relaxation, guided visualization, or imagining.

1. This is a revised version of a transcribed lecture given on May 26, 1986, at Vermont College's Noble Hall, Montpelier, Vermont.

First published in 1987 in *Sinister Wisdom: A Multicultural Journal by and for Lesbians*, this short essay illustrates Anzaldúa's use of postcolonial theory to revisit the issues of accountability and identity explored in earlier writings like "La Prieta." After positing "whiteness" as an oppressive epistemological and social framework which we have all internalized, Anzaldúa uses this critique to challenge women of colors and others from marginalized groups to move beyond simple forms of us-against-them oppositionality and develop new individual and communal identities. She also explores new configurations of intersubjectivity (relational identity) and offers an early articulation of her theory of nos/otras, expressed here as "see[ing] through the eyes of the Other."

# En Rapport, In Opposition
*Cobrando cuentas a las nuestras*

Watch for Falling Rocks

The first time I drove from El Paso to San Diego, I saw a sign that read "Watch for Falling Rocks." And though I watched and waited for rocks to roll down the steep cliff walls and attack my car and me, I never saw any falling rocks. Today, one of the things I'm most afraid of are the rocks we throw at each other and the resultant guilt we carry like a corpse strapped to our backs for having thrown rocks. We colored women have memories like elephants; the slightest hurt is recorded deep within. We do not forget the injury done to us and we do not forget the injury we have done another. Unfortunately, we do not have hides like elephants. Our vulnerability is measured by our capacity for openness, intimacy. And we all know that our own kind is driven through shame of self-hatred to poke at all our open wounds. And we know they know exactly where the hidden wounds are.

> I keep track of all distinctions. Between past and present. Pain and plea-sure. Living and surviving. Resistance and capitulation. Will and circum-stances. Between life and death. Yes. I am scrupulously accurate. I have become a keeper of accounts. — IRENA KLEPFISZ[1]

One of the changes that I've seen since *This Bridge Called My Back* was published is that we no longer allow white women to efface us or suppress us.[2] Now we do it to each other. We have taken over the missionary's "let's civilize the savage role," fixating on the "wrongness" and moral or political inferiority of some of our sisters, insisting on a profound difference between oneself and the Other. We have been indoctrinated into adopting the old imperialist ways of conquering and dominating, adopting a way

111

of confrontation based on differences while standing on the ground of ethnic superiority.

In the "dominant" phase of colonialism, European colonizers exercise direct control of the colonized, destroy the native legal and cultural systems, and negate non-European civilizations in order to ruthlessly exploit the resources of the subjugated with the excuse of attempting to "civilize" them. Before the end of this phase, the natives internalize western culture. By the time we reach the "neocolonialist" phase, we've accepted the white colonizers' system of values, attitudes, morality, and modes of production.[3] It is not by chance that in Texas the more rural towns' Chicano neighborhoods are called *colonias* rather than *barrios*.

There have always been those of us who have "cooperated" with the colonizers. It's not that we have been "won" over by the dominant culture, but that it has exploited preexisting power relations of subordination and subjugation within our native societies.[4] The Great White Ripoff—and they are still cashing in. Like our exploiters who fixate on the inferiority of the natives, we fixate on the fucked-upness of our sisters. Like them we try to impose our version of "the ways things should be"; we try to impose one's self on the Other by making her the recipient of one's negative elements, usually the same ones that the Anglo projected on us. Like them, we project our self-hatred on her; we stereotype her; we make her generic.

Just How Ethnic Are You?

One of the reasons for this hostility among us is the forced cultural penetration, the rape of the colored by the white, with the colonizers depositing their perspective, their language, their values in our bodies. External oppression is paralleled with our internalization of the oppression, and our acting out from the oppression. They have us doing to those within our own ranks what they have done and continue doing to us—Othering people. That is, isolating them, pushing them out of the herd, ostracizing them. The internalization of negative images of ourselves, our self-hatred, poor self-esteem, makes our own people the Other. We shun the white-looking Indian, the "high yellow" Black woman, the Asian with the white lover, the Native woman who brings her white girlfriend to the Pow Wow, the Chicana who doesn't speak Spanish, the academic, the uneducated. Her difference makes her a person we can't trust. Para que sea "legal," she must pass the ethnic legitimacy test we have devised. And it is exactly our internalized whiteness that desperately wants boundary lines (this part of me is Mexican, this Indian) marked out. Woe to any sister or any part of us that steps out of our assigned places, woe to anyone who doesn't measure up to our standards of ethnicity. Si no califica, if she fails to pass the test, le aventamos mierda en la cara, le aventamos piedras, la aventamos. We throw shit in her face, we throw rocks, we kick her out. Como gallos de pelea nos atacamos unas a las otras — mexicanas de nacimiento contra the born-again mexicanas. Like fighting cocks, razor blades strapped to our finger, we slash out at each other. We have turned our anger against ourselves. And our anger is immense. Es un ácido que correo.

Internal Affairs o las que niegan a su gente

> Tu traición yo la llevo aquí muy dentro,
> la llevo dentro de mi alma
> dentro de mi corazón.
> Tu traición.
> —CORNELIO REYNA[5]

I get so tired of constantly struggling with my sisters. The more we have in common, including love, the greater the heartache between us, the more we hurt each other. It's excruciatingly painful, this constant snarling at our own shadows. Anything can set the conflict in motion: The lover getting more recognition by the community, the friend getting a job with higher status, a break-up. As one of my friends said, "We can't fucking get along."

So we find ourselves entreguerras,[6] a kind of civil war among intimates, an in-class, in-race, in-house fighting, a war with strategies, tactics that are our coping mechanism, that once were our survival skills and which we now use upon one another,[7] producing intimate terrorism — a modern form of las guerras floridas, the war of the flowers that the Aztecs practiced in order to gain captives for the sacrifices. Only now we are each other's victims, we offer the Other to our politically-correct altar.

El deniego. The hate we once cast at our oppressors we now fling at women of our own races. Reactionary — we have gone to the other extreme — denial of our own. We struggle for power, compete, vie for control. Like kin, we are there for each other, but like kin we come to blows. And the differences between us and this new Other are not racial but ideological, not metaphysical but psychological. Nos negamos a sí mismas y el deniego nos causa daño.

Breaking Out of the Frame

I'm standing at the sea end of the truncated Berkeley pier. A boat had plowed into the black posts, gouging out a few hundred feet of structure, cutting the pier in two. I stare at the sea, surging silver-plated between me and the lopped-off corrugated arm, the wind whipping my hair. I look down, my head and shoulders, a shadow on the sea. Yemayá pours strings of light over my dull jade, flickering body, bubbles pop out of my ears. I feel the tension easing and, for the first time in months, the litany of work yet to do, of deadlines, that sings incessantly in my head, blows away with the wind.

> Oh, Yemayá, I shall speak the words
> you lap against the pier.

But as I turn away I see in the distance, a ship's fin fast approaching. I see fish heads lying listless in the sun, smell the stench of pollution in the waters.

From where I stand, queridas carnalas—in a feminist position—I see, through critical lens with variable focus, that we must not drain our energy breaking down the male/white frame (the whole of western culture) but turn to our own kind and change our terms of reference. As long as we see the world and our experiences through white eyes—in a dominant/subordinate way—we're trapped in the tar and pitch of the old manipulative and strive-for-power ways.

Even those of us who don't want to buy in get sucked into the vortex of the dominant culture's fixed oppositions, the duality of superiority and inferiority, of subject and object. Some of us, to get out of the internalized neocolonial phase, make for the fringes, the Borderlands. And though we have not broken out of the white frame, we at least see it for what it is. Questioning the values of the dominant culture which impose fundamental difference on those on the "wrong" side of the good/bad dichotomy is the first step. Responding to the Other not as irrevocably different is the second step. By highlighting similarities, downplaying divergences, that is, by rapprochement between self and Other it is possible to build a syncretic relationship. At the basis of such a relationship lies an understanding of the effects of colonization and its resultant pathologies.

We have our work cut out for us. Nothing is more difficult than identifying emotionally with a cultural alterity, with the Other. *Alter*: to make different; to castrate. *Altercate*: to dispute angrily. *Alter ego*: another self or another aspect of oneself. *Alter idem*: another of the same kind. Nothing is harder than identifying with an interracial identity, with a mestizo identity. One has to leave the permanent boundaries of a fixed self, literally "leave" oneself and see oneself through the eyes of the Other. Cultural identity is "nothing more nor less than the mean between selfhood and otherness . . ."[8] Nothing scares the Chicana more than a Latina who lumps her with the norteamericanas. It is easier to retreat to the safety of the difference behind racial, cultural, and class borders. Because our awareness of the Other as object often swamps our awareness of ourselves as subject, it is hard to maintain a fine balance between cultural ethnicity and the continuing survival of the culture, between traditional culture and an evolving hybrid culture. How much must remain the same, how much must change.

For most of us our ethnicity is still the issue. Ours continues to be a struggle of identity—not against a white background so much as against a colored background. Ya no estamos afuera o atrás del marco de la pintura—we no longer stand outside nor behind the frame of the painting. We are the foreground, the background, and the figures predominating. Whites are not the central figure; they are not even in the frame, though the frame of reference is still white, male, and heterosexual. But the white is still there, invisible, under our skin—we have subsumed the white.

## El Desengaño

And yes, I have some criticism, some self-criticism. And no, I will not make everything nice. There is shit among us we need to sift through. Who knows, there may be some fertilizer in it. I've seen collaborative efforts between us end in verbal abuse, cruelty, and trauma. I've seen collectives fall apart, dumping their ideals by the wayside and treating each other worse than they'd treat a rabid dog. My momma said, "Never tell other people our business, never divulge family secrets." Chicano dirt you do not air out in front of white folks, nor lesbian dirty laundry in front of heterosexuals. The things cultural stay with la Raza. Colored feminists must present a united front in front of whites and other groups. But the fact is we are not united. (I've come to suspect that unity is another Anglo invention like their one sole god and the myth of the monopole.[9]) We are not going to cut through la mierda by sweeping the dirt under the rug.

*We have a responsibility* to each other, certain commitments. The leap into self-affirmation goes hand in hand with being critical of self. Many of us walk around with reactionary, self-righteous attitudes. We preach certain political behaviors and theories and we do fine with writing about them. Though we want others to live their lives by them, we do not live them. When we are called on it, we go into a self-defensive mode and denial just like whites did when we started asking them to be accountable for their race and class biases in 1980–81.

Las Opuestas

In us, intra- and cross-cultural hostilities surface in not so subtle put-downs. Las no compremetidas, las que niegan a su gente. Fruncimos las caras y negamos toda responsabilidad. Where some of us racially mixed people are stuck in now is denial and its damaging effects. Denial of the white aspects that we've been forced to acquire, denial of our sisters who for one reason or another cannot "pass" as 100% ethnic—as if such a thing exists. Racial purity, like language purity, is a fallacy. Denying the reality of who we are destroys the basis from which to talk honestly and deeply about the issues between us. We cannot make any real connections because we are not touching each other. So we sit facing each other. Before the words escape our mouths the real issues are blanked out in our consciousness, erased before they register because it hurts too much to talk about them, because it makes us vulnerable to the hurt the carnal may dish out, because we've been wounded too deeply and too often in the past. So we sit, a paper face before another paper face—two people who suddenly cease to be real. La no compasiva con las complaciente, lo incomunicado atorado en sus gargantas.

   We, the new Inquisitors, swept along with the "swing to the right" of the growing religious and political intolerance, crusade against racial heretics, mow down with the sickle of righteous anger our dissenting sisters. The issue (in all aspects of life) has always been when to resist the changes and when to be open to them. Right now, this rigidity will break us.

Recobrando

Una luz fría y cenicienta bañada en la plata pálida del amanecer entra a mi escritorio and I think about the critical stages we feminists of color are going through, chiefly those of learning to live with each other *as carnalas, parientes, amantes, as kin, as friends, as lovers*. Looking back on the road that we've walked during the last decade, I see many emotional, psychological, spiritual, political gains—primarily developing an understanding and acceptance of the spirituality of our root ethnic cultures. This has given us the ground from which to see that our spiritual lives are not split from our daily acts. En recobrando our affinity with nature and her forces (deities), we have "recovered" our ancient identity, digging it out like dry clay, pressing it to our current identity, molding past and present, inner and outer. Our clay-streaked faces are acquiring again images of our ethnic self and self-respect taken from us by the colonizadores. And if we've suffered losses, if often in the process we have momentarily "misplaced" our carnalahood, our sisterhood, there beside us always are the women, las mujeres. And that is enough to keep us going.

By grounding in the earth of our native spiritual identity, we can build up our personal and tribal identity. We can reach out for the clarity we need. Burning sage and lighting Guadalupe candles by themselves won't cut it, but can be a basis from which we act.

And yes, we are elephants with long memories, but scrutinizing the past with binocular vision, training it on the juncture of past with present, identifying the options on hand, and mapping out future roads will ensure us survival.

So if we won't forget past grievances, let us forgive. Carrying the ghosts of past grievances no vale la pena. It is not worth the grief. It keeps us from ourselves and each other; it keeps us from new relationships. We need to cultivate other ways of coping. I'd like to think that the in-fighting we presently find ourselves doing is only a stage in the continuum of our growth, an offshoot of the conflict that the process of biculturation spawns, a phase of the internal colonization process, one that will soon cease to hold sway over our lives. I'd like to see it as a skin we will shed as we are born into the twenty-first century.

And now in these times of the turning of the century, of the harmonic convergence, of the end of El Quinto Sol (as the ancient Aztecs named our present age), it is time we began to get out of the state of opposition and into rapprochement, time to get our heads, words, ways out of white territory. It is time that we broke out of the invisible white frame and stood on the ground of our own ethnic being.

.

Notes

1. Irena Klepfisz, *Keeper of Accounts* (Montpelier, Vermont: Sinister Wisdom Books, 1982), 85.

2. According to Chela Sandoval, the publication of *Bridge* marked the end of the

second wave of the women's movement in its previous form. "U.S. Third World Feminist Criticism: The Theory and Method of Oppositional Consciousness," a dissertation in process. [After completing her dissertation at the University of California, Santa Cruz, Sandoval revised and published it as *Methodology of the Oppressed* (Minneapolis: University of Minnesota Press, 2000).]

3. Abdul R. JanMohamed, "The Economy of Manichean Allegory: The Function of Racial Difference in Colonialist Literature," *"Race," Writing, and Difference*, ed. Henry Louis Gates Jr. (Chicago: University of Chicago Press, 1985), 80–81.

4. JanMohamed, "The Economy of Manichean Allegory," 81.

5. A Chicano from Texas who sings and plays *bajo-sexto* in his *música norteña/conjunto*. "*Tu Traicion*" is from the album 15 *Exitasos* (Reyna Records, 1981).

6. *Entreguerras, entremundos / Inner Wars Among the Worlds* is the title of my next book [This book has not yet been published.]

7. Sara Hoagland, "Lesbian Ethics: Intimacy & Self-Understanding," *Bay Area Women's News* 1 no. 2 (May/June 1987): 7.

8. Nadine Gordimer, quoted in JanMohamed's essay, p. 88.

9. Physicists are searching for a single law of physics under which all other laws will fall.

This previously unpublished poem was first drafted in 1984 and revised in 1990. In it, Anzaldúa narrates a recurring experience from her doctoral years in Austin, Texas, during the mid-1970s. For more on this experience, see her discussion in the interview with Linda Smuckler (in part 1). Like most poetry, "The Presence" is open to multiple interpretations; I believe that it illustrates some of the spirit-inflected dimensions of Anzaldúa's worldview, as well as her theory of knowing.

## The Presence

Yes, I've seen spirits
out of the corner of my eye.
But when I've whirled around
fast, they've dived just behind the
behind the edge of my vision.
But I feel them in the room.
I remember one in particular,
a he-spirit. I called him my writing daemon
because whenever I wrote
he'd always stand just behind
my left shoulder. He'd tell me what to write
what to write. No, not aloud.
In my head. I didn't have to
think the words, the words just
flowed out of my fingertips
into my pen, spilling on the paper.
Sometimes this spirit would follow me
to the homes of friends
to the university, but after a couple
of blocks he would get further and further
behind as if afraid he'd forget the way back
to my apartment. He'd always be there
when I returned.
                                    I never told a soul,
but one day a friend I was out with
said, "You know that ghost
or whatever? Well, it's following
us again." My mouth fell.
He described the spirit

exactly as I'd seen it, saying,
"It's the spirit of your dead
father." But it wasn't. It was
a spirit helper or a guardian spirit.
Or some sort of primordial image,
an archetype like the animus or something.
Behind my thoughts was a thinking
without words, a thinking in pictures
flashing so fast that when I tried to
catch them they'd disappear behind me,
slide out the edge of my mind's eye
or blend into a camouflage of curtains,
plants, furniture. I could almost track
it by its smell. Then the thinking covered
its spoor like fine sand obliterated
even my memory of it. If I had told anyone
I had followed the workings of consciousness
and that it was a spirit looking over my left shoulder
my left shoulder, they would have held
finger to temple and made circles.
Yes, there at the edge where the
blankness resides, where the
physical eyes don't follow, is
is the spirit. Don't whirl around.
Stay very still and you'll see them.

Written shortly after the publication of *Borderlands / La Frontera*, this short essay picks up where *Borderlands*'s sixth prose chapter, "Tlilli, Tlapalli / The Path of the Red and Black Ink," left off, elaborating on what I call Anzaldúa's shaman aesthetics. I describe Anzaldúa's theory and praxis of imagination as "shaman aesthetics" to underscore her belief in art's healing, transformative power and her shape-shifting approach to language and the body. An earlier version of this essay was published in *Conversant Essays: Contemporary Poets on Poetry*, edited by James McCorkle (Detroit: Wayne State University Press, 1990).

# Metaphors in the Tradition of the Shaman

"We are all prisoners of our own self-images."
—ANDREW KAPLAN, *Scorpion*

Right after *Borderlands/La Frontera* came out, I focused on what was weak or lacking in it and everything that was "wrong" with my life. I repeatedly represented (both with pictures and words in my head and with internal feelings) how things were in such a negative way that I put myself in a disempowering state and eventually made myself sick. As is true with all humans, the working of my imagination acted upon my own body. Images communicated with tissues, organs, and cell to effect change. Once again it came home to me how powerful the image and the word are and how badly I needed to control the metaphors I use to communicate with myself. Sí, la imaginación es muy poderosa.

And now, eight months after *Borderlands/La Frontera* hit the bookstores, the answer to the questions interviewers keep asking me—Just what exactly had I written and why—came to me. I realize that I was trying to practice the oldest "calling" in the world—shamanism—and that I was practicing it in a new way. The Sanskrit word for shaman, *saman*, means *song*. In non-literate societies, the shaman and the poet were the same person. The role of the shaman is, as it was then, to preserve and create cultural or group identity by mediating between the cultural heritage of the past and the present everyday situations people find themselves in. In retrospect I see that this was an unconscious intention on my part in writing *Borderlands/La Frontera*.

To carry the poet-shaman analogy further, through my poet's eye I see "illness," lo que daña, whatever is harmful in the cultural or individual body. I see that "sickness" unbalances a person or a community. That it may be in the form of disease, or disinformation/misinformation perpetrated on women and people of color. I see that always it takes the form of metaphors.

La curación—the "cure"—may consist of removing something (dis-indoctrination), of extracting the old dead metaphors. Or it may consist of adding what is lacking—restoring the balance and strengthening the physical, mental, and emotional states of the person. This "cure" leads to a change in our belief system, en lo que creemos. No longer feeling ourselves "sick," we snap out of the paralyzing states of confusion, depression, anxiety, and powerlessness and we are catapulted into enabling states of confidence and inner strength. In *Borderlands/La Frontera*, I articulate the debilitating states that women and the colonized go through and the resulting dis-empowerment. It is not easy to get out of these states. All cultures and their accompanying metaphors resist change. *All Mexicans are lazy and shiftless* is an example of a metaphor that resists change. This metaphor has endured as fact even though we all know it is a lie. It will endure until we replace it with a new metaphor, one that we believe in both consciously and unconsciously.

We preserve ourselves through metaphor; through metaphor we protect ourselves. The resistance to change in a person is in direct proportion to the number of dead metaphors that person carries.[1] But we can also change ourselves through metaphor. And, most importantly, we can share ourselves through metaphor—attempt to put, in words, the flow of some of our internal pictures, sounds, sensations, and feelings and hope that as the reader reads the pages these "metaphors" will be "activated" and live in her.

Because we use metaphors as well as hierbitas or curing stones to effect changes, we follow in the tradition of the shaman. Like the shaman, we transmit information from our consciousness to the physical body of another. If we're lucky we create, like the shaman, images that induce altered states of consciousness conducive to self-healing. If we've done our job well we may give others access to a language and images with which they can articulate/express pain, confusion, joy, and other experiences thus far experienced only on an inarticulated emotional level. From our own and our people's experiences, we will try to create images and metaphors that will give us a handle on the numinous, a handle on the faculty for self-healing, one that may cure the depressed spirit, the frightened soul.

En posesión de la palabra. Despite language, class, and identity differences and conflicts there exist strong cultural links among Chicana, mexi-cana, Latina, Native, Asian, Black, and other women. We can safeguard and strengthen these links through communication. People in possession of the vehicles of communication are, indeed, in partial possession of their lives.

1. William J. J. Gordon and T. Poze, *The Metaphorical Way of Learning and Knowing* (Cambridge, Mass.: Porpoise Books, 1971), 224.

The introduction to her edited collection *Making Face, Making Soul / Haciendo Caras: Creative and Critical Perspectives by Women of Color* (1990), this piece offers important insights into Anzaldúa's shaman aesthetics (or what she describes here as "making face, making soul") and her worldview during the late 1980s and early 1990s as she explores the relationship between identity, art, and resistance; theory-as-process; cultural appropriation; and other issues. As Anzaldúa's capitalization of "Racism" and her occasional overly simplistic descriptions of "white"-raced people might suggest, this essay is one of her most oppositional essays; unlike later pieces such as "(Un)natural bridges" (see part 3), "Haciendo caras" contains some stark self/other binary oppositions and over-generalizations.

## Haciendo caras, una entrada

**Masks and Interfaces/***Caras y máscaras.*** Among Chicanas/*mexicanas, haciendo caras,* "making faces," means to put on a face, express feelings by distorting the face—frowning, grimacing, looking sad, glum, or disapproving. For me, *haciendo caras* has the added connotation of making *gestos subversives,* political subversive gestures, the piercing look that questions or challenges, the look that says, "Don't walk all over me," the one that says, "Get out of my face." "Face" is the surface of the body that is the most noticeably inscribed by social structures, marked with instructions on how to be *mujer, macho,* working-class, Chicana. As mestizas—biologically and/or culturally mixed—we have different surfaces for each aspect of identity, each inscribed by a particular subculture. We are "written" all over, or should I say, carved and tattooed with the sharp needles of experience.

The world knows us by our faces, the most naked, most vulnerable, exposed, and significant topography of the body. When our *caras* do not live up to the "image" that the family or community wants us to wear and when we rebel against the engraving of our bodies, we experience ostracism, alienation, isolation, and shame. Since white Anglo-Americans' racist ideology cannot take in our faces, it, too, covers them up, "blanks" them out of its reality. To become less vulnerable to all these oppressors, we have had to "change" faces, *hemos tenido que cambiar caras "como el cambio de color en el camaleón—cuando los peligros son muchos y las opciones son pocas."*[1] Some of us are forced to acquire the ability, like a chameleon, to change color when the dangers are many and the options few. Some of us who already "wear many changes / inside of our skin" (Audre Lorde)[2] have been forced to adopt a face that would pass.

The masks—las máscaras we are compelled to wear—drive a wedge between our intersubjective personhood and the persona we present to the world. "Over my mask / is your mask of me" (Mitsuye Yamada). These masking roles exact a toll. "My mask is control / concealment / endurance / my mask is escape / from my / self" (Mitsuye Yamada). "We are all bleeding, rubbed raw behind our masks."[3] After years of wearing masks we may become just a series of roles, the constellated self limping along with its broken limbs.

In sewing terms, "interfacing" means sewing a piece of material between two pieces of fabric to provide support and stability to collar, cuff, yoke. Between the masks we've internalized, one on top of another, are our interfaces. The masks are already steeped with self-hatred and other internalized oppressions. However, it is the place—the interface—between the masks that provides the space from which we can thrust out and crack the masks.

In this anthology and in our daily lives, we women-of-color strip off the máscaras others have imposed on us, see through the disguises we hide behind, and drop our personas so that we may become subjects in our own discourses. We rip out the stitches, expose the multi-layered "inner faces," attempt to confront and oust the internalized oppression embedded in them, and remake anew both inner and outer faces. We begin to displace the white and colored male typographers and become, ourselves, typographers, printing our own words on the surfaces, the plates, of our bodies. We begin to acquire the agency of making our own caras. "Making faces" is my metaphor for constructing one's identity. "[U]sted es el moldeador de su carne tanto como el de su alma."[4] You are the shaper of your flesh as well as of your soul. According to the ancient nahuas, one was put on earth to create one's "face" (body) and "heart" (soul). To them, the soul was a speaker of words and the body a doer of deeds. Soul and body, words and actions, are embodied in Moyocoyani, one of the names of the Creator in the Aztec framework, "the one who invents himself/herself . . . the Builder Kachina himself/herself."[5] In our self-reflexivity and in our active participation with the issues that confront us, whether it be through writing, front-line activism, or individual self-development, we are also uncovering the interfaces, the very spaces and places where our multiple-surfaced, colored, racially gendered bodies intersect and interconnect. This book aims to make accessible to others our struggle with all our identities, our linkage-making strategies, and our healing of broken limbs.

How the Book Was Made and Why

**Comienzos/Origins.** For years I waited for someone to compile a book that would continue where *This Bridge Called My Back* left off. A book that would confront the Racism in the white women's movement in a more thorough, personal, direct, empirical, and theoretical way. A book that would deepen the dialogue between all women and that would take on the various issues — hindrances and possibilities — in alliance-building. A book that would explode the neat boundaries of the half dozen categories of marginality that define us and unflinchingly bring us *cara a cara* with our own *historias*. A book that would bear unmistakable witness. I got tired of hearing students say that *Bridge* was required in two or three of their women's studies courses; tired of being a resource for teachers and students who asked me what texts by women-of-color they should read or teach and where they could get these writings. I had grown frustrated that the same few women-of-color were asked to read or lecture in universities and classrooms, or to submit work to anthologies and quarterlies. Why weren't other women-of-color being asked? Repeatedly tokenizing the same half dozen *mujeres* was stymieing our literary/political movement. Drained of our energy, we few tokens had little left to deploy into the development of our own literary and political movements.

The urge to anthologize, to bring more voices to the foreground, grew stronger. Then, in the spring of 1988, when I came to Santa Cruz to teach for U.C. Santa Cruz's Women's Studies, I realized that there were no recent anthologies of women-of-color writings. I stopped waiting. In the midst of my unpacking, I worked around the clock frantically locating, reading, copying, compiling, and organizing material for a class reader which I titled *Haciendo caras*. On the last day of this whirlwind task, Chela Sandoval and I sat down on my living room floor and together we looked at my six piles of papers. What was left after discarding and rearranging became a framework for this book.

Section one focuses on the degradations and horrors that Racism inflicts, the various ways we are wounded and scarred by its corrosive legacy. Section two focuses on how we combat Racism and sexism and how we "work through" internalized violence, how we attempt to decolonize ourselves and find ways to survive personally, culturally, and racially. Love, humor, and optimism are the feelings that permeate the third section. The silencing strategies of the privileged, the repression of our voices and our painful passage from psychic numbing into utterance and creation of our own *paroles* — how we learn to (in Kit Quan's words) metaphorically "sing" our songs—is the gist of section four. Section five focuses on the woman of color as writer/artist, intellectual. Section six explores debates about alliances and how we work within our own communities, with other ethnic groups, and with marginalized whites. The last section focuses on the intellectual, critic and theorist, and on our critical theories and theories of consciousness as well as the intellectual spaces we are beginning to occupy. It is about other ways, including traditional ethnic modes, of perceiving and knowing.

Originally, I had intended the anthology to consist entirely of previously published historical documents, but as I worked on it, I found myself (as we had with *This Bridge*) wanting to include the unknown, little published or unpublished writers. Because there is little publication support for our writings, I've made a special effort to work with women who do not consider themselves writers, or at least not yet. The book provides space for some ethnic mestizas who have been silenced before uttering a word, or, having spoken, have not been heard. A few pieces give fresh, immediate voice to the issues facing women who, in university surroundings, are often thrown into confusion about their ethnic and/or racial identity.

**Montage and fragmented discourse.** Let the reader beware—I here and now issue a *caveat perusor*: s/he must do the work of piecing this text together. The categories in this work reflect our fragmented and interrupted dialogue which is said to be a discontinued and incomplete discourse. The method of organizing the book was largely that of poetic association, another way of organizing experience, one that reflects our lives and the ways our minds work. As the perspective and focus shift, as the topics shift, the listener/reader is forced into participating in the making of meaning—she is forced to connect the dots, to connect the fragments.

This anthology is meant to engage the reader's total person. I do not believe that "distance" and "objectivity" alone help us come to terms with our issues. Distancing cannot be a major strategy—only a temporary breather. Total feeling and emotional immersion, the shocking drench of guilt or anger or frustration, wakes us up to some of our realities. The pieces in this book awaken the emotions—our emotional bodies "take in" and process the whole spectrum of states of consciousness from waking to dreaming. The intellect needs the guts and adrenaline that horrific suffering and anger, evoked by some of the pieces, catapult us into. Only when all the charged feelings are unearthed can we get down to "the work," la tarea, nuestro trabajo—changing culture and all its oppressive interlocking machinations. These pieces are not only *about* survival strategies, they are survival strategies—maps, blueprints, guidebooks that we need to exchange in order to feel sane, in order to make sense of our lives.

Besides being a testimonial of survival, I wanted a book which would teach ourselves and whites to read in nonwhite narrative traditions—traditions which, in the very act of writing, we try to recoup and to invent. In addition to the task of writing, or perhaps included in the task of writing, we've had to create a readership and teach it how to "read" our work. Like many of the women in this anthology, I am acutely conscious of the politics of address. *Haciendo caras* addresses a feminist readership of all ethnicities and both genders—yes, men too. Contrary to the norm, it does not address itself *primarily* to whites, but invites them to "listen in" to women-of-color talking to each other and, in some instances, to and "against" white people. It attempts to explore our realities and identities (since academic institutions omit, erase, distort, and falsify them) and to unbuild and rebuild them. We have always known that our lives and identities are simultaneously mediated, marked, and influenced by race, class, gender, and vocation. Our writings and scholarship, built on earlier waves of feminism, continue to critique and to directly address dominant culture and white feminism. But that is not all we do; these pieces attest to the fact that more and more we are concentrating on our own projects, our own agendas, our own theories.

### Everything About Racism Evades Direct Confrontation

> I am from an island whose history is steeped in the abuses of Western imperialism, whose people still suffer the deformities caused by Euro-American colonialism, old and new. Unlike many third world liberationists, however, I cannot claim to be a descendent of any particular strain, noble or ignoble. I am, however, "purely bred," descendent of all the parties involved in that cataclysmic epoch. I despair, for the various parts of me cry out for retribution at having been brutally uprooted and transplanted to fulfill the profit-cry of "white" righteousness and dominance. My soul moans that part of me that was destroyed by that callous instrument . . . the gun, the whip, the book. My mind echos with the screams of disruption, desecration, destruction. —ROSA VILLAFANE-SISOLAK[6]

Racism, the word nobody likes. Whites who don't want to confront Racism and who don't name themselves white recoil in horror from it, shun it like the plague. To mention the word in their company disrupts their comfortable complacency. To call a text or methodology under discussion in a classroom or conference "racist," or to call a white person on her or his Racism, is to let loose a stink bomb. Like a tenacious weed, Racism crops up everywhere—it has a stranglehold on everyone. It is cultivated and produced in families, churches, temples, and state institutions. The psychological effects of Racism have been greatly underestimated.

The people who practice Racism—everyone who is white in the United States—are victims of their own white ideology and are impoverished by it. But we who are oppressed by Racism internalize its deadly pollen along with the air we breathe. Make no mistake about it, the fruits of this weed are dysfunctional lifestyles which mutilate our physical bodies, stunt our intellects, and make emotional wrecks of us. Racism sucks out the life-blood from our bodies, our souls. As survivors of Racism, women-of-color suffer chronic stress and continual "post-traumatic stress syndrome" (suffered by survivors of wars). We are at high risk, and not just from AIDS.

Racism is a slippery subject, one which evades confrontation, yet one which overshadows every aspect of our lives. And because so few (white) people are directly and honestly talking about it, we in this book have once again had to take on the task. Making others "uncomfortable" in their Racism is one way of "encouraging" them to take a stance against it.

**A Classic Example.** Racism is especially rampant in places and people that produce knowledge. I want to describe the dynamics in the U.S. Women-of-color class I taught at U.C. Santa Cruz because it may help prepare teachers who will use this text in similar courses. Two of the goals I had were for the 120 students to identify and interpret instances of Racism ("internalized dominance")[7] and to both recognize their internalized Racism and oppression and develop strategies against them. I wanted students of color to become aware of, and get out from under, conditioned subservience; I wanted to call attention to the dynamic of avoidance among us, of not acknowledging each other—an act of dehumanizing people like ourselves. Yet another goal was to encourage students to emerge from "blank-outness" and openly combat the dominant groups' denial and erasure of ethnic subjectivity by allowing the students a relatively safe space (there is no completely safe space) to speak up and "expose" their feelings.

At first, what erupted in class was anger—anger from *mujeres* of color, anger and guilt from whites, anger, frustration, and mixed feelings from Jewish women who were caught in the middle (being white but often sympathizing with colored), and anger and frustration on my part from having to mediate between all these groups. Soon my body became a vessel for all the tensions and anger, and I dreaded going to class. Some of my students dreaded going to class. But gradually the *mujeres-de-color* became more assertive in confronting and holding whites accountable for their unaware, "blocked," and chronically oppressive ways. They "agitated" other students into actively demanding that the school system address their needs. When whitewomen or Jewishwomen attempted to subvert the focus from women-of-color's feelings to their own feelings of confusion, helplessness, anger, guilt, fear of change, and other insecurities, the women-of-color again and again redirected the focus back to *mujeres-de-color*. When several whitewomen stood up in class and either asked politely, pleaded, or passionately demanded (one had tears streaming down her face) that women-of-color teach them, when whitewomen wanted to engage women-of-color in time-consuming dialogues, *las mujeres-de-color* expressed their hundred years weariness of trying to teach whites about Racism. They were eloquent in expressing their skepticism about making alliances with whites when most whitewomen focused exclusively on their own feelings and needed reassurance, acceptance, and validation from *mujeres-de-color*.

Many whitewomen did not acknowledge that they were agents of oppression, while others became more aware of their racial "blank spots," stating in class how Racism undermined the integrity of their personhood and how guilt had a debilitating effect in their lives. Most of the white Jewishwomen in the class did not want to identify as white (I'm not referring to the Jewish women-of-color). Some declared that they felt they "belonged" more to the women-of-color group than they did to the white group. Because they felt isolated and excluded, they felt that their oppressions were the same or similar to those of women-of-color. Some *mujeres-de-color* questioned the concept of "same" oppressions and claimed that all oppressions were being collapsed into one. The problem was that whitewomen and white Jewishwomen, while seeming to listen, were not really "hearing" women-of-color and could not get it into their heads that this was a space and class on and about women-of-color. As one student of color wrote: "I think the hardest thing for me was having to understand that the white students in class . . . [could not] understand the experiences that we have lived."[8] Though there were important lessons learned, the inability to listen and hear—along with the confusion, anger, and doubts about ever being able to work together—almost tore our class apart.

**"Selective Reality" and "Blank Spots."** Failure to empathize with (empathy may open the door to understanding) another's experience is due, in part, to what I call "selective reality," the narrow spectrum of reality that human beings select or choose to perceive and/or what their culture "selects" for them to "see." Perception is an interpretive process conditioned by education. That which is outside of the range of consensus perception is "blanked out." Lorna Dee Cervantes' piece, "Poem for the Young White Man Who Asked Me How I, An Intelligent, Well-Read Person, Could Believe in the War Between Races," is a perfect example of the young man's "selective reality." Racism and internalized oppression result from this "editing" of reality. "You do not see me because you do not see yourself and you do not see yourself because you declare yourself outside of culture," writes María Lugones. According to Lugones, dis-engagement is a sanctioned ethnocentric racist strategy. Whites not naming themselves white presume their universality; an unmarked race is a sign of Racism unaware of itself, a "blanked-out" Racism.

## Diversity and Difference: Tactics to Avoid Confronting Racism

"Diversity" and "difference" are vague, ambiguous terms, defined differently by whitefeminists and feminists of color. Often whitefeminists want to minimize racial difference by taking comfort in the fact that we are all women and/or lesbians and suffer similar sexual-gender oppressions. They are usually annoyed with the actuality (though not the concept) of "differences," want to blur racial difference, want to smooth things out—they seem to want a complete, totalizing identity. Yet in their eager attempt to highlight similarities, they create or accentuate "other" differences such as class. These unacknowledged or unarticulated differences further widen the gap between white and colored. In the act of pinpointing and dissecting racial, sexual, or class "differences" of women-of-color, whitewomen not only objectify these differences, but also change those differences with their own white, racialized, scrutinizing, and alienating gaze. Some white people who take up multicultural and cultural plurality issues mean well, but often they push to the fringes once more the very cultures and ethnic groups about whom they want to disseminate knowledge. For example, the white writing about Native peoples or cultures displaces the Native writer and often appropriates the culture instead of proliferating information about it. The difference between appropriation and proliferation is that the first steals and harms; the second helps heal breaches of knowledge. (The author Lynn Andrews is a prime example of a white woman who "rips off" people of color, examining Native spirituality and myth with a white collector's mentality. She passes off fiction as fact and distorts the true picture of Native peoples in a way they, as writers, would not. Tony Hillerman, on the other hand, is an example of a white man who, through his fiction and reference to works by Native writers, spreads factual information that widens our knowledge of the Hopi and Navajo cultures.)

In June 1989, I was asked to speak at the Texas Lesbian Conference in Houston, Texas, where "diversity" was stressed. Many different groups belonging to Chicana, Latina, German, Italian, and other white ethnic Texan groups attended. There was an assumption that all these groups were in the same boat—after all, all the women were lesbians. But ethnic colored people in this country are not on an equal footing with other ethnic American groups. We're never just "one of the guys." The pull to believe we can "belong," that we can blend in, that we can be accepted like any other "American" can seduce us into putting our energies into the wrong battles and into picking allies who marginalize us further. Dwelling on "diversity" and multiculturalism (a euphemism for the imperializing and now defunct "melting pot") is a way of avoiding seriously dismantling Racism—by both whitewomen and women-of-color. We want so badly to move beyond Racism to a "postracist" space, a more comfortable space, but we are only prolonging the pain and leaving unfinished a business that could liberate some of our energies.

In Which Voice/With Which Voice

**The Silence That Hollows Us.** For silence to transform into speech, sounds, and words, it must first traverse through our female bodies. For the body to give birth to utterance, the human entity must recognize itself as carnal—skin, muscles, entrails, brain, belly. Because our bodies have been stolen, brutalized, or numbed, it is difficult to speak from/through them. *No hables de esas cosas, de eso no se habla. No hables, no hables. ¡Cállate! Estate quieta.* Seal your lips, woman! When she transforms silence into language, a woman transgresses. Women-of-color in the U.S. must not only transform silence into our native speech, but as immigrants, Chicanas/Latinas, and speakers of Black or different varieties of Asian English as well as other dialects, we must learn a foreign tongue—standard American English, a language laden with alien ideologies which are often in direct opposition to those in our own cultures. To speak English is to think in that language, to adopt the ideology of the people whose language it is and to be "inhabited" by their discourses. *Mujeres-de-color* speak and write not just against traditional white ways and texts but against a prevailing mode of being, against a white frame of reference. Those of us who are bilingual, or use working-class English and English in dialects, are under constant pressure to speak and write in standard English. Linguistic code-switching, which goes against language laws and norms, is not approved of.

We cross or fall or are shoved into abysses whether we speak or remain silent. And when we do speak from the cracked spaces, it is *con voz del fondo del abismo*, a voice drowned out by white noise, distance, and the distancing by others who don't want to hear. We are besieged by a "silence that hollows us."[9] As "present" beings, though ones who have been "blanked out" and whose voices are heard as static, women-of-color have difficulty speaking within a discourse and within a group of speakers who (be they white or colored) exclude her. And, in the case of Kit Quan, a discourse whose speakers take pleasure in disdaining and belittling her as a triply marginalized woman of color and do so in the name of feminist or leftist politics.

A Chicana graduate student talked to me about not knowing how to argue against the professors who were trying to shove their methods and theories down her throat. "I don't have the language, the vocabulary," she said, sobbing. Like many *mujeres* of color in graduate school, she felt oppressed and violated by the rhetoric of dominant ideology, a rhetoric disguised as good "scholarship" by teachers who are unaware of its race, class, and gender "blank spots." It is a rhetoric that presents its conjectures as universal truths while concealing its patriarchal privilege and posture. It is a rhetoric riddled with ideologies of Racism which hush our voices so that we cannot articulate our victimization.

While Kit Quan and the Chicana graduate student are not permitted a voice, Lynda Marín's protagonist in "Her Rites of Passage" cannot speak in first person. She is in that place where there is no language. So thoroughly has she been made to identify with the position of object to someone else's subject that she seems doomed to silence until her young daughter, struggling against the same silencing forces, evokes in her mother a claim to her own subjecthood. Her "rites of passage" locate her outside the patriarchal system of language, but corporeally in charge of her resistance to that system, her body finally responding to what she could not earlier allow herself to be fully aware of. "Silence. It breaks with all the force of a tidal wave. You may be deafened in the ending of silence. You may be crushed under its power."[10]

¿En qué voz? When we do acquire a voice, we often become periquitas (parrots), as in Carmen Morones' poem, imitators, loquacious in a foreign tongue. Untied, our tongues run away from themselves. When we come into possession of a voice, we sometimes have to choose with which voice (the voice of the dyke, the Chicana, the professor, the master), in which voice (first person, third, vernacular, formal) or in which language (Black English, Tex-Mex, Spanish, academese) to speak and write. When we, the objects, become the subjects, and look at and analyze our own experiences, a danger arises that we may look through the master's gaze, speak through his tongue, use his methodology—in Audre Lorde's words, use the "master's tools." Some feminist theorists of color write jargonistically and abstractly, in a hard-to-access language that blocks communication, makes the general listener/reader feel bewildered and stupid. These theorists often mistakenly divide theory and lived experience and are more off-putting than many of the masters they ape. Operating here may be defense mechanisms that an intellectually colonized person adopts. I too am seduced by academic language, its theoretical babble insinuates itself into my speech and is hard to weed out. At the same time I feel that there is a place for us to use specialized language addressed to a select, professional, vocational, or scholarly group—doctors, carpenters, and seamsters use language that only those in their own particular work can understand. We should not give up these "languages" just because they are not accessible to the general public.


Creativity is a Coping Strategy

A woman of color who writes poetry or paints or dances or makes movies knows there is no escape from race or gender when she is writing or painting. She can't take off her color and sex and leave them at the door of her study or studio. Nor can she leave behind her history. Art is about identity, among other things, and her creativity is political.

Remember again the Náhuatl concept: the soul speaks, the body acts. The hand is an extension of our will; it holds the pen, the brush, the lump of clay. It is both a symbol and a vehicle of communication. Without the hand the voice is helpless. "La lengua necesita la mano para dar villa a los pensamientos," writes Margo Glantz. The tongue needs the hand to give thoughts life. "La lengua se monta sobre la mano y produce la escritura."[11]

The tongue mounts the hand and produces writing. When tongue and hand work together, they unite art and politics and attack the dominant ideology. For many of us the acts of writing, painting, performing, and filming are acts of deliberate and desperate determination to subvert the status quo. Creative acts are forms of political activism employing definite aesthetic strategies for resisting dominant cultural norms and are not merely aesthetic exercises. We build culture as we inscribe in these various forms.

Inherent in the creative act is a spiritual, psychic component — one of spiritual excavation, of (ad)venturing into the inner void, extrapolating meaning from it and sending it out into the world. To do this kind of work requires the total person — body, soul, mind, and spirit. Ultimately alone with only the hum of the computer, accompanied by all my faces (and often yours as well), the monitor's screen reflects back the dialogue among "us." I talk to myself. That's what writers do, we carry on a constant dialogue between language and hands and images, one or another of our identities trying desperately to get in a word, an image, a sound.

But language, fine arts, and literature do not belong to women-of-color, and culture and the social system enslave our hands in clerical, factory, field, or secretarial work to service it. We are forced to steal a bit of visual, oral, or written language, to escape and hide out long enough so that with half a hand we can struggle to rearrange or create "new" patterns that will contribute to building, creating, and being an integral part of the molding we are encased in. Art is a struggle between the personal voice and language, with its apparatuses of culture and ideologies, and art mediums with their genre laws — the human voice trying to outshout a roaring waterfall. Art is a sneak attack while the giant sleeps, a sleight of hands when the giant is awake, moving so quick they can do their deed before the giant swats them. Our survival depends on being creative.

Even when our bodies have been battered by life, these artistic "languages," spoken from the body, by the body, are still laden with aspirations, are still coded in hope and "*un desarme ensangretado*," a bloodied truce.[12] By sending our voices, visuals, and visions outward into the world, we alter the walls and make them a framework for new windows and doors. We transform the *posos*, apertures, *barrancas, abismos* that we are forced to speak from. Only then can we make a home out of the cracks.

*Haciendo teorías*

Theory originally meant a mental viewing, an idea or mental plan of the way to do something, and a formulation of apparent relationships or underlying principles of certain observed phenomena which had been verified to some degree. To have theory meant to hold considerable evidence in support of a formulated general principle explaining the operation of certain phenomena.[13] Theory, then, is a set of knowledges. Some of these knowledges have been kept from us—entry into some professions and academia denied us. Because we are not allowed to enter discourse, because we are often disqualified and excluded from it, because what passes for theory these days is forbidden territory for us, it is vital that we occupy theorizing space, that we not allow whitemen and women solely to occupy it. By bringing in our own approaches and methodologies, we transform that theorizing space.

What does being a thinking subject, an intellectual, mean for women-of-color from working-class origins? It means not fulfilling our parents' expectations, it means often going against their expectations by *exceeding them*. It means being in alien territory and suspicious of the laws and walls. It means being concerned about the ways knowledges are invented. It means continually challenging institutionalized discourses. It means being suspicious of the dominant culture's interpretation of "our" experience, of the way they "read" us. It means being what Judy Baca terms "internal exiles."

What is considered theory in the dominant academic community is not necessarily what counts as theory for women-of-color. Theory produces effects that change people and the way they perceive the world. Thus we need *teorías* that will enable us to interpret what happens in the world, that will explain how and why we relate to certain people in specific ways, that will reflect what goes on between inner, outer, and peripheral "I"s within a person and between the personal "I"s and the collective "we" of our ethnic communities. *Necesitamos teorías* that will rewrite history using race, class, gender, and ethnicity as categories of analysis, theories that cross borders, that blur boundaries—new kinds of theories with new theorizing methods. We need theories that will point out ways to maneuver between our particular experiences and the necessity of forming our own categories and theoretical models for the patterns we uncover. We need theories that examine the implications of situations and look at what's behind them. And we need to find practical application for those theories.

We need to de-academize theory and to connect the community to the academy. "High" theory does not translate well when one's intention is to communicate to masses of people made up of different audiences. We need to give up the notion that there is a "correct" way to write theory.

Theorists of color are in the process of trying to formulate "marginal" theories that are partially outside and partially inside the western frame of reference (if that is possible), theories that overlap many "worlds." We are articulating new positions in these "in-between," Borderland worlds of ethnic communities and academies, feminist and job worlds. In our literature, social issues such as race, class, and sexual difference are intertwined with the narrative and poetic elements of a text, elements in which theory is embedded. In our *mestizaje* theories we create new categories for those of us left out or pushed out of the existing ones. We recover and examine non-western aesthetics while critiquing western aesthetics; recover and examine non-rational modes and "blanked-out" realities while critiquing rational, consensual reality; recover and examine indigenous languages while critiquing the "languages" of the dominant culture. And we simultaneously combat the tokenization and appropriation of our literatures and our writers/artists.

Some of the tasks ahead of us, then: to go beyond explaining why women-of-color aren't writing more theory, why our work isn't being published or distributed, and, instead, to strategize about ways to get our work out; to change the focus from the topic of whitewomen's exclusionary practices to address the quality of what has been included and the nature of this inclusion. If we have been gagged and disempowered by theories, we can also be loosened and empowered by theories.

*La tarea que nos queda por delante*

**Left-Handed Guardians.** Looking at how far we've come and what we've had to endure to maintain what little space we've managed to wrest from the dominant culture, I see incredible hard work and amazing results. We are busy beavers (and like them also an endangered species), doers, determined and willing to work at building our arts and our theories and actualizing our dreams. Though we've accomplished much, for us it is *never* enough. In the midst of our laboring, we've had to watch our backsides, we've had to develop very sharp teeth to protect our creations. Because we've had to be cautious, we've often mistrusted each other. Wherever we are, we make sure there are several entrances and exits, that our homes have alternate escape routes, and we don't let ourselves get painted into corners. In spite of all this, we have a sense of teamwork and honor and respect for the abilities of other women, and we work hard at building community. In trying to settle our differences, we look for alternative solutions. This makes us visionaries, people with vision, with new things to say and new perspectives to say them from.

Our strength lies in shifting perspectives, in our capacity to shift, in our "seeing through" the membrane of the past superimposed on the present, in looking at our shadows and dealing with them. A medicine story tells of Crow's fascination with her own shadow. "She kept looking at it, scratching it, pecking at it, until her shadow woke up and became alive. Then Crow's shadow ate her. Crow is Dead Crow now. . . ."[14] Crow is the Left-Handed Guardian who does not let the past eat us up. Encrucijadas, haunted by voices and images that violated us, bearing the pains of the past, we are slowly acquiring the tools to change the disabling images and memories, to replace them with self-affirming ones, to recreate our pasts and alter them—for the past can be as malleable as the present. So, throwing caution to the wind, rechazamos esas falsas imágenes, we refute those false images, quebramos los falsos espejos para descubrir las desconocidas sombras, we break the false mirrors in order to discover the unfamiliar shadows, the inner faces, las caras por dentro. To make face is to have face—dignity and self-respect.

Among the strengths working for us is the ability to see through our self-sabotaging behaviors. Our inner payasa, clown-face, is always aware of what's going on and uses humor to volley back the racial slurs. We have the ability to enter other levels, to listen to our gut knowledge and acknowledge that some of us do know where we are in particular stages of our lives. We are cultivating our ability to affirm our knowing. Jauntily we step into new terrains where we make up the guidelines as we go.

We are in the present, with both feet on the ground and one eye to the future. Chela Sandoval wrote: "We had each tasted the shards of 'difference' until they had carved up our insides; now we were asking ourselves what shapes our healing would take." Our healings take many forms: our ability to laugh at ourselves, to see through our own foolishness, our pride, hope, love. We are continuing in the direction of honoring others' ways, of sharing knowledge and personal power through writing (art) and activism, of injecting into our cultures new ways, feminist ways, mestiza ways. Adaptability, when we forget to stand firm on some issue or when we allow others to choose the terms of our relationships, can be our biggest weakness. But adaptability is also our biggest strength.

**We have not one movement but many.** Our political, literary, and artistic movements are discarding the patriarchal model of the hero/leader leading the rank and file. Ours are individual and small group *movidas*, unpublicized *movimientos*—movements not of media stars or popular authors but of small groups or single *mujeres*, many of whom have not written books or spoken at national conferences. Though unnoticed, right now in small towns women are organizing, attending meetings, setting up retreats or demonstrations. Our movements, like the wind, sweep through the sea of grass in California, cut swaths in Texas, take root in Maine, sway public opinion in North Dakota, stir the dust in New Mexico. Now here, now there, *aquí y allá*, we and our *movimiento*'s art, firmly committed to transforming all our cultures.

## Notes

1. Rosario Castellaños, "*Apuntes: Para una declaración de fe*," *Poesía no eres tú* (my translation). (México: Secretaría de Educación Pública, Colección Séptima Setentas 83, 1975), 25.

2. Subsequent unfootnoted references refer to pieces in this book.

3. Chrystos, from a letter to me.

4. Rosario Castellaños, "El Mar," *Poesia no eres tú*, 92.

5. Inés Hernández, "'Triumph is a sweet song-the one you know': The Voices of Gloria Anzaldúa, Wendy Rose, and Joy Harjo," presentation at MLA Conference, December, 1988.

6. Rosa Villafañe-Sisolak, from an unpublished paper.

7. This is a phrase used by Gail Pheterson. I have slightly modified her definition. See "Alliances Between Women: Overcoming Internalized Oppression and Internalized Domination," *Signs: Journal of Women in Culture and Society* vol. 12, no. 1 (1986).

8. Jodi Stephens, *Women-of-Color Class Anthology*, 7. Segments from that anthology are presently being used in core courses at UCSC and the editors are now seeking a publisher.

9. Amber Coverdale Sumrall, "Coming Home," *Porter Gulch Review* 9 (Fall/Winter, 1989), 74.

10. Amethyst Uchida, *Women-of-Color Class Anthology*, 8.

11. Margo Glantz, *La lengua en la mano* (Puebla, México: Premia Editora Tlahuapan, 1983), 9.

12. Ixok Amargo, *Central American Women's Poetry for Peace*, ed. Zoe Anglesey (Penobscot: Granite Press, 1987), 205.

13. *Webster's New World Dictionary of American Language*, College Edition, 1959.

14. Jamie Sams and David Carson, *Medicine Cards*, illus. Angela C. Werneke (Santa Fe: Bear and Company, 1988), 133.

First published in 1990 in the collection *Bridges of Power: Women's Multicultural Alliances* (edited by Lisa Albrecht and Rose M. Brewer), this essay is a much-expanded version of Anzaldúa's keynote address delivered in June 1988 at the Lesbian Plenary Session of the annual conference for the National Women's Studies Association (NWSA). In addition to exploring the linkages between identity and alliance-making, Anzaldúa offers suggestions for activists interested in engaging in coalition work. The essay illustrates some of the ways Anzaldúa's theories were developing during the 1980s: it looks back, toward her theorization of bridges and her alliance work in *This Bridge Called My Back: Writings by Radical Women of Color*, and forward, toward her radically inclusionary theorization of "(Un)natural bridges," shifting perspectives, and new tribalism.

# Bridge, Drawbridge, Sandbar, or Island

*Lesbians-of-Color Hacienda Alianzas*[1]

> Hablando se entienden las cosas.
> (People understand each other by talking)
> —Mexican proverb

Buenos días marimachas, lesberadas, tortilleras, patlaches,[2] dykes, bulldaggers, butches, femmes, and good morning to you, too, straight women. This morning when I got up I looked in the mirror to see who I was (my identity keeps changing), and you know how hair looks when you've washed it the night before and then slept on it? Yes, that's how mine looked. Not that I slept that much. I was nervous about making this talk and I usually never get nervous until just before I'm on. I kept thinking, What am I going to tell all those women? How am I going to present and represent myself to them and who, besides myself, am I going to speak to and for? Last night lying in bed in the dorm room I got disgusted with my semi-prepared talk so I wrote another one. I threw that out too. Then I skimmed several papers I was working on, looking for ideas. I realized that I couldn't use any of this material and ordered my unconscious to come up with something by morning or else. This morning I walked over here, picking lint off my shirt, feeling wrinkled, and thinking, Here I am, I'm still the poor little Chicanita from the sticks. What makes me think I have anything useful to say about alliances?

Women-of-color such as myself do have some important things to say about alliance and coalition work. The overlapping communities of struggle that a mestiza lesbian finds herself in allows her to play a pivotal role in alliance work. To be part of an alliance or coalition is to be active, an activist. Why do we make alliances and participate in them? We are searching for powerful, meaning-making experiences. To make our lives relevant, to gain political knowledge, to give our lives a sense of involvement, to respond to social oppression and its debilitating effects. Activists are engaged in a political quest. Activists are alienated from the dominant culture but instead of withdrawing we confront, challenge. Being active meets some basic needs: emotional catharsis, gratification, political epiphanies. But those in an alliance group also feel like a family and squabble and fight like one, complete with a favorite (good child) and a scapegoat (bad child).

## The Fracture: At Homeness / Estrangement

I look around me and I see my carnalas, my hermanas, the other half and half's, mita' y mita'* (as queer women are called in South Texas), and I feel a great affinity with everyone. But at the same time I feel (as I've felt at other conferences) like I am doing this alone; I feel a great isolation and separateness and *differentness* from everyone, even though I have many allies. Yet as soon as I have these thoughts—that I'm in this alone, that I have to stand on the ground of my own being, that I have to create my own separate space—the exact opposite thoughts come to me: that we're all in this together, juntas, that the ground of our being is a common ground, la Tierra, and that at all times we must stand together despite, or because of, the huge splits that lie between our legs, the faults among feminists like the fractures in the earth. Earthquake country, these feminisms. Like a fracture in the Earth's crust splitting rock, like a splitting rock itself, the quakes shift different categories of women past each other so that we cease to match, and are forever disaligned—colored from white, Jewish from colored, lesbian from straight. If we indeed do not have one common ground but only shifting plots, how can we work and live and love together? Then, too, let us not forget la mierda between us, a mountain of caca that keeps us from "seeing" each other, being with each other.

Being a mestiza queer person, una de las otras ("of the others") is having and living in a lot of worlds, some of which overlap. One is immersed in all the worlds at the same time while also traversing from one to the other. The mestiza queer is mobile, constantly on the move, a traveler, callejera,

* Shortened form of "mitad y mitad."

a cortacalles. Moving at the blink of an eye, from one space, one world, to another, each world with its own peculiar and distinct inhabitants, not comfortable in any one of them, none of them "home," yet none of them "not home" either. I'm flying home to South Texas after this conference, and while I'm there, I'm going to be feeling a lot of the same things that I'm feeling here—a warm sense of being loved and of being at home, accompanied by a simultaneous and uncomfortable feeling of no longer fitting, of having lost my home, of being an outsider. My mother, and my sister and my brothers, are going to continue to challenge me and to argue against the part of me that has community with white lesbians, that has community with feminism, that has community with other mujeres-de-color, that has a political community. Because I no longer share their world view, I have become a stranger and an exile in my own home. "When are you coming home again, Prieta," my mother asks at the end of my visit, of every visit. "Never, Momma."[3] After I first left home and became acquainted with other worlds, the Prieta that returned was different, thus "home" was different too. It could not completely accommodate the new Prieta, and I could barely tolerate it. Though I continue to go home, I no longer fool myself into believing that I am truly "home."

A few days ago in Montreal at the Third International Feminist Book Fair (June 1988), I felt a great kinship with women writers and publishers from all over the world. I felt both at home and homeless in that foreign yet familiar terrain because of its strangeness (strange because I had never been there). At the conference, and most especially at the lesbian reading, I felt very close to some white lesbian separatist friends. Then they would make exclusionary or racist remarks and I would feel my body heating up, I would feel the space between us widening. Though white lesbians say that their oppression in a heterosexist, homophobic society is similar to the suffering of racism that people-of-color experience, they can escape from the more overt oppressions by hiding from being gay (just as I can). But what I can't hide from is being Chicana—my color and features give me away. Yes, when I go home I have to put up with a lot of heterosexist bullshit from my family and community, from the whole Chicano nation who want to exclude my feminism, my lesbianism. This I have in common with women-of-all-colors. But what really hurts, however, is to be with people that I love, with you mujeres-de-todos-colores, and to still feel, after all our dialogues and struggles, that my cultural identity is still being pushed off to the side, being minimized by some of my so-called allies who unconsciously rank racism a lesser oppression than sexism. Women-of-color feel especially frustrated and depressed when these "allies" participate in alliances dealing with issues of racism or when the theme of the conference we are attending is racism. It is then that white feminists feel they have "dealt" with the issue and can go on to other "more important" matters.

At the Montreal Conference I also felt an empathy with heterosexual women-of-color and with the few men who were there, only to be saddened that they needed to be educated about women-only space. It also made me sad, too, that white lesbians have not accepted the fact that women-of-color have affinities with men in their cultures. White lesbians were unconsciously asking women-of-color to choose between women and men, failing to see that there is more than one way to be oppressed. Not all women experience sexism in the same way, and for women-of-color sexism is not the only oppression. White lesbians forget that they too have felt excluded, that they too have interrupted women-of-color-only space, bringing in their agenda and, in their hunger to belong, pushed ours to the side.

Alliance work is the attempt to shift positions, change positions, reposition ourselves regarding our individual and collective identities. In alliance we are confronted with the problem of how we share or don't share space, how we can position ourselves with individuals or groups who are different from and at odds with each other, how we can reconcile one's love for diverse groups when members of these groups do not love each other, cannot relate to each other, and don't know how to work together.

## The Activist y la Tarea de Alianzas

Alliance-coalition work is marked or signaled by framing metacommunication, "This is alliance work."[4] It occurs in bounded specific contexts defined by the rules and boundaries of that time and space and group. While it professes to do its "work" in the community, its basis is both experiential and theoretical. It has a discourse, a theory that guides it. It stands both inside (the community one is doing the work for) and outside ordinary life (the meeting place, the conference). Ideally one takes alliance work home.

In alliance-coalition work there is an element of role playing, as if one were someone else. Activists possess an unspoken, untalked about ability to recognize the unreality and game-playing quality of their work.[5] We very seriously act/perform as well as play at being an ally. We adopt a role model

or self-image and behave as if one *were* that model, the person one is trying to be. Activists picture themselves in a scenario: a female hero venturing out and engaging in nonviolent battles against the corrupt dominant
world with the help of their trusted comadronas. There are various narratives about working at coalition, about making commitments, setting
goals, and achieving those goals. An activist possesses, in lesser or greater
degree, a self-conscious awareness of her "role" and the nature of alliance
work. She is aware that not only is the alliance-coalition group struggling
to make specific changes in certain institutions (health care, immigration
laws, etc.) but in doing so the group often engages in fighting cultural
paradigms — the entire baggage of beliefs, values, and techniques shared
by the community.[6] But in spite of all cultural inscriptions to the contrary,
the activist with her preconceived self-image, her narrative, and her self-
reflectivity resists society's "inscribing" cultural norms, practices, and
paradigms on her. She elects to be the one "inscribing" herself and her
culture. Activists are agents.

## In Collusion, in Coalition, in Collision

For now we women-of-color are doing more solidarity work with each
other. Because we occupy the same or similarly oppressed cultural, economic space(s) or share similar oppressions, we can create a solidarity
based on a "minority" coalition. We can build alliances around differences, even in groups which are homogenous. Because people-of-color
are treated generically by the dominant culture — seeing and treating us
as parts of a whole, rather than as individuals — this forces us to experience ourselves collectively. I have been held accountable by some white
people for Richard Rodríguez's views and have been asked to justify César
Chávez's political strategies. In classes and conferences I am often called
to speak on issues of race and am thereafter responsible for the whole
Chicano/Mexican race. Yet, were I to hold a white woman responsible for
Ronald Reagan's acts, she would be shocked because to herself she is an
individual (nor is her being white named because it is taken for granted
as the norm).

I think we people-of-color can turn this fusion or confusion of indi-
vidual/collectivity around and use it as a tool for collective strength and not
as an oppressive representation. We can subvert it and use it. It could serve
as one base for intimate connection between the personal and collective in
solidarity work and in alliances across differences. For us the issue of alli-

ances affects every aspect of our lives—personal growth, not just social. We are always working with whitewomen or other groups unlike ourselves toward common and specific goals during the time the work of coalition is in process. Lesbians-of-color have always done this. Judit Moschkovitz wrote: "Alliances are made between people who are different."[7] I would add between people who are different but who have a similar conscience that impels them toward certain actions. Alliances are made between persons whose vague unconscious angers, hopes, guilts, and fears grow out of direct experiences of being either perpetrators or victims of racism and sexism.

Feelings of anger, guilt, and fear rose up nine years ago at Storrs, Connecticut, at the 1981 NWSA Women Respond to Racism Conference, when issues of alliances and racism exploded into the open. Along with many women-of-color I had aspirations, hopes, and visions for multiracial comunidades, for communities (in the plural) among all women, of mundos zurdos (left-handed worlds). Cherríe Moraga and I came bringing an offering, *This Bridge Called My Back: Writings by Radical Women of Color*; it made its debut at that conference. Some of my aspirations were naive, but without them, I would not have been there nor would I be here now. This vision of comunidad is still the carrot that I, the donkey, hunger for and seek at conferences such as this one.

At the 1981 conference we laid bare the splits between whitewomen and women-of-color, white lesbians and lesbians-of-color, separatists and nonseparatists. We risked exposing our true feelings. Anger[8] was the strongest in/visible current at that conference, as it is at this one, though many of us repressed it then and are still repressing it now. Race was the big issue then, as it is now for us. Race, the big difference. When asked what I am, I never say I'm a woman. I say I am a Chicana, a mestiza, a mexicana, or I am a woman-of-color—which is different from "woman" (woman always means whitewoman). Monique Wittig claims that a lesbian is not a woman because woman exists only in relation to men; woman is part of the category of sex (man and woman) which is a heterosexual construct.[9] Similarly, for me a woman-of-color is not just a "woman;" she carries the markings of her race, she is a gendered racial being—not just a gendered being. However, nonintellectual, working-class women-of-color do not have the luxury of thinking of such semantic and theoretical nuances, much less exempting themselves from the category "woman." So though I myself see the distinction, I do not push it.

A large part of my identity is cultural. Despite changes in awareness since the early eighties, racism in the form of "Your commitment has to be to feminism, forget about your race and its struggles, struggle with us not them" is still the biggest deterrent to coalition work between whitewomen and women-of-color. Some white feminists, displacing race and class and highlighting gender, are still trying to force us to choose between being colored or female; only now they've gone underground and use unconscious covert pressures. It's all very subtle. Our white allies or colleagues get a hurt look in their eyes when we bring up their racism in their interactions with us and quickly change the subject. Tired of our own "theme song" (Why aren't you dealing with race and class in your conference, classroom, organization?) and not wanting to hurt them and in retaliation have them turn against us, we drop the subject and, in effect, turn the other cheek. Women-of-color need these and other manipulations named so that we can make our own articulations. Colored and whitewomen doing coalition work together will continue to reflect the dominated/dominator dichotomy UNLESS whitewomen have or are dealing with issues of racial domination in a "real" way. It is up to them how they will do this.

Estranged Strangers: A Forced Bonding

Alliance stirs up intimacy issues, issues of trust, relapse of trust, intensely emotional issues. "We seem to be more together organizationally and estranged individually."[10] There is always some, no matter how minimal, unease or discomfort between most women-of-color and most whitewomen. Because they can't ignore our ethnicity, getting our approval and acceptance is their way to try to make themselves more comfortable and lessen their unease. It is a great temptation for us to make whitewomen comfortable. (In the past our lives may have depended on not offending a white person.) Some of us get seduced into making a whitewoman an honorary woman-of-color—she wants it so badly. But it makes us fidget, it positions us in a relationship founded on false assumptions. A reversed dependency of them upon us emerges, one that is as unhealthy as our previous reliance on them. There is something parasitic about both of these kinds of dependencies. We need to examine bondings of this sort and to "see through" them to the unconscious motivations. Both white and colored need to look at the history of betrayal, the lies, the secrets and misinformation both have internalized and continue to propagate. We need to ask: Do women-of-color want only patronage from white women? Do white feminists only need and expect acceptance and acknowledgment from women-of-color? Yet there is an inherent potential for achieving results in both personal and political cross-racial alliances. We could stick to each other like velcro, whose two different sides together form a great bond—the teeth of one fasten onto the fabric of the other half and hold with a strength greater than either half alone.

Though the deepest connections colored dykes have is to their native culture, we also have strong links with other races, including whites. Though right now there is a strong return to nationalist feeling, colored lesbian feminists in our everyday interactions are truly more citizens of the planet. "To be a lesbian is to have a world vision."[11] In a certain sense I share this vision. If we are to create a lesbian culture, it must be a mestiza lesbian culture, one that partakes of all cultures, one that is not just white in style, theory, or direction, that is not just Chicana, not just black. We each have a choice as to what people, what cultures, and what issues we want to live with and live in and the roles we want to play. The danger is that white lesbians will "claim" us and our culture as their own in the creation of "our" new space.

### "Chusando"[†] Movidas / A Choice of Moves

There are many roles, or ways of being, of acting, and of interacting in the world. For me they boil down to four basic roles: bridge, drawbridge, sandbar, and island. Being a bridge means being mediator between yourself and your community and white people, lesbians, feminists, white men. You select, consciously or unconsciously, which group to bridge with—or they choose you. Often the you that's the mediator gets lost in the dichotomies, dualities, or contradictions you're mediating. You have to be flexible yet maintain your ground, or the pull in different directions will dismember you. It's a tough job; not many people can keep the bridge up.

Being a drawbridge means having the option to take two courses of action. The first is being "up," i.e., withdrawing, pulling back from physically connecting with white people (there can never be a complete disconnection because white culture and its perspectives are inscribed on us/into us). You may choose to pull up the drawbridge or retreat to an island in order to be with your colored hermanas in a sort of temporary cultural separatism. Many of us choose to "draw up our own bridges" for short periods of time in order to regroup, recharge our energies, and nour-

[†] From the English word "choosing."

ish ourselves before wading back into the frontlines. This is also true for whitewomen. The other option is being "down"—that is, being a bridge. Being "down" may mean a partial loss of self. Being "there" for people *all the time, mediating all the time* risks being "walked" on, being "used." I and my publishing credentials are often "used" to "colorize" white women's grant proposals, projects, lecture series, and conferences. If I don't co-operate I am letting the whole feminist movement down.

Being an island means that there are no causeways, no bridges—maybe no ferries, either—between you and whites. I think that some women-of-color are, in these reactionary times, in these very racist times, choosing to be islands for a little while. These race separatists, small in numbers, are disgusted not only with patriarchal culture, but also with white feminism and the white lesbian community. To be an island, you have to reject certain people. Yet being an island cannot be a way of life; there are no lifelong islands because no one is totally self-sufficient. Each person de-pends on others for the food she eats, the clothes she wears, the books she reads, and though these "goods" may be gotten from within the island, sequestering oneself to some private paradise is not an option for poor people, for most people-of-color.

At this point in time, the infrastructures of bridge and drawbridge feel too man-made and steel-like for me. Still liking the drawbridge concept, I sought and found the sandbar, a submerged or partly exposed ridge of sand built by waves offshore from a beach. To me the sandbar feels like a more "natural" bridge (though nature too, some argue, is a cultural con-struction). There is a particular type of sandbar that connects an island to a mainland—I forget what it is called. For me the important thing is how we shift from bridge to drawbridge to sandbar to island. Being a sandbar means getting a breather from being a perpetual bridge without having to withdraw completely. The high and low tides of your life are factors which help you to decide whether or where you're a sandbar today, tomorrow. It means that you're functioning as a "bridge" (maybe partially underwater, invisible to others) and that you can somehow choose who you'll allow to "see" your bridge, who you'll allow to walk on your "bridge"—that is, who you'll make connections with. A sandbar is more fluid and shifts loca-tions, allowing for more mobility and more freedom. Of course there are sandbars called shoals, where boats run amuck. Each option comes with its own dangers.

So what do we, lesbians-of-color, choose to be? Do we continue to func-tion as bridges? Do we opt to be drawbridges or sandbars? Do we isolate ourselves as islands? We may choose different options for different stages of our process. While I have been a persistent bridge, I have often been forced to "draw the bridge," or have been driven to be an island. Now I find myself slowly turning into a sandbar—the thing is that I have a fear of drowning.

Mujeres-de-color, mujeres blancas, ask yourselves what are you now, and is this something that you want to be for the next year or five years or ten? Ask yourself if you want to do alliance-coalition work and if so what kind and with whom. The fact that we are so estranged from whitewomen and other women-of color makes alliance work that much more imperative. It is sad that though conferences allow for short-term alliances, the potential for achieving some feminist goals are short-circuited by participants' politically correct "performances" instead of more "real" and honest engagement. Choosing to be a bridge, a drawbridge, and a sandbar allows us to connect, heart to heart, con corazónes abiertos. Even islands come to NWSA conferences—perhaps they come to find other islands.

Terms of Engagement

Mujeres-de-color, there are some points to keep in mind when doing coalition work with whitewomen. One is to not be lulled into forgetting that *coalition work attempts to balance power relations and undermine and subvert the system of domination-subordination* that affects even our most unconscious thoughts. We live in a world where whites dominate colored and we participate in such a system every minute of our lives; the subordination/ domination dynamic is that insidious. We, too, operate in a racist system whether we are rebelling against it or are colluding with it. The strategies of defense we use against the dominant culture we also knowingly and unknowingly use on each other.[12] Whites of whatever class always have certain privileges over colored people of whatever class, and class oppression operates among us women-of-color as pervasively as among whites.

Keep in mind that if members of coalitions play at the deadly serious and difficult game of making alliances work we must set up some ground rules and define the terms we use to name the issues. We need to "see through" some common assumptions. One is that there is no such thing as a common ground. As groups and individuals we all stand on different plots. Sisterhood in the singular was a utopian fantasy invented by whitewomen, one in which we women-of-color were represented by whitewomen, one in which they continued to marginalize us, strip us of our individuality. (One must possess a sense of personhood before one can develop a sense of sisterhood.) It seems to me that through extensive coalitions, various "hermanidades"‡ may be created—not one sisterhood but many. We don't all need to come together, juntas (total unity may be another utopian myth). Some of us can gather in affinity groups, small grassroots circles and others can bridge more broadly. All parties involved in coalitions need to recognize the necessity that women-of-color and lesbians define the terms of engagement: that we be listened to, that we articulate who we are, where we have come from (racial past), how we understand oppression to work, how we think we can get out from under oppression, and what strategies we can use in accomplishing the particular tasks we have chosen to perform. When we don't collectively define ourselves and our locations, the group will automatically operate under white assumptions, white definitions, white strategies. Formulating a working definition, preferably one subject to change, of alliance/coalition, racism, and internalized racism will clear the floor of patriarchal, white, and other kinds of debris and make a clean (well, sort of clean) space for us to work in. I've given you my definitions for alliance and coalition. Racism is the subjugation of a cultural group by another for the purpose of gaining economic advantage, of mastering and having power over that group—the result being harm done, consciously or unconsciously, to its members. We need to defy ethnocentrism, the attitude that one culture is superior to all others. Ethnocentrism condones racism. Racism is theory, it is an ideology, it is a violence perpetuated against colored ethnic cultures.

The intensity of the violence may range from hidden, indirect forms of discrimination (housing) through overt forms of ethnocidal practices (enforced schooling, religious harassment) to forms of physical and direct violence culminating in genocide (holocaust). . . . It becomes structurally institutionalized as the basis of hegemony, it turns into systematic racism.[13]

> Internalized racism means the introjecting, from the dominant culture, negative images and prejudice against outsider groups such as people-of-color and the projection of prejudice by an oppressed person upon another oppressed person or upon her/himself. It is a type of "dumping."[14]

On the phone the other day I was telling my mother that I'd confronted my neighbor—a black man who "parties" everyday, from morning till

‡ Anzaldúa's variation on "hermandades."

night, with a dozen beer-drinking buddies—and demanded that he not intrude on my space with his noise. She said, "No, don't tell them anything, black men kill. They'll rape you." This is an example of internalized racism; it is not racism. Chicanos as a group do not have the power to subjugate black people or any other people. Where did my mother learn about blacks? There are very few black people in the Rio Grande Valley of South Texas. My mother has internalized racism from the white dominant culture, from watching television, and from our own culture which defers to and prefers light-skinned güeros and denies the black blood in our mestizaje—which may be both a race and class prejudice, as darker means being more indio or india, means poorer. Whites are conditioned to be racist, colored are prone to internalize racism and, for both groups, racism and internalized racism appear to be the given, "the way things are." Prejudice is a "stabilized deception of perception."[15] I call this "deception" "selective reality"—the narrow spectrum of reality that human beings choose to perceive and/or what their culture "selects" for them to "see."[16] That which is outside the range of consensus (white) perception is "blanked-out." Color, race, sexual preferences, and other threatening differences are "unseen" by some whites, certain voices not heard. Such "editing" of reality maintains race, class, and gender oppressions.

Another point to keep in mind is that feminists-of-color threaten the order, coherence, authority, and concept of white superiority; this threat makes some white feminists uncomfortable and some assimilated colored women uneasy. Feminists-of-color, in turn, are made uncomfortable by the knowledge that, by virtue of their color, white feminists have privilege and white feminists often focus on gender issues to the exclusion of racial ones. After centuries of colonization, some whitewomen and women-of-color, when interacting with each other, fall into old and familiar patterns: the former will be inclined to patronize and to "instruct," the latter inclined to fall into subservience and, consciously or unconsciously, model herself after the whitewoman. The woman-of-color might seek white approval or take on gradations of stances, from meek to hostile, which get her locked into passive to aggressive to violently reactive states.

But how are you to recognize your aliada, your ally in a roomful of people? Coalition work is not a sport where members of a particular team go bare-chested or wear T-shirts that say AMIGA (which stands for an actual organization in Tejas). It can get confusing unless you can distinguish each other. And, once you identify each other, how will you work together?

When calling a foul, do you harangue the other person in a loud voice? Do you take on a matador defense–neglect to guard the opposing player in favor of taking the limelight to inflate your ego? Will your organization be a collective or a hierarchy? Should your modus operandi be hands-on or hands-off? Will your offensive strategies consist of nudges, bumps, shoves, or bombs? You may have to accept that there may be no solutions, resolutions, or even agreement ever. The terms *solution, resolution, progressing,* and *moving forward* are western-dominant cultural concepts. Irresolution and disagreement may be more common in life than resolutions and agreements. Coalition work does not thrive on "figurehead" leaders, on grandstanding, "leadership always makes you master and the others slaves."[17] Instead, coalition work succeeds through collective efforts and individual voices being heard. Once we focus on coalition/alliance we come to more questions: How long should we stay together? Should we form temporary *carnalaship* of extended family which leads to strong familial and tribal affiliations but which work against larger coalitions?

If You Would Be My Ally

Ideally as allies (all lies), we can have no major lies among us, and we would lay our secrets—the ones we've internalized and the ones we propagate—on the conference table. In looking at the motivation of those we are in solidarity with (women-of-color) and those who want to make alliances with us (whitewomen), we not only need to look at who they are, the space(s) they occupy, and how they enter our space and maneuver in it, but we have to look at our own motivations. Some issues to ponder and questions to ask ourselves. If all political action is founded on subconscious irresolutions and personal conflicts, then we must first look at that baggage we carry with us before sorting through other folks' dirty laundry.

Having examined our own motives we can then inquire into the motivations of those who want to be our allies: Do they want us to be like them? Do they want us to hide the parts of ourselves that make them uneasy, i.e., our color, class, and racial identities? If we were to ask white lesbians to leave their whiteness at home, they would be shocked, having assumed that they have de-conditioned the negative aspects of being white out of themselves by virtue of being feminist or lesbian. But I see that whiteness bleeds through all the baggage they port around with them and that it even seeps into their bones. Do they want to "take over" and impose their values in order to have power over us? I've had white and colored friends tell me that I shouldn't give my energy to male friends, that I shouldn't go to horror movies because of the violence against women in them, that I should only write from the perspective of female characters, that I shouldn't eat meat. I respect women whose values and politics are different from mine, but they do not respect me or give me credit for self-determining my life when they impose trendy politically-correct attitudes on me. The assumptions they are making in imposing their "political correctness" on me is that I, a woman, a chicana, a lesbian should go to an "outside" authority rather than my own for how to run my life.

When I am asked to leave parts of myself out of the room, out of the kitchen, out of the bed, these people are not getting a whole person. They are only getting a little piece of me. As feminists and lesbians, we need all of us together, tlan (from the Náhuatl meaning close together), and each one of us needs all the different aspects and pieces of ourselves to be present and totally engaged in order to survive life in the late twentieth century.

Do they only want those parts of us that they can live with, that are similar to theirs, not different from them? The issue of differences continues to come up over and over again. Are we asked to sit at the table, or be invited to bed, because we bring some color to and look good behind the sheets? Are we there because those who would be our allies happen to have ancestors that were our oppressors and are operating out of a sense of guilt? Does this whitewoman or woman-of-color or man-of-color want to be our ally in order to atone for racial guilt or personal guilt? Does this person want to be "seen" and recognized by us? According to Lacan, every human action, even the most altruistic, comes from a desire for recognition by the Other and from a desire for self-recognition in some form.[18] For some, love is the highest and most intense recognition.

María Lugones, a Latina philosopher, a woman who is at this conference, wrote a paper with a whitewoman, Vicky Spelman, "Have We Got a Theory For You: Feminist Theory, Cultural Imperialism, and the Demand for the Woman's Voice,"[19] in which they posit that the only motivation for alliance work is love and friendship. Nothing else. I have friends that I totally disagree with politically, friends that are not even from the same class, the same race, the same anything, but something keeps us together, keeps us working things out. Perhaps Lugones and Spelman are right. Love and friendship can provide a good basis for alliance work, but there are too many tensions in alliance groups to dismiss with a light comment that bonds are based on love and friendship. This reminds me of Dill's

critique of sisterhood being based on common (white) interests and alike-
ness.[20]

What may be "saving" the colored and white feminist movements may
be a combination of all these factors. Certainly the tensions between opposing theories and political stances vitalize the feminist dialogue. But
it may only be combined with respect, partial understanding, love, and
friendship that keeps us together in the long run. So mujeres think about
the carnalas you want to be in your space, those whose spaces you want to
have overlapping yours.

## Ritualizing Coalition and Alliance Building

Speaking and communicating lay the groundwork, but there is a point
beyond too much talk that abstracts the experience. What is needed is
a symbolic behavior performance made concrete by involving body and
emotions with political theories and strategies, rituals that will connect
the conscious with the unconscious. Through ritual we can make some
deep-level changes.

Ritual consecrates the alliance. Breaking bread together, and other
group activities that physically and psychically represent the ideals, goals,
and attitudes promote a quickening, thickening between us.

Allies, remember that the foreign woman, "the alien," is nonacayocapo
which in Náhuatl means one who possesses body (flesh) and blood like
me. Aliadas, recuerden que la mujer extranjera también es nonacayocapo,
la que tiene cuerpo y sangre como yo. Remember that our hearts are full
of compassion, not empty. And the spirit dwells strong within. Remember
also that the great emptiness, the hollowness within the psyches of whitewomen propels them to coalition with colored. Oh, white sister, where is
your soul, your spirit? It has run off in shock, susto, and you lack shamans
and curanderas to call it back. Sin alma no puedes animarte pa' nada.[§]
Remember that an equally empty and hollow place within us allows that
connection, even needs that linkage.

It is important that whitewomen go out on a limb and fight for women-
of-color in workplaces, schools, and universities. It is important that
women-of-color in positions of power support their disempowered sisters. The liberation of women is the private, individual, and collective responsibility of colored and white men and women. Aliadas por pactos de

§ Shortened form of "para nada."

alianzas, united by pacts of alliances, we may make some changes—in ourselves and in our societies.

After reading this paper consider making some decisions and setting goals to work on yourself, with another, with others of your race, or with a multiracial group as a bridge, drawbridge, sandbar, island, or in a way that works for you. En fin quiero tocarlas de cerca, I want to be allied to some of you. I want to touch you, kinswomen, parientas,‖ compañeras, paisanas, carnalas, comrades, and I want you to touch me so that together, each in our separate ways, we can nourish our struggle and keep alive our visions to recuperate, validate, and transform our histories.

## Notes

Rather than discussing anti-Semitism, a dialogue I choose not to take on in this paper for reasons of length, boundaries of topic, and ignorance on my part of all its subtleties (though I am aware that there is a connection between racism and anti-Semitism I am not sure what it is), I've decided not to take it on nor even make a token mention of it. I realize that this is a form of "If you don't deal with my racism I won't deal with yours," and that pleading ignorance is no excuse.

1. This essay is an elaboration and reworking of a speech given at the Lesbian Plenary Session, "Lesbian Alliances: Combatting Heterosexism in the 80's," NWSA, June 1988. Quiero darle las gracias a, I want to thank, Lynet Uttal for her generous critical reading of this text. I also want to thank Jaime Lee Evans, Helen Moglen, Joan Pinkvoss, Lisa Albrecht, Audrey Berlowitz, Rosalinda Ramírez, and Claire Riccardi for the various ways they encouraged and helped my writing of this paper.

2. The words *marimachas* and *tortilleras* are derogatory terms that mujeres who are lesbians are called. *Patlache* is the Náhuatl term for women who bond and have sex with other women. *Lesberadas* is a term I coined, prompted by the word *desperado*.

3. Gloria Anzaldúa, "Never, Momma," a poem published in *Third Woman*, Fall 1983.

4. The concept of framing meta-communication was articulated by Gregory Bateson in *Steps to an Ecology of Mind* (New York: Ballantine, 1972).

5. Ibid.

6. For a definition of cultural paradigms see T. S. Kuhn, *The Structure of Scientific Revolutions* (Chicago: University of Chicago Press, 1970).

7. Judit Moschkovich. ["But I Know You, American Woman," in *This Bridge Called My Back*, 79–84.]

8. This was documented by Chela Sandoval, "Feminism and Racism," a report on

‖ Anzaldúa coins a new word by gendering the neutral "parientes" and making it feminine.

the National Women's Studies Association Conference held in Storrs, Connecticut, 1981 in *Making Face, Making Soul / Haciendo Caras: Creative and Critical Perspectives by Feminists of Color*, ed. Gloria Anzaldúa (San Francisco: Aunt Lute, 1990). See also Audre Lorde, "The Uses of Anger: Women Responding to Racism," in *Sister Outsider: Essays and Speeches* (Trumansburg, N.Y.: Crossing Press, 1984), 145–75.

9. Monique Wittig, "One Is Not Born A Woman," *Feminist Issues* 1, no. 2 (winter 1981).

10. Lynet Uttal, from commentary notes of her reading of this text, February 1990.

11. Elana Dykewomon, talk given in June 1988 in Montreal at the Third International Feminist Book Fair for a panel on Lesbian Separatism.

12. See Anzaldúa, "En Rapport, In Opposition: Cobrando cuentas a las nuestras," in *Making Face, Making Soul / Haciendo Caras*. The essay first appeared in *Sinister Wisdom* 33 (fall 1987).

13. *Minority Literature in North America: Contemporary Perspectives*, ed. Wolfgang Karrer and Hartmut Lutz, unpublished manuscript. [Published by Peter Lang (New York), 1988.]

14. Gail Pheterson defines internalized domination as "the incorporation and acceptance by individuals within a dominant group of prejudices against others." "Alliances Between Women: Overcoming Internalized Oppression and Internalized Domination," in this collection [*Bridges of Power: Women's Multicultural Alliances*, ed. Lisa Albrecht and Rose M. Brewer (Philadelphia: New Society, 1990), 34–48].

15. Alexander Mitscherlich's definition of prejudice in *Minority Literature in North America: Contemporary Perspectives*, ed. Wolfgang Karrer and Hartmut Lutz, 257.

16. See my introduction to *Making Face, Making Soul / Haciendo caras* cited above. My rationale for hyphenating *women-of-color*, capitalizing *Racism*, and making *whitewomen* one word is in this introduction. [See "Haciendo caras, una entrada" in this volume.]

17. María Lucía Santaella, "On Passion as (?)Phanevou (maybe or almost a phenomenology of passion)," *Third Woman: Texas and More* 3, nos. 1 and 2 (1986): 107.

18. Jacques Lacan, *Écrits, A Selection*, trans. Alan Sheridan (New York: W. W. Norton, 1977).

19. María Lugones and Elisabeth V. Spelman, "Have We Got A Theory for You! Feminist Theory, Cultural Imperialism and the Demand for 'The Woman's Voice,' " *Women's Studies Int. Forum* 6, no. 6 (1983): 573–81. Reprinted in *Making Face, Making Soul / Haciendo caras*.

20. Lynet Uttal, from commentary notes of her reading of this text, February 1990. Uttal refers to Bonnie Thornton Dill, "Race, Class, and Gender: Prospects for an All Inclusive Sisterhood," *Feminist Studies* 9 (1983): 131–48.

This humorous, surrealistic short story, first published in Charles Tatum's edited collection *New Chicana/Chicano Writing* (1992), gives us a peek into Anzaldúa's more playful, humorous side. Anzaldúa first drafted this story in 1990 and revised it several times in order to include it in *La Prieta*, what she calls her "novel/collection of stories."

## Ghost Trap / Trampa de espanto

At first Ursula la Prieta had been devastated by the death of her husband. She had thrown her plump short body into the grave on top of his coffin shrieking, "¡Ay viejito! ¿Por qué me dejaste? Yo te quería tanto. I loved you so much!" Everyone else was dry-eyed. In between sobs she heard someone say, "Hasta que se lo llevó el diablo al miserable." Another said, "Let him burn in hell." She only wept louder. For days she wailed. People felt skeptical, then uneasy at the drama and started referring to Prieta's cries as "La Llorona."

"It's not like he treated you that good," her comadre reminded her.

Often she would wake in the middle de la noche in a sweat, the echo de su grito/llanto still throbbing in her throat and feeling like the atmosphere. Her house was not the same. She would turn to him to be consoled, not that he would soothe her with a calm voice—he had only paid attention to her cuando quería algo. But she missed cushioning his skinny body and his sharp hip bones and knees. The presence de otro cuerpo had been a source of comfort in the silence of the night. Upon opening her eyes, she would find the bed empty. She would pace from room to room at night thinking about him, feeling numb and decepcionada. Gradually her loneliness soured and her grief turned into anger. Why, why, why had he deserted her? Actually his liver had deserted her. Cirrhosis.

One night, two months after his death, a snoring woke her. Se despertó to find him, or rather his ghost, in bed with her. "¡Viejo!" she cried out, astounded. She smiled for the first time since his death. She reached for him, then suddenly drew back her hand and clutched her corazón.

Durante el día he would follow her around the house, only her steps creaked the floor boards. She was amazed at just how small her house had become. He dogged her steps or hovered nearby while she hoed up and down the rows and rows of corn, squash, and beans of her immense jardín. Still, he would never go beyond the front gate when she left to do her mandados. She began to spend more time in the homes of her comadres o se iba a pasear con ellas.

"Ay, Doña Ursula, you never used to spend time chismeando with us?" said one of her comadres.

"Sí, comadrita y ahora tú eres la alcahueta."

After a couple of weeks, as they were in the living room watching T.V. she asked him "Viejo, why do you keep coming back every night? Did you forget something? Did you leave something unfinished? Is there some business you want to complete? Tell me y yo te ayudo a hacerlo. If only you'd tell me what you want."

"Vieja, prietita linda, bring me clean clothes," his voice was thin as a trail of smoke.

"Bah, estás muerto, you're dead ¿pa' qué necesitas ropa?" she whispered back. He repeated his request, his voice getting louder and louder, finally driving her to the closet. Of course his clothes were missing, she'd given them away. Now she would have to go into the shop to buy men's things and face the look of censure on the shopkeeper's face at how fast she had replaced her marido con otro pelado.

"Vieja, vieja, fix me some dinner," he said in a harsh mutter. Le guisó carnitas, his favorite dish, and set it on the table. But a ghost can't eat, so the comida sat on the table gathering moscas. "Vieja, viejita linda, tráeme una cerveza." Off she would go to la tiendita de la esquina to get the beer. La gente de la colonia began to talk about how her grief had driven her to drink. She would pull the tab and place the can of beer en la mesa by "his" chair. "You know I only drink Tecate," he growled. But a ghost can't drink. The beer would go flat. She was tempted to drink his cerveza to alleviate her increasing irritation.

Instead, she thought of all the cositas she would make with popsicle sticks. She would give them away as gifts or sell during fiesta days. She would make altar pieces, frames to hold photos of dead ancestors. She would paint them with bright colors.

Tending to his ghost seemed to take all of her time. She began to resent the time she had spent washing and cooking and trimming his hair and toenails when el pelado had been alive. She realized that she missed her solitude. Hadn't he made her feel wanted and protected? Well, now his constant presence stifled her. Just when she thought herself free, el pendejo was back and even more trouble than when he was alive. Her only consolation was that she didn't have to wash his smelly calcetines and dirty underwear. She had been two weeks without him. Pero su nueva vida de dos semanas sin él ya no era suya. She wanted her new life back. Yes, now that she was free of taking care of others, now that she lived alone, now that she had time to get together with las comadres things were different. Now, how was she going to stop her marido muerto from returning?

One day inspiration brought a smile to her face. She made a little model of her house with popsicle sticks and glue and placed it in a safe spot halfway between his grave in the nearby camposanto and her home. One of her comadres had told her that ghosts have no sense of perspective. Her chair creaked on the porch as she waited and rocked, hoping el espanto would enter the model house thinking it was hers.

That night nothing woke her. In the morning cuando despertó she turned towards the side where su viejo had been sleeping the past thirty years. His ghost was not there, nor was it there the following night. While she didn't want it to return, she had a feeling it would come back and waited all nerviosa for it to appear. But suppose someone found la casita and accidentally opened the door and let the ghost out. Some element of nature—a strong wind or a fire—could destroy the flimsy cage and her dead husband would get out. The tiny house was too fragile to be buried— the earth would crush it and the ghost would escape. She went to where she had left la casita and barred the door with a popsicle stick. Now she had to put it somewhere safe and out of the reach of others.

After several days of deliberation, she carefully carried the ghost trap into her house and placed it under the bed where mischievous nietos would not find it.

That night a voice woke her. It called out, no longer at a whisper, "Vieja, vieja todavía estás buenísima. Ándale, déjame probar ese cuerpazo. Let me touch ese cuerpo exquisito." El pelado chiflado was back. She thought she felt his body stirring under the bedcovers. Half dreaming, half awake, she pushed him away, saying "Vete viejo aguado." But he kept climbing on top of her.

"I wish you were alive so I could wring your neck." Both were surprised by the sharpness in her voice.

"You shouldn't talk to me like that."

"Why not? You've always said mean things to me."

All night she refused to open her legs to him.

The next morning she woke with deep grooves down the corners of her mouth and bruises on her breasts, arms, and inner thighs. She peered under la cama and saw that the mattress had squished the cage, forcing the door to crack open. She walked from room to room looking for el pinche desgraciado and muttering to herself. "¡Ya me voy a deshacer de ese cabrón!" She considered going to the local curandera and asking her to drive his soul into el pozo, better yet, al infierno. Huh, or she could look through the yellow pages to find an hechicera.

Ah, no, if my loneliness has summoned him, my anger will drive him away. I'll do it myself, she said to herself. "Afuera desgraciado. Get out of here. Be gone you ghost. If you don't leave te voy a maldecir."

Just in case her words failed, she plugged in the vaccum cleaner and put it by her bed. To make it harder for his hands to reach her body, she tugged on two of her sturdiest corsets, several pairs of pants, and three shirts, turned off the lights, and got into bed. Almost immediately she jumped out of bed to fetch her heavy sartén just in case he'd taken on more substance than the vacuum could handle. But if the suction wouldn't get him maybe the noise would drive him back to the cemetery and into the other world. She hid it under las cobijas. "Come on cabrón, hijo de la chingada, vente pendejo," she said under her breath. "Viejito, viejito lindo, come into my bed. I'm waiting for you," dijo con voz de sirenita.

She saw his ghostly body edge cautiously into the room. "¿No estás enojada, viejita?" he asked softly.

"¡Apúrate viejo! que te quiero dar algo."

Translations

marido, *husband*
Ay viejito ¿por qué me dejaste? Yo te quería tanto, *Why did you leave me old man? I loved you so much*
La Llorona, *the weeping woman [see Appendices for more information]*
decepsionada, *disillusioned, disenchanted, disappointed*
despertó, *she woke up*
viejo, *old man*
corazón, *heart*
Durante el día, *during the day*
jardín, *garden*
mandados, *errands*
comadres, *co-mothers, very good female friends*
o se iba a pasear con ellas, *or she'd go for a ride with them*
Chismiando, *gossiping*
y a hora tú eres la alcahueta, *and now you're the instigator*
y yo te ayudo a hacerlo, *and I'll help you do it*
Vieja, prietita linda, *woman, sweet lady (Prietita is the diminutive of Prieta, the dark one)*

Ba, estás muerto, ¿pa' que necesitas ropa, *Agh, you're dead. What do you need clothes for?*

marido con otro hombre, *husband with another man*

Le guisó carnitas, *She cooked him beef seasoned with spices*

comida, *food*

moscas, *flies*

traéme una cerveza, *bring me a beer*

la tiendita de la esquina, *the little corner store*

La gente, *People (began to talk)*

en la mesa, *on the table*

cositas, *small things*

el pelado, *the good-for-nothing*

el pendejo, *the stupid asshole*

calcetines, *socks*

pero su nueva vida de dos semanas sin él ya no era suya, *but her new two-week-old life without him was not hers anymore*

marido muerto, *dead husband*

camposanto, *graveyard*

el espanto, *ghost*

cuando despertó, *when she woke up*

nerviosa, *nervous*

nietos, *grandchildren*

Vieja, vieja todavía estás buenisima. Ándale, déjame probar ese cuerpazo, *You're still really hot. Come on, let me have a taste of that big, beautiful body.*

ese cuerpo exquisito, *that exquisite body*

El pelado chiflado, *the scoundrel*

Vete viejo aguado, go, *get away from me you flabby old man (one with flabby genitals, i.e. who is sexually wasted or worn out)*

la cama, *the bed*

el pinche desgraciado, *that no good son of a bitch*

Ya me voy a deshacer de ese cabrón, *I'm going to rid myself of that stubborn man*

curandera, *healer, medicine woman*

el pozo, *hole*

al infierno, *to hell*

hechicera, *female sorcerer*

afuera desgraciado, *get out you damned man*

te voy a maldecir, *I'm going to curse you*

sartén, *iron skillet*

cobijas, *bed covers*

cabrón, hijo de la chingada, vente pendejo, *go you old goat, son of a bitch, come here stupid*

viejito lindo, *sweet old man*

dijo con voz de sirenita, *she said with a siren's voice*

"¿No estás enojada, viejita?" *You aren't angry, are you, old lady?*

"¡Apúrate viejo! que te quiero dar algo." *Hurry up, old man, I want to give you something*

This essay was first published in Betsy Warland's edited collection *Inversions: Writing by Dykes, Queers, and Lesbians* (1991). When Warland invited Anzaldúa to contribute to the proposed collection, Anzaldúa decided to begin with a recorded conversation and convert the transcript into an essay. After recording a conversation between herself and Jeffner Allen, Anzaldúa transformed her part of the dialogue into this essay. (See Anzaldúa's *Interviews/Entrevistas*, chapter 3, for a transcript of the original discussion.) As with "La Prieta" and some of Anzaldúa's other earlier writings, this piece illustrates the formative role she played in developing queer theory. (See, for instance, Anzaldúa's discussion of identity labels and queer as a meaning-making process.) And as with "En Rapport, In Opposition: Cobrando cuentas a las nuestras," "Haciendo caras, una entrada," and other writings, this piece makes important contributions to "whiteness" studies. "To(o) Queer the Writer" also explores issues related to solidarity, theorizing, reading, and the writing process. Anzaldúa continued revising this essay after its original publication and planned to include it in a book of essays. The version here is the early one from 1990.

# To(o) Queer the Writer—Loca, escritora y chicana

## Queer Labels and Debates

I believe that while there are lesbian perspectives, sensibilities, experiences and topics, *there are no "lesbian writers."*

For me the term lesbian es un problema. As a working-class Chicana, mestiza[1]—a composite being, amalgama de culturas y de lenguas—a woman who loves women, "lesbian" is a cerebral word, white and middle-class, representing an English-only dominant culture, derived from the Greek word *lesbos*. I think of lesbians as predominantly white and middle-class women and a segment of women of color who acquired the term through osmosis much the same as Chicanas and Latinas assimilated the word "Hispanic." When a "lesbian" names me the same as her, she subsumes me under her category. I am of her group but not as an equal, not as a whole person—my color erased, my class ignored. Soy una puta mala, a phrase coined by Ariban, a tejana tortillera. "Lesbian" doesn't name anything in my homeland. Unlike the word "queer," "lesbian" came late into some of our lives. Call me de las otras. Call me loquita, jotita, marimacha, pajuelona, lambiscona, culera—these are words I grew up hearing. I can identify with being "una de las otras" or a "marimacha," or even a jota or a loca porque—these are the terms my home community uses. I identify most closely with the Náhuatl term patlache. These terms situate me in South Texas Chicano/mexicano culture and in my experiences and recuerdos. These Spanish/Chicano words resonate in my head and evoke gut feelings and meanings.

I want to be able to choose what to name myself. But if I have to pick an identity label in the English language I pick "dyke" or "queer," though these working-class words (formerly having "sick" connotations) have been taken over by white middle-class lesbian theorists in the academy. Queer is used as a false unifying umbrella which all "queers" of all races, ethnicities and classes are shoved under. At times we need this umbrella to solidify our ranks against outsiders. But even when we seek shelter under it we must not forget that it homogenizes, erases our differences. Yes, we may all love members of the same sex but we are not the same. Our ethnic communities deal differently with us. I must constantly assert my differentness, must say, This is what I think of loving women. I must stress: The difference is in my relationship to my culture; white culture may allow its lesbians to leave—mine doesn't. This is one way I avoid getting sucked into the vortex of homogenization, of getting pulled into the shelter of the queer umbrella.

What is a lesbian writer? The label in front of a writer positions her. It implies that identity is socially constructed. But only for the cultural "other." Oblivious to privilege and wrapped in arrogance, most writers from the dominant culture never specify their identity; I seldom hear them say, I am a white writer. If the writer is middle class, white, and heterosexual s/he is crowned with the "writer" hat—no mitigating adjectives in front of it. They consider me a *Chicana* writer, or a lesbian Chicana writer. Adjectives are a way of constraining and controlling. "The more adjectives you have the tighter the box."[2] The adjective before writer marks, for us, the "inferior" writer, that is, the writer who doesn't write like them. Marking is always "marking down." While I advocate putting Chicana, tejana, working-class, dyke-feminist poet, writer-theorist in front of my name, I do so for reasons different than those of the dominant culture. Their reasons are to marginalize, confine, and contain. My labeling of myself is so that the Chicana and lesbian and all the other persons in me don't get erased, omitted, or killed. Naming is how I make my presence known, how I assert who and what I am and want to be known as. Naming myself is a survival tactic.

I have the same kinds of problems with the label "lesbian writer" that I do with the label "Chicana writer." Sí, soy chicana, and therefore a Chicana writer. But when critics label me thus, they're looking not at the person but at the writing, as though the writing is Chicana writing instead of the writer being Chicana. By forcing the label on the writing they marginalize it.

I've had the legitimacy issue thrown at me by another Chicana lesbian, Cherríe Moraga. In a book review of *Borderlands/La Frontera*, she implied that I was not a real lesbian because I did not stress my lesbian identity nor did I write about sexuality. I gathered that she wanted me to focus on lesbian sexuality. Her criticism implies that there is such a thing as a lesbian writer and that a lesbian writer should only write about lesbian issues and that lesbian issues are about sexuality.[3] It is ironic that some straight Chicanas/os, seeing only sexual difference because to them it is a glaring difference, also stress lesbian and gay aspects of my identity and leave out the culture and the class aspects. Always the labeling impacts expectations. In this double bind, one reader may view the label as a positive attribute, another as a way to marginalize.

This anthology's topic, "lesbian writers writing about their own writing," assumes the existence of a "lesbian" writer. It follows the tradition in which white middle-class lesbians and gay men frame the terms of the debate. It is they who have produced queer theory and for the most part their theories make abstractions of us colored queers. They control the production of queer knowledge in the academy and in the activist communities. Higher up in the hierarchy of gay politics and gay aesthetics, they most readily get their work published and disseminated. They enter the territories of queer racial ethnic/Others and re-inscribe and recolonize. They appropriate our experiences and even our lives and "write" us up. They occupy theorizing space, and though their theories aim to enable and emancipate, they often disempower and neo-colonize. They police the queer person of color with theory. They theorize, that is, perceive, organize, classify, and name specific chunks of reality by using approaches, styles, and methodologies that are Anglo-American or European. Their theories limit the ways we think about being queer.

Position is point of view. And whatever positions we may occupy, we are getting only one point of view: white middle-class. Theory serves those that create it. White middle-class lesbians and gays are certainly not speaking for me. Inevitably we colored dykes fall into a reactive mode, counter their terms and theories — as I am doing, as I have to do before I can even begin to write this essay. We focus on the cultural abuse of colored by white and thus fall into the trap of the colonized reader and writer forever reacting against the dominant. I feel pushed into trying to "correct" the record, to speak out against it while all the time realizing that colored queers are not responsible for educating white lesbians and gays.

What I object to about the words "lesbian" and "homosexual" is that they are terms with iron-cast molds. There are assumptions made, by both insiders and outsiders, when one identifies with these terms. The words "lesbian" and "homosexual" conjure up stereotypes of differences that are different from those evoked by the word "queer." "Queer" also provokes different assumptions and expectations. In the '60s and '70s it meant that one was from a working-class background, that one was not from genteel society. Even though today the term means other things, for me there is still more flexibility in the "queer" mold, more room to maneuver. "Lesbian" comes from a Euro-Anglo American mold and "homosexual" from a deviant, diseased mold shaped by certain psychological theories. We non-Euro-Anglo Americans are supposed to live by and up to those theories. A mestiza colored queer person is bodily shoved by both the heterosexual world and by white gays into the "lesbian" or "homosexual" mold whether s/he fits or not. La persona está situada dentro de la idea en vez de al revés.

I struggle with naming without fragmenting, without excluding. Containing and closing off the naming is the central issue of this piece of writing. The core question is: What is the power and what is the danger of writing and reading like a "lesbian" or a queer? Can the power and danger be named and can queer writing be named? How does one give queer writing labels while holding the totality of the group and the person in one's mind? How do we maintain the balance between solidarity and separate space, between the güeras/os and the morenas/os? "Where are our alliances, with our culture or our crotch?"[4] En vez de dejar cada parte en su región y mantener entre ellos la distancia de un silencio, mejor mantener la tensión entre nuestras cuatro o seis partes/personas.

Identity is not a bunch of little cubbyholes stuffed respectively with intellect, race, sex, class, vocation, gender. Identity flows between, over, aspects of a person. Identity is a river—a process. Contained within the river is its identity, and it needs to flow, to change to stay a river—if it stopped it would be a contained body of water such as a lake or a pond. The changes in the river are external (changes in environment—river bed, weather, animal life) and internal (within the waters). A river's contents flow within its boundaries. Changes in identity likewise are external (how others perceive one and how one perceives others and the world) and internal (how one perceives oneself, self-image). People in different regions name the parts of the river/person which they see.

La busqueda de identidad—How Queer is Queer?

Often I am asked, "What is your primary identity, being lesbian or working-class or Chicana?" In defining or separating the "lesbian" identity from other aspects of identity I am asked to separate and distinguish all aspects from one another. I am asked to bracket each, to make boundaries around each so as to articulate one particular facet of identity only. But to put each in a separate compartment is to put them in contradiction or in isolation when in actuality they are all constantly in a shifting dialogue/relationship—the ethnic is in conversation with the academic and so on. The lesbian is part of the writer, is part of a social class, is part of a gender, is part of whatever identities one has of oneself. There is no way that I can put myselves through this sieve, and say okay, I'm only going to let the "lesbian" part out, and everything else will stay in the sieve. All the multiple aspects of identities (as well as the sieve) are part of the "lesbian." I can understand that impulse to nail things down, to have a checklist which says that for you to be a dyke, a radical lesbian, or an s/m lesbian, you must pass certain criteria. But when those criteria are applied to people who fall outside the characterizations defined by white, middle-class lesbians and gays (such as racial ethnic/Others), it feels very totalitarian. It feels more totalitarian for dykes of color than for lesbians because the checklist and criteria come from gay white ideology, whether its proponents are white or colored.

Different lesbians and gays scrutinize the cultural/Other to see if we're correct—they police us out of fear of instability within a community, fear of not appearing united and fear of attack by non-gay outsiders. But I fear a unity that leaves out parts of me, that colonizes me, i.e., violates my integrity, my wholeness, and chips away at my autonomy. We police ourselves out of fear as well. Because of our mestizaje, colored queers have more communities to deal with (ethnic, class, white lesbians, etc.) that analyze us to determine if we "pass."

The same thing is true of the dyke community: it wants to pinpoint the dykes who are in the closet, the lesbians who are out, the queers who are activists, gays who are writers. You are privileged differently if you are out there being a model of "the good lesbian." And if you're not, if you happen to be a lesbian and you write a story in which the protagonist is male or a straight woman, then you're criticized for supporting the patriarchy by writing traditionally, for writing about concerns that are not seen as "lesbian concerns." But yet, what these lesbian readers fail to see is that a lot of times, in presenting traditional content or characters that the gay community thinks support the patriarchy, they may not be "seeing" that the queer colored writers are doing something radical or critical via the form and/or style. The story may depict violence of men against women. The white lesbian "reads" this as a text perpetuating the oppression of women. Often in showing "how it really is," colored dykes actually effect changes in the psyches of their readers. Often the lesbian reader misses the subtle subversive elements and hidden messages. Her binocular vision, focusing on the trees, misses the forest.

## Reading Them Reading Me

A strange thing happens when I attend poetry or prose readings where two or three lesbian feminists read. Often nothing they say moves me because it is too predictable, too "white" and racist in its ignorance of colored gay experiences. I have done a number of readings within the white lesbian community and almost always have received a very generous reception. They may squirm when I bring up racism and class oppression, but they seem to swallow what I say. I've also read in the Latino/Chicano Mission community (where I have drawn smaller crowds) and have felt they would rather I had checked my queerness at the door. On the other hand, poems and stories dealing with race and class are received with much fervor.

Once in the Haight district I read to an audience of white and colored hippies, straight beats and non-literary people. Later in a poem I tried to express the feelings of "at-home-ness" I experienced with them. I realized that they had been open and receptive to my work and that class had something to do with it. When I read poems dealing with colored queer or Chicana issues, the audience didn't have any preconceptions. I felt accepted, respected, and valued in a more total way than I had experienced in the "lesbian" or the Mission communities in San Francisco. These feelings are central to the interaction between writer, reader and text. Class y el conflicto de clases is at the core of this paper, perhaps more than dealing with being "queer of color."

In the past the reader was a minor character in the triangle of author-text-reader. More and more today the reader is becoming as important if not more important than the author. Making meaning is a collaborative affair. Similar class, ethnic, and sexual identity is a strong component of the bond between writer and reader. This intimate interactive relationship I have with readers has to do with a colored queer feminist mestiza identity. Not all writers experience this interaction. This interaction comes with the realization that writing is a collaborative, communal activity not done in a room of one's own. It is an act informed and supported by the books the author reads, the people s/he interacts with, and the centuries of cultural history that seethe under her skin. The idea of shared writing is not yet part of the consensual reality of most writers.

A lot of my poems, stories, and essays (what I call *autohistorias*) are about reading—not just reading as in the act of reading words on a page, but also "reading" reality and reflecting on that process and the process of writing in general. The Haight poem is about me reading, about other people reading me and me reading them reading me. Most of these people at the Haight reading were straight, and a lot of them were men—what you would consider chauvinist and anti-feminist—yet they were there for me in a way that the other groups such as the politically correct or the politically aware groups weren't. What was it about them that was open and receptive? They would call out encouragement, would rock and hum to my words—they were listening with their bodies and not just their intellects. They weren't "reading" me the usual way. They were "reading" my readings in front of me. Their faces were not blank nor passive. They saw me as vulnerable, a flesh-and-blood person and not as a symbol of representation, not as a "Chicana" writer. They saw me as I wanted to be seen then—as an embodied symbol.

## Reading Like a Lesbian

Reading like a queer feminist, which includes listening like one, may be how one would distinguish dyke-feminist or feminist from non-dyke/feminist. Queer readers want to interact, to repeat back or reflect or mirror, but also do more than just reflect back and mirror—to add to the dialogue. White lesbians feel that colored dykes have important things to communicate or perhaps they want to really "listen to" and "read" us better in order to mitigate and correct their ethnocentrism. And that might be why dykes of color have such a low patience with texts and public events that don't allow us to participate fully. When I attend white women's music concerts there's so little part of me that gets to interact that there's nothing there for me. When I read Emma Pérez or Terri de la Peña or watch comedians Mónica Palacios and Margo Gómez perform and when I study the art of Ester Hernández I realize what is missing from white lesbian texts—colored queer rites of passage.[5]

Though the Haight-Ashbury audience responded best (back then in 1980–81), in 1991 lesbian and gay readers and audiences (who have learned to "read" me in their classrooms) not only are beginning to reflect back my ideas but to also actively engage with me and my theories.

Queering the Writer and Reading With a Queer Facultad

We queers also label ourselves. It is we as well as white, middle-class heterosexuals who say, "S/he's a gay writer." The gay community wants so badly to have pride in its artists and writers; it wants to shout it from the rooftops. There is a hunger for legitimacy in queers who are always trying to "discover" gay movie stars and great writers.

Can a straight woman or a man write a lesbian story? The questions are, Are you a dyke writer because you're a dyke, or are you a lesbian writer because the concerns that you write about are lesbian concerns? In other words, Is there such a thing as a lesbian language, dyke style, lesbian terminology, dyke aesthetics, or is it all up to the individual who's writing, regardless of whether she's a dyke or a straight woman, or a man? This is the same question that theorists asked in earlier debates—can a man write as a straight woman, can a man read as a woman? *We all know that women read as men and women write as men, because that's how we were taught.* We were trained to read as men. Little girls read the books that boys read, but the boys never read the books with little girl heroines, and so women are taught to read westerns and spy novels and mysteries, and the "serious" literature,[6] but we also read "women's literature," watch soap operas, read romances, read women's mysteries. But men aren't taught to read women. How and why do we break with this gender socialization? Isn't the departure as significant as establishing the criteria? Reading affects the development of female and male identity. I, for one, define my life and construct my identities through the process of reading and writing—dyke detective novels, cultural theory, Latin American fiction. Can we apply this in the same way to the lesbian readers and the lesbian writers?

A straight woman reader of dyke writings would likely not catch a lot of the undercurrents having to do with dyke sexualities or sexual experiences (unless, of course, she has a lot of lesbian friends). Queers (including cultural Others) can fill in the gaps in a lesbian text and reconstruct it, where a straight woman might not. I am arguing for a lesbian sensibility, not a lesbian aesthetic.

Reading is one way of constructing identity. When one reads something that one is familiar with, one attaches to that familiarity, and the rest of the text, what remains hidden, is not perceived. Even if one notices things that are very different from oneself, that difference is used to form identity by negation—"I'm not that, I'm different from that character. This is me, that's you." Yet readers have an attraction to the unfamiliar, a curiosity. Which is why straight readers read gay literature. When a straight writer writes about us, perhaps also out of curiosity, or latent queerness or to capitalize on a trendy forbidden lifestyle, s/he often ends up appropriating our lives, paying them token attention and focusing on sex instead of the full complexity of our lives. So while we do write for straight readers, they don't write for us.

Identity formation is a component in reading and writing whether through empathy and identification or through disidentification. If it's a lesbian who's reading, she will have more incentive to keep reading when she reaches a dyke-concerns-laden passage in my writing. There will be more doors and windows through which she can access the text than if she's a non-lesbian. If she's a working-class dyke of color, however, there are even more entradas, more identity-making opportunities. If she's a Chicana lesbian she's got the greatest possibility of finding herself represented in my writing. But some Chicana dykes, such as urban dwellers or younger ones, may be excluded from my writing, while others bearing other kinds of "otherness" may plug into my writing. Just as we speak in different ways, we read in different ways, write in different ways. Educational and lived experiences change the way we speak, hear, read, and write.

However, there are straight, white, academic women who sometimes "see into" and "see through" to unconscious falsifying disguises by penetrating the surface and reading underneath the words and between the lines. As outsiders, they may see through what I'm trying to say better than an insider. For me then it is a question of whether the individual reader is in possession of a mode of reading that can read the subtext, and can introject her experiences into the gaps. Some conventionally trained readers do not have the flexibility (in identity) nor the patience in deciphering a "strange," that is, different, text. Reading skills may result from certain ethnic, class, or sexual experiences which allow her to read in non-white ways. She looks at a piece of writing and reads it differently.

I'm also a reader of my own work. And as a reader, I usually have more in common with the Chicana dyke than I do with the white, middle-class feminist. I am in possession of both ways of reading—Chicana working-class, dyke ways of reading, and white middle-class heterosexual and male ways of reading. I have had more training in reading as a white, middle-class academic than I do reading as a Chicana. Just like we have more training reading as men.

Reading With One's Foot In One's Mouth

Learning to read is not synonymous with academic learning. Working-class and street people may go into an experience — for example an incident taking place on the street — and "read" what is taking place in a way that an academic couldn't. One always writes and reads from the place one's feet are planted, the ground one stands on, one's particular position, point of view. When I write about different ideas, I try to flesh out and embody them rather than abstract them. But I don't always spell things out. I want the reader to deduce my conclusions or at least come up with her own. Often the working-class person or the colored dyke will automatically identify with that experience and say, "Oh, yeah, I've lived it, or my friend has told me she's lived that," or whatever. The white, middle-class academic woman might see it in terms of where the author positions herself; whether she is "rereading" (reinterpreting) or reinscribing certain patriarchal signs; whether s/he locates herself in a specific historical period; whether she is self-reflective about her writing. These are approaches and moves she has learned to make as a feminist critic, and they are different from the moves that the street-wise person utilizes. The street reader looks at an experience as something that's alive and moving or about to move, whereas the academic looks at the flattened out, abstract theory on these pages that is not connected to the actual experience. Being queer, being of color, I consider myself standing in the Borderlands (the actual crossroads or bridge) of these two "readings." I may be able to read the situation in the street from the point of view of a streetwise person, and I can look at these abstract theoretical writings and be able to read them academically because of the schooling that I've had.

One of the things that I've discovered about people critiquing my writing is that they want me to flesh out more of the gaps, provide more transition. I suppose this is so they don't have to do as much work. "In my instruction in tutoring writing," commented Vicki Alcoset, my writing intern, who is Chicana and Jewish, "this is the main hidden agenda that defines 'good' writing in the U.S. The point is to assume the reader is lazy, wants everything spelled out for her/him. If the reader has to work to get meaning, the writing is no 'good.'" Another reason that people sometimes want me to elaborate is because they want to know my meaning as well as their own. Roz Spafford, a college composition writing instructor at UCSC,[7] suggests that perhaps the reader is looking for fullness and complexity, and a desire not to project their experience/thinking onto mine, a desire to listen fully. But for me, what's fun about reading is those gaps where I can bring my experience into the piece of writing and use concrete images to go off into my own experience. It makes the writing richer because I can bring more into it. But we haven't been taught to read in that manner. We have, in fact, been taught not to trust it. I think that I can "read" that way because I'm in my inner world, my psychic and imaginary worlds so much that I've developed the facultad to navigate such texts. The more I interact with the text the better. The more entrances, the more access for all of us.

## White Lesbian Formula Writing

One of the things that I find very boring about some lesbian writing—fiction and non-fiction—is an almost formulaic impression or imposition on the writing of what lesbians should think about—a kind of politically correct way of writing that feels very sterile, very flat. One formula leads to the underlying belief that to be a lesbian writer you have to write about sexuality, and that the predominant concern of our work should be sexual relationships or sexuality. It's a given. This ideological imprint makes us view our sexuality in a preconstructed way. It tells us dykes how to think and feel about our bodies. Perhaps if we weren't supposed to write about sex so much, the writing would be more vital and vibrant. Besides, not all dykes want to write about sex or sexuality. Which brings us back to an earlier point: Is lesbian writing called such when it's not about lesbianism/sexuality but is by a lesbian?

Certain tropes that are considered lesbian properties—the coming-out story, the lesbian couple relationship, the break-up—have become formulaic. The formula is very white and mostly middle-class and so prevalent that it is almost a genre. A coming-out story is different if it is written from the perspective of some "other"—racial, cultural, class, ethnic, or for whatever reason a lesbian has been "othered." A lot of cultural Others take the white lesbian patterns as models. So that whatever freshness of perspective, of presentation, of self-confrontation, encountering oneself as a lesbian and confronting one's community as a lesbian, instead of having that fresh, unique presentation of it, what we do is we copy this other model that's white middle-class. It kills our writing. If it's not possible to entirely change the formula I'd at least like to see it be more representative of the diverse realities of queers, to read it and write it through other cultural lenses. I think that dykes have breached an opening in the dialogue about women connecting with our bodies. Dykes bridged some of the political, theoretical, cultural, critical concepts/ beliefs with concrete experience—external/internal, sexual and corporeal. And that was really good.

A rainbow is a bridge. The word is used politically by Native Americans— it derives from Native American people symbolizing the way different people communicate and relate with each other. It's the vision that Native Americans have of the red and the white and the black and the yellow being able to communicate and make alliances. According to the Native Americans, they were the keepers of the Earth and they were the ones that would facilitate this rich, multi-alliance, multi-bridging. A bridge excludes racial separatism. So the concept has taken a beating recently because of the reactionary times we're going through and the upsurge in racism and white supremacy. But I can see that in the '90s a rainbow *serpent* bridge composed of new mestizas/os, bi- and multi-racial queer people who are mixed and politicized will rise up and become important voices in our gay, ethnic, and other communities.

Notes

This essay is in progress and is excerpted from a longer piece. It started as a take-off on the transcription of my part in an interview/dialogue with Jeffner Allen. Gracias a mis interns Dianna Williamson, Vicki Alcoset, Audrey Berlowitz, and Michelle Ueland, and also to Betsy Warland and Roz Spafford, who made comments: grammatical, stylistic, and conceptual.

1. The new mestiza queers have the ability, the flexibility, the malleability, the amorphous quality of being able to stretch this way and that way. We can add new labels, names, and identities as we mix with others.

2. Dianna Williamson, commentary on this text, April 1991.

3. Cherríe Moraga, "'Algo secretamente armado': A Review of Gloria Anzaldúa's *Borderlands/La Frontera: The New Mestiza*," *Third Woman* (Fall 1989): 151–56.

4. Dianna Williamson, commentary on this text, April 1991.

5. See *Chicana Lesbians: The Girls Our Mothers Warned Us About*, edited by Carla Trujillo (Berkeley: Third Woman Press, 1991).

6. The debate is not settled as to what's "serious" literature as opposed to woman-centered literature. The terms are suspicious ones to embrace. Does this

imply that what women read is not "serious," i.e., not important? However, this piece is not the place to take on that discussion.

7. The book Spafford uses for Lit 203 at the University of California at Santa Cruz, *Facts, Artifacts and Counterfacts: Theory and Method for a Reading and Writing Course*, by David Bartholomae and Anthony Petrosky (Portsmouth, N.H.: Boynton Cook, 1986) suggests that reading is misreading.

This essay, like "Bearing Witness: Their Eyes Anticipate the Healing" (in part 3), illustrates another side of Anzaldúa: her intense interest in the world of visual art. Originally published in the San Diego Museum of Contemporary Art's *La Frontera/The Border: Art about the Mexico/United States Border Experience* (1993), "Border Arte" describes Anzaldúa's experience viewing "AZTEC: The World of Moctezuma" exhibition at the Denver Museum of Natural History. In addition to offering important insights into Anzaldúa's shaman aesthetics, "Border Arte" contains her first extensive description and interpretation of Coyolxauhqui (Ko-yol-sha-UH-kee) as well as elaborations on her theories of el cenote, nepantla, and autohistoria. This piece also demonstrates Anzaldúa's shift from borderland to nepantla theory and her ongoing interest in revisionist mythmaking, trans issues, and the relationship between identity, nationalism, and art. Although some readers, particularly those who identify as "white," as male, and/or as members of the dominating culture, have felt as though Anzaldúa excludes them from portions of this piece, "The New Mestiza Nation" and other later writings indicate that the aesthetics and artists she describes here are inclusionary, and apply to other artists as well.

# Border Arte

*Nepantla, el Lugar de la Frontera*

The gatekeeper at the museum takes our ticket. We enter the simulation of the Aztec capital city, Tenochtitlán, as it was thought to exist before the European colonizers destroyed it. It is opening day of the "AZTEC: The World of Moctezuma" exhibition at the Denver Museum of Natural History. El legado indígena. Here before my eyes is the culture of nuestros antepasados indígenas. Sus símbolos y metáforas todavía viven en la gente chicana/mexicana. I am again struck by how much Chicana/o artists and writers feel the impact of ancient Mexican art forms, foods, and customs. We consistently reflect back these images in revitalized and modernized versions in theater, film, performance art, painting, dance sculpture, and literature. La negación sistemática de la cultura mexicana-chicana en los Estados Unidos impide su desarrollo haciendo esto un acto de colonización. As a people who have been stripped of our history, language, identity, and pride, we attempt again and again to find what we have lost by digging into our cultural roots imaginatively and making art out of our findings. I ask myself, What does it mean for me, esta jotita, this queer Chicana, this mexica-tejana to enter a museum and look at indigenous objects that were once used by her ancestors? Will I find my historical Indian identity here, along with its ancient mestizaje? As I pull out a pad to take notes on the clay, stone, jade, bone, feather, straw, and cloth artifacts, I am disconcerted with the knowledge that I too am passively consuming and appropriating an indigenous culture. I, and the Chicano kids from Servicio Chicano Center I walked in with, are being taught our cultural roots by whites. The essence of colonization: rip off a culture, then regurgitate the white version of that culture to the "natives."

This exhibit bills itself as an act of good will between North America and Mexico, a sort of bridge across the border. The Mexico/United States border is a site where many different cultures "touch" each other, and the permeable, flexible, and ambiguous shifting grounds lend themselves to hybrid images. The border is the locus of resistance, of rupture, implosion and explosion, and of putting together the fragments and creating a new assemblage. Border artists cambian el punto de referencia. By disrupting the neat separations between cultures, they create a culture mix, una mezcla in their artworks. Each artist locates her/him self in this border "lugar," and tears apart and rebuilds the "place" itself.

The museum, if it is daring and takes risks, can be a kind of "borderlands" where cultures co-exist in the same site, I think to myself as I walk through the first exhibit. I am jostled amidst a white middle-class crowd. I look at videos, listen to slide presentations, and hear museum staff explain portions of the exhibit. It angers me that all these people talk as though the Aztecs and their culture have been dead for hundreds of years when in fact there are still 10,000 Aztec survivors living in Mexico.

I stop before the dismembered body of la diosa de la luna, Coyolxauhqui, bones jutting from sockets. The warrior goddess with bells on her cheeks and serpent belt calls to mind the dominant culture's repeated attempts to tear the Mexican culture in the U.S. apart and scatter the fragments to the winds. This slick, prepackaged exhibition costing $3.5 million exemplifies that dismemberment. I stare at the huge round stone of la diosa. To me she also embodies the resistance and vitality of the Chicana/mexicana writer/artist. I can see resemblances between the moon goddess' vigorous and warlike energy and Yolanda López's *Portrait of the Artist as the Virgin of Guadalupe* (1978), which depicts a Chicana/mexicana woman emerging and running from the oval halo of rays with the mantle of the traditional virgen in one hand and a serpent in the other. *Portrait* represents the cultural rebirth of the Chicana struggling to free herself from oppressive gender roles.[1] The struggle and pain of this rebirth is also represented eloquently by Marsha Gomez in earthworks and stoneware scuptures such as *This Mother Ain't For Sale*.

The sibilant whispery voice of Chicano Edward James Olmos on the walkman interrupts my thoughts and guides me to the serpentine base of a reconstructed sixteen-foot temple where the human sacrifices were flung down, leaving bloodied steps. Around me I hear the censorious, culturally ignorant words of the whites who, while horrified by the bloodthirsty Aztecs, gape in vicarious wonder and voraciously consume the exoticized images. Though I, too, am a gaping consumer, I feel that these artworks are part of my legacy. I remember visiting Chicana tejana artist Santa Barraza in her Austin studio in the mid-1970s and talking about the merger and appropriation of cultural symbols and techniques by artists in search of their spiritual and cultural roots. As I walked around her studio I was amazed at the vivid Virgen de Guadalupe iconography on her walls and drawings strewn on tables and shelves. The three "madres," Guadalupe, La Malinche, y La Llorona are culture figures that Chicana writers and artists "re-read" in our works. And now, sixteen years later, Barraza is focusing on interpretations of Pre-Columbian codices as a reclamation of cultural and historical mestiza/o identity. Her "códices" are edged with milagros and ex votos.[2] Using the folk art format, Barraza paints tin testimonials known as retablos, traditional popular miracle paintings on metal, a medium introduced into Colonial Mexico by the Spaniards. One of her devotional retablos is of La Malinche with maguey (the maguey cactus is Barraza's symbol of rebirth). Like many Chicana artists her work explores indigenous Mexican "symbols and myths in a historical and contemporary context as a mechanism of resistance to oppression and assimilation."[3] Once more my eyes return to Coyolxauhqui. Nope, she's not for sale and neither are the original La Lupe, La Llorona, and La Chingada and their modern renditions.

Olmos's occasional musical recitations in Náhuatl further remind me that the Aztecs, their language, and indigenous cultures are still very much alive. Though I wonder if Olmos and we Chicana/o writers and artists also are misappropriating Náhuatl language and images, hearing the words and seeing the images boosts my spirits. I feel that I am part of something profound outside my personal self. This sense of connection and community compels Chicana/o writers/artists to delve into, sift through, and rework native imagery.

I wonder about the genesis of el arte de la frontera. Border art remembers its roots—sacred and folk art are often still one and the same. I recall the nichos (niches or recessed areas) and retablos (altar pieces) that I had recently seen in several galleries and museums such as the Denver Metropolitan State College Art Museum. The altar pieces are placed inside open boxes made of wood, tin, or cardboard. The cajitas contain three-dimensional figures such as la virgen, photos of ancestors, candles, and sprigs of herbs tied together. They are actually tiny installations. I make mine out of cigar boxes or vegetable crates that I find discarded on streets before garbage pickups. The retablos range from the strictly traditional to the modern more abstract forms. Santa Barraza, Yolanda M. López, Marsha Gomez, Carmen Lomas Garza, and other Chicanas connect the everyday life with the political, sacred, and aesthetic with their art.[4]

I walk from the glass-caged exhibits of the sacred world to the Tlate-lolco, the open mercado, the people's market, with its strewn baskets of chiles, avocados, nopales on petates, and ducks in hanging wooden cages. I think of how border art, in critiquing old, traditional, and erroneous representations of the Mexico/United States border, attempts to represent the "real world" de la gente going about their daily lives. But it renders that world and its people in more than mere surface slices of life. If one looks beyond the obvious, one sees a connection to the spirit world, to the underworld, and to other realities. In the "old world," art was/is functional and sacred as well as aesthetic. At the point that folk and fine art separated, the metate (a flat porous volcanic stone with rolling pin used to make corn tortillas) and the huipil (blouse)[5] were put in museums by the western curators of art. Many of these officiators believe that only art objects from dead cultures should end up in museums. According to a friend[6] who recently returned from Central America, a museum in Guate-mala City solely houses indigenous clothing as though they were garments of the past. There was little mention of the women she saw still weaving the same kind of clothing and using the same methods as their ancestors. However, the men in the Guatemalan community, Todos Santos, wear red pants while men from another area wear another color. Indigenous peoples were forced to wear clothing of a certain color so that their pa-trones could distinguish "their" peons from those of other bosses. The men's red pants reflect a colonization of their culture. Thus, colonization influences the lives and objects of the colonized and artistic heritage is altered.

I come to a glass case where the skeleton of a jaguar with a stone in its open mouth nestles on cloth. The stone represents the heart. My thoughts trace the jaguar's spiritual and religious symbolism from its Olmec origins to present-day jaguar masks worn by people who no longer know that the jaguar was connected to rain. Who no longer remember that Tlaloc and the jaguar and the serpent and rain are tightly intertwined.[7] Through the cen-turies a culture touches and influences another, passing on its metaphors and its gods before it dies. (Metaphors *are* gods.) The new culture adopts, modifies, and enriches these images, and it, in turn, passes them on. The process is repeated until the original meanings of images are pushed into the unconscious. What surfaces are images more significant to the prevailing culture and era. However, the artist on some level still connects to that unconscious reservoir of meaning, connects to that nepantla state of transition between time periods, and the border between cultures. Chicana/o artists presently are engaged in "reading" that cenote, that nepantla, and that border.

Art and la frontera intersect in a liminal space where border people, especially artists, live in a state of "nepantla." Nepantla is the Náhuatl word for an in-between state, that uncertain terrain one crosses when moving from one place to another, when changing from one class, race, or sexual position to another, when traveling from the present identity into a new identity. The Mexican immigrant at the moment of crossing the barbed wired fence into a hostile "paradise" of el norte, the U.S., is caught in a state of nepantla. Others who find themselves in this bewildering transitional space may be the straight person coming out as lesbian, gay, bi, or transsexual, or a person from working-class origins crossing into middle-classness and privilege. The marginalized starving Chicana/o artist who suddenly finds her/his work exhibited in mainstream museums or sold for thousands in prestigious galleries, as well as the once neglected writer whose work is in every professor's syllabus, for a time inhabit nepantla.

I think of the borderlands as Jorge Luis Borges's Aleph, the one spot on earth which contains all other places within it. All people in it, whether natives or immigrants, colored or white, queers or heterosexuals, from this side of the border or del otro lado are personas del lugar, local people—all of whom relate to the border and to the nepantla states in different ways.

I continue meandering absently from room to room, noticing how the different parts of the Aztec culture are partitioned from others and how some are placed together in one room and a few feet apart but still seem to be in neat little categories. That bothers me. Abruptly I meet myself in the center of the room with the sacrificial knives. I stand rooted there for a long time, thinking about spaces and borders and moving in them and through them. According to Edward Hall, early in life we become oriented to space in a way that is tied to survival and sanity. When we become disoriented from that sense of space we fall in danger of becoming psychotic.[8] I question this—to be disoriented in space is the "normal" way of being for us mestizas living in the borderlands. It is the sane way of coping with the accelerated pace of this complex, interdependent, and multicultural planet. To be disoriented in space is to be en nepantla. To be disoriented in space is to experience bouts of dissociation of identity, identity breakdowns and buildups. The border is in a constant nepantla state and it is an analog of the planet. This is why the borderline is a persistent metaphor in el arte de la frontera, an art that deals with such themes of identity, border crossings, and hybrid imagery. "Imágenes de la Frontera" was the title of the Centro Cultural Tijuana's June 1992 exhibition.[9] Malaquías Montoya's *Frontera Series* and Irene Pérez' *Dos Mundos* monoprint are examples of the multi-subjectivity, split-subjectivity, and refusal-to-be-split themes of the border artist creating a counter art.

The nepantla state is the natural habitat of artists, most specifically for the mestizo border artists who partake of the traditions of two or more worlds and who may be binational. They thus create a new artistic space— a border mestizo culture. Beware of el romance del mestizaje, I hear myself saying silently. Puede ser una ficción. I warn myself not to romanticize mestizaje—it is just another fiction, something made up like "culture" or the events in a person's life. But I and other writer/artists of la frontera have invested ourselves in it.

There are many obstacles and dangers in crossing into nepantla. Border artists are threatened from the outside by appropriation by popular culture and the dominant art institutions, by "outsiders" jumping on their bandwagon and working the border artists' territory. Border artists also are threatened by the present unparalleled economic depression in the arts gutted by government funding cutbacks. Sponsoring corporations that judge projects by "family values" criteria are forcing multicultural artists to hang tough and brave out financial and professional instability. Border art is becoming trendy in these neo-colonial times that encourage art tourism and pop culture rip-offs, I think, as I walk into the Aztec Museum shop. Feathers, paper flowers, and ceramic statues of fertility goddesses sell for ten times what they sell for in Mexico. Of course, there is nothing new about colonizing, commercializing, and consuming the art of ethnic people (and of queer writers and artists) except that now it is being misappropriated by pop culture. Diversity is being sold on TV, billboards, fashion lines, department store windows, and, yes, airport corridors and "regional" stores where you can take home Navaho artist R.C. Gorman's *Saguaro* or Robert Arnold's *Chili Dog*, a jar of Tex-Mex picante sauce, and drink a margarita at Rosie's Cantina.

I touch the armadillo pendent hanging from my neck and think, frontera artists have to grow protective shells. We enter the silence, go inward, attend to feelings and to that inner cenote, the creative reservoir where earth, female, and water energies merge. We surrender to the rhythm and the grace of our artworks. Through our artworks we cross the border into other subjective levels of awareness, shift into different and new terrains of mestizaje. Some of us have a highly developed facultad and may intuit what lies ahead. Yet the political climate does not allow us to withdraw completely. In fact, border artists are engaged artists. Most of us are politically active in our communities. If disconnected from la gente, border artists would wither in isolation. The community feeds our spirits and the responses from our "readers" inspire us to continue struggling with our art and aesthetic interventions that subvert cultural genocide.

A year ago I was thumbing through the *Chicano Art: Resistance and Affirmation* catalog. My eyes snagged on some lines by Judy Baca, Chicana muralist: "Chicano art comes from the creation of community. . . . Chicano art represents a particular stance which always engages with the issues of its time."[10] Chicana/o art is a form of border art, an art shared with our Mexican counterparts from across the border[11] and with Native Americans, other groups of color, and whites living in the vicinity of the Mexico/ United States border or near other cultural borders elsewhere in the U.S., Mexico, and Canada. Both Chicana/o and border art challenge and subvert the imperialism of the U.S., and combat assimilation by either the U.S. or Mexico, yet they acknowledge its affinities to both.[12]

"Chicana" artist, "border" artist. These are adjectives labeling identities. Labeling impacts expectations. Is "border" artist just another label that strips legitimacy from the artist, signaling that s/he is inferior to the adjectiveless artist, a label designating that s/he is only capable of handling ethnic, folk, and regional subjects and art forms? Yet the dominant culture consumes, swallows whole the ethnic artist, sucks out her/his vitality, and then spits out the hollow husk along with its labels (such as Hispanic). The dominant culture shapes the ethnic artist's identity if s/he does not scream loud enough and fight long enough to name her/his self. Until we live in a society where all people are more or less equal and no labels are necessary, we need them to resist the pressure to assimilate.

I cross the room. Codices hang on the walls. I stare at the hieroglyphics. The ways of a people, their history and culture put on paper beaten from maguey leaves. Faint traces in red, blue, and black ink left by their artists, writers, and scholars. The past is hanging behind glass. We, the viwers in the present, walk around and around the glass-boxed past. I wonder who

I used to be, I wonder who I am. The border artist constantly reinvents her/himself. Through art s/he is able to re-read, reinterpret, re-envision, and reconstruct her/his culture's present as well as its past. This capacity to construct meaning and culture privileges the artist. As cultural icons for her/his ethnic communities, s/he is highly visible. But there are drawbacks to having artistic and cultural power—the relentless pressure to produce, being put in the position of representing her/his entire pueblo and carrying all the ethnic culture's baggage on her/his espalda while trying to survive in a gringo world. Power and the seeking of greater power may create a self-centered ego or a fake public image, one the artist thinks will make her/him acceptable to her/his audience. It may encourage self-serving hustling—all artists have to sell themselves in order to obtain grants, get published, secure exhibit spaces, and receive good reviews. But for some, the hustling outdoes the artmaking.

The Chicana/o border writer/artist has finally come to market. The problem now is how to resist corporate culture while asking for and securing its patronage and dollars without resorting to "mainstreaming" the work. Is this complicity on the part of the border artist in the appropriation of her or his art by the dominant dealers of art? And if so, does this constitute a self-imposed imperialism? The impact that money and making it has on the artist is a little explored area though the effect of lack of money has been well-documented (as evidenced in the "starving artist" scenario).

Artistic ideas that have been incubating and developing at their own speed have come into their season—now is the time of border art. Border art is an art that supercedes the pictorial. It depicts both the soul of the artist and the soul of the pueblo. It deals with who tells the stories and what stories and histories are told. I call this form of visual narrative *autohistorias*. This form goes beyond the traditional self-portrait or auto-biography; in telling the writer/artist's personal story, it also includes the artist's cultural history. The altars I make are not just representations of myself; they are representations of Chicana culture. El arte de la frontera is community- and academically-based—many Chicana/o artist have MAs and PhDs and hold precarious teaching positions on the fringes of universities. To make, exhibit, and sell their artwork, and to survive, los artistas band together collectively.

Finally, I find myself before the reconstructed statue of the newly unearthed el dios murciélago, the bat god with his big ears, fangs, and protruding tongue representing the vampire bat associated with night, blood sacrifice, and death. I make an instantaneous association of the bat man with the nepantla stage of border artists—the dark cave of creativity where they hang upside down, turning the self upside down in order to see from another point of view, one that brings a new state of understanding. I wonder what meaning this bat figure will have for other Chicanas/os, what artistic symbol they will make of it and what political struggle it will represent. Perhaps like the home/public altars, which expose both the United States' and Mexico's national identity, the murciélago god questions the viewer's unconscious collective and personal identity and its ties to her/his ancestors. In border art there is always the specter of death in the backgrounds. Often las calaveras (skeletons and skulls) take a prominent position—and not just of el día de los muertos (November 2nd). De la tierra nacimos, from earth we are born, a la tierra retornamos, to earth we shall return, a dar lo que ella nos dió, to give back to her what she has given. Yes, I say to myself, the earth eats the dead, la tierra se come a los muertos.

I walk out of the Aztec exhibit hall and turn in the walkman with the Olmos tape. It is September 26, mi cumpleaños. I seek out the table with the computer, key in my birthdate, and there on the screen is my Aztec birth year and ritual day name: 8 Rabbit, 12 Skull. In that culture I would have been named Matlactli Omome Mizuitzli. I stick my chart under the rotating rubber stamps, press down, pull it out, and stare at the imprint of the rabbit (symbol of fear and of running scared) pictograph and then of the skull (night, blood sacrifice, and death). Very appropriate symbols in my life, I mutter. It's so raza. ¿y qué?

At the end of my five-hour "tour," I walk out of the museum to the parking lot with aching feet and questions flying around my head. As I wait for my taxi, I ask myself, What direction will el arte fronterizo take in the future? The multi-subjectivity and split-subjectivity of border artists creating various counter arts will continue, but with a parallel movement where a polarized us/them, insiders/outsiders culture clash is not the main struggle, where a refusal to be split will be a given.

The border is a historical and metaphorical site, un sitio ocupado, an occupied borderland where single artists and collaborating groups transform space, and the two home territories, Mexico and the United States, become one. Border art deals with shifting identities, border crossings, and hybridism. But there are other borders besides the actual Mexico/United States frontera. Juan Dávila's (a Chilean artist who has lived in Australia since 1974) Wuthering Heights (1990) oil painting depicts Juanito Leguna, a half-caste, mixed breed transvestite. Juanito's body is a simulacrum parading the phallic mother.[13] Another Latino artist, Rafael Barajas (who signs his work as "El Fisgón"), has a mixed media piece titled *Pero eso sí . . . soy muy macho* (1989). It shows a Mexican male wearing the proverbial sombrero taking a siesta against the traditional cactus, tequila bottle on the ground, gunbelt hanging from a nopal branch. But the leg protruding from beneath the sarape-like mantle is wearing a high-heeled shoe, hose, and garterbelt. It suggests another kind of border crossing — gender-bending.[14]

As the taxi whizzes me to my hotel, my mind reviews image after image. Something about who and what I am and the 200 "artifacts" I have just seen does not feel right. I pull out my "birth chart." Yes, cultural roots are important, but I was not born at Tenochitlán in the ancient past nor in an Aztec village in modern times. I was born and live in that in-between space, nepantla, the borderlands. There are other races running in my veins, other cultures that my body lives in and out of, and a white man who constantly whispers inside my skull. For me, being Chicana is not enough. It is only one of my multiple identities. Along with other border gente, it is at this site and time, where and when, I create my identity along with my art.

## Notes

I thank Dianna Williamson, my literary assistant, for her invaluable and incisive critical comments and suggestions, Natasha Martínez for copyediting this essay. Gracias also to Servicio Chicano Center in Denver for the pricey and hard-to-get ticket to the opening of the Aztec exhibition.

1. See Amalia Mesa-Bains's article "El Mundo Femenino: Chicana Artists of the Movement—A Commentary on Development and Production," in the catalog, CARA, *Chicano Art: Resistance and Affirmation*, eds. Richard Griswold Del Castillo, Teresa McKenna and Yvonne Yarbro-Bejarano (Los Angeles: Wight Art Gallery, University of California, 1991).

2. See Luz María and Ellen J. Stekert's untitled art catalog essay in [the catalog for the exhibition] "Santa Barraza," March 8–April 11, 1992, La Raza / Galería Posada, Sacramento, California.

3. Santa Barraza, quoted in Jennifer Heath's, "Women Artists of Color Share World of Struggle," *Sunday Camera*, March 8, 1992, 9C.

4. See Carmen Lomas Garza's beautifully illustrated children's bilingual book, *Family Pictures / Cuadros de familia* (San Francisco: Children's Book Press, 1990), in particular "Camas para soñar / Beds for Dreaming." Garza has three pieces in "La Frontera / The Border: Art About The Mexico / United States Border Experience" exhibition of the Museum of Contemporary Art and El Centro Cultural de la Raza in San Diego, California.

5. The Maya huipiles are large rectangular blouses which describe the Maya cos-

mos. They portray the world as a diamond. The four sides of the diamond represent the boundaries of space and time; the smaller diamonds at each corner, the cardinal points. The weaver maps the heavens and underworld.

6. Dianna Williamson, June 1992.

7. Roberta H. Markman and Peter T. Markman, eds., *Masks of the Spirit: Image and Metaphor in Mesoamerica* (Berkeley: University of California Press, 1989).

8. The exact quote is: "We have an internalization of fixed space learned early in life. One's orientation in space is tied to survival and sanity. To be disoriented in space is to be psychotic." Edward T. Hall and Mildred Reed Hall, "The Sounds of Silence," in *Conformity and Conflict: Readings in Cultural Anthropology*, eds. James P. Spradlley and David W. McCurdy (Boston: Little, Brown and Co., 1987).

9. The exhibition was part of El Festival Internacional de la Raza 92. The artworks were produced in the Silkscreen Studios of Self Help Graphics, Los Angeles and in the Studios of Strike Editions in Austin, Texas. Self Help Graphics and the Galería Sin Fronteras, Austin, Texas, organized the exhibitions.

10. See *Chicano Art: Resistance and Affirmation*, eds. Richard Griswold Del Castillo, Teresa McKenna, and Yvonne Yarbro-Bejarano (Los Angeles: Wight Art Gallery, University of California, 1991), 21. For a good presentation of the historical context of Chicana/o art see Shifra M. Goldman and Tomás Ybarra-Frausto's "The Political and Social Contexts of Chicano Art," in CARA, 83–95.

11. For a discussion of Chicano posters, almanacs, calendars, and cartoons that join "images and texts to depict community issues as well as historical and cultural themes," metaphorically link Chicano struggles for self-determination with the Mexican revolution, and establish "a cultural and visual continuum across borders," see Tomás Ybarra-Fausto's "Gráfica/Urban Iconography" in the art catalog *Chicano Expressions: A New View in American Art*, April 14–July 31, 1986 (New York: INTAR Latin American Gallery, 1986), 21–24.

12. Among the alternative galleries and art centers that combat assimilation are the Guadalupe Cultural Arts Center in San Antonio, Mexic-Arte Museum and Sin Fronteras Gallery in Austin, Texas, and the Mission Cultural Center in San Francisco.

13. See Guy Brett, *Transcontinental: An Investigation of Reality* (London: Verso, 1990). The book, which accompanied the exhibit at Ikon Gallery in Birmingham and Cornerhouse, Manchester, explores the work of nine Latin American artists: Waltercio Caldas, Juan Dávila, Eugenio Dittborn, Roberto Evangelista, Victor Grippo, Jac Leirner, Cildo Meireles, Tunga, Regina Vater.

14. See "ex profeso, recuento de afinidades colectiva plástica contemporánea: imágenes: gay-lésbicas-eróticas," put together by Círculo Cultural Gay in Mexico City and exhibited at Museo Universitario del Chope during la Semana Cultural Gay de 1989, junio 14–23.

This never before published essay began as a talk Anzaldúa gave to Dorrinne Kondo's class at Pomono College on February 6, 1991; five years later, she revised the transcript for publication. Due to her ongoing health difficulties, as well as several writing deadlines, she filed the essay away for future publication. Although this piece is not as polished as some of Anzaldúa's later work, it offers useful background information on *Borderlands / La Frontera*, her writing process, and her theory of the interconnections between reading and writing. This essay also includes Anzaldúa's insightful discussion of her poem "Poets have strange eating habits," which is included in *Borderlands / La Frontera*.

# On the Process of Writing
## *Borderlands | La Frontera*

### Genesis

I was in Vermont, it was winter, and it was snowing. The snow was very white. The people were very white. I would walk into a store and be stared at because there are not that many people of color in Vermont. I think that because Vermonters are used to seeing black and white, they couldn't quite figure out this mestiza in-between.

Later in the spring as I walked the streets of Montpelier, I saw brightly colored bags — trashbags stuffed with raked-up leaves — in people's front yards. The bags were taped just so, the twisters twisted just so. . . . Everything was so neat and orderly. The houses were mostly three-story houses, white clapboard. I was so homesick for Texas. In the Southwest, Chicanos live in pink and purple houses–what I call Chicano architecture. Junk cars parked in the front yard or driveway are part of that architecture. It was quite a contrast between growing up in Texas and the Southwest and living in New England. Because of that homesickness, I began writing *Borderlands*.

You are closer to home when you're further away. As a writer I can write about places after I've left them, rather than when I'm still there. This is especially true when I write about home. These feelings of being an outsider, an alien, generated in me the impetus to explain things to myself and others. Communicating feelings often makes me feel like a tea kettle letting off steam. While writing and speaking act as a safety valve, they are also political acts that spring from the impulse to subvert, resist, educate, and make changes. So I let the anger generated by the racism I was experiencing (I was teaching creative writing and women's studies at the ADP program at Vermont College) fuel my writing. I was angry at the homophobia and class bias. I was the only woman of color, the only working-class woman, the only lesbian, and the only teacher who taught in a non-academic way. In that snowy land I felt like a person from another planet might feel.

Of course, some of the poems in *Borderlands/La Frontera* came from an earlier period. When I have a manuscript going, I look through all my files to find additional material for it. As I sort through my files I'll say, "Well, this piece is about what it means to grow up bilingual; it could fit into the section about language and identity. This one is a poem about the oppression women suffer, this one is about the violation of women's bodies." I link the violation of women's bodies with the violation of the land, then with the particular appropriation of Indian and Chicano lands in the Southwest—and decide that both poems could go in the loss-of-the-land section.

I intended to *spread* as well as *produce* knowledge about Chicana/os and the border for other Chicana/os, people of color, and whites such as these New Englanders that I had been living among. It was for people who had no idea what it meant to be a seventh-generation Chicana who had grown up in Texas near the border. When I lived in Brooklyn (or Boston, or New Haven, or South Bend) both whites and some Latinas/os would often ask, "Well, when did you come from Mexico?" Or "Are you Latin American from—like, South America or Central America?" I heard these questions from people who thought they were in tune with the Latino community and Latina identity, but didn't know how to distinguish between Puerto Ricans, Cubans, Chicanas, or Mexican immigrants. In this little town, Montpelier, Vermont, people didn't even know Chicanos existed.

Purpose

As I said earlier, I intended *Borderlands* not only to spread, but also to produce knowledge. The whole time I've been in school the producers of knowledge have been middle- and upper-class white people—those with power in the universities, science establishments, and publishing and art houses. They produce the theories and books that we read. They produce the unconscious values, views, and assumptions about reality, about culture, about everything. We internalize, we assimilate, these theories.

So I had a problem because I wanted to produce artworks, to produce knowledge, but I was from a campesina-working class, a woman from a racial minority who's a lesbian. How do you get past all those obstacles?

And I wanted to do it my way, using my approach, my language. I didn't want to do what Audre Lorde describes as using the master's tools; I did not want to ape the master. I wanted to write in a mestiza style, in my own vernacular, yet also use the knowledges and histories of the white cultures, of other ethnic cultures. I wanted to be able to deal with certain theories, to be able to philosophize. I wanted my cake and I wanted to eat it too.

Most people can't get away with doing all of this—they may not have the faith or the stubbornness or their jobs are up for review or tenure or in other ways they're threatened. There may not be a market for their writing, or if the market is there they may not be able to get one foot in the door. Art and literature are exclusive. If you are a professor of color, you are required to write like a white professor. (For instance, journals and quarterlies often have very specific guidelines.)

My writings (and I) had been repeatedly rejected by the Chicano male-stream, so I decided to continue with the feminist presses because they had supported me. After teaching in the Texas public school system, I decided (years before) that I wasn't going to be a professional academic. But because I loved teaching so much (it was the administrative aspect of it that I hated), I decided that I would do short teaching stints (teach a month here, a quarter there) and thus support my chief vocation—writing. By freelancing, I would remain my own boss. Though this way of making a living is not without its drawbacks, it allows me to give writing primacy.

As a dyke of color, I have to take pretty big risks in my teaching, speaking engagements, and writing. I push against the boundaries of what's acceptable and traditional in these three lines of work. *Borderlands* could have fallen flat on its face. It's accessible to certain audiences but inaccessible to others. It's accessible or inaccessible depending on how much work you want to do in reading it. There are lots of gaps between passages—its style is elliptical and spiral. I start with a theme, figure, or symbol, and then that symbol becomes a motif and gets maybe hinted at in another chapter and then explored further in another chapter; at the final chapter you come around back to the beginning, and the symbol eventually ends up recurring in some of the poems. The reader has to fill in a lot of the gaps.

Another thing that's difficult or easy—again, depending on whether the readership is Chicanas/os who can read Spanish or people of color and whites who can't—is the code-switching in language. It's not comfortable if you don't know Spanish or Chicano Spanish; even Spanish speakers sometimes feel uncomfortable because I'm not using Castilian, I'm using Chicano Spanish. Not only do I code-switch in language, but I jerk the reader around by also code-switching in genre: mixing genres, crossing genres from poetry to essay to narrative to a little bit of analysis and theory. The reader has to put it all together at the end. Hopefully when you read the whole book the poems become integrated with the essays and the book will make sense.

Another way *Borderlands* is accessible is that I narrate certain specific historical happenings — my uncle who got sent to the other side, got picked up by la migra when he didn't have his papers, my experiences as a campesina. I give you contexts for the theories I attempt to put forth. People can hook specifically into these snippets of lived experience, can hook into the pain. Thus the reader gets hooked.

Interaction between Reader and Writer

In *Borderlands* (as well as in the two book projects I'm currently working on now, *Prieta*, a novel/collection of stories I call "autohistorias," and *Lloronas, Women Who Wail: Self-Representations and the Production of Writing, Knowledge, and Identities*), I intended to problematize the relationship between reader, writer, and text — specifically the reader's role in giving meaning to the text. It is the reader (and the author reading as reader) who ultimately makes the connections, finds the patterns that are meaningful for her or him. There's a leeway for the reader to interact with the text because of the gaps. As the reader is reading along s/he may get pissed or angry or frustrated and then s/he may think, "Yeah. Last week I had a dialogue with a girlfriend or a boyfriend or a professor and it was about my feeling of invisibility . . ." Such passages in *Borderlands* arrest the reader and make her think of her own experiences, especially experiences where s/he has been abused or violated intellectually, emotionally, or physically. In this way the reader brings into the text her own experience.

The reader's co-creation of the book makes me, the author, realize that I am not the sole creator. There are certain things that the author sets up for the reader, but the reader is, to some degree, a co-author. This is even more true when the reader responds to the book in writing — with a book review, a critical paper, etc. The text is not a fixed text. The words will always be the same words, right? As long as they keep printing the book, the words remain the same. But the text will be different with each reader and each reading. The text will move and reveal something new every time you read it. If you read *Borderlands*, for example, ten years from now you will have a different identity and therefore will give it a different interpretation. You will be positioned in a different space, a different location, and you'll be thinking from that new bedrock—you will have a different perspective. Perhaps things that you miss in the reading now, will resonate ten years from now. Things that you were excited about the first time you read the text, you won't even notice during the next read. I read *Jane Eyre* thirteen times from when I was nine until now, thirteen times, and each time was a different reading because my identity had changed. As a feminist I read it in a feminist way—I give it a feminist reading. My feminist reading gives me a different interpretation about Jane's and Bertha's characters. I now see something I missed when a younger reader: the racial dynamics between Rochester, Jane, and Bertha, who's a Creole/mestiza from Jamaica. I now am looking at how sexuality operates in the novel and how Jane Eyre's sexuality is not only repressed but is also projected onto Bertha, the madwoman in the attic, the wild woman. It's safe for Jane Eyre to have a sexuality because the uncontrolled sexuality is projected. I now see things in the book that I didn't see when I was twelve, thirteen, fourteen, fifteen, and sixteen. Now, as a dyke feminist, I see more consciously through an aware, politicized perspective.

## Reception of *Borderlands / La Frontera*

I am surprised that *Borderlands* has been received so well. First, I thought that Chicanas would not like it because I talk bad about my culture. (In many ways all of our cultures are really fucked up. My culture is fucked up—maybe not as fucked up as the white culture. It is ethnocentric but not racist—if a culture that is smaller than the dominant culture, members of the smaller culture can't be racist. It does not have the power to oppress white people, okay?) But the Chicanas and other women of color received it very well; even a woman from Hawai'i said, "I know you're writing about the Southwest, but you know, this sounds like my life, this sounds like where I come from." An Asian woman, a Latina, and a black woman came up to me (at different times); they were very angry about the code-switching. They weren't so much angry at me as they were frustrated at living in this country and being deprived of their language, being ripped off of their tongue. Here I was using Spanish, and they were so envious that I could write Spanish whereas their languages had been erased. They were mad at themselves, at their parents, and at society. Then there were the white readers who felt, "Oh, here's a book that does not shut me out." Using the concept of the mestiza, I talk about people like us who are bio-

logical mestizas, and cultural, and intellectual, and psychological mestizas—that's us colored folk. But there are also white women, working-class
women who by virtue of their experience have had so many dealings with
other cultures, either through learning in universities or through having a
lover who's black or Chicana or Asian or Native, or through being raised in
a barrio along with colored people. These whites have crossed over; they've
become cultural mestizas. Okay, so that made the white women feel good
and the white men feel good, because they could also access the book.

On the other hand some of the Chicanas and women of color said,
"You're being too nice to the white people. They shouldn't be able to access
this book. We want them to know that there's a real difference between
being biologically mestiza—the dark color, the features, the oppression
that goes with it—and a cultural mestiza with white skin privilege."

I also found that Borderlands was either really appreciated, and used with
appreciation, or else it was appropriated. When it was appropriated, it was
taken over and used in a token way by white theorists who would write
about gender but make brief references to race and class and mention my
name, or mention Audre Lorde or Maxine Hong Kingston, but as an aside.
They never integrated our theories into their writing. Instead, they were
using us to say, "Here I am a progressive, liberal, white theorist. I know
women of color. See? I'm mentioning these folks." Also, they would look
at some of the conclusions and concepts and theories in Borderlands and
write about them, saying that my theories were derived from their work.
They had discovered these theories. They insisted that I got these theories from Foucault, Lacan, Derrida, or the French feminists. But I was not
familiar with these theorists' work when I wrote Borderlands. I hadn't read
them. So what they were saying was, "She got it from these white folks and
didn't even cite them."

In my current writings, I explore in an autobiographical mode my own
theories about what happens to students of color in universities and to
people of color in this country. I find that white feminists expect me to cite
authority figures, to get quotations and inspiration from master writers—
writers who never had our experiences. Instead of using my own experience, I am supposed to quote from their disembodied theories.

In their theoretical work the big theoretical guns implied that women
of color's writings prove that postmodernism and poststructuralism exist;
one has only to look at our fractured lives and fragmented writings. This
kind of inter-referentiality between different texts and lived experiences
they consider to be characteristic of postmodernism, as are the conditions of our lived experiences—being jerked around from one world to

the other, from one situation to the other. We, writers of color, verified for the European theorist the fact that theirs was not an exclusive school of thought. After all, they were not only just talking about themselves, they were also talking about colored people. We were the quintessential example of the postmodern condition. They missed the boat somewhere along the way—but that's another talk.

## Process

I want to talk a bit about the process of writing *Borderlands*. One thing I urge you to do when you are reading and writing is to figure out, literally, where your feet stand, what position you're taking: Are you speaking from a white, male, middle-class perspective? Are you speaking from a working-class, colored, ethnic location? For whom are you speaking? To whom are you speaking? What is the context, where do you locate your experience? In the Bronx, in Southern California? Why are you doing this research? What are your motivations? What are the stakes, what's at stake—to use a popular theoretical expression. In other words, what's in it for you? What are the terms of the debate and who set up these terms? Everybody has a stake; you're doing it because you are affirming your ethnic identity; you want to document your experience; you want to find meaning in it; you want to find acceptance and legitimacy; you don't want your voice erased. These may be some of the stakes for people of color. As a white person you may have similar stakes or you may be doing it because you're tired of living in a racist country, you're tired of your ignorance and you want to learn about other peoples, other cultures. You may want to make a better world in which we all can live in relative peace. Or you may do it out of guilt. You may say to yourself, "Well, I took Dorinne Kondo's class," or "I read some of this," or "my best friend is," and you feel good as a white person because you're not racist.

A lot of times I don't even know my motivations until after the fact. Maybe you're the same way, or you may have overt motivations and then covert, hidden ones. So you try and figure out why you're doing this writing and reading. Are you appropriating or appreciating? We all delve into other cultures. We are curious. I have studied Tibetan Buddhism, the Pre-Columbian peoples of Mexico, European philosophy, English novels. All of us have a curiosity about the Other—it's a way of learning. Earth is a small planet, and we're all on it together—we're dependent on each other, that's our link.

But if you are getting material from other cultures only because it benefits you personally . . . When I started writing children's stories, I noticed that 99% of all children's stories were written by whites and that most stories about ethnic kids were written by whites. They write about the desert, Native Americans, hawks. Some of these stories are beautifully written, but their authors are appropriating the lives and spirits of a people that they tried to exterminate. They take the religion, the land—incarcerating Indians in reservations which are really concentration camps. Today whites are stealing the last things Indians have clung to—their art, their spirituality, and their religious traditions. Every white person who had written a children's book about Indian peoples displaced a Native person who could have written it. White publishers, the ones in power, publish the white people. Some of these whites may not even know they are excluding because of race—it may not be a consciously racist act, it may be just ignorance. Nonetheless, the writer of color gets rejected and the white rip-off writer gets published and gets rich off of marginalized people.

There is another kind of appropriation—one that is true to the culture it is borrowing from. Tony Hillerman is an example of a white man who's respected and whose mystery novels are well-received in the Hopi-Navaho communities. According to some Native people that I've spoken with, he's done his homework, researched well. Lynn Andrews is an example of the rip-off artist; she misrepresents Native spirituality and lies, passing off her books as nonfiction when they are really fiction. It would be fine if the author was honest, telling readers: "This is fictitious; I was never an apprentice to a medicine woman/shaman." I realize there is a thin line between fiction and nonfiction—it's a line I myself constantly cross over in my work. In a sense, all writing is fiction—but again, that is a discussion for another paper.

I will read a poem and get into the process of writing with you, and then I'm going to stop talking and listen to you. When I shut up and you talk, I would like to hear from the women of color. In the academy we get silenced and it becomes a habit. We let that kind of intellectual space be taken away from us and occupied by the white students and professors. It's very risky as a person of color to speak up; we always feel like we didn't get as good an education—the upper-class black or Chicana who went to Yale may have received a good education but has other internalized negative self-images to contend with. I'm talking about those of us who feel that if we open our mouths we're going to say something ignorant. This is part of the racism we've internalized. Those of us who possess the self-confidence to speak may hold back because of class or cultural injunctions. With Chicano/mexicanos it is a sign of respect to not challenge somebody who's older, especially a maestra. We are not supposed to challenge a teacher. S/he's always muy respetada, very much respected. Competitive challenging in a classroom is alien, something we have to teach ourselves to do. I have to force myself to be aggressive. It's hard for us to speak up in a classroom or an auditorium.

Prohibited speech, the white student experiences being a disfranchised outsider; for a few seconds s/he wears another's shoes—and the fit pinches. But this experience teaches her to listen. S/he can't jump in as soon as somebody opens their mouth. This teaches you how to listen to other people's experience. So I'm asking that las mujeres de color contribute to the dialogue, also lesbians and working-class people of all colors, people who get marginalized. Mostly the majority of the students in a classroom are straight, and they have a lot of blank spots about how pervasive racism and heterosexuality are. To counter racism and homophobia every day of our lives takes a lot of energy. When a person of color, a lesbian or a gay man, is sitting in a classroom, s/he is already putting out a lot of energy just maintaining—surviving emotionally and intellectually. For her to speak out is not only risky but also means putting out more energy than she may have.

In one of my poems about the process of writing, I use the metaphor of the horse. The horse is a very important symbol for me. I was telling Dorinda in her office that I have a story called "She Ate Horses" which you'll see in another text that you're reading, *Lesbian Cultures and Philosophies*; the version in this text is the second version. I now have a third version which I'm going to give her to give to you so you can, if you want, compare them. If I could borrow somebody's *Borderlands* I'll read "Poets have strange eating habits."

(insert the poem.)*

Before we get into the discussion, there are a couple of things I want to mention. Did you notice how I go from the "she" to the "I?" When a poet is immersed in the act of writing, there is a movement from close up to back off to see what s/he's doing. The distancing persona becomes the "she," while plunging into the immediacy of the experience becomes the "I." Here we all are: Gloria the author, the I who's the narrator who's immersed in the writing of the poem—often the boundary between au-

---

* These are Anzaldúa's original instructions. Due to the *Borderlands* publisher's restrictions, the poem is not reproduced here.

thor and narrator get erased so that I become the I of the poem. When I look at it, when I read it, the reading and the writing go together and the "I" becomes a "she," because there's two of us now. Then there is a third entity, the characters "I" and "she" which in the writing become more than the writer or the narrator; they've taken on fictional aspects because of the elements that I, the author, choose to focus on in my experience as a writer, leaving out, because of time and page limitations, many other feelings and experiences about writing.

There are other metaphors besides the horse that symbolize the act of writing. The mouth, la boca, labios y lengua, and the hands are symbols of self-expression. You use your mouth and throat chakra for speaking, hands for communicating and expressing yourself. The mare with the wounds and the scabs are the wounds that I'm writing about. For me to write about an experience that's been painful, there's a wound, and it's got a scab. To write I have to peel the scab off, get back into the pain and the blood, tú sabes. Even when I write about the good things, the joys—the pain and the joy come together. Writing is like jumping off a cliff. It's opening your stomach and examining your entrails and telling others, "This piece of gut is about the time such and such happened and it is connected to other people and the world in this way and that." You expose your innermost feelings, you walk out in the street without any clothes on. Another motivation for writing Borderlands was to heal the wounds—which necessitated opening the wounds anew. That's why I state "wounding is a deeper healing." Even if it's self-wounding, if you're doing incest survival therapy, if you're doing rape therapy, if you're doing couples therapy, you're opening up those wounds, and hopefully the air will start healing them as they are out in the open. Of course, writing is concealing, too. One can hide in the writing.

Writing is like spreading your legs. People are going to come in. They're going to enter through your orifices. When you read me you're coming into me. There are intimate secrets lodged in my body that I go around exposing to perfect strangers. Every writer is a bit of an exhibitionist. Exposing myself is a conscious act. As soon as I reveal myself to you, open my legs up to you, take my clothes off to you and open my heart to you, I also hide myself. This back-and-forth movement—revealing, concealing, revealing, concealing—goes on throughout Borderlands—and even more in Prieta. The reader has to figure out where the author conceals and where s/he reveals. In every piece of writing there's a subtext—a hidden text, an underbelly—which the author may not even be conscious of, things that I don't want people to know about me but which the reader may pick up or which the writer as reader may pick up years later.

As a writer I not only carry a lot of baggage in the form of memories on my back but I also have to carry the stresses of my life—the public speaker, the teacher, the sister, the daughter, the friend, the lover, the woman of color, the dyke, the feminist—but I also take on the stresses of the people I create in the writing.

This previously unpublished poem, whose title can be translated as "The vulva is an open wound," is one of Anzaldúa's most overtly autobiographical and intimate works. I first read this poem in 1991 when she gave it to me during her week-long gig at the University of Arizona; she explained that she had decided not to read it at the public event because she was worried that it could leave the audience in a depressed state. Anzaldúa drafted this poem around 1990 and revised it throughout much of the 1990s.

## La vulva es una herida abierta/
## The vulva is an open wound

> !Qué no quiero verla!
> Dile a la luna que venga,
> que no quiero ver la sangre.
> —FEDERICO GARCÍA LORCA, "Llanto," 156

Thunder    the heartbeat of the mother    pumping blood into her
she pushes    kicks    she wants out    the vast cathedral of the belly
shrinking    contracting    pushing her    out    the bloodline severing
She nuzzles the Breast    that familiar thump    that taste    that smell of
milk and her mother's skin    fill her    are her
La madre la baña y la empolva    le cambia los pavicos cuando
orina.    Her mouth seeks the Breast    does not find it    rage pounds
its three-month-old fists Her mother's young breasts    cannot hold the
milk.
She screams, refuses la tetera    until her mother puts a black nipple
on it Her mouth softening it    worrying it for months until    she
gnaws a hole through    She turns her face away from the bottle
nipple    whenever her mother tries to put it into her mouth    so
Papi drives all over el valle    buscando un mamón negro    searching
for a black nipple    In the meantime she fasts    You've always been
stubborn    her mother tells her.
They were husking mazorcas one day    La dejaron sola in the shed    Su
mamá heard her screaming vino corriendo    Among the dry corn
leaves    se la halló bañada de sudor y lágrimas    Cuando le cambió her
diaper    she saw a huge gusanote echado    lying entre los labios    en
sus nalgitas    huellas coloradas 'onde* le había quemado    The worm

* Shortened form of "donde."

had burned a red trail on her flesh    Tenía tres meses    At three
months    her body started leaking    small pink spots on her pavico.
Eskimo girls start their periods early    le dijo el doctor a su
mamá    Prietita feels as though a bird with a sharp beak    inhabits her
belly    Le pica    le pica    She bleeds 10 días de cada 24    She watches
a chicken, neck wrung, twitch all over the yard. It bleeds then lays still.
Dead. At night she stays awake to keep death away. Chickens peck each
other when confined in small spaces. She is afraid. No not of the blood
but of what happens when someone or something bleeds.
Other children do not double over    with lightning stabs    have 106
degree fiebres that turn their curly hair straight    do not live with a dull
persistent dolor
do not wash bloody garras    gagging on the menstrual odors    hanging
them on shrubs    escondiéndolas from brothers    uncles    cousins    A
los seis años other children do not have budding rose tits under tight
muslin girdles    wear a rag pinned to their calzones    refuse to take
communal showers    cúbrete, escóndelo    do not have pimples or
secretos    cannot be mothers    They do not shoot up to tower    skinny
and hunched    over second graders    are not gangly    awkward
with translucent    faint blue veins    orejas you can see light
through    The eyes de los otros niños    track her steps    She feels
naked and ashamed.    She knows the children have guessed something
was    wrong    with her
She watches the deer hanging from the trees slowly rotating, dripping
blood from the severed jugular. Mami skinning the deer already gutted
by Papi, salting the thin strips. Days later taking down la ropa de
carne seca oliendo a humo.    Red like dried blood on stained cotton
rags    cover it up    hide it
She digs caves into the soft sides of ravines    plays hide and seek en el
monte
Plays the onion game    y se convierte en cebolla enroscada alrededor de
su hermana Knock knock ¿Quién es?    es la Vieja Inés    cerquita de la
noria    Que no se te olvide    keep your legs shut
She feeds the chickens and the hogs    shells the corn    Standing on
a chair by the sink    she pumps the handle    watches the windmill
turn    spurt out water
She is seven    her skin paper thin    Wringing the necks of
chickens    right hand closing over chicken's head    Skin    paper
thin    the world streaming in right arm thrust away    the quick twist

cranking    tossing broken neck and chicken on the ground before    the
blood starts spurting    hen flopping    banging into things becoming
still    jerking    the last twitch    But she can't kill    the vulture inside her
She is a sponge absorbing the metallic smell    skin paper thin    has to
shut down where the pain is    her mother cooking repollo con pollo
Una herida, tenía una herida abierta, a foul smelly place from where
blood drips. Nalgas hediondas, she heard mother, aunts and others say,
of the female private parts.
Panocha apestosa, verijas mugrosas—these bad words the only ones she
knew
Men, she heard, were not as dirty and smelly as women. Thick folds of
stained cotton skin-paper thin    thunder pumping blood    she shrinks
behind her skin    as she cuts up old rags with scissors    she severs    the
second umbilical to her body.
She would take the bloody garras    smelling of sulfur    with their
burgundy creased stains    and folds of decomposed tissue    out into the
shed    y las lavaba    En la cubeta    she'd stir the rags    stained from a
thousand bleedings    with a stick in the backyard    where her    brothers
wouldn't see her    The big secret    the big shame    She would hang
them low entre los nopales    instead of the clothesline
Tenía miedo que alguien la viera    She was afraid    someone would
catch her with the bloody evidence en sus manos    Horrified at the
pains    that would sweep through her    Her insides    coming up
up    vomiting    shrinking into herself when the jabs came    when
pain    the vulture    pecked her insides Cuando se bañaba    she didn't
use the same water to wash her face or hair that she used to clean her
lower body.
Su mamá le dijo not to tell    So Prieta swallowed the secret    se lo tragó
That night she could hear it    moving quietly    slithering from her
chest    to her stomach    It wandered inside her    whole body    from her
little toe    to her little finger
Whenever it entered her esophagus    she would swallow hard    and
push it back down.
Occasionally el secreto would gurgle    up    to rebel its confinement
and she would squelch it down    with a waterfall    Cuando el vaso was
empty    el secreto was left floundering    in her bladder    swimming
around and around    grabbing at the smooth sides    trying to hang
on    She wanted to tell her secret    to push it out of her body    but it
stubbornly hung on    Prieta could feel it getting larger    and knew that
soon it would    transform itself    The knowledge ate away at her.

As she grew older the bouts of    dizziness    and nausea    would attack
her when she least expected them    Se vomitaba    but el secreto hid
in the forest of her lungs    or swam in the lakes of her stomach    and
refused to be dislodged    She felt the beak stab her lower belly again
and again    She lost weight    yet strangely her stomach comenzó
a crecer    Su pelo    began to fall off in chunks    The bathtub drain
would clog with her hair    She snapped at her girlfriend    se peleó
con su publisher    Sus amigas stopped calling her    She stopped
writing    Keeping el secreto sealed up inside herself    was causing
havoc in her life.

Prieta could no longer even talk    to herself    The constant
chatter    suddenly stilled was the most shocking thing she had
ever experienced    The silence was complete and stretched in all
directions    En medio de su desierto blanco    of blank pages something
moved    was alive    Her stomach protruded even more    Something
nudged her stomach    as though seeking a way out    Each day
its movements grew more vigorous    until she felt it ramming
itself    against her ombligo.

Una noche while she was sleeping    it got past her garganta    and
entered her ear canal    She woke to an excruciating    pain    and
when she put her hand to touch her ear    her fingers touched the
wet    slippery    worm-like body of an    axolotl    the larvae stage de la
salamandra

Translations

La vulva es una herida abierta, *The vulva is an open wound*
¡ Qué no quiero verla! / Dile a la luna que venga, / que no quiero ver la
    sangre." *I don't want to see her | Tell the moon to come | (that) I don't want to
    see the blood.*
La madre la baña y la empolva, *The mother bathes and powders her*
le cambia los pavicos cuando orina, *she changes her diapers when she urinates*
la tetera, *the baby bottle*
buscando un mamón negro, *searching for a black nipple*
Un día estaba deshojando mazorcas. La dejaron sola en el cuarto. Su
    mamá la oyó gritar y vino corriendo. Sobre hojas secas la halló bañada
    de sudor y lágrimas. Cuando le cambió el pavico vió un gusanote
    echando entre sus labios, en sus nalgitas huellas coloradas donde le
    había quemado. *One day they were husking the corn. She was left alone in the
    shed. Her mother heard her screaming and came running. Among the dry corn*

> leaves she found her, damp with sweat and tears. When she changed her diaper she
> saw a huge worm lying between her labia. The worm had burned a red trail on her
> flesh. She was three months old.

cúbrete, *cover yourself up*

escóndelo, *hide it*

la ropa, *the clothes*

carne seca, *dried meat*

oliendo a humo, *smelling like smoke*

es una cebolla enroscada alrededor de su hermana, *she is an onion curled
around her sister*

es la Vieja Inés cerquita de la noria, *she is the Old Hag Inés near the well*

repollo con pollo, *cabbage with chicken*

nalgas hediondas, *stinky behind*

panocha apestosa, *smelly crotch*

verijas mugrosas, *dirty cunt*

Based on a talk delivered at St. Olaf College on March 7, 1992, this previously unpublished essay, which Anzaldúa worked on at various points from 1995 through 2001, offers both a summary of her position in *Borderlands* and an important extension into the next phase of her theoretical development. Anzaldúa provides an expanded definition of her theory of the "new mestiza," emphasizing that, as she defines the term, *mestizaje* can take multiple forms, including some that go beyond biological/racial identity categories to include intellectual, spiritual, aesthetic, and more. This essay explores a variety of additional topics, including multiculturalism, education, disciplinary boundaries, nos/otras, new tribalism, and the "Trojan mula," which she defines as subversive intellectuals and academics of any color, those who challenge the status quo. Anzaldúa also draws on her own experiences to discuss some of the difficulties women of colors and other racial/ethnic, intellectual, and/or emotional mestizas might experience in the academy.

# The New Mestiza Nation
*A Multicultural Movement*

As we near the turn into the twenty-first century, we face a backlash and a dangerous regressive state inside and outside of education. The visibility of hate groups, the KKK, neo-nazis and other white supremacy groups has increased in the last few years. They proclaim that racial/ethnic others, working-class people, people of color are taking over their white territory and using affirmative action to drive them out of jobs. White supremacists, right-wingers, the advocates of family values, and academic elitists have made the political climate ripe for neo-conservatives who accuse multiculturalists of diluting the national identity, weakening the literary canon, and giving people of color, working-class people, gay men, and lesbians hegemonic control. They denounce the wave of multiculturalism on campuses, referring to it as a new tyrannical form of being "politically correct." When some of us criticize racism or homophobia in the academy they respond by pointing the finger at us and shouting their right-wing buzzwords like political correctness to silence dissenting voices.

True multiculturalism endangers white males and forces them to feel ashamed of their culture by presenting the histories and perspectives of ethnic groups. Multiculturalists disrupt the fantasy that has dominated the State's official version of this country's history. These radical multiculturalists seek to split open the fantasy of a monocultural nation, interrogate the history of internal and external colonialism by the U.S. government, and protest U.S. wars against the Third World and imperialist domination of the Americas. We stress that Others can't be lumped together, our issues collapsed, our differences erased. Women of color, working-class and gay people are refusing to let our histories, stories, and theories be appropriated, made invisible, or turned against ourselves. We resist neo-conservative attempts to invert notions of power which supposedly make us powerful and them powerless. We expose this notion as a form of racism designed to discount the voices of those who form the backbone of the heritage of the U.S. There are a few disciplines—Women's Studies, Ethnic Studies, and some segments of American Studies and Latin American Studies—that are progressive and open to other ways of thinking and to the literatures of people of color. But most administrations and disciplines are firmly entrenched. They have had this power from the beginning of this nation, and they're not going to relinquish it easily.

Amidst this attack by conservatives, people of color, working-class people, and progressive whites in the academy continue to struggle fiercely to define multiculturalism as a movement that reflects and represents the real United States—the mixed, hybrid, mestiza, character of this country.

I consider myself a mestiza multiculturalist teacher and writer[1] informed by my identity as a Chicana Tejana dyke from a working-class background. I am involved in the anti-colonial struggle against literary assimilation, claiming linguistic space to validate my personal language and history. Mestiza feminists such as myself seek the means to transform pedagogical and institutional practices so that they will represent ethnic people and protect students of color, gay men, and lesbians against racist and heterosexist violence. Women of color and working-class people have been at the forefront of this multicultural movement, before multicultural was even a term widely used. We have been articulating the need for curriculums that represent us, pedagogical approaches that do not silence us, and scholarship that challenges existing power hierarchies. We want our histories, our knowledge, our perspectives to be accepted and validated not only in the universities but also in elementary, junior high, and high schools. The roots of multicultural education lie in the lived experiences and struggles of women of color and working-class people. Not that others have not also worked for this, but we have been there all along, knowing that education depends upon incorporating all different points of view, white, colored, and mestiza, drawing on and from las lenguas of our peoples.

Through our multi-layered experiences as mestizas, women of color, working-class, and gay people we claim multicultural education as a centerpiece of the mestiza nation. In 1920 José Vasconcelos, a Mexican philosopher, envisioned a mestizo nation, a cosmic race, a fifth race embracing the four major races of the world.[2] We are creating ways of educating ourselves and younger generations in this mestiza nation to change how students and teachers think and read by de-constructing Euro-Anglo ways of knowing; to create texts that reflect the needs of the world community of women and people of color; and to show how lived experience is connected to political struggles and art making.

We bring to the present our political experience which is why we are wary of the ways concepts like multiculturalism, difference, and diversity can get co-opted. These terms can, and have, been used against us, making it seem as though difference and diversity are power neutral, thus diluting or stripping these terms of their emancipatory potential. A radical political agenda is often reduced to superficial efforts to serve international foods, wear ethnic clothes, and decorate corporate complexes and airports with native colors and art. This multicultural appropriation/misappropriation is an attempt to control difference by allocating it to bordered-off sections in the curriculum. Diversity is then treated as a superficial overlay that does not disrupt any comfort zones. It is reduced to a footnote or an appendix in people's psyches. Our cultures, languages, thinking, and art are color-coded, made into commercial products, and reified as exotic cultural tales devoid of human agency. The racial/ethnic other or "nos/otras" — a word I split to show that we and they are both us and other — seeks terms that identify our heritages. Mestiza, which is actually an old term, speaks to our common identity as mixed bloods. I have been exploring this as a new category which is more inclusive than a racial mestizaje. Most Chicanos, Latinos, Asians, and Native Americans are mixed bloods. Many are half and half: half Chicano/half white, half Japanese/half white, and so on. The new mestiza is a category that threatens the hegemony of the neo-conservatives because it breaks down the labels and theories used to manipulate and control us. Punching holes in their categories, labels, and theories means punching holes in their walls.

The Trojan mulas in the academy, those who have been educated and assimilated in universities, run the risk of being white-washed in the academy's acid. They are held captive in the academic Tower, bashed by high theory discourses. They are tired of their minds being occupied by white men, cansadas de la reconquista de la mente, tired of being occupied and driven out of our minds. They are tired of being shot down by language, writing, theoretical discourse. The pen is a weapon used against them. The pen is the sword that renders us war prisoners in intellectual mind factories. But we are learning to wield the pen. Many of the terms that are now going around are not used by people of color, progressive whites, working-class whites, gays, lesbians, or disabled people. They are terms given to us by the new conservatives in the administration, in the faculty, and in the boardrooms. These conservative educators and students overshadow the few people of color and progressive whites in the academy.

Identity Crisis

As leaders of this movement, the new mestizas are among those who often feel worn down by the costs of exclusionary education. These costs have been high for feminists of color, queer scholars, activists, and artists who are producing new scholarship and who see the possibility of self-representation in higher education. We, the mestiza multiculturalists, know well the dangers of this border crossing, dangers to be reckoned with as we continue to walk across the firing lines. As a Chicana tejana patlache mujer del nuevo mundo, I am tired of being the counteremancipatory voice, tired of being the return of the repressed, the token woman with the prominent Indian features.

The United States is struggling with a crisis of identity. The new conservatives want to keep higher education a Euro-Anglo institution. They want to keep a Euro-Anglo country, expanding a Euro-Anglo world, imperializing into the Third World. But we problematize their hegemony. We say, "Yo también soy América." For me, America does not stop at the Mexican and Canadian borders. It encompasses North America, Central America, South America, and Canada. We have to stop appropriating the word America to only fit the United States. It is all of this, el Nuevo Mundo.

This crisis of identity is not restricted to the monocultural white heterosexuals denouncing the wave of multiculturalism on campuses. The crisis is also felt by mestizas, people of color, mujeres, and lesbians of color who inhabit so many different worlds. This new racism has pounded hegemonic theories into us, making us feel like we don't fit. We are alienated. We are exiled. Not only are they undermining us by assimilating us, but in turn, we are using these very same theories, concepts, and assumptions that we have bought into against ourselves. Mestizas internalize those theories, concepts, and labels that manipulate and control us. We buy into these distortions and then we use them on ourselves. Many of us have become split from our ethnic, racial, and class communities. We are trying to figure out terms and ways of being in the world so that we will not be destroyed, so that we will not be co-opted or assimilated, so that we can make sense out of and teach our histories to ourselves and those who come after us. As we create a more diverse curricula we learn ways of teaching and knowing that are more representative of a mestiza nation.

The new mestiza finds herself inside the ivory tower, inside white-colored walls. It is hard to get through that gate and many do not make it. But once she passes through that gate, she becomes a sort of Trojan horse, a Trojan mula who has infiltrated in order to subvert the system, bringing new ideas with her. This work becomes such a weighty job because she does triple duty. She studies the dominant culture through the scholarship her professors require her to read. She tries to learn about her own culture, seeks permission to explore topics, write papers, and design a thesis that interests her. But her interests may extend beyond English or white American scholarship. Overwhelmed by her multiple tasks, she often ends up seduced and subverted by the system instead of subverting it.

If she is a progressive white teacher, she has to fight not only her own white sisters, but also those people of color who think, "What is that gringa doing with our stuff?" As a faculty member of color she does double, triple, quadruple work. She becomes a Trojan mula, stumbling with all this baggage. And sometimes the academy starts chipping away at her walls as she rams the academy's walls with her head to make room for others like herself; she ends up on the floor with a bloodied head as she comes up against classrooms where she and her communities are completely invisible. The mestiza must constantly find the energy to develop strategies, meet with people, form organizations, and build coalitions. And all of this depends upon funding so that she can do the Spanish festival, have lesbian, gay, and bisexual awareness week, invite a woman of color scholar or artist to the speaker series, build alliances among her own people and with other groups.

After the first, second, or third year in college, or by the time the mestiza is in graduate school, chances are she has been stepped on a lot—she has boot tracks on her face. Her head is already bloodied from going up against the walls. I call this *Pisando su sombra*, and it takes its toll. She may get subverted instead of doing the subverting. In such instances, her mind and imagination are taken over, and the mestiza is internally colonialized: She is mined for her art, words, writing, and music, for her clothes, hair, and the way she walks. She is mind-mugged, violated intellectually as she faces the crisis of representation for women of color, queers, and other mestizas. This mind-mugging robs her of her soul, her spirit, and leaves her tired, lethargic. She has been turned into una sombra, a shadow person, just another statistic in struggle.

These walls and gates around fields of study and around the actual buildings are designed to keep us out or to hold us captive if we do get inside. The mestiza is asked somehow or other to scale thick and tall walls. Without acknowledging the difficulties involved in bridging more than one reality, she is left on her own to do the best she can. Being true to and maintaining ties with her ethnic communities is sometimes at odds with developing her intellectual identities, especially if this intellectualism denies any notion of difference.

My experience is a case in point. When I first entered graduate school, I was one of only two Chicanas in the entire graduate program of the Comparative Literature Department at the University of Texas in Austin. I felt very isolated and marginalized. I left after completing all of my course work when a couple of advisors told me that we were living in "America" and there was no such thing as Chicano literature. In the early and mid 1970's feminist studies and feminist theory were not yet legitimate topics of study or research. I was not allowed to apply a multicultural approach to feminist theory, Chicano literature, and Spanish literature. I was dissatisfied with studying only American English and Latin American literature. Now I am all but dissertation in my second venture in graduate school, this time at the University of California at Santa Cruz. I am still dissatisfied with the methods of literary study. Like other graduate students of color, I've tried to de-construct the orals and dissertation criteria. Because of my privilege as a published author and a person who gets paid for her words as a speaker, professors listen to me. Whether they hear what I say is another matter.

For mestizas such as myself, the areas of study that professors want us to concentrate on do not appeal. We want new books, new areas of inquiry, and new methodologies. We want to study non-English and non-Euro-American literatures. We want more work by women of color on the reading lists. We are bookworms gnawing holes in the canon; we are termites undermining the canonical curriculum's foundations.

We struggle to make room for ourselves, to change the academy so that it does not invalidate, stamp out, or crush our connections to the communities we come from. For working-class and colored people this means breaking down the barred windows that have kept us out of the universities.

I come from working-class roots, and it has been quite a struggle to negotiate the privilege I have received as a writer. Before gaining privilege, I was shut up, made invisible. As I move from the underclass to working class to middle class, I travel from being on the side of the "have-nots" to finding myself somewhat crossing over into the territory of the "haves," whom I've always viewed as oppressors. I am doing a lot of border crossing. Crossing over into the oppressors' terrain makes for a complex identity (and an identity complex). It problematizes who and what I am. Our attitudes toward money are programmed by our own class of origin. The indoctrination we receive is imprinted so deeply within us that it is hard to break through it. People from working-class origins find it difficult to get through the class barriers that exist in institutions of learning, writing, and art—barriers to being in school, to speaking out, to making our voices heard.

The new mestizas have a connection with particular places, a connection to particular races, a connection to new notions of ethnicity, to a new tribalism that is devoid of any kind of romantic illusions. The new mestiza is a liminal subject who lives in borderlands between cultures, races, languages, and genders. In this state of in-betweenness the mestiza can mediate, translate, negotiate, and navigate these different locations. As mestizas, we are negotiating these worlds every day, understanding that multiculturalism is a way of seeing and interpreting the world, a methodology of resistance.

## Theories of mestizaje: border inscriptions

People who are initiating a new politics of difference and who are the carriers of difference must have boundary-crossing visions. As multiculturalists they are developing theories of mestizaje—border inscriptions which draw on a combination of cultural values and traditions that show how certain kinds of knowledge have been conquered and colonized. Notions of mestizaje offer another "reading" of culture, history, and art—that of the dispossessed and marginal. Multicultural texts show the writer's or artist's struggle to decolonize subjectivity. For mestizas it is not sufficient simply to reinscribe the traditional culture they emerged from and set up a we-are-right/they-are-wrong binary opposition. Perspectives based on representation problematize these binaries, asking how people negotiate multiple worlds every day. My identity is always in flux; it changes as I step into and cross over many worlds each day—university, home community, job, lesbian, activist, and academic communities. It is not enough for me to say I am a Chicana. It is not enough for me to say I am an intellectual. It is not enough for me to say I am a writer. It is not enough for me to say I am from working-class origins. All of these and none of these are my primary identity. I can't say, this is the true me, or that is the true me. They are all the true me's.

Progressive whites who have friends from different worlds and who study different cultures become intellectual mestizas. They may not be emotional mestizas and certainly are not biological mestizas. But there can be empathy between people of color and progressive, sensitive, politically aware whites.

### Discovery Theories

As political conservatives continue to put boundaries around knowledge and history, it is up to us, new mestizas, to tell the multiple histories and the influence that colonized and immigrant people have had on the construction of this country. If you study the waves of immigration, indigenous history, and the theories of the discovery, you will find that Africans came here hundreds and hundreds of years before Columbus. There are books that verify the existence of Africans in Mexico and South America. There is also a theory that Chinese and Japanese came over long before Columbus.

Foundational theories of the "discovery" show the devastation of colónnialism (a word I've coined after Colón). Ours is a 500-year struggle against colonialism that continues as the U.S. government spends 87 billion dollars to publicize the commemoration of the 500 years of "discovery." They are sailing three ships—the Niña, the Pinta, and the Santa María—from England to three different U.S. cities: New York, Washington, D.C., and Boston. Some of the commemorators are saying, "Yes, let's show a little bit of Indian history." But that little bit is tokenized and assimilated, made palatable just as they make palatable their hegemonic "discovery" theory. We're not celebrating genocide and the resurgence of un nuevo racismo y la reconquista de al mente.

### Creating work that cannot be assimilated

We need to create poetry, art, research, and books that cannot be assimilated, but is accessible. For example, take Borderlands / La Frontera: you can access that book, but hopefully it won't get consumed out of existence or tokenized or assimilated to death. I know that as you read the ideas you will reinterpret them, but the ideas can't be melted down. The components are distinct; they're there to dialogue with one another. The different races and communities that make up the Chicana do not disappear, they are not repressed. In reading *Borderlands*, the intellectual Gloria, the published writer and the person with an academic identity, are present. Behind these Glorias are others: Gloria the campesina, Gloria the clerk worker in temp jobs, the unemployed Gloria who subsisted on potatoes, the coming-into-middle-class Gloria, Gloria the lesbian, Gloria the ex-campesina are all present. When I speak at an academic conference, Gloria the intellectual might take center stage. If I am with a group of Chicanas, the ethnic me comes forward and the other Glorias withdraw backstage. In a room full of socializing and partying dyke friends, a different me comes out. But it doesn't mean that in the different communities some parts of me are repressed; all of me is there. Nor does this mean that I am a fake when I present different faces.

As a mestiza, I have many true faces, depending upon the kind of audience or the area I find myself in. Using *mestiza* as an umbrella term means acknowledging that certain aspects of identity don't disappear, aren't assimilated or repressed when they are not in the foreground. Identity is a changing cluster of components and a shape-shifting activity. To refer to a person who is changing identity I use the Náhuatl term *nagual*. The nagual is a shapeshifter, a person who changes from human form to animal form. We shift around to do the work we have to do, to create the identities we need to live up to our potential.

### Con los ojos y la lengua como pluma en la mano izquierda

Staying alive and not getting too battered in the university requires strategies to fight back—strategies of survival and resistance. One strategy brings together three different abilities—communicating, knowing, and doing which I represent in my hieroglyph of a left hand on whose palm are pictured a pair of eyes, a mouth with a tongue hanging out and the writing tip of a pen at the tip of the tongue. Los ojos represent seeing and knowing which can lead to understanding or conocimiento. It means getting to know each other and, as mestizas from many cultures, seeing from multiple points of view, from the viewpoint of a multiculturalist who takes in and tries to incorporate all the different perspectives. It means looking in, looking from more than one direction at the same time. La lengua is a symbol for speech, for breaking silence by talking, communicating, and writing. The split forked tongue of a serpent is my signal for communicating bilingually.*

To activate the conocimiento and communication we need the hand. The hand is an agent of action. It is not enough to speak and write and talk and communicate. It is not enough to see and recognize and know. We need to act upon what we know, to do something about it. The left hand has always been seen as sinister and strange, associated with the female gender and creativity. But in unison with the right, the left hand can perform great things. It is not enough to theorize and intellectualize—theory needs to connect with action, with activism. When theorizing, we need to ask of ourselves and others: *What does this theory have to do with working-class people, women of color, single women with children? What is the ideological and political function of this particular theory? How is this theory being used as an ideological weapon?*

Multiculturalist mestizas want to connect to all our different communities: the job, straight, and activist communities. The mestiza is in a position to make links. First of all, she is a borderland person, a bridge person. She connects from her ethnic community to the academic community, from the feminist group to non-political groups, from the Spanish language to the English language. She has the choice to be a bridge, a drawbridge, a sandbar, or an island in terms of how she relates to and defines herself in the world. She chooses when to do coalition and alliance work.[3] If she is colored, being a bridge means that she is always out there with white people, translating and mediating. As a drawbridge, she withdraws part of the time and says, "I don't want to have anything to do with straights, whites, males, etc. I need time to be with myself, my people. I need time to recharge, regenerate my batteries." The person who opts to be an island says, "I don't want to have anything to do ever with the straight or white folks." Being an island is basically impossible because we all depend on each other for necessities such as shelter and food. A symbol for another kind of bridge is a sandbar. One type of sandbar goes from island to mainland. That is my choice of a bridge because it's natural and it's under water, which means I can be alone when I desperately need to, or I can connect to people. My creativity starts with solitude,[4] but it also needs close contact with others in my different communities where we discuss mutual cultural

---

* For a later version of this image, see figure 9 (and note that the later version includes an ear, thus indicating an important development in Anzaldúa's theorizing). Significantly, Anzaldúa associated this later version with her theory of spiritual activism.

and literary issues and support each other with our theories, experiences, and writing.

Doing bridge work brings up many questions, such as: *Where do I come from? What's my culture like? How do I position myself?* For whites this question means being clear about who you are and what privileges you bring into the group's dynamics. It means asking: *What can I do with my privileges? How can I use them for nos/otras? Instead of women of color being a resource for me, how can I be a resource for them? What kinds of knowledge can I offer nos/otras?* This means using your connections, your networks. It may mean making a way for nos/otras to get recognition, funds, or a grant. Or it could mean just being an empathetic ear.

I've seen that when white people align themselves with the struggles of women of color, their understanding of the struggles changes. When a white woman offers to work with nos/otras, we ask her the same thing we ask ourselves: What's in it for you? What is the motivation behind your crossing? More often than not she'll ask herself: *Am I one more white woman ripping off yet another culture? Am I one more white woman bringing her guilt and wanting to be exonerated? Am I one more white woman coming over and saying, "Look at me, I am not racist; otherwise I wouldn't be working with you."*

All of us carry multiple unconscious motivations—both positive and negative. Half the time we don't know why we do things. Ten years down the road a woman of color may deduce, "Oh! I did that because I wanted white people to like me." Because people of color have been oppressed by white people so much we often seek their validation, love, and acceptance. Because we have been violated, we demand so much, we hunger for that acceptance and love. Muchas veces when we don't get it some of us become hostile or rebellious, some of us knuckle under and assimilate, and still others become bridges. Most of the time we don't know exactly why we respond in certain ways. Ten years down the road when we identify as feminists or lesbians or post-feminists, we might look back and say, "Oh yeah. Back then my thinking was screwed up. What I wanted from these white folk, ethnic community, dykes, etc., was for them to tell me I was okay." This desire is dangerous for both women of color and white women because we get into this dialectic of the la patrona, the great white mother, and the needy colored kid.

Sometimes the tables are turned and it is the white person that wants something from the colored student. The white feminist, professor, wants to be accepted and validated, to hear, "This a great syllabus. You are being really multicultural. You are dealing with racism." Meanwhile, the student realizes that the professor doesn't want to hear her call herself Chicana or Indian. She doesn't want the student to have any interaction with her ethnic community. The professor wants the university student to be cut off from all her cultural roots. The professor's rhetoric professes that student and teacher are on an equal footing when that is not the case. Within this dynamic, students play the role that professors assign them. The greater the cultural and class difference, the more intense the dynamic between them. Power is at the center of this dynamic. In the past, faculty were always in the position of power. But now things are changing—at least on the surface. In classrooms, a white professor and white students may defer to a black or Latina student. The professor will say, "Tell me about your culture, tell me about your writers, tell me about your art." The mighty weight to represent her culture is put on the colored student. Because she is supposed to come up with all the political and cultural theories, a tremendous amount of power is given to her. But this power can overwhelm her.

When whites tell nos/otras that white people have no culture, they are oblivious to the fact that this whole country and the dominant culture is their culture. What white people watch on television is their culture. The films that they see on the VCR, the foods they eat and the clothes they buy, the vacations they take—it is from their culture, yet they keep saying, "I have no culture." This statement means that the majority of whites don't have a sense of their historical roots, roots that may go back to ancient Ireland or England. They don't know what Celtic means, for instance. That's why they want to appreciate or appropriate black, Latino, Native, or Asian cultures. Appropriation is a dangerous act, es muy peligroso, if they are serious about doing coalition work.

Origins

In the last few years, "origins" has become a bad word because the deconstructionists see everything as socially constructed. According to them there is no such thing as "origins." Deconstructionists and some feminist theorists assert that origins are falsely romanticized and idealized. In some ways this assertion is true. We do tend to romanticize origins and culture, but the new mestiza is aware of the tendency to romanticize. She tries to look at the past and examine the aspects of culture that have oppressed women. The past is constantly being constructed in a number of ways. First, the perspective of the viewer of that history changes from one epoch to another; the perspective of a person changes from year to year. Second, the past has not been represented "truthfully" in history books. Written by the conquerors, history books distort and repress the histories of women and people of color.

Perhaps white theorists say that origins are passé or unattractive because they don't want to delve into their past. They may be afraid to discover that one of their ancestors enslaved people, raped indigenous women, or ripped off the land from Indians. As a mestiza, I also look at my white ancestors who did exactly that. I look at the Aztecs and their cruelty. I look at things in my past that are not attractive. But it is scary for white people to think, "Who am I? Who are my people?" It is scary to see that a lot of the European immigrants were released from jails or came here as deserters of various causes, as convicts and criminals.

Crossing cultural and class borders requires that one look at the blood in one's veins, examining the history of one's people, including its religious and spiritual practices. Taken back far enough, one discovers some kind of shamanism in their cultural pasts. Look for and build on the positive.

There is such a thing as collective guilt, just as there is individual guilt. I don't mean that the father's guilt automatically, genetically, is handed down to his children. If today a white person is operating under the same white supremacist ideology as his great great grandfather—the notion that white people are better than people of color—then that person is as guilty as his ancestors. If that white person is not living that ideology, has said, "No, this is not my ideology," then he is not accountable or responsible for the sins of his ancestors. However, the ideology that operated during the slave and early colonial times is still operating today. When Bush opens his mouth, you can still hear that old ideology.

As we continue the struggle with the new conservatism's onslaught, we find ourselves at an impasse—but we can't go back. We need a reminder of what this struggle is all about. At this time when the term multiculturalism is being completely subverted, it is important that this concept be sharply defined. Forcing down foreign concepts into our minds is analogous to the insistence on maintaining "family values"—a sign of how desperate they are to keep things the way they once were, because things have changed. But it's too late, the walls have chinks in them, and we refuse to give up our positions no matter how insistent their backlash. To allow depression or disillusionment to stop our struggle would lose the ground we've gained.

Multiculturalism is about including stories of difference. Se trata de otras narrativas. It is about alter-narratives. The stories of multiculturalism are stories of identity, and narratives of identity are stories of location. A story is always a retelling of an older story. This is my retelling.

## Notes

1. I am a seventh-generation American whose ancestors lived in a part of Texas that used to be Mexico; before, it was Indian territory. My ancestors were Tejanos from Mexico. Long ago a boundary got drawn up and the Anzaldúas found themselves on this side of the border while the other Anzaldúas (who call themselves Anzaldua without the accent) found themselves split on the other side, and we lost touch with each other. This is what has happened to the Chicano/Mexicano race in this country. We are an in-between race. We are still Mexican in terms of racial ancestry but are Norteamericanos who have been educated in U.S. schools and raised imbibing and consuming the dominant values and customs. I am also a dyke Chicana. I call myself *patlache* which is the Aztec Náhuatl word for dyke. The word *lesbian* does not fit my background, my experience. The term comes from Lesbos, the Greek Island, and is a term of identity for white middle-class lesbians.

2. See José Vasconcelos, *La Raza Cósmica: Mission de la Raza Ibero-Americana* (México: Aguilar S.A. de Ediciones, 1961). For more discussion of this work and concept, see my "La Consciencia de la Mestiza: Toward a New Consciousness," in *Making Face, Making Soul / Haciendo Caras*, ed. Gloria Anzaldúa (San Francisco: Aunt Lute, 1990).

3. See my "Bridge, Drawbridge, Sandbar or Island," *Bridges of Power: Women's Multicultural Alliances*, edited by Lisa Albrecht. [Included in this volume.]

4. I promise myself I am going to do some unscheduled relaxation, even if it's only for five minutes. In my life everything is scheduled, even fun. I tell myself that I need to lie down or go out in the sun, even for just five minutes without trying to think about anything and leave the worries behind. The truth is I always have a list in my mind: I gotta do this speech, get ready for this gig, turn this paper in to a professor, do the revisions on my novel, or critique someone else's work. If I happen to be in a classroom or a bus or a car when I am trying to relax I do deep breathing (into my stomach) real slow. I listen to music. I have a tape of the sounds of dolphins, sea otters, and humpback whales. I play it in the airport while I am writing and waiting to board my plane. I do a lot of my writing in airplanes now.

# Part Three

## Gallery of Images

> In creating artistic works, the artist's creative process brings to the page/canvas/ wood the unconscious process of the imagination. . . . By awakening and activating the imagining process in the viewer, la artista empowers us. La imaginación gives us choices and options from which to free ourselves from las jaulas that our cultures lock us in.
>
> —From "Bearing Witness: Their Eyes Anticipate the Healing"

Anzaldúa valued many forms of art—the visual as well as the verbal. As she explains in several interviews, she seriously considered focusing her energies on painting or sculpture, rather than on writing. Even after she committed herself to the written word, she did not abandon the visual arts: she included many elaborate sketches and informal doodles in her journals; created flyers for her writing workshops and events like El Mundo Surdo Reading Series (figure 1); recommended and sketched out designs for some of her book covers; added little drawings with her signature when autographing books or signing letters; wrote about contemporary and indigenous paintings and murals; and used what she calls "pictograms" or "glifos" to illustrate her talks. For Anzaldúa, images and ideas are intimately interrelated. As she explains in a later manuscript version of "Border Arte," "Over twelve years ago I switched from using flow charts during my speaking engagements to using what I call pictograms or rough glifos (hieroglyphs) I sketch on transparencies. The images I place on overhead projectors 'illustrate' my ideas and theories." This section honors Anzaldúa's commitment to multiple art forms. While most of these images are glifos drawn by Anzaldúa herself for use in her speaking engagements, this gallery also includes black-and-white reproductions of two of Liliana Wilson's paintings (discussed in "Bearing Witness").

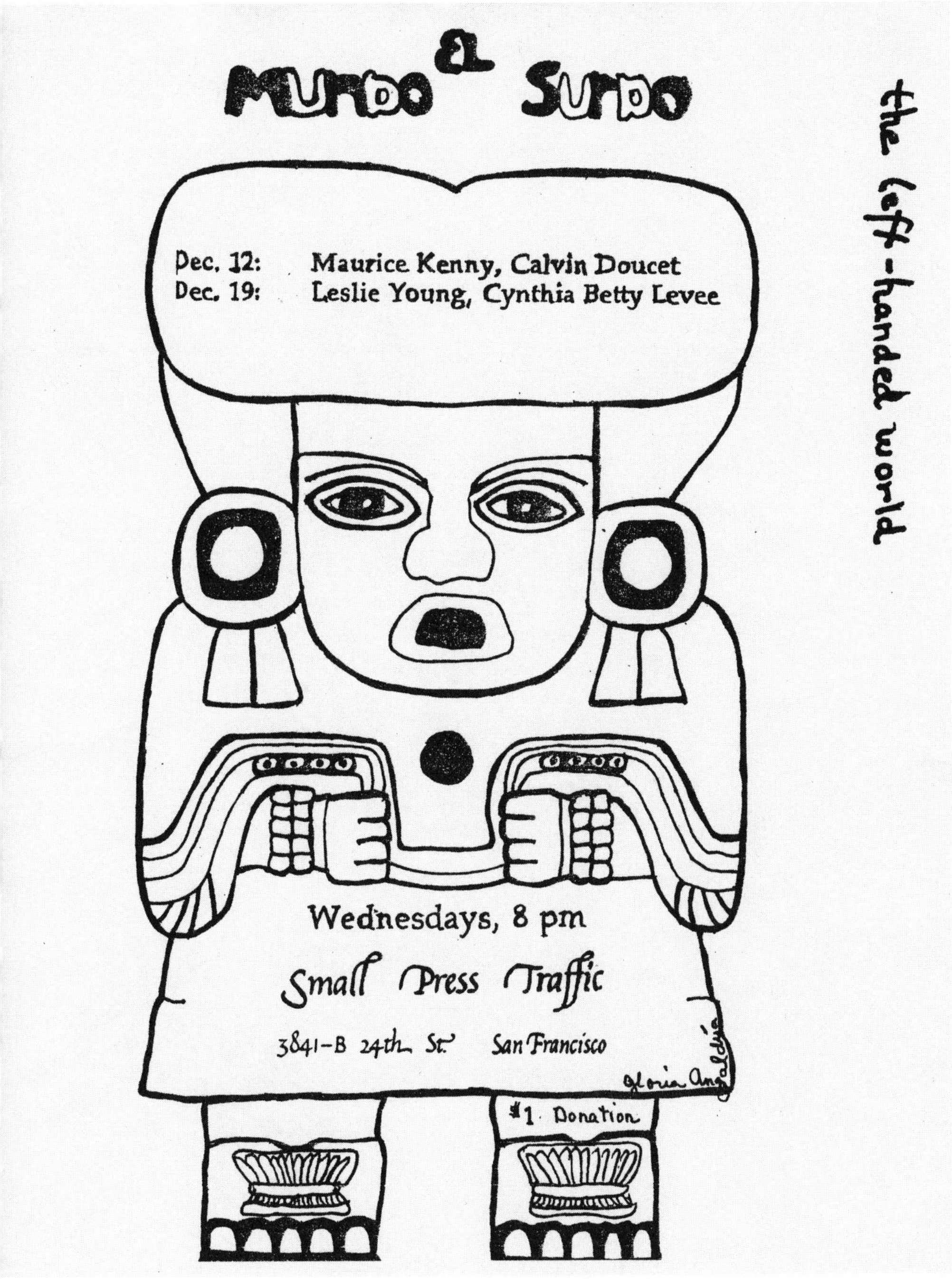
El
Mundo Surdo
the left-handed world
Dec. 12: Maurice Kenny, Calvin Doucet
Dec. 19: Leslie Young, Cynthia Betty Levee
Wednesdays, 8 pm
Small Press Traffic
3841-B 24th St. San Francisco
Gloria Anzaldúa
$1 Donation

1. El Mundo Surdo Reading Series flyer, designed by Gloria Anzaldúa

2. "The Way Station (Changing Identities),"
by Gloria Anzaldúa

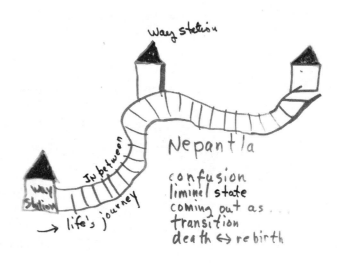

Changing identities
Forming identities

Way station

In between

Way Station

→ life's journey

Nepantla

confusion
liminal state
coming out as...
transition
death ↔ rebirth

movidas

3. "Nepantla," by Gloria Anzaldúa

nepantla

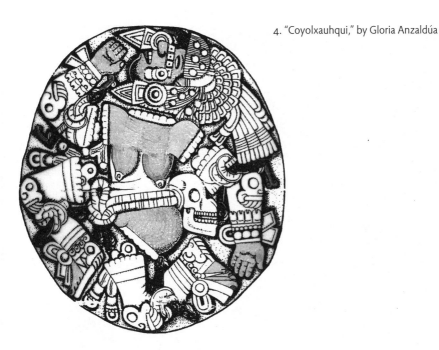

4. "Coyolxauhqui," by Gloria Anzaldúa

5. "Feet in Multicultures," by Gloria Anzaldúa

6. *Memorias de Chile* (2001), by Liliana Wilson

7. *La Diosa del amor* (2003), by Liliana Wilson

fissure
crack
Aperture
gate
rajadura
agujero
hueco
rapture

cross threshold

Pool of images

el cenote

8. "El cenote," by Gloria Anzaldúa

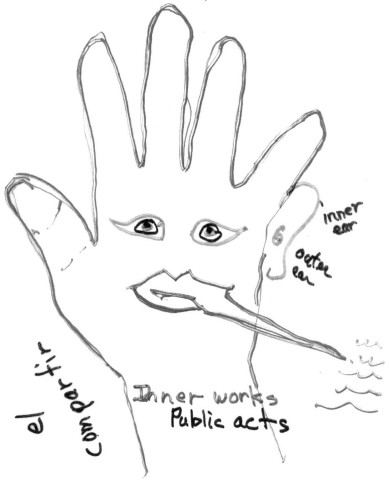

9. "Spiritual Activism: Acts of Vision," by Gloria Anzaldúa

Identity
always
under construction.

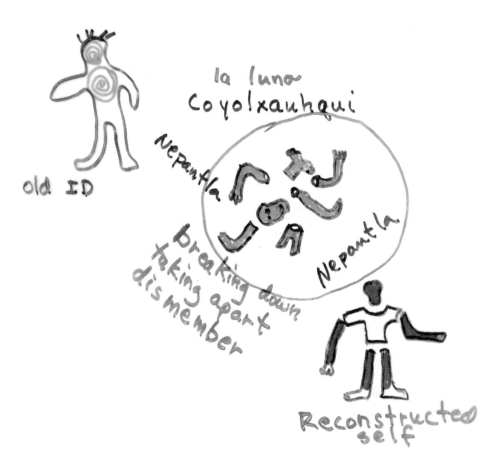

old ID

la luna
Coyolxauhqui

Nepantla

Nepantla

breaking down
taking apart
dismember

Reconstructed
self

10. "Identity Is Always Under Construction," by Gloria Anzaldúa

# Part Four

## "Later" Writings

With the imperative to "speak" esta herida abierta (this open wound) before it drowns out all voices, the feelings I'd buried begin unfurling. Vulnerable once more, I'm clawed by the talons of grief. I take my sorrow for a walk along the bay near my home in Santa Cruz. With the surf pounding in my ears and the wind's forlorn howl, it feels like even the sea is grieving. I struggle to "talk" from the wound's gash, make sense of the deaths and destruction, and pull the pieces of my life back together. I yearn to pass on to the next generation the spiritual activism I've inherited from my cultures. If I object to my government's act of war I cannot remain silent. To do so is to be complicitous. But sadly we are all accomplices.

—From "Let us be the healing of the wound: The Coyolxauhqui imperative—la sombra y el sueño"

Anzaldúa wrote this short piece for *Cassell's Encyclopedia of Queer Myth, Symbol and Spirit* (1996), edited by her close friends Randy Conner, David Sparks, and Mariya Sparks. In addition to challenging conventional understandings of knowledge and overly simplistic binaries between social constructionism and essentialism, this brief essay offers useful insights into the roles that spirituality (or what she describes as "spiritual mestizaje") played in Anzaldúa's life. From the late 1990s and until her death she was working on an expanded version titled "Spiritual Mestizaje, An Other Way."

## Foreword to *Cassell's Encyclopedia* of *Queer Myth, Symbol and Spirit*

For many years what kept my spiritual flame lit was the memory of the picture of la Virgencita de Guadalupe, a Mexican manifestation of the Virgin Mary, that Mamagrande Ramona kept on her dresser-top altar alongside las velas, the votive candles, and snapshots of family members, muertos y vivos, the dead and the living. That memory led me to haciendo altares (the making of altars), curanderismo (healing), nagualismo (shamanism), and other indigenous Mexican traditions.

After being mugged and later suffering a near-death experience and a host of other traumas, I realized that I would go mad if I did not honor the spirit world. Meditational practice, altar-making, and other rituals helped me to cope with fear, depression, loneliness, poverty, and oppression. I learned that when I could not change external circumstances, I could at least alter my perspective regarding them. Altering my perception often led to the transformation of outer reality.

For me, spirituality is a source of sustenance, a way of knowing, a path of survival. Like love, spirituality is a relational activity leading to deep bonds between people, plants, animals, and the forces of nature. Spirituality not only transforms our perceptions of "ordinary" life and our relationships with others, but also invites encounters with other realities, other worlds.

When I began to suspect that I might be una de las otras, "one of the others," una mita' y mita', "half and half," I went to one of those places I always go to for solace, for guidance, and to better understand myself and others—books. That part of myself which is of European heritage— primarily Spanish and Basque—finds resonance in the term "lesbian" and in the vision of Sappho's thiasos on the island of Lesbos. That part of myself which is of indigenous American heritage takes delight in "patlache," Náhuatl for an Amazon-like, woman-loving woman. Yet I hunger for a spirituality that will embrace my mestiza ("mixed") as well as my queer self.

I remember a night in the winter of 1980, when we were all living on Noe Street in San Francisco, shoving a note under Randy and David's door, asking, "Is there a queer spirituality?" My question led us to many discussions over lattes at Cafe Flore.

As I read *The Encyclopedia of Queer Myth, Symbol and Spirit*, I feel a sense of belonging to a vast community of jotos, "queers," who participate in the sacred and mythic dimensions of life. Again and again, I see parts of myself reflected in many of its narratives and symbols. Like one who was starving, once I tasted such articles as "Shamanism," "Tlazolteotl," and "Xochiquetzal," and other kernels of Aztlán (the mythical homeland of the ancient peoples of Mexico), I quickly lapped up the queer stories of cultures beyond my own.

Years ago, when I first studied the Mayan glyph, or pictogram, that depicts a king covered in part by a jaguar pelt, and read that the glyph is called "The Way," the word and the image resonated throughout my being. "The Way" has multiple meanings. It refers simultaneously to the shaman, to an animal and/or spirit companion, to metamorphosis, to the art of "dreaming" worlds. For a "postcolonial" mestiza like myself, any single way is not "the" way. A spiritual mestizaje weaves together beliefs and practices from many cultures, perhaps including elements of Shamanism, Buddhism, Christianity, Santería, and other traditions. Spiritual mestizaje involves the crossing of borders, incessant metamorphosis. It is a spirituality that nurtures the ability to wear someone else's skin, its central myth being shapeshifting. In its disturbance of traditional boundaries of gender and desire and its narratives of metamorphosis—as amply presented here—as well as in its traversing of cultural and historical borders, Queer Spirit qualifies as a kind of spiritual mestizaje.

This encyclopedia may disturb some queer theorists and other academics in its focus on the mythic and spiritual aspects of erotic and gendered experience. It is time for us to move beyond confining parameters of what qualifies as knowledge. When we refuse to consider the value of knowledge that is rooted in the body, in the psyche, in paralogical experience, we fail to challenge colonialist, post-Renaissance, Euro-Western conceptions of reality. We need to move beyond the facile dichotomy of "essentialism" and "constructionism" to embrace other theoretical paradigms inclusive of embodied and in-spirited knowledge. In its comprehensiveness and inclusiveness, this encyclopaedia is a valuable reference work. But it is not simply a reference work. It challenges us to read history—the history of sexuality as well as the history of the sacred—differently, giving voice to knowledges that are deeply rooted in the realm of spirit.

At long last, here is an encyclopedia for jotas y jotos and all others who seek to recover, reinscribe, and re-vision myths and symbols of gender metamorphosis and same-sex desire.

This never before published poem, which reads almost like a page out of a writing manual, hints at Anzaldúa's intense, prolonged revision process as well as her shaman aesthetics. Last revised in January 1997, "How to" contains allusions to "Speaking in Tongues" (included in part 1) and "the presence" (included in part 2) and offers useful insights into Anzaldúa's perspectives on reading and writing.

## How to

free associate or shift
into automatic writing. Let it all out.
Put the vomit away for a week.

Cut and paste
into some kind of order.
let the presence
of the poem find itself.

Discard a word
or add another, let meaning grapple
for its existence

let the words
fight it out in your head,
but if the fight doesn't end
up in your gut,
you don't have a poem.

It's not on paper you create
but in your innards
you always have help
someone or something stands
over your shoulder.

After the fight
you weed out the losers
you move the winners
closer to the light,
you prune, you polish
                    the remainder
is the soul of the poem
the feeling is the space around it

the space between the words and
       in the words
Sometimes that space
lays
      there like a wet towel
and
      muffles meaning and feeling.
At other times it's an explosive
gas
defying shape and reason.

Or it may arrest words
in their tracts and congeal feeling
allowing it only a gelatin quiver
or two

Sometimes it solidifies like cement
before it can let the reader in—

             Committed or esthete,
they want to know, as if the horse
comes before the cart.

     It may or may not be enough
to unmask the villain
     to vent your anger against him
Some say you must present
     the solution
     not just the problem.
Theories tend to be trendy
who knows what it'll be this time next year.

     back to the problem

When you're far away from it—
you know, the someone-else-wrote-this
-not-the-me-I-am-right-now,
you're no longer afraid of it

now you can read it to others

Don't worry if everyone
misses the whole point.

Pretend that's what you
meant to say anyway,

> Wait awhile
> before mailing it out
> poems like wine mellow with time,
> or else if cheap will turn to vinegar

Don't hold your breath
chances are
???????

This previously unpublished excerpt from one of Anzaldúa's many writing projects hints at the origins of her vocation as a writer, as its title suggests. Using the third person, Anzaldúa describes the "calling" and decision to write, as well as her subsequent "apprenticeship" and "detribalization." This short autohistoria, which was last revised in November 1997, complements "La Prieta" and "Dream of the Double-Faced Woman" (also included in this volume) and demonstrates the intimate relationship between Anzaldúa's writing and her pursuit/ creation of new knowledge.

## Memoir—My Calling; or, Notes for "How Prieta Came to Write"

In her early years it was too painful to inhabit her flesh, fully. She was afraid of her impulses; she locked herself in a world of ideas. Books were her great love. In them she sought the answers to the riddles of life, of death, of immortality. Books were her refuge from a world in which she didn't belong. There was an escape from the intimacy of flesh struggling against flesh in pain, an escape to the cool distant regions of abstract thought. She buried her head in Kierkegaard's *Fear and Trembling* and *Sickness unto Death* and found a despair equaling her own. She became acquainted with the void.

Prieta tenía un amor al conocimiento, a love of knowledge. Her head was always in a book. The encyclopedia, *Æsop's Fables, The Call of the Wild*—which she read thirteen times. She read *Jane Eyre* and *Meditations* of Marcus Aurelius thirteen times, too. Don Quixote, pocketbook westerns—anything she could lay her hands on. Almost everyone disapproved of her reading. Her mother said that so much studying would make her brain soft. She would go crazy. But her father and Mamagrande Locha were proud of mi'jita. Unlike most other Mexicans, Mamagrande kept books in her trunk along with her clothes and camphor. When Prieta came to visit, her grandmother would dig them out. After that, books always had a certain smell. Prieta would sit reading, undistracted by the animated voices of Mamí, Papí, and tías y tíos y Mamagrande. There were the squawking of chickens, the grunting of pigs, and the lowing of cows. She loved to listen to the grownups tell their tales, especially Mamgrande Ramona's story of La Jila, a resident ghost woman from a nearby church who followed people down the road late at night. She loved to listen to her father tell her mother about the apparitions that appeared to him as he drove his red truck through the monte. She inherited those stories in the oral tradition of her people.

She was a misfit, and she took refuge from a world where she did not belong. She hid herself in books, in mysticism, metaphysics, and alchemy, in witchcraft, magic, hidden wisdom.

Philosophy and psychology were her favorite subjects. Jungian psychology. Mythology. Religion. She read occultism, mysticism. The night passed in study, precious hours, her favorite. Philosophy from the Greek, Philos = love; Sophia = of wisdom. Philosophy, Psychology, Religion, Metaphysics. She loved it. Love of wisdom. She became a reader of dictionaries. Each word opened up a new world. Books gave her permission to do things. Reading David Seabury's *The Art of Selfishness* was a transformative event. Seabury argued that it was okay to take chunks of time for oneself in order to study or do other things. This was a great shock to her, and in fact it would be years before she completely stopped feeling guilty and "selfish" when doing things for herself, like reading and writing.

She read to escape—retreated into fantasy and books—romance, suspense, western, detective, espionage, science fiction, reading far into the middle of the night. She came across forbidden, marvelous acts of perversion, a sweet compulsion. She got aroused, she wet herself.

Prieta oyó la llamada and she answered the call. Next to animals she liked books most. Books called to her. Later they called her to writing. She had to choose. Either she answered the call, or she did not. If she denied it she would have to repress the knowledge of other realities and sink into the familiar entrancement, blanking out those new realities. If she accepted the call she would have to leave home, but refusing the call would lead to sickness.

So it began: her apprenticeship. The first stage was detribalization. She was forced to recognize the illusory and arbitrary nature of social norms. She tried to escape these norms, first through counter-cultural defiance, and next by examining the cultural biases and restrictions, pointing them out to her mother, sister, brothers, and anyone else who would listen.

She was forced into this detribalization by a crisis of life-altering proportions. Whenever she began to slump into complacency, another crisis would snap her eyes open. She had five confrontations with death. She also had confrontations with spirits, where the mask of reality lifted and she could see behind it to the hidden reality, and several powerful dreams and visions.

Her training began. She attempted to strengthen her will, concentration, and memory. Every day she wrote in her journal. She fasted, went through sleep deprivation. She prayed and meditated. She spent periods in solitude and isolation in the wilderness. She let herself starve rather than expend her energies doing shit work. She wanted to know, to become a knower, while she turned away from society and towards herself. Gradually, too, she turned back to her community. As soon as she alleviated or came to understand her suffering she tried to translate her insight into shareable form so that others could use it. Her life became a series of alternating withdrawals and returns, of sudden breakthroughs. She experienced numerous visions and changes in the configurations of her identity.

This very short prose poem, which originated in Anzaldúa's writing notas, depicts one stage of her writing process. Like the other poems in this section, this one has not been previously published. Note the ways Anzaldúa intertwines identity, writing, and consciousness.

## When I write I hover

When I write I hover above myself and sometimes I zoom in and out. I am both me and not me, the eye that looks at things is my eye yet another's eye. When I write I am both most myself and least myself. When I write I escape my condition but the writing always takes me back to confront my condition because to write is to live in made up worlds. I write not just to escape reality but to create a new reality. I write because it's my calling, my task to do in the world. I write. It is a ritual, a habit, a propensity bred in my bones. It is what I do. I write because I like to think on paper. I write because I like to think, and to track my thoughts. I write because I want to leave a discernable mark on the world.

In 2001 Anzaldúa and Cherríe Moraga received the prestigious Bode-Pearson Prize for Outstanding Contributions to American Studies presented by the American Studies Association for their groundbreaking multicultural edited collection *This Bridge Called My Back*. In part, the nominators wrote, "Their voices have sprung open the ways in which American studies has been understood. The image of the 'virgin land' has been replaced by the border/land; the 'machine in the garden,' by mestiza consciousness. By this, we mean to recognize the paradigm shift in theorizing national identity that their work accomplished." Although this award was granted for Anzaldúa's co-edited work, the nominators' references to "border/land" and "mestiza consciousness" subtly acknowledge the enormous impact Anzaldúa's *Borderlands / La Frontera: The New Mestiza* has made on issues of national identity and, by extension, American studies. Due to financial concerns and health issues, Anzaldúa could not attend the conference where the award was presented, but she prepared this short talk, which was read by Deborah Vargas.

# Transforming American Studies
## 2001 Bode-Pearson Prize Acceptance Speech

I am honored to be a co-winner of the American Studies Bode-Pearson Prize. I wish to thank the American Studies Association, particularly the award committee members, Gary Okihiro, Paula Rabinowitz, and Vicki Ruiz. I dedicate this acceptance speech to Raza students and teachers in American Studies.

I am an outsider/insider in academic circles. This allows me to look at American Studies from three points of view: the distance of the outsider, the closeness of the insider, and the in-between zone, the space between worlds I call "nepantla." Tonight I speak to you from nepantla, el espacio entre medio.

Though American Studies is already an interdisciplinary project and we've made a concerted effort to make it a "true" American Studies, I urge us to investigate the intersections among various groups and countries. Social movements cross borders—a discipline like American Studies must also cross borders in order to live up to the name "American." I encourage us to explore our relationship to the other Americas, and in our teaching and research find ways of collaborating back and forth across borders on issues of cultural and racial differences within and outside the U.S. such as Mexico–U.S. relations, migration, immigration, and border restrictions.

Within our borders I see the need to explore inclusivity in terms of inter-relationships and commonalities, neither as difference nor sameness but as complex interplay among difference, sameness, and similarities. Let us open our internal borders, let us not be afraid of cultural mestizaje. Though we've opened American Studies to include people of color, there are still gaps in the areas of sexualities, gender, class, religions, regions, and "race"/ethnicity, an area that many teachers ignore. It's not enough to keep reading and assigning *This Bridge Called My Back* or *Borderlands / La Frontera*. Educators need to create fertile ground for the coming generations of women and men of color and "white" students; otherwise we relegate all to an impoverished education. How do we create a fertile ground? By educating ourselves: Teaching and learning are transformative experiences. Self-education requires that we open all of our senses, not just our minds, and allow ourselves to be changed by the books and perspectives of other people. It requires that we unleash our passion for social justice rather than using our energy to compete with our colleagues for reputation and publication.

As teachers, all of us occupy positions of "power." We have the power to change not only our students' lives but our own. Our classrooms can be places for social transformation, but only if we teachers continually educate ourselves. Without the mentorship of a few teachers along the way I would not be receiving this award today. The seed for *This Bridge Called My Back* came to me in the mid-seventies in a graduate English class taught by a "white" male professor at the University of Texas, Austin. As a seventh-generation Chicana American born on this side of the border I felt invisible, alienated from the gringo university, and dissatisfied with both el movimiento chicano and the feminist movement. I resisted academic assimilation by using writing to confront my frustrations and make sense of my experiences. Writing most of my papers in an autobiographical politically-engaged voice rather than the dispassionate, disembodied language of academic discourse pushed on graduate students did not endear me to my professors. When one of my "white" male professors championed my writing his teaching makes all the difference.

This year *This Bridge Called My Back* celebrates its twentieth anniversary. I am happy to announce that Third Woman Press is issuing its third edition. The motivating force for putting *This Bridge* together is still the same twenty years later—the fact that there were few articles about women of color or educators who discussed the existence of women-of-color. There were no books like *This Bridge Called My Back* or *Borderlands / La Frontera*. There are few books like *this bridge we call home*, an anthology AnaLouise Keating and I have just finished editing and which Routledge is publishing next year. The reason I edit and write books today is in part due to the lack of pertinent materials in the classes and universities I attended. A writer writes about what she or he wants to learn. Similarly, a teacher teaches what she or he needs to learn. Transformation does not happen unless we explore what threatens us as teachers and students; what we sweep under our desks; what we silence; what we're angry about; what causes us anxiety; what brings us into open conflict and disagreement; and what cultural prescriptions and cultural teachings we're rebelling against. The shadow of American Studies hides under these desconocimientos, as do our individual shadow beasts.

When we experience boundary shifts, border violations, bodily penetrations, identity confusions, a flash of conocimiento (understanding) may sear us, shocking us into a new way of reading the world. I urge us to look at the underbelly of American Studies, to recognize its shadow beast, confront its fictions, and examine its practice of desconocimientos—of ignoring what it as a collective body does not want to know.

It requires courage to carve out a separate distinct eye/perspective from the field we're in, particularly when we're dependent upon it, me on you teaching my books, you for your paychecks. It requires nerve to explore the discipline's unsavory aspects, its unaddressed issues and underlying conflicts. It takes courage to tear the field apart and reconstruct it. Let's challenge each other to examine, in our classrooms, our own inherited or acquired privileges, our social positions, and to take responsibility for our assumptions about people who are different from us. Let's challenge each other to spread conocimiento (knowledge). The power to act and make choices is the only power we have. I invite all of you to become academic activists and join women of color in exploring developing peace, spiritual, and social movements, and in bringing about social change. Let us teach our students to become world citizens and move at ease among diverse cultures, countries, and customs.

Contigo en la lucha,
Gloria E. Anzaldúa
November 9, 2001

Throughout much of her adult life, Anzaldúa felt particularly close to Yemayá, the Yoruban orisha (goddess) associated with the oceans and other waters. Anzaldúa's house in Santa Cruz was located about one block from the Pacific Ocean. Almost every day Anzaldúa took a long walk along the ocean, on West Cliff Drive. This previously unpublished poem, last revised in January 2001, reflects Anzaldúa's intimate relationship with the ocean Yemayá.

# Yemayá

I come to you, Yemayá,
ocean mother, sister of the fishes.
I stop at the edge of your lip
where you exhale your breath on the beach—
into a million tiny geysers.
With your white froth I anoint my brow and cheeks,
wait for your white-veined breasts to wash through me.

Yemayá, your tongues lick me,
your green mouths nibble my feet.
With your brine I inhale the beginnings of life.
Your silver tongues hiss then retreat
leaving hieroglyphs and silence on the sand.

Take me with you, Yemayá.
Let me ride your flaking tortoise shell,
dance with your serpents and your seals.
Let me roar down the marble cliffs of your shoulders
varooming into waterfalls—
chipping into a million emeralds!

Beached at the edge of your lilac skirt,
you lay driftwood, a feather, a shell at my feet.
Your silver tongues hiss then retreat.
I wipe the salt spray from my face.
Yemayá, ocean mother,
I take you home in a bottle.
Tonight I will sleep on your rolling breasts.
Esta noche sueño contigo.

What did Anzaldúa think about the impact of *This Bridge Called My Back*? Did she feel that it transformed feminist movement? And how did her own views change over the years? This short essay, first published in 2002 as the foreword to *this bridge we call home: radical visions for transformation*, addresses these questions, among others. As the word (un)natural, with its prefix in parentheses, might suggest, Anzaldúa both affirms and questions her earlier bridging strategies. She also expands her theories of new tribalism and nepantleras and insists on the role of imagination in effecting social change.

# (Un)natural bridges, (Un)safe spaces

At sunset I walk along the bluffs gazing at the shifting sea, a hammered sheet of silver. A full moon rises over the cliffs of Natural Bridges like an opalescent ball. Under my feet pressure and heat are continuously changing the layers of sedimentary rock formed 100,000 years ago. It took the waves thousands of years to cut out a remnant headlands and thousands more to wear holes or arches through its flanks and shape three stone bridges. Year after year these same waves expanded the arches until the weight of the overlying rock collapsed the outermost bridge twenty-one years ago. In a few seconds the 1989 Loma Prieta earthquake brought down the innermost bridge. Today only the middle one remains, a lone castle-like seastack with an arched hole for an eye.

Whenever I glimpse the arch of this bridge my breath catches. Bridges are thresholds to other realities, archetypal, primal symbols of shifting consciousness. They are passageways, conduits, and connectors that connote transitioning, crossing borders, and changing perspectives. Bridges span liminal (threshold) spaces between worlds, spaces I call nepantla,[1] a Náhuatl word meaning tierra entre medio. Transformations occur in this in-between space, an unstable, unpredictable, precarious, always-in-transition space lacking clear boundaries. Nepantla es tierra desconocida, and living in this liminal zone means being in a constant state of displacement—an uncomfortable, even alarming feeling. Most of us dwell in nepantla so much of the time it's become a sort of "home." Though this state links us to other ideas, people, and worlds, we feel threatened by these new connections and the change they engender. I think of how feminist ideas and movements are attacked, called unnatural by the ruling powers when in fact they are ideas whose time has come, ideas as relentless as the waves carving and later eroding stone arches. Change is inevitable, no bridge lasts forever.

I used to cross a trestle bridge near the Boardwalk until a winter storm demolished it. Recently I watched the workers rebuild this historic landmark, leaving intact some of the original foundation but supporting it with heavy buttresses and integrating it with other new materials. In this bridge we call home: radical visions for transformation we've taken the model provided by This Bridge Called My Back and given it a new shape—hopefully without compromising the inherent character and structure of the original. Every generation that reads This Bridge Called My Back rewrites it. Like the trestle bridge, and other things that have reached their zenith, it will decline unless we attach it to new growth or append new growth to it. this bridge we call home is our attempt to continue the dialogue, rethink the old ideas, and germinate new theories. In these pages we move from focusing on what has been done to us (victimhood) to a more extensive level of agency, one which questions what we're doing to each other, to those in distant countries, and to the earth's environment. The knowledge that we are in symbiotic relationship to all that exists and co-creators of ideologies—attitudes, beliefs, and cultural values—motivates us to act collaboratively.

As swells break against the Santa Cruz mudstone promontories I feel that we who struggle for social change are the waves cutting holes in the rock and erecting new bridges. We're loosening the grip of outmoded methods and ideas in order to allow new ways of being and acting to emerge, but we're not totally abandoning the old—we're building on it. We're reinforcing the foundations and support beams of the old puentes, not just giving them new paint jobs. While trying to hold fast to the rights feminists, progressives, and activists have carved out for us with their fingernails, we also battle those who are trying to topple both old and new bridges.

Twenty-one years ago we struggled with the recognition of difference within the context of commonality. Today we grapple with the recognition of commonality within the context of difference. While This Bridge Called My Back displaced whiteness, this bridge we call home carries this displacement farther. It questions the terms "white" and "women of color" by showing that whiteness may not be applied to all whites, as some possess women-of-color-consciousness, just as some women of color bear white consciousness. This book intends to change notions of identity, viewing it as part of a more complex system covering a larger terrain, and demonstrating that the politics of exclusion based on traditional categories diminishes our humanness.

Today categories of race and gender are more permeable and flexible than they were for those of us growing up in the pre-1980s. *this bridge we call home* invites us to move beyond separate and easy identifications, creating bridges that cross race and other classifications among different groups via intergenerational dialogue. Rather than legislating and restricting racial identities it tries to make them more pliant. The personal and cultural narratives are not disinterested, objective questionings of identity politics but impassioned and conflicted engagements in resistance. They show the ruptures y los desconocimientos (ignored knowledge) around identity issues, revealing how much has shifted in the last twenty years, but also how little has changed. In our efforts to rethink the borders of race, gender, and identity, we must guard against creating new binaries.

Expanding on *This Bridge Called My Back* we incorporate additional underrepresented voices such as those of transgendered people, Arab-, and South Asian/Indian- Americans. We attempt to break the impasse between women of color and other groups. By including women and men of different "races," nationalities, classes, sexualities, genders, and ages we complicate the debates within feminist theory both inside and outside the academy and inside and outside the U.S. Gathering people from many geographies in a multicultural approach is a mark of inclusivity, increased consciousness, and dialogue. This inclusivity reflects the hybrid quality of our lives and identities — todas somos nos/otras. Living in multicultural communities and the complexities of our age demand we develop a perspective that takes into account the whole planet.

Our goal is not to use differences to separate us from others, but neither is it to gloss over them. Many of us identify with groups and social positions not limited to our ethnic, racial, religious, class, gender, or national classifications. Though most people self-define by what they exclude, we define who we are by what we include — what I call the new tribalism. Though most of us live entremundos, between and among worlds, we are frustrated by those who step over the line, by hybridities and ambiguities, and by what does not fit our expectations of "race" and sex.

I fear that many mujeres de color will not want whites or males to be contributors in our book. We risk their displeasure. It would have been easier for AnaLouise and me to limit the dialogue to women of color. Many women of color are possessive of *This Bridge Called My Back* and view it as a safe space, as "home." But there are no safe spaces. "Home" can be unsafe and dangerous because it bears the likelihood of intimacy and thus thinner boundaries. Staying "home" and not venturing out from our own group comes from woundedness and stagnates our growth. To bridge means loosening our borders, not closing off to others. Bridging is the work of opening the gate to the stranger, within and without. To step across the threshold is to be stripped of the illusion of safety because it moves us into unfamiliar territory and does not grant safe passage. To bridge is to attempt community, and for that we must risk being open to personal, political, and spiritual intimacy, to risk being wounded. Effective bridging comes from knowing when to close ranks to those outside our home, group, community, nation, and when to keep the gates open.

Sometimes we feel most unsafe with people of our own group. On September 11 as I listened to the rhetoric of retaliation and war, I realized it masked feelings of bewilderment, sorrow, and fear—the U.S. borders of "safety" had been violated and many people could no longer see our country the same way. Rather than reflect on this arrebato (breach), some of us screamed for revenge. I recalled the internal strife flaring up months earlier in the postings of the listserv we set up for our contributors. I think the listserv conflict also masked feelings of fear—this supposedly safe space was no longer safe. The contentious debates among Palestinian women and Jews of Latina, Native, and European ancestry churned a liquid fire in our guts.

Conflict with its fiery nature can trigger transformation depending on how we respond to it. Often delving deeply into instead of fleeing from it can bring an understanding (conocimiento) that will turn things around. In some of the responses to the heated discussions I saw genuine attempts to listen and respect all sides. With generous conciliatory responses a few contributors tried to heal las rajaduras split open by mistrust, suspicions, and dualisms. Where others saw borders these nepantleras saw links; where others saw abysses, they saw bridges spanning those abysses. For nepantleras to bridge is an act of will, an act of love, an attempt toward compassion and reconciliation, and a promise to be present with the pain of others without losing themselves to it.

A bridge, such as this book, is not just about one set of people crossing to the other side; it's also about those on the other side crossing to this side. And ultimately, it's about doing away with demarcations like "ours" and "theirs." It's about honoring people's otherness in ways that allow us to be changed by embracing that otherness rather than punishing others for having a different view, belief system, skin color, or spiritual practice. Diversity of perspectives expands and alters the dialogue, not in an add-on fashion but through a multiplicity that's transformational, such as in mestiza consciousness. To include whites is not an attempt to restore the privilege of white writers, scholars, and activists; it is a refusal to continue walking the color line. To include men (in this case, feminist-oriented males) is to collapse the gender line. These inclusions challenge conventional identities and promote more expansive configurations of identities—some of which will soon become cages and have to be dismantled.

The anthology we originally conceived was even more inclusionary. The challenge AnaLouise and I faced was to be as inclusive as possible within the page/word limitation set by our publisher. Due to the current economics in the book industry and the subsequent conviction that teachers would not include a big and pricey book in their syllabi, we had to reduce our original 1,300-page manuscript to 850 pages, the original 108 pieces to 80, and the 113 contributors to 87. In order to keep our commitment to all our contributors we moved an entire section into a second book, one on telling stories and bearing witness. Making these changes took more time and energy than we expected. We agonized over the cuts. Lengthier pieces had to be trimmed and every piece tightened, a task we embraced with repugnance but also with dedication. What kept our shoulders to the task was our vision of empowering others, encouraging conocimiento (deep awareness), and striving for social justice.

For positive social change to occur we must imagine a reality that differs from what already exists. The wish to repair, to heal our wounds—what I call the Coyolxauhqui imperative—animates the creation of this book, our teaching, and activism. To treat the wounds and mend the rifts we must sometimes reject the injunctions of culture, group, family, and ego. Activism is the courage to act consciously on our ideas, to exert power in resistance to ideological pressure—to risk leaving home. Empowerment comes from ideas—our revolution is fought with concepts, not with guns, and it is fueled by vision. By focusing on what we want to happen we change the present. The healing images and narratives we imagine will eventually materialize.

Este libro celebra y encarna el espíritu y linaje of *This Bridge Called My Back*. With it we honor las luchadoras que nos dejaron un legado de protesta y activismo por medio de la pluma. Ours is the responsibility of marking the journey and passing on the torches and rituals left by those who have already crossed many types of bridges. The 87 voices in this collection transmit knowledge and wisdom, plant ideas in our minds, and initiate us into awareness, igniting the passion that sparks activism. We honor those whose backs are the bedrock we stand on, even as our shoulders become the ground for the generations that follow, and their bodies in turn will become the next layer of strata. Though we're aware of the danger of losing our individuality to the collective fires and the risking of our safe spaces, this undertaking empowers us to become sentinels, bearers of witness, makers of historias.

I descend down the steep bluffs to the tide pool terraces between sea and cliffs. Squatting, I stare at a sea anemone in a pocket of water on the pitted rock. Biologically, we are a single gene pool with minor variations and superficial cultural and genetic differences; we are interconnected with all life. I prod the anemone; it shudders and shakes, contracting into a protective ball. We all respond to pain and pleasure in similar ways. Imagination, a function of the soul, has the capacity to extend us beyond the confines of our skin, situation, and condition so we can choose our responses. It enables us to re-imagine our lives, rewrite the self, and create guiding myths for our times. As I walk back home along the cliffs, a westerly wind buffeting my back, the crashing breakers scour the shoulders of the bluffs slowly hewing out keyholes, fledgling bridges in the making.

Gloria E. Anzaldúa,
November 2001

1. I use the word *nepantla* to theorize liminality and to talk about those who facilitate passages between worlds, whom I've named nepantleras. I associate nepantla with states of mind that question old ideas and beliefs, acquire new perspectives, change worldviews, and shift from one world to another.

Throughout her career but especially in the final two decades of her life, Anzaldúa often explored issues related to wounding and healing. This previously unpublished poem, last revised in August 2002, provides a glance into her exploration of the relationship between the two.

## Healing Wounds

I have been ripped wide open
by a word, a look, a gesture—
from self, kin, and stranger.
My soul jumps out
scurries into hiding
i hobble here and there
seeking solace
trying to coax it back home
but the me that's home
has become alien without it.
Wailing, i pull my hair
suck snot back and swallow it
place both hands over the wound
but after all these years
it still bleeds
never realizing that to heal
there must be wounds
to repair there must be damage
for light there must be darkness.

Also titled "Dreaming la Prieta" and "Los Entremados de PQ," this previously unpublished fiction story has undergone many changes and exists in many versions, stretching back to the 1970s when the protagonist was a man, named PQ, who was related to Andrea de la Cruz, the protagonist of "El paisano is a bird of good omen" (included in part 1). Anzaldúa was revising the version included here at the time of her passing; she planned to include "Reading LP" in *La Prieta, The Dark One*, her novel-in-stories, which she described in her writing notas as a book "about transformation and metamorphosis, about the relation between nature and culture, between humans and animals. The stories interweave the surreal, unconscious subreality of the inner world of thought, fantasy and dream and the world of the spirit with the everyday life. All converge at the liminal space I call nepantla, the interface space between all the worlds. Prieta experiences a sense of self that is and is not tied to time, space, or society. She experiences unusual events—a shamanistic event which awakens her, or a paranormal event where different realities converge. She undergoes a radical shift in the way of seeing the world, a coming-to-consciousness results in changes in her identity." I include this lengthy description because it so closely applies to Prieta's experience in this story.

## Reading LP

The splash. Her body slicing the water. Water backing up through her nostrils, hitting her throat. Her hands and arms thrashing en el agua. She can't swim. The shock of finding herself at the bottom of the irrigation canal pulses through her. A thump, her right hand hits the cement wall and pain shoots up her arm. She bounces up sputtering, coughing, gasping, and spewing out the putrid water. Through waterlogged lashes she sees the rim, her right hand shoots up to grab it. And misses. Her body slides down the cement, the sting of scraped skin on forearms and elbows.

She sinks back into dead leaves and water. Again she arches, reaching up, grabbing blindly for the rim. Again she misses. As she slides down the grainy side, a fingernail breaks off. Again she hurls her body up. Her fingers grasp the edge and cling, the weight of her body wrenching the muscles in her arm. She hoists her torso out, swings one leg over the rim, pulls her upper body onto it and balances on her stomach, the rim digging into her middle. Then she twists her body and rolls over onto the grass-covered ground.

Standing on shaky legs, she peers down at the ten foot deep canal. ¡Cagada! What the hell made her fall? The last thing she remembers is lying on her stomach on the patch of grass by the canal reading the book. She shakes her head and body and swings her arms around, scattering drops of water in the air. The clothes are plastered to her body. Already she feels the hot summer sun beginning to dry them. Groaning, she bends to pick up the book lying open on the grass. She thumbs through it, comes to the page she was last reading: ". . . wind ruffles and turns the pages. Like pale gray moths . . ." No answer there.

She gazes at la Tigra,* looks around at her patchwork of fields, pastures, lagoon, woods, culverts, ditches, and fences. Everything still here: windmill, barn, garage, corrals, and cows. She sees her work everywhere. La Tigra, the land she's plowed, planted, and mulched. La tierra that mothers her, feeds her, comforts her. The buildings and fences she's pounded, patched, and painted. The cows she milked, fed, and watered.

She turns to the ranch house, the two-hundred-year-old sprawling white frame house with wraparound porch, surrounded by tall mesquite trees. La cara de su casa, its size and shape holding the imprint of her forebears. She studies the landscape as she would a painting but she can't maintain the distance necessary to be merely an observer. She is embedded in it. To look at it is to look at herself. She could solve the mystery of what's just happened to her if only she could read the landscape, as if the land could give her a message through its feel, sounds, and smells.

Bo, her German shepherd, comes running up to her and sniffs her wet clothes. Boots swish sucking, and still trailing water, she staggers from the backyard to the house and up the porch steps. She props herself against the kitchen's outside wall. Tremors course through her body, chilling her. The sun filtering through las ramas de mesquite, leaves shifting, casting filigree patterns on her body. She sticks her finger in her ear and flicks out water. The strident sound of chicharras rushes into the silence and throbs in her head. She pushes herself off la pared, opens the screen door and enters the kitchen. She drops the book on the table and walks toward the dining room.

The room's doorway frames the living room door, and inside that frame is the full-length mirror on the opposite wall. Something about the layout stops her eye. As she walks toward it, she sees a slight dripping shape. It takes her a second to realize it's her own reflection. Though she's looked at these walls hundreds of times, this time algo feels different. She shivers, cold to her huesos.

As she walks toward the bathroom she's surprised at how the doorway de cada cuarto frames another doorway and that el espejo reflects two more doorways—those of the bedroom and bathroom.

* Anzaldúa's version of "Tigresa."

She tosses her clothes over the towel rack and, grabbing a used towel from the hamper, mops up the water on the floor. She showers quickly in water hot as she can stand. She rinses off the stagnant smells and gurgles out the taste of canal water. In the bathroom mirror, her cheekbones are stark against her washed-out face, her cropped hair sticks up in wet spikes. The white band on her forehead where her hat roosts looks paler. In the mirror she sees el espejo de la sala and all it reflects. Walls within walls and the spaces in between supported by beams and entremados. Putting on her blue comfortable but worn bathrobe, she pads barefoot to the kitchen. How did she fall into the canal?

The last thing she feels like is eating, but Bar-Su will be hungry. Out of the corner of her eye, she sees *the book* on the red-and-white gingham oil cloth. With half shrug, she opens the refrigerator, takes out tortillas, cucumber, tomato, onion, a jar of tahini butter, places them on the counter. Maybe some tea will sooth her nervios. She grabs a fistful of orange leaves from a paper sack and drops them into a pot of water then turns on the burner. She stares at the book, then places the honey bear, a quart of milk, and a cup on the counter by the stove. Her head cocks: tires crunching on gravel, car engine shuts off, a door slams, a shadow falls across the door, and then a tall woman enters, leather sandals squeaking.

"Hi, honey. I know, vengo tarde. What you up to?" says Bar-Su.

"Quiubo† corazón. I was just about to fix you something to eat. ¿Tienes hambre?" la Prieta asks, stretching to give the tall woman a smacking kiss on the lips.

"Sí, pero no por comida. What's this, LP, mi Prietita consentida con los ojos soñadores?" she says cupping LP's breasts, one in each hand, squeezing them, thumbs strumming nipples.

"Ay qué fresca. Those, I'll have you know, are my two best assets. Show some respect, ruca. I wanted to be ready, pa' no gastar tiempo. I'd pounce on you as you walked in, tear your clothes off in one swoop," says la Prieta, making a tearing sound. "And then we'd take a running dive into la cama."

"Oh, yeah? I'd say these are your best assets," the tall woman says, palms stroking then slowly rotating on LP's buttocks. "Your tetas aren't bad either, pero tu panocha y gusanito estan a toda madre," she whispers in Prieta's ear, putting her palm over Prieta's pubis and pressing down. "Forget the bed, we could fuchi-fuchi right here. . . ."

† Shortened, popular form for "Qué hubo."

Then looking intently into LP's face she says, "What's wrong?"

"I fell into the canal."

"Whoa, what did you say? You fell?"

"Yeah, it was really weird," says LP.

"Are you okay, honey? Here, let me look at you. Hey, you don't look so good."

LP glances at the book on the table. "Water got into my ear." She bends her head and hits the side of it against the edge of her hand.

"How'd you fall?"

"I don't know. One minute I was reading that book and the next I was at the bottom of the canal."

"But that's crazy," Bar-Su says. "I told you, el trabajo te está matando."

"Yeah, tell me about it."

"How'd you get out?"

"It wasn't easy."

"I wish you'd learn how to swim; dog paddling doesn't cut it, Prieta."

Prieta reaches for the whole wheat tortillas. Bar-Su swats her hands. "Deja eso," she says. "That healthy stuff may be good for you but it tastes awful. Here, I'll fix us some real Tex-Mex taquitos."

Bar-Su begins to clear the table. Picking up the book, she says, "You know, you spend more time with this book than you do with me. Every time I turn around it's in your hand."

"Something about it fascinates me. Besides I've got to write my paper, want to do good in school."

"Yeah, I know. What an eerie-looking cover," Bar-Su says.

They both stare at the black whirlpool disappearing into a light blue background.

"Where's the title? asks Bar-Su. "It's strange for a book cover not to have a title."

"That, querida, is one of the reasons I chose it for my paper. Besides . . . it *does* have a title. This glyph aquí represents words, only you have to know the language. It means 'entremados.' I had a hard time persuading el cabrón English prof to let me write my paper on it."

Bar-Su sits down and pulls LP onto her lap. LP leafs through the book with Bar-Su looking on.

"Who's that author? Never heard of him," says Bar-Su.

"I think the author's a her. The style and other stuff feels like a woman's. Or maybe I think the author is a woman because I'm reading like one."

"You mean you're projecting your stuff into the book?"

"Yeah. John Q . . . you remember him? You met him at Sabas Q's funeral. He lives by this book, says it's the best thing he's ever read and he's read everything. You've seen his house, it's a library; even the bathroom is full of books."

"Sounds familiar, ¿eh? Well, John Q's a queer one. But then they're all locos, your cousins. Does it by any chance run in your family?" she asks jerking the book out of LP's hands and putting it on the window sill. She clasps her arms around Prieta.

"My family's swimming in two dollar bills. Y tu familia doesn't like that a whole lot," LP says, looking into her novia's eyes. "Can you stay tonight?"

"Why? So I can wait for you to do your chores then read this book yet again and then fall into bed exhausted never noticing if I'm in bed with you?"

"Don't start, Bar-Su. I don't have the energy for it."

"Sorry, babe. I can't stay anyway. Mi pobre madrecita—I couldn't get Joe to stay with her tonight. I can't leave her alone. What if she has another stroke while you and I are here fucking? Or while I'm thinking of fucking and you're reading this book."

LP scrunches her face, then, catching the look in Bar-Su's eyes, says, "Hey, hon, I do want to spend more special time with you. Really. And your brothers should take more responsibility with your mother. I want a live-in lover, not a part-time one."

An hour later after they've eaten, Bar-Su is sitting on the wide backporch swing, one foot pushing it back and forth. LP's head is propped across her middle. LP looks at the western sky, its faint streaks of purple and orange. Then she picks up the book and reads a passage aloud.

"There's something weird about this book. You heard how the main character falls into a lake?"

"So? I wish you'd stop reading that thing."

"Well, words from this book were running in my head when I fell into the canal. I think John Q. gave me this book for a reason."

Bar-Su sits up and looks at her. "I don't think I like what I think you're saying."

"You're not the only one! It was creepy, Bar-Su. I lost track of . . . well, me, for a few minutes. It was like I'd stepped out of time. I don't know where I went. I mean I, me, this self that I am sort of got lost. Maybe it was just for a few seconds. No, don't look like that."

"Now where are you going?"

"Gotta fix the fence," says LP. "The cattle will get out and I'll spend all day tomorrow rounding them up."

She goes out to the shed, straps on the staple gun and hammer, puts on her work gloves and picks up the posthole digger. She strings barbed wire, stapling it to the posts. When it grows too dark to see she turns on the lights attached to the tall railroad ties encircling the homestead's perimeter and continues working for another hour.

At midnight Barbara-Susana stands up and paces from one end of the wrap-around porch to the other. The chicharra's shrill sounds drown the sound of her footsteps on the creaking wood. "I'm getting pretty tired of how you're always so busy with la siembra and school and now this. When you're with me you're not really with me."

"I know, hon, I really do. I am trying to do better."

"That's what you always say." After a few minutes of silence Bar-Sue jumps off the porch and leaves behind a shower of gravel.

LP stands and stares at the plume of dust rising behind the taillights' reddish tingle, listens to the shushing sounds of leaves as the wind works through them. She flips off the high-powered lights in the yard and corrals. Everything is pitch black.

Book in hand, she walks into the house and to the bedroom where she falls into bed and starts reading. As she reaches the last page, she hears the bantam rooster crowing from the skeletal ebony tree. Stretching and yawning she looks at the clock, 2:31 a.m. Shit! two hours eaten up by the book. Dos pinches horas and where was she all that time?

La luz de la luna slipping in through Venetian blind slats cuts vertical strips across her body. The rest of the room is dark. She falls asleep. When she wakes, her breathing is shallow. The cool perspiration on her bare body has roused her out of a dream. En el sueño una mujer in a familiar landscape is inside a hollow, gutted, round book. The giant cover flapped open and shut, open and shut. As her right thumb prods her ear, LP becomes aware of the pain in her left side and turns over. She loses the rest of the dream and slips into sleep once more.

She wakes up at about 5:00. The first thing she thinks of es el libro. Time to get her ass out of bed and start her chores.

She walks out to the cotton fields and checks the plants for insects, blights, rusts, smuts, wilts, rots, and fungi. She bends down and palms a handful of dirt. Feels the soil, rubs it between her fingers: Is it too coarse and gritty, too silty and clay-like? Maybe she should test the pH. Maybe in the fall she'll sow some green manuring. Yeah, plant alfalfa or clover right here, then plow it under while still tender and young. Return the crop to the soil for decomposition, give the land back the nutrients she's taken from it. And hope the wind won't blow away the top soil. Uh huh, she'll cultivate a rich layer of humus. She'll borrow a chisel plow, maybe one with straight shanks, go in deep and break up the compacted subsoil. Or maybe she should just stubble mulch.

At lunch, she goes to the family plot and sprawls on a grave under the shade of a copse of mesquite trees. After she eats her papas con chorizo in flour tortillas and drinks her thermos of iced tea, she walks up and down looking at the headstones, reading the names of the people who had left their signature on the land but whose bodies had years since moldered into dust. Weather and erosion had dulled the names and dates carved in stone. Her mother and brother stopped tending the cemetery years ago. When she bought their parcels, the dead became hers, too. She bends down over her mamagrande's grave and straightens the wreath of cempazúchitl flowers, its orange blossoms beginning to fade. Hoof-and-mouth disease and unpaid taxes did her grandmother in, forcing her to sell a big chunk of the land in order to keep a few hundred acres. Her roots, her history. As she walks among the graves she treads a moving current. She is part of a continuum. She doesn't own the land, it owns her. She is its caretaker. She was supposed to marry and leave her home. Not for women their homeland. Andrea, another Prieta, had been forced to leave . . . or had chosen to leave. But not LP. She refuses.

She takes the book out of her lunch bag. She'll read a few minutes then go back to work.

Finishing the afternoon chores she returns home to get something to eat and make a few calls. When she hangs up the phone, she picks up the book. Antes de que se de cuenta, she's read the book from cover to cover. Read the whole thing without stopping. Where in the hell does she go when she's reading? She's not here, that's for sure. She looks outside through the window, gauging how low the sun's sunk, then she looks at her watch. ¡Jíjole! This time it took her only an hour and forty-five minutes to finish the book, less time than before. She pokes her ear with her finger then places the same hand on the sheet-rock wall. Its cool solidity reassures her. But it's not that solid, there are the hollow spaces, entremados, between the walls. She could stick her head through it.

Next morning she wakes muttering, "gotta get away from that book." She pushes her fist through the sleeve of her faded denim jacket, the one with the tawny embroidered jaguar on its top left pocket, and shoves bare feet into her scuffed boots. Semi-naked, she strides out into the backyard. Breathing in the cool morning smells, she peers into the rosy sky looking for the rising sun. Mist envelops the top of the mesquites and brings a chill to her bare legs. The fog from the lagoon hovers over the tractor, shed, and shrubs. She watches dawn dissolve the night mist and gradually shroud the tree and rooftops. The sun is a diffused yellow light.

Her eyes track Bo trotting across the field. She whistles. The dog stops, raises his head, cocks his ears, and runs toward her. He leaps up to lick her face and then bounds away, wanting a game of catch. LP runs after him, bare legs pumping, blood surging. Bo turns around and jumps her; she falls and rolls around, hugging him. Cool hard ground, dew-wet dog smell, warm panting breath, rasping tongue on her face. She buries her face in his fur, blocking out the sun. When she comes up for air, the dog shakes his body, dispersing drops of water like pollen in the wind.

"When was the last time I gave you a bath?" she asks, cuffing the dog's head. "Enough, Bo. Time to work, now. Ándale, go, go, go. Vámonos, round up the cows."

The dog lopes quickly across the cowpen. With short, mock-angry barks, he dashes in and out among the cows, nipping at their shanks. A slow-moving, heavy-uddered Guernsey lumbers toward her. Prieta swings the corral door open, the bottom scraping the ground. She spreads silage in the trough and as la vaca lowers her head to it, she picks up the stool, puts it down near the cow's rear, and straddles it. She leans her forehead against the cow's shank and places her right hand on the gaunt hip bone, listens to the intestines gurgling and the tail switching off flies. With a moist rag she wipes the udders clean and begins wringing milk from las chichis. The milk sputters and hisses as it hits the bucket. The smell of warm milk engulfs her. Shoving the stool back, she kneels on the ground, lips and mouth reaching for a tit. Her tongue and palate pull the milk into her mouth and throat. She wonders what it would be like to suck milk from Bar-Su's breasts.

She goes to the feed bins and scatters corn for the chickens. After cleaning out the cow pen with a fork, she shovels the manure into a wheelbarrel and pushes it to the orchard where she spreads it around the trees. She no longer minds the stink of ammonia from the cow pies, but she hates cleaning out the pig pen. She finishes repairing the windmill pump and hurries through the rest of her morning chores. She's done them thousands of times. Daily rituals.

LP drops her gloves on the ground and bends over the sink pump over the trough. She works the handle up and down; when the water gushes out she splashes cold water over her neck and arms.

She gets into her pickup truck and heads into town, making a list as she drives: feedstore, post office, grocery and hardware stores. Behind her she leaves twin plumes of rising dust and sounds of tire sucking sand and gravel. The fresh breeze coming off the green fields feels good against her short wet hair.

Returning from her errands, LP approaches her ranch from the west entrance. She stops, jumps out of the pickup and unlocks the gate tied to the center post. The sign hanging above the entrance to her ranch is swinging on its chains in the wind. LP stretches up, her fingers trace the words *El Rancho la Tigra* carved into the belly of a wooden jaguar. One of her abuelos had named el rancho *El Tigre* after the Mexican jaguars that crossed into south Texas from Mexico. Neither her brothers nor her mother had wanted to pay the back taxes to hold onto the land. LP had. She changed the ranch's gender to go with hers.

LP opens la puerta de la cerca, gets back in her pickup, drives through. She stops, turns off the engine, jumps out again and swings the gate shut. Bringing two fingers of the right hand to her straw hat, LP salutes the plastic snake curled around the top of the post. How like Bar-Su to enshrine the gate she calls "LP's altar" with a plastic snake. That was three years ago. They've been novias for four years.

She leans her back against the thick log for a minute and thinks about her crops and how or where she can steal a few hours away from them to give Bar-Su. "Here I am again, mi tigra. Venga por favor, dueña de la tierra, show yourself, madre mía. Once more I call on you. No, I don't want you to send this land rain. Help me figure out what's happening to me. If you could only send me a small sign—anything that would point me in the right direction."

She continues in a sing-song voice for a few minutes, then gets back into the pickup, pulls into the backyard, backs up to the shed door, un-latches and pulls down the tailgate, and unloads the feed bags. Dropping her boots on the porch she goes in. She pops the Vangelis Papathanassiou tape into the cassette player, and the sounds of "Can You Hear the Dogs Barking?" pulse throughout the house and yard from both the inside and outside speakers.

It's almost dusk, yet the temperature is still in the mid 90s. She walks outside and watches the ruddy blaze in the western horizon and the orange glow on the road and fences.

LP plops down, belly up onto the grass under el palo verde, sinking into its pungent smell. The ground's coolness soothes her; the tension drops from her shoulders. As the music quickens its tempo, she rises and begins to whirl around, clicking her feet together in the air. She must really be crazy to dance in this heat—and the evening chores to get done. The air seems thick enough to sustain her weight for slow seconds, there between earth and sky. When she was twelve she dreamed of going to Paris to study dance. But of course her legacy was heavy boots, grease, and green growing plants.

She twirls around the graves of el camposanto, weaving in and out among them, startling the sparrows in the dark-green ebony trees. She breathes in the hot evening air fragrant with the smell of dry earth. The sky reels as she dances, the light dims gradually amidst the ear-splitting sound of chicharras and Bo barking in the distance. Distracted by an image from the book, she stumbles and falls as the last orange band finally sinks into the horizon. She lies there, blinking into the darkness, seeing a glowing bed of coals, feeling the light breeze fanning them. She sees herself adding pieces of paper to a fire, sees herself watching the fire consume them. This image slowly fades.

That night, just as sleep begins overtaking her, her knee jerks and she resurfaces, sinks and surfaces. Her hand reaches toward the night table. Reading often puts her to sleep. *Why do I feel this compulsion to read the book again?* Something in it bothers her, but she doesn't know what, —and that bothers her more. It takes her even less time than before to read the entire book—an hour and a half. The image of the bed of coals in the book is slightly different from the one she saw that afternoon. In going from the printed word in the book to the words in her mind, the events and people in the book change in subtle ways. Or is it she who subtly changes? Yeah, she thinks, that would make a good topic for the Lit Crit paper: the intrusion of the fiction. Except the intrusion doesn't seem to stop when she closes the book's covers. The book is a trigger of some sort. Suddenly she is afraid again.

"¡Íjíjole!" She flings the book across the room, it slides across the floor. She's more awake than ever. Damn. She remembers Mrs. McAlastair, her preschool teacher, reading aloud from a book. She can't remember the book or its topic. Just that every time Mrs. McAlastair read it, something would draw LP to look out the window. She'd stare at the green field bordered by blue bonnet, the wind bending their fragile stems. LP wanted to be out there on the lush grass, but she wanted to take Mrs. McAlastair and the dream her words created with her. The wind whispering the words just beneath Mrs McAlastair's voice. Then something would shift, like a string snapping, and LP would turn back to Mrs. McAlastair sitting at her desk. And now thirty years later it was happening again.

LP stretches and turns to look out the window, hand reaching for the light and finds herself between two walls. Se halla entre paredes. ¡Epa! Keep calm. Taking deep breaths, she pictures each plane and partition of the house she designed and built with the help of her primas. Click. The light is on and she's back and the house is itself again.

"¡Chingao!"‡ Gotta move the bed away from this wall, it's too close— but she doesn't know what it's too close to. Even now, she feels the book calling. She looks around the room, then shoves and pulls the bed against la otra pared. As she's shifting the night table, she stubs her toes against the book. She grasps her injured foot and topples the floor lamp.

By the time she runs the vacuum over the brighter patches where the bed and table used to be, light is streaking in through the curtains. 5 a.m. and morning chores. She straightens the framed snapshots of her mother, brothers, and assorted familiares on top of the dresser. She takes one last glance at the new arrangement, then walks into the kitchen. Wolfing down a tortilla with cheese, beans, and salsa, she walks out into the coral light.

After the morning chores she pulls on her gloves, puts diesel in the gas tank, and rouses the cranky tractor. She backs it to the discs, hooks them up, and drives to the edge of her north forty. Lowering the fluorescent green discs, she begins to turn the sod. Behind the slow-moving tractor a ribbon of the dark plowed ground flattens the weeds, leaving a cleared, smooth surface that will give the harvesters easier access to the crop. She watches the black tierra turn and the birds following the plow seeking the worms exposed by the discs. A tendril from her mind locks into the familiar task. Tierra y sol. Soon the unrelenting sun and tractor roar empty her brain of all thought.

Sometime later she surfaces, dazed. Why has she stopped discing? How long has she been stopped, shaking with the tractor's idling vibrations? She catches the tail end of a scene, a woman on her hands and knees in the mud, rain pelting her body. Ay diosita, not another scene from the book. Her arms and legs turn weak and sweat breaks across her forehead. She shakes her head, trying to shake loose the scene. She may be that woman.

‡ Popular form of "chingado."

It may rain soon, the crops would be ruined. Stop it! She's letting her fear get ahead of herself.

She lurches off the tractor and walks around, trying to find her legs. She pauses, rubs scuffed boots against disced earth, bends, picks up some dirt. Straightening, she rubs it between her fingers testing the texture: Rich, loamy. She sniffs it. Not too much hydrogen. She forces herself back up on the tractor, finishes the discing, then heads back to the house.

At home she pulls off her sweat-stiffened jeans and, in shirt and boots, goes out behind the shed to finish patching la cerca. If she could get away with it she'd never wear clothes. Too confining. But the work is hard on her body, she needs the denim for protection.

She finds herself in the bathroom not knowing how or when she got there. A remnant of memory flashes and disappears like fish in the water. In the mirror she sees red-rimmed eyes and a face darkened with dirt. She removes her cap. Her hair is matted to her head, the white line on her forehead in stark contrast to her red neck. She strips off the shirt sticking to her. Doubled over the sink, she is aware of the compactness of her body, bones, muscles, skin. No, she contains her body. Her body holds her in, her skin protects her from zancudos y mosquitos y el sol. But her skin doesn't keep out. . . . She rinses her face, then stares at the water swirling and gurgling down the drain. She gropes for the nearest towel, pats her face, and digs her thumbs into her ears. What the hell is going on?

She goes into the bedroom for a nap but can't sleep. Pinche libro. She rolls to the edge of the bed, lowers her head to the floor, and peers underneath. Despite her resolution not to get near the book again, she hauls it out and lets it fall open at the beginning. Picking a line at random, she begins to read.

Seventy-five minutes later she reaches the last sentence. She's beginning to realize why she feels a compulsion to read this book over and over. The book is about. . . . Gotta hide it. Maybe if it's out of sight the compulsion to read it won't kick in. She glances around the room, picks a place, and hides the book.

Just as she's drifting into sleep she hears a woman's voice saying softly: "When you read fiction you enter its reality. When it's compelling enough it will enter your reality."

Chinga tu madre! Where's the voice coming from? She bolts out of bed and, head first, dives under it. El libro, ¿en dónde lo escondió? She crawls out from under la cama and starts rummaging through her chest of drawers. El altar, she thinks—I hid it in the compartment under the altar.

She picks up a writing tablet and, with the book in her hands, goes out to the back porch and sits on the swing. She looks at the sky, hoping not to see the clouds that come before the dark thick clouds of rain. The book opens to page 3: "Yesterday the book fell open when I dropped it onto the kitchen table . . ." LP rocks and creaks for an hour through the hot afternoon reading the book. With her tongue between her teeth she sits hunched over the writing tablet scratching across the yellow lines.

Afterwards she again decides to hide it. This time in the shed. In the back of the steel shelf, by the calendar of the adelita with a bugle in her hand, the low bodice, the exposed thighs. LP goes outside. The afternoon feels ponderous, oppressive. She looks at the broad flat landscape all around her, then up at the sky. Dark clouds.

Chingao. Suffocating humidity. Sure sign of a big weather change. Looks like it'll rain soon. Rain, rain, por favor go away. The squash and watermelons would rot where they lay. Just last month she'd been praying for rain, hoping not to have to pay $300 an acre to irrigate. No hurricanes, okay? she tells the Jaguar rain god. Not until all the hay is baled.

She empties out the stock tank, cleans it with a broom, hoses it down and refills it. She tosses off her sweat-stiffened canvas gloves, goes to the sink pump outside and dunks her head under the cold gushing water.

Going inside, she makes tuna sandwiches which she downs with big gulps of lemonade straight from the two-quart jar. She's tired. Beyond tired. She sits down on the porch swing for a few minutes and makes a mental list of all the chores yet to do this week.

She wakes up on the porch swing. She's dreamed every scene in the book—all compacted into a few minutes of dream time. But this time it's different—this time she held onto herself, remembered who she was for a few seconds. She wasn't totally lost in. . . . whatever/wherever she was. If only she could remember it all! But she'd never had good recall—never could memorize anything, not even the ballads of García Lorca which her former lover Llosí adored so much. Llosí her first heartbreak. Llosí of the slightly dazed look who had married LP's primo. While LP wrote love poems to Llosí, her husband wrote love poems to Prieta. Prieta had been almost tempted when he'd suggested a three-way. Now Prieta realizes why—she'd been as captivated by him as Llosí had been. Now finally she could admit it. But being a part-time student, full-time marimacha, and a sembradora with two hundred acres to farm in the back monte of the southernmost tip of Tejas left her no time to experiment with yet another type of relationship. It was hard enough being una de las otras. She had more than enough in her hands trying to cope with Bar-Su's family, so resistant to queers.

Later she finds herself sitting on an idling tractor listening to the same voice reciting passages from the book . . . When she comes to, she is almost done with the baling. Ese libro desgraciado me va a volver loca. Y este pinche sol. She curses the book, the sun, the cost of the tractor, the baler, water, seed, gasoline, and state land and school taxes. She takes out her taquitos and thermos of decaf con leche.

When she finishes baling she drives the tractor back to the garage. She pulls the long iron pipe attached to the round smooth socket, and unhooks the baler from the tractor all the while praying, Please don't let it rain, mi tigra. Weather prone to sudden changes in South Texas.

Bo runs up to her, barking. Exhausted, she stumbles into the kitchen with Bo leaning his shoulder against her leg. She washes up, grabs a container of yogurt and a bag of granola, and plumps down at the kitchen table with a box of papers. She'll do some bookkeeping, write out checks for the farm bills, and if there is time, she'll read up on the new developments with fertilizers in this month's issue of Farm and Ranch.

She falls onto her bed, exhausted—just a little nap. But sleep is nudged out again and again. Just as she's about to go under, her hand reaches out for Bar-Su on the other side of the bed, but comes back empty. Don't, don't you dare reach for that book again. You know what Bar-Su will say, that you're addicted to reading that damn book. Palms moist, she gets up, goes out to the shed, finds the feed sack, and takes out the book. She comes back and flops down on the living room couch. Before she knows it she's reading the first sentence: "A tall woman enters, 'Hi, what you up to?'"

An hour later: she has re-read todo el pinche libro. Each reading takes less time than the one before. Flinging the book against the wall she hurries outside to feed the animals, milk the cow, and gather the eggs.

Prieta se va de un chore to another, trying to beat the encroaching darkness. But the shadows fatten. She stops, watches the sun sink into the earth leaving smears of orange, amber, and bronze across the horizon. Thin pinpoints of light begin to appear in the sky. The cicadas intensify their shrill cacophony. The more intently she listens to the sounds the louder they grow.

She turns on the shed light and fiddles with the jacked-up Ford. Diosa mía, marooned at the farm with her chariot of the rusting fenders. As she runs the red rag over her greasy hands she mentally tallies her property, which will for sure get repossessed if it rains. The haymaker, sweeper, haycutter, tractor, cotton picker: total worth $100,000. The corn harvester belongs to her cousin. Si se da la cosecha she'll trade in the old tractor for a newer model, one with air-conditioning.

She lowers the jack, pulls it out from under, and tosses it into the tool-box in back of the pickup. She turns the key but the engine won't turn over. ¡Chinpiotes! Now she can't go over to her novia's house. Bar-Su can come to her only on Wednesday afternoons and Saturday nights anyway. Chinga tu madre. What a hypochondriac—she's sick all the time. *Haven't I been understanding? Damn right. I've been a saint not bugging Bar-Su. Una santa. Of course, Bar-Su's right—if she came more often I wouldn't have time for her. Well, así es la vida.*

She raises the pick-up's hood, checks the battery cables, then sits on the ground. She falls back and, supine, slowly wiggles her body under la troca.

Feeling a cramp in her hand, she looks down and finds she's been grip-ping the wrench too tightly. She must have lain there a long time, immo-bile, displaced out of herself.

She scuttles out from underneath the truck, stands up and stares at her small calloused hands and the black grease oozing between her fingers. Tiene miedo. Again while under the truck she'd heard a voice. This time it sounded like water racing along a river. Images had appeared, then were swept away by the rushing water. That's all she remembers.

Pero no es nada. Nothing's happened to her. El mal aire le había en-trado, es todo. Something had entered her body. Algo le había entrado. Possessed by some spirit. The spirit of the book? Naw, libros don't have spirits. Do they? A curandera could suck whatever it was out of her body. And the fear along with it.

"Jefita, where are you?" Pedro, her hired hand, gets out of his troca and comes toward her. She didn't even hear him drive into the yard.

"Quiúbole§ jefa, vine a ver si quieres que trabaje mañana. You have work for me tomorrow?"

"No, no te voy a necesitar. I'll be using the tractor so I won't need you until Monday. Quiero que comiences muy de mañanita."

She notices that he's eyeing her bare legs. "¿Qué miras?"

He turns to the side, spits, and scratches his crotch.

§ Shortened form of "Qué húbole."

"Nada, jefa. ¿Y si llueve?" he says, looking up at the sky.

"If it rains quiero que me ayudes a fix esta pinche pickup."

"Bueno, jefa. Ójalá que no llueva porque si llueve vas a perder toda la cosecha. ¿Qué tienes, 'tas enferma? You don't look so good."

She shakes her head, "No, I'm not sick. Not exactly. Es que me desvelé anoche."

Inside the house, she turns on the TV in the living room. Any program will do, anything to drown out the images and voice. After a while she discovers that though her eyes are on the TV screen, the scene she's watching is not on TV. A small woman sits cross-legged staring into space. The woman's back is turned towards LP. The image is so strong Prieta smells the tallow from the candles surrounding the woman.

LP leaps up, punches the television's off button, and rushes around the room searching for the book. She snatches it up, along with her cigarettes and lighter, and races out to the backyard.

Caliche stings the soles of her feet and the cooling night air clears her head. She looks up at the moon. It hangs low in the graying sky. Bo trots beside her and pokes his cold nose in her palm, then smells the book and whines. He leans his shoulder against her leg.

"Watch this, Bo. It's going to be fun. We're going to get rid of lo no invitado — it's worn out its welcome."

Her bare foot hits a log, which crumbles to ash under her foot. Soft ceniza oozes through her toes, immersing her feet in the cool powdery ash from an earlier fire. She pitches the half-burned brush she'd cleared from the pastures into the fire bed and feels a fingernail break off. ¡Chin! she examines her calloused hands. Yep, she's got the hands of a marimacha, a real country femme.

She hurries into the shed and searches frantically among tractor implements, mildewed tarp, spools of barb-wire, and old saddles suspended from a beam until she finds a can of gasoline and returns to the pile of brush.

As she drenches the branches with gasoline, she stumbles, icy liquid sloshes over her foot. She can't find a rag, so she takes off her panties and wipes her foot with them. Trying not to breathe in the gas fumes, she picks up the book and begins tearing out a leaf. She stops and begins to read. No, don't start, don't start, you'll get sucked in again. She forces herself to stop reading.

The wind ruffles and turns the pages. Like pale gray moths in the moonlight, they flutter softly with each sigh of the wind. She lights a cigarette, takes a few jerky sucks, then tosses it into the heap. It flares up. Explodes. Lights and shadows flicker over her body as she stands motionless watching the flames. When the fire has dwindled to brasas she realizes how odd she would have looked to others—standing there naked, holding a book to her breasts. Pero no hay otra alma for miles.

Wincing at the small rocks under her feet, she walks painstakingly to the house. In the bathroom she bends over the sink. The hot water stings her face and chest but she is at peace. It was getting too scary and she was getting in way over her head.

In bed, at the onslaught of sleep, she strains to hear the shrill whine of a wire stretched to its breaking point. As she stretches out her arms toward the wall on her left, her hands disappear. ¡Ay diosita! She jumps back. Then she sits there with goosebumps all over her body. She looks at her hands. Still the same scarred manos, except they're shaking badly. She thinks she hears a voice.

"Bar-Su?" she calls out. She listens. Silence. Then she remembers that her girlfriend is at her mother's. She hears a sound—a whine. There behind her, growing louder and louder. Sweat breaks out under her armpits. Swiftly she turns to the sound, and is suddenly caught off balance. She grabs the bedpost to right herself, but instead her hand goes straight through. It does not appear at the other side—and the bedpost is only three inches thick.

Slowly her whole body falls forward and follows her arm. She finds herself buffeted by a thick wind that feels like a river of gelatin. There is no bedpost, no wall, no bedroom. She's alone, listening to her breath sawing in and out, almost drowning out the soft whimpering sounds coming from her throat. Alone, in thick blue air.

With trembling hands she touches her face and then the space around her and behind her head. She tucks her face into the crook of her elbow and shields her head with the other arm as she is whirled around and around. In her mind the words from the book—"Tres peras peladas prisoned en la pared. She took a fall. Right through the wall"—repeat over and over.

Suddenly, everything is still and she finds herself lying in a huddle against a stone wall. Her arms reach back and grope for an entrance to the other side, back to her tierra, her tractor, y su ranchito. Her heart is pounding so hard she can't hear her thoughts, can't swallow the knot in her throat.

All of a sudden, she is catapulted once more through the dark mouth of the cave. Someone is screaming—her. She stuffs her fist into her mouth. Immediately, she's bombarded by vibrations of sounds she feels but can't hear. Shadows dive toward her, then fall away before reaching her. Ah! she is about to get it, an inkling of what's going on, of what's really happening, but that too is sucked away by el silencio.

Then all is still. She holds her breath. To her it looks like she's caught in a sticky gauze of carded cotton. She can only move a few inches in one direction. Even if she hacked herself free there might be a wall beyond this one, y otra pared behind it. She's in some kind of tunnel. Or she's inside a serpent—yeah, she's been devoured by the earth serpent. No, this is more like a birth canal. Madness is being caught between worlds, sanity is reaching either side.

Agua.

Huge drops beat her head and back. She lifts her face to the sky, rain buzzard beaks stab at her eyes, feathers flail her face. Senses stifled as if wrapped in sheets of plastic, and she, all fingers and nails, piercing holes in it, but not fast enough. She sits up. Her body makes a sucking sound. She sees herself as others might: a mud-covered scarecrow staggering in the rain, bolts of lightning flickering around her. "Mud-covered scarecrow staggering in the rain" . . . is that a phrase from the book?

Her feet slosh through shifting quicksand.

No not quicksand, only mud.

What is she doing in the middle of a field, pelted by sheets of rain? Well, there goes la cosecha. The cotton is ruined. Thousands of dollars lost to the rain. She can almost see her corn bent double, tassels drooping down to the mud. She tries to total up the damage: it's too much for her to figure out. She'd be lucky if the bank repossesses every piece of junk in the place. ¡Chinga tu madre! Es la noche del tigre, the time of Tláloc, diosito del agua, jaguar face.

She hears someone calling her.

"Prieta linda, what are you doing here? Soaked to the bone?"

"Bar-Su. You? Here in the middle of the night? Is it your mother?"

"No, she's fine, Prieta, and it's mid-afternoon. How did you get here?"

Prieta looks around and finds she's standing in the field behind Bar-Su's mother's house. The sun is shining brightly, there's not a cloud in the sky, and the dirt is bone dry under her buttocks and hands.

"I fell through the bedpost."

"What?!?"

"Jíjole, I thought I was going crazy. It was so real."

"What was so real?" Bar-Su hovers over her, staring intently. "Maybe you *are* going crazy."

LP feels the tug of Bar-Su's hands on her upper arms as Bar-Su pulls her up from the ground and steers her toward her car.

"Hush now. You can tell me all about it when I get you home," says Bar-Su, taking a blanket from the trunk and wrapping it around LP. Then she gently pushes LP into the passenger seat.

When they reach La Tigra, LP opens the car door and waits for Bar-Su to come around the front of the car to her side. She throws herself against Bar-Su's thin body, breathing in her familiar scent. Tremors from the cold and from arousal rise up in waves from the pit of her stomach into her mouth.

They stand arms clasped around each other. Bar-Su tugs LP slowly into the house, helps her shower, and tucks her into bed. Leaving the bedroom, Bar-Su returns about ten minutes later with a cup of orange leaf tea with milk and honey. Then she gets into bed and, cradling Prieta in her arms, gently rocks her.

"OK, baby, ¿Qué pasó?"

LP hiccups, "I must have triggered the rain by fooling around in the other place."

"What rain?"

"The rain en el otro lugar. Gracias a diosita that it didn't rain on this side. I didn't lose the crop. But the bedpost . . ."

"What about the bedpost?"

"Well, I went through it and when I got out the other end I was at your mom's place. Fue bien fácil, Bar-Su. First the sounds, then my hand went through the post, then my head, shoulders, and the rest of me. I slipped right in, smooth as butter. There was only a slight resistance."

She extends her hand toward the wall, then stops short.

"I bet I could do it again. But I'm scared. What if I don't come out the other side? What's happening to me?" She begins to cry.

"Shush, shush," Bar-Su keeps saying as she holds her.

"Listen, I was thinking about you, wanting to be with you when I went through the post. When it started happening, me cagué de miedo. That's where I messed up, I shouldn't have fought it. That's why it took so long."

"I felt you, honey. I sensed you calling me. I thought your hand had gotten caught in one of the machines."

"Chin, it takes me away."

"I'm going to call Joe. I left Mamí all by herself. If I can't find someone to stay with her, I'll have to go back."

"OK."

"What takes you away?"

"The book. It's opened up some kind of passage. And now I don't even need the book to get to the other place. When I'm en ese otro lugar I'm not the same as the me here and now. It's like there's two of me." LP presses her face between Bar-Su's breasts and gradually her taut body softens under Bar-Su's slow strokes.

"Hush now, try to get some sleep. That's it, my Pretty-Quick, just rest. I gotta make the call." A few minutes later Bar-Su returns. "Well, Joe's not a home," she says.

After Bar-Su leaves, LP sits up and goes over and over what happened to her. She remembers her body stretching, traveling.

Before going to sleep LP picks up the phone and dials.

"Hello, Bar-Su?"

"How are you feeling, Hon?"

"A little shaky but otherwise fine. Don't want to face it, whatever's happening to me. Don't want to know. And don't know when I'll get my nerve back. I'm trying to psyche myself into trying it again, maybe aim to come out in your bedroom at your mother's."

"Don't you dare! It's too risky. Why are you doing this, LP?"

"I don't know, maybe something is missing in my life. All I do is work from before sunup to after sundown. Maybe what's missing is on the other side."

"What do you mean? What's missing?"

"Pos, I don't know. Maybe I need to learn more about who I am, what I want from life."

"You've got me, honey. Doesn't that count?"

"I don't think this is about you."

They smooch good night and hang up.

Next day they're lying close together on the old mattress on the porch. Prieta sits up and takes a sip from her third cup of té de hojas de naranjal.

"Look, Bar-Su, I went through that pole and I came out ten miles away."

"Sí, yo sé, the book possessed you."

"No, the book was just the trigger. I don't need the book to access the gate or whatever to that other place. It's just a twist of attention, like turning a switch.

"I don't think I want to hear this. Forget the whole thing, LP. It's too dangerous."

"Well, then let's do it together. You're always saying we need to do more stuff together."

"Sure. La gente will really have something to talk about then. Two women who fuck each other now passing into otros mundos. That'll be the absolute limit. We'll get burned alive."

They were quiet for a while.

"Maybe you're right," LP says. "It is dangerous. Unless I can hold on, remember who I am and not get totally sucked in by the other world."

"And how will you do that?"

"I need to be in the two states of mind, here and there, at the same time."

"This is crazy, sweetheart. I'm starting to get really concerned about you. You don't have time to be taking these trips. You barely get any sleep as it is," says Bar-Su.

"I'm not crazy, this is really happening. Time doesn't matter. I mean, I sort of step out of time. At first I was gone for three hours—that's how long it took me to read the book. The second and the third rereadings took me less time. And this fourth rereading, I got ahead of myself."

"What do you mean?"

"It was night when I fell through and I got to your mom's place in the afternoon. Of the same day. See? I didn't lose time, I gained it."

After Bar-Su leaves, LP finishes her cup of té. The nausea is gone. She walks around the house, poking her hands in the air and in the walls, trying to find a spot that feels different. She doesn't have to go through walls. There are veins, streams, currents, or whatever, all around. When she finds one she'll just lean into it and end up near wherever she wants.

She goes outside and walks around in circles for an hour, holding out her hands here and there.

A rock or a leaf will do—if she just . . . really looks at it. Bo runs up to her, barking. Of course. Should she do it? She's afraid. And exhausted. Tomorrow, yes, mañana she'll try. She walks to the tool shed, picks up the hammer and saw and goes back inside the house, the screen door snapping shut behind her.

The dining room doorway frames the door to the living room and the mirror on the opposite wall reflects three more doorways where there should actually only be two. Which wall should she take apart first?

Translations

en el agua, *in the water*
chicharras, *cicadas*
la pared, *the wall*
la puerta, *the doorway, or door*
la sala, *in the living room*
algo, *something*
huesos, *bones*
de cada cuarto, *of each room*
el espejo, *the mirror*
entremados, *support beams or spaces between the walls*
nervios, *nerves*
vengo tarde, *I'm late*
¿Quiubo corazón?, *What's up sweetheart?*
¿Tienes hambre?, *Are you hungry?*
ay qué fresca, *my but you're fresh*
sí, pero no comida, *yes, but not for food*
ruca, *Pachuco word for girl*
pa' no gastar tiempo, *so I wouldn't waste any time*
la cama, *the bed*
tetas, *tits*
pero tu panocha y gusanito estan a toda madre, *but your pussy and clit are
    hot shit*
querida, *dear, lover*
aquí, *here*
el cabrón, *that asshole*
y tu familia, *and your family*
novia, *girlfriend, lover*
mi pobre madrecita, *my poor mama*
'ta bueno, *it's alright*
dos pinches horas, *two fucking hours*
la luz de la luna, *the moonlight*
en el sueño una mujer, *in the dream a woman*
antes de que se de cuenta, *before she realizes it*
zempasuchitl, *a kind of morning glory called "flowers for the dead"*
jíjole, *shit, damn*
ándale, *come on*
vámanos, *let's go*

la vaca, *the cow*

chichis, *tits*

cuando esta ordeñando, *when she is milking*

primas, *cousins (female)*

chinga tu madre, *(literally) fuck your mother*

chingao, *fucked*

una de las otra, *one of them*

monte, *woods, thicket, chaparral*

Ese libro desgraciado me va volver loca, *That no good book is going to drive me nuts.*

todo el, *all the*

diosa mía, *my goddess*

chin, *damn*

y este pinche sol, *and the goddamn sun*

troca, *pick-up*

una santa, *a saint*

curandera, *healer*

pero no es nada, *but it's nothing*

El mal aire le había entrado, es todo. Algo le había entrado. *The bad spirits had entered her, that's all. Something had gotten into her.*

Quiúbole jefa, vine a ver si quieres que trabaje mañana. *What's up boss, I came to see if you want me to work tomorrow.*

No, no te voy a necesitar hasta el lunes. Quiero que comiences muy de mañanita con la pizcadora de algodón. *I'm not going to need you 'til Monday. I want you to start picking the cotton early in the morning.*

Y ¿si llueve? *And if it rains?*

¿Qué miras? Nada, jefa, *What are you looking at? Nothing, boss.*

Quiero que me ayudes a componer esa pinche troca, *I want you to help me fix that goddamn truck.*

Bueno, jefa. Ojalá que no llueva. Ojalá que no pierdas toda tu cosecha. ¿Qué tienes, 'tas enferma? *Alright, boss. Hopefully it won't rain. Hopefully you won't lose your harvest. What's the matter? Are you sick?*

No, es que no dormí anoche, *No, I just didn't sleep last night.*

caliche, *coarse rock used on dirt roads*

brasas, *coals*

y otra pared, *and another wall*

ceniza, *ash*

tres peras peladas, *three peeled pears*

agua, *water*

noche del tigre, *the night of the tiger*
troquero, truck driver, *one who hauls harvested crops*
chinga tu puta madre, *fuck your mother of a whore*
fue bien fácil, *it was so easy*
me cagué de miedo, *I was so scared, I shit my pants*
té de hojas de naranja, *orange leaf tea*
sí, yo sé, *yes, I know*
la gente, *the people*

This playful interview between Anzaldúa and her character LP (La Prieta) offers additional insights into Prieta, her author, and "Reading LP." Note also LP's shifting view of reality.

## A Short Q & A between LP and Her Author (GEA)

GEA: "What do you want?"

LP: "I want to be free of constraints. You know, I'm tied down to this farm and yes this is what I want but sometimes I just want to fly, to soar. I want to imagine something and have it come true right away, in a second, in less than a second," she says, raising her arms up toward the sky and stomping the ground hard with her boots.

GEA: "What or who is standing in your way?"

LP: "Myself mostly, my assumptions about reality, about what is possible to do and not do. I feel rooted to the ground, can't indulge in fantasy, in dreams. I want time to dream, time to savor life. Instead I'm always running behind, too many chores, not enough hours."

"I have to be practical, nobody else in my family is. They would have just lost the old homestead. My ancestors would have worked themselves to death for nothing. I feel I have to be the one to hold on to the land, to make it work."

"Not many women farmers, folk don't approve. Say I act too much like a man. Teté embodies all these criticones, busybodies. If it wasn't for Bar-Su encouraging me to do what I want, for always understanding, I'd chuck it all."

"I just want to be free of this feeling of being stuck, of being too solid, too practical."

GEA: "What's your greatest strength?"

LP: La Prieta tips back her hat, takes it off and slaps it against her thigh, with her fingers, rakes her hair from nape to crown. "I guess I would say my perseverance, I just keep at it until I find out what I need to find out."

GEA: "What do you need to find out?"

LP: "Why the crack exists and why I fell through it. I mean here I was: sun burning strong, my body sweating, flexing, pulsing. The sky up there, the ground down here and all of a sudden everything shifts and I'm having this weird experience. Why is it happening at all? What about the laws of physics, gravity? And why is it happening to me? Am I alone in experiencing this?"

GEA: "Why do *you* think it's happening?"

LP: "To show that dreams happen, that they are real. That it's dangerous to get too rigid and fixated on a certain kind of reality—that this reality is not all it appears to be. There are cracks in the picture. Maybe other worlds exist and they sometimes bleed into this one through the cracks."

GEA: "Why is it happening to *you*?"

LP: "Maybe to show that it goes both ways—it bleeds into my world and I bleed into its. I think that maybe I'm supposed to go back and forth, journey there, you know, like the nagualas, the shamans. It's something I need to learn. Maybe so I can cope with not having enough time to do all I want. Only right now, in the beginning, it is taking more time away from me rather than freeing it up."

GEA: "Do you think it happens to other people?"

LP: "Yeah, sure. At least in fiction. It happens to the woman, the protagonist, in the book I'm reading."

GEA: "What gets you into the most trouble?"

LP: "I knew you'd ask that! What gets me into the most trouble is my persistence. Amá calls it my being terca, stubborn, mule-headed. Unstoppable. Like a runaway tractor, a bull with only one thing in his mind. I just never give up, just keep pressing, pushing until I get what I want."

GEA: "So what do you really want?"

LP: "I want to be invincible, powerful. But also fluid, flexible, bending, accommodating. I want to stay here in my land, yet I want to travel, too."

GEA: "What are you going to do to resolve your dilemma?"

LP: "Either leave it alone, forget it, or keep at it until I figure it out."

This previously unpublished poem, last revised in 2002, gives us another glimpse into Anzaldúa's writing process.

## Like a spider in her web

Rain drums against the roof
Wind slaps the window panes
Daylight thrusts against the door
Trying to get in.

To keep out the world
I burrow under blankets
And like a spider in her web
Spin images and words
Fashioning another kingdom
More real than the outer
El sueño del mundo—
The sum of the collective—
Is dimmer than my soul's dream

In my cave of bed and comforter
Faces come and go
People cry, people laugh
I'm abandoned, then embraced
In my cave of bed and blankets
I'm walking in the woods
Or standing on a mountain top
Looking at ocean waves
Dash against the cliffs below

In my cave of bed and quilt
Sueño another world.
While el otro mundo dreams me.

Like "Border Arte" (in part 2), "Bearing Witness" illustrates Anzaldúa's interest in the visual arts. Here Anzaldúa discusses her aesthetics of decolonization, her innovative theories of desconocimiento and nepantla, and the epistemological implications of "seeing through" consensual reality. Anzaldúa wrote this piece in the summer of 2002 for the catalog of Liliana Wilson's art exhibit at the Esperanza Peace and Justice Center in San Antonio. Wilson and Anzaldúa were close friends, and Anzaldúa suggested the title for the painting *Bearing Witness*, which Wilson worked on while visiting Anzaldúa in Santa Cruz.

# Bearing Witness
*Their Eyes Anticipate the Healing*

The paintings of Liliana Wilson fill their frames with well-balanced, un-crowded espacios y figuras possessing a clean solidness about them while simultaneously emanating an other-worldly presence. Sus pinturas often depict girls, young men, and androgynous figures in still, trance-like stances, immobile, almost frozen in place. Their gazes are attuned to some inner voice o imágenes inolvidables de la memoria. In *Bearing Witness* (2002) Liliana succeeds in establishing the interiority of the figure, one of the most difficult feats to achieve in a painting. *Bearing Witness* portrays a double or dual-conscious consciousness. Border artists are in the precarious position of having our feet in different worlds: the dominant, the ethnic, and the queer, which often induces a double being-ness.

In *Bearing Witness* the third eye of the artist is informed by "seeing," a sort of detached witnessing in order to remember. I consider esta figura as both a real and an imaginal being who's shifted from ordinary normal perception to a different type of "seeing," one that "sees" through the illusions of consensual reality. The watching inner eye está viendo como en sueños, in a kind of controlled waking dream. In *Memories of Chile* (2002) there's an unwillingness to "see" or of being forced not to look. [See figure 6.] This is the subject of other paintings where leaves veil the eyes or the figure covers his or her eyes. I call this *desconocimiento*,[1] being overwhelmed by reality and not wanting to confront it. Desconocimiento is the opposite of *conocimiento*; it's the shadow side of "seeing." In this painting como en toda la obra de Liliana, her textured, detailed architecture of vision makes the background y los espacios vacíos seem like subjects in their own right and as important as las imágenes y figuras.

There are parallels between conscious dreaming and the imaginative process of fiction, painting, dancing, music, and other art forms. I use the word *ensueños* to describe this process that all artists engage in. Las pinturas de Liliana son ensueños que se quieren hacer realidad. Los ensueños she depicts attempt to bridge the reality of the dream with physical reality. In her work el ensueño de la pintura becomes embodied, physically real. But upon looking away from it the viewer realizes que la artista has successfully captured us in a lucid waking dream merely through the medium of painted images on a flat surface, blurring the boundaries between the reality of the picture and that of our lives.

In her most successful paintings the conscious aspects never overwhelm the unconscious elements, but are held in *nepantla*,² the midway point between the conscious and the unconscious, the place where transformations are enacted. Both aspects are poised on the edge of balance, sustained and held by a palpable tension, as in *Mekaya* (2002), a piece depicting a cage hanging in midair over a young androgynous figure with bent head and face hidden on crossed arms over bended knees.

In creating artistic works, the artist's creative process brings to the page/canvas/wood the unconscious process of the imagination as in Liliana's surrealistic *La diosa del amor* (2002). [See figure 7.] Looking at Liliana's art, especially the boy with two heads in *Deterioros* (2002), for long periods will transport the viewer into imaginative flights or other states of consciousness as she struggles to make meaning of its mystery. By awakening and activating the imagining process in the viewer, la artista empowers us. La imaginación gives us choices and options from which to free ourselves from las jaulas that our cultures lock us in.

El arte fronterizo like Liliana's deals with the themes of shifting identities, border crossings, and hybrid imagery—all strategies for decolonization. Good "border" arte decolonizes identity and reality: that is, it teaches us to "unlearn" mainstream cultural identity labels, unlearn consensual reality. It teaches us to "see" through the roles and descriptions of reality that we ourselves, la gente, and our cultures impose on us. It makes holes in the assumptions and beliefs self/others/communities have about reality. El arte de la frontera is about resistance, rupture, and putting together the fragments.

Liliana's paintings often depict someone caged, blindfolded, bleeding, breaking down, falling through the air, splintering, and falling to pieces. Yet even when the figures are falling apart, witnessing, or remembering injustice, they hold the clues to liberate themselves. At first glance estas figuras are about to land on their heads, but their bodies point toward something else, toward la esperanza of upward flight, toward achieving equilibrium. Their minds are not in the spaces their bodies occupy, but trying to soar toward freedom. After being split, dismembered, or torn apart la persona has to pull herself together, re-member and reconstruct herself on another level. I call this the *Coyolxauhqui process* after the dis-membered Aztec moon goddess. Estas pinturas narrate testimonios of violence y de exilio. First they lead the viewer to imagine and reenact the trauma that initiated the fall, the falling apart, and the splintering, which la artista perhaps experienced as a young girl in her native Chile during the dictator's regime. Examples of these Coyolxauhqui-like images are *Calvario* (2002) and *Hombre ensangrentad* (2002), and dozens of other pinturas. As the viewer continues to look at these paintings she imagines, as do the subjects of the painting, how such a healing process could be enacted.

The beauty of Liliana's paintings lies in their understated optimism. Even as las figuras realize that some part of them will always bear wounds, something in their eyes shows us that they know that after a long struggle they will cross to the distant shore where they will integrate themselves into a wholeness of sorts. Their eyes, anticipating the healing, envision reaching el otro lado.

## Notes

1. See my piece, "now let us shift: the path of conocimiento–inner work, public acts" in *this bridge we call home: radical visions for transformation*, eds. Gloria E. Anzaldúa and AnaLouise Keating (New York: Routledge, 2002) for discussion of desconocimiento, conocimiento, "seeing," Coyolxauhqui, and other concepts that appear in this piece. Liliana's *Girl and Snake* (2001) also appears in that anthology.

2. See "Border Arte: Nepantla, el Lugar de la Frontera" which first appeared in the catalog *La Frontera/The Border: Art About the Mexico/United States Border Experience*. Curators of the exhibition: Patricio Chávez and Madeleine Grynsztejn, Exhibition and Catalogue Coordinator Kathryn Kanjo (San Diego, CA: Centro Cultural de la Raza and Museum of Contemporary Art, 1993). It was later reprinted in MACLA 27, no. 1 (July/August 1993) under the title "Chicana Artists: Exploring nepantla, el lugar de la frontera." ["Border Arte" is also included in part 2 of this collection.]

This previously unpublished poem, written in September 2003, illustrates Anzaldúa's playfulness as well as her revisionist mythmaking. Sometimes referred to as the "Weeping Woman," Llorona is a central figure in Mexican, Mexican American, and Chicano/a folklore, as well as an important presence in Anzaldúa's work. There are many different versions of the story, but in most of them Llorona is the ghost of a beautiful young woman, seduced and abandoned by a man, who kills (usually by drowning) her children. She is destined to wander forever crying for her lost children. Note the ways Anzaldúa revises these conventional stories.

# The Postmodern Llorona

The apparition smelling of sulphur, smoke
has shed her ancient mythical white dress
for white jeans and a white sweatshirt
with the words SERPENT WOMAN
in fluorescent lime green.
She's exchanged her huaraches
for white high top sneakers.
She sports a short spiked asymmetrical haircut with a magenta swathe,
having long ago shorn her long black pelo
and thrown it into the river.
Attached to her key ring is a pen knife
and a tiny cradle.
The young woman is not afraid of La Llorona
she has become La Llorona
Her high-pitched yell is curdling the blood of her parents,
raising the hair on the back of their necks.
Most days she floats through the air on a natural high.
If she ever remembers the macho
who abandoned and betrayed her
it does not render her paralyzed in susto and grief.
She is the macha woman, the femme,
La Llorona is a lesbian, and abandonment and betrayal
are now mediated by both parties or in couples therapy.
The weeping woman walks our streets,
does her laundry at Ultramat.
La Llorona attends UCSC, goes on picnics
and to the movies.

La Llorona writes poems.
The dismembered missing children are not
the issue of her womb—she has no children.
She seeks the parts of herself
she's lost along the way.
Her eyes still shine yellow in the night
but you will only hear her screaming
at Take Back The Night Rallies.
If she dreams at night
only her shrink knows if they're nightmares.

Throughout her career, and even before she became a published author, Anzaldúa was intensely interested in the relationship between Native and Chicana identities and in the concept of indigeneity more generally. This e-mail dialogue (written in 2002 at the request of her good friend, Inés Hernández-Ávila) represents one of Anzaldúa's most extensive discussions of these issues, focusing especially on the importance of indigenous knowledges to her work. I was reluctant to include this piece; it is not as polished or as carefully revised as most of Anzaldúa's published work, due to her poor health and pressing publication deadlines. However, in addition to providing a sustained discussion of indigenous issues, Anzaldúa offers one of her most detailed discussions of her theory of new tribalism as well as additional insights into her theories of el cenote and nepantlera. "Speaking Across the Divide" was originally published, in slightly different form, in the fall-winter 2003 issue of *Studies in American Indian Literatures*.

## Speaking across the Divide

1. How did you come to an understanding of your indigenous identity?

I don't call myself an india, but I do claim an indigenous ancestry, one of mestizaje. I first became aware of la india in me when I was a child. When I came out of my mother's body, Mamagrande Locha told everyone that I was "pura indita" because I had dark blotches on my nalgas (buttocks). Because I have a face como una penca de nopal, because I was a dark brown girl who had darker skin than my siblings and other Anzaldúas, my family started calling me la "Prieta," the dark one. People said I had the demeanor (whatever that is) of los indios as I used to lie down on the bare earth to soak up the sun or crouch over the holes of snakes waiting for them to slither out. I would watch las urracas prietas fluff their feathers and caw. I learned that these images had power; these images allowed me an awareness of something greater, an awareness of the interconnectedness of people and nature and all things, an awareness that people were part of nature and not separate from it. I knew then that the india in me ran deep. Later I recognized myself in the faces of the braceros that worked for my father. Los braceros were mostly indios from central Mexico who came to work the fields in south Texas. I recognized the Indian aspect of mexicanos by the stories my grandmothers told and by the foods we ate. Still later I realized that making art is my way of connecting to the tribe, to my indigenous roots. Creative work feeds my soul, gives me spiritual satisfaction.

2. What does it mean to you to have Indian ancestry?

To have Indian ancestry means that mi cuerpo (my body), soul, and spirit have raíces (roots) in this continent. El árbol de mi vida has indigenous roots. I think that about 75% of DNA is an amorphous record of all past lives and past lives of ancestors. If this is true, la india in me will never be lost to me.

To have an Indian ancestry means to fear that la india in me that has been killed for centuries continues being killed. It means to suffer psychic fragmentation. It means to mourn the losses — loss of land, loss of language, loss of heritage, loss of trust that all indigenous people in this country, in Mexico, in the entire planet suffer on a daily basis. La gente indígena suffer a loss that's cumulative and unrecognized by the masses in this country, a loss generations old, centuries old. To have Indian ancestry means to bear a relentless grief. To have indigenous ancestry also means to bear the promise of psychic integration. As broken and shattered people we are driven to re-gather our spirits and energies, to reorganize ourselves. To have Indian ancestry is to envision a moon that is always rising, to see the sky rear up, to have entry into new imaginings.

I think it's not enough for me to be a Chicana or an Indian; it's not enough for anyone to base their identity on race, gender, class, sexuality, or any of the traditional categories. All of us have multiple identities. Besides lo indio, el mestizaje that I'm comprised of includes the biological mixtures of Basque, Spanish, Berber Arab, and the cultural mix of various cultures of color and various white cultures. I call this expanded identity "the new tribalism." In 1991, I "appropriated" and recycled the term "new tribalism" from David Rieff[1] who used it to criticize me for being "a professional Aztec" and for what he sees as my naïve and nostalgic return to indigenous roots. He takes me to task for my "romantic vision" in Borderlands / La Frontera, and claims that Americans should think a little less about race and a little more about class. I use the term "new tribalism" to formulate a more inclusive identity, one that's based on many features and not solely on race. In order to maintain its privileges the dominant culture has imposed identities through racial and ethnic classification. The new tribalism disrupts this imposition by challenging these categories. The new tribalism is a social identity that could motivate subordinated communities to work together in coalition.

3. Why do you think there is such resistance from some individuals to see Mexicanos and Chicana/os as Indians? What kind of resistance do you see? In other words, when someone resists seeing Mexicanos as Indians, what are they resisting?

There is definitely resistance from both sides. Some Raza (Mexicans and Chicanas/os) hate the Mexican (and therefore the Indian) in themselves. They only acknowledge their Spanish blood. Muchos tienen an unconscious vergüenza for being Mexican, for being part Indian. This self-hatred is projected onto Native women when Chicanas treat them sin respeto (disrespectfully). When Chicanas and other mujeres de color treat Native women and their issues as less important, we demote them to pawns for our movimientos. We make las indias the other. Nosotras gets divided into nos/otras, into an us/them division. The us/them dichotomy locks us into a who-is-more-oppressed dynamic. Internalized racism and internalized shame get played out. We all re-enact the colonialism and marginalization the dominant culture practices on Natives and people of color.

Then there's the question of who is "Indian." It would take a book to even begin dealing with this issue! Some Native Americans don't accept Chicanas as indias. Some think of Chicanas (and other women of color) as "appropriationists." During the "Color of Violence" conference in Santa Cruz organized by Andy Smith, la caca between Chicanas and Native women surfaced with a lot of finger pointing, basing the conflict on "intra-racism at the kitchen table." They saw Chicanas' use of the indigenous as a continuation of the abuse of native spirituality and the Internet appropriation of Indian symbols, rituals, vision quests, and spiritual healing practices like shamanism. Some natives put Chicanas/os on the side of the dominators and claim that our fantasies are similar to those of "whites." Similar conflicts between Chicanas and Native women surfaced in the "Conference Against Violence of Women of Color" in Chicago.

Right now Chicanos/as and Native Americans in ethnic studies departments like University of California, Berkeley's are experiencing internal rifts and have polarized into separate groups, each entrenched in their positions. People on both sides are angry and bitter, and both are passionate about their cultures. Emotions run deep, but also close to the surface, and often gush up in anger and frustration. We open old heridas, wounds of genocidal colonization and marginalization that have never formed scabs because they've continued to bleed for centuries. Each group reinforces its borders in automatic defense mechanisms. Estos pleitos are hard to witness because both Native Americans and Chicanos share a long history of theft of entitlement. What sets off these bursts of contention are issues related to resources, teaching positions, grant distributions, and power in decision making. On many campuses the battles between different ethnic groups are reaching critical mass.

4. What's behind the fighting? Why do you think the rift is happening?

The underlying cause is systemic racism and internalized racism. The in-fighting manifests itself as verbal and emotional violence. What's particular about this violence is that it doubles back on itself. Instead of joining forces to fight imperialism we're derailed into fighting with each other, into maneuvering for power positions. Each struggles to be heard. Chicanas want to present their side of the indigenous narrative, so we take over the table. Chicanas and other people of color further silence Native women, already rendered invisible by the dominant culture and the corporate universities. Internalized racism gets "gendered" or "sexed" between Native women and mestizas, people who historically were the most chingadas (fucked). This history of oppression erupts with violence toward each other. This doesn't just happen between Native women and Chicanas. It's happening between other ethnic groups, between Chicana/os and Asians, between Afro-Americans and other groups. Ethnic groups are thrown a few crumbs in the form of teaching positions, grants, decision-making in hiring, etc., and we fight each other for them. It's the old divide-and-conquer strategy. There are some instances in which the different ethnic studies programs work in solidarity with each other, particularly when they are independent of each other.

5. Why do you think there aren't more Chicanas doing Native American studies and more Native Americans doing Raza studies?

One reason may be because we construct identity differently. Another reason may be because each group is defending their identities and territories against the encroachment of the other. Who has legitimate right to do scholarship dealing with identity, language, and other areas pertaining to both groups? The issue of "blood quantum" (the measuring stick this country beats the Indians with) is one of the most explosive in the discussion of what constitutes tribal identity and indigenous legitimacy. In an earlier email, Inés mentioned the viciousness of the "assault on blood." ¿Cuáles gotas me van a quitar para "delegitimarme"? she asks. This makes me think about the "one drop" of black blood that makes you an African American, the one-eighth of Native American blood that makes you an Indian. In the case of Chicanas/os, where una nueva raza of mixed-bloods was created when Spaniards raped Mexican Indian women, the number of drops of blood doesn't seem to matter because most of us identify as mestizas. We weren't raised on reservations, nor were we raised identifying as Indian. Some Chicanas/os are angry at having to state the obvious—that biologically we have Indian blood.

I come from a state (Texas) that decimated every Indian group, including the Mexican indigenous. I don't look European, but I can't say I'm Indian even though I'm three quarters Indian. But the issue is much more complex than how many drops of indigenous blood Indians and Chicanas have. I've always claimed indigenous ancestry and connections, but I've never claimed a North American Indian identity. I claim a mestizaje (mixed-blood, mixed culture) identity. In participating in this dialogue I fear violating Indian cultural boundaries. I'm afraid that what I say may unwittingly contribute to the misappropriation of Native cultures, that I (and other Chicanas) will inadvertently contribute to the cultural erasure, silencing, invisibility, racial stereotyping, and disenfranchisement of people who live in real Indian bodies. I'm afraid that Chicanas may unknowingly help the dominant culture remove Indians from their specific tribal identities and histories. Tengo miedo que, in pushing for mestizaje and a new tribalism, I will "detribalize" them. Yet I also feel it's imperative that we participate in this dialogue no matter how risky.

Chicanas are damned for ripping off Native culture if they claim their Indianness and they are damned for going over to "whites" when gringos crook their fingers saying, "Come over to our side, you too are Caucasian." At other times "whites" will point their finger and say, "You belong over there with the dirty Indians." Chicanos weren't raised on reservations, nor were we raised identifying as Indian. I grew up in a Mexican ranch community, not an Indian community. Chicanas cannot claim to be members of indigenous people of Norte América unless their particular mix pertains to U.S. tribes. We can't represent Indian women, nor tell their stories.

Native women and Chicanas construct their indigenismo differently. It's a question of how you identify. Some Chicanas may have more Indian blood, but they might not identify with their indigeneity. Other Chicanas do not acknowledge their mixed blood. Unless it's culturally nourished, what's in the blood lies dormant. People who biologically may have less Indian blood than Chicanas, like Louise Erdrich or Paula Gunn Allen, are able to claim their Indianness (they both acknowledge their mixed-blood status as well). Deborah Miranda (Esselen/Chumash—non-federally recognized tribes) claims that if mixed-blood Indians identify as mestizas and not as Indian their indigeneity would vanish completely ("Footnoting Heresy"). This is tantamount to suicide/genocide. Until the indigenous in Indians and Chicana/os are ensured survival, establishing a new tribalism, a mestiza nation, remains merely a vision. But dream we must. The mestizaje and the new tribalism I envision adds to but does not dispossess Indians (or others) from their own history, culture, or home-ethnic identities.

The question is how much is nature, how much nurture, how much culture. Maybe identity depends more on which community you identify with, how you are reared, and less on the drops of blood in your veins. But roots are important; who was here on this continent first does matter. The Indian in all of us is indigenous to this continent and has been here for thousands of years; the white, Spanish, black, Asian aspects of our heritage are diasporic and came later.

Yet we're all mestizos. Mestizaje in Chicano identity and mestizaje in indigenous identity are two branches of the same tree. Mestizaje is the chief metaphor in the construction of both Raza and indígena identities. I fault Raza for ignoring the underlying Indian aspect of mestizo identity, for not embracing the Indian in our mestizaje in ways that don't misuse the appropriation of lo indio. Many of us are aware that we can't continue to claim indigenous origins and ignore what's happening to indígenas in Mexico and in the United States. Though Chicanas, like Indians, emerged from a colonized history, we can't ignore the fact that Indians are still under the imperialist thumb, are still undergoing colonialism. When Chicanas (and other women of color) take up the cause of silenced Native women, we don't hold ourselves responsible for how we use the history of colonization of Natives, a colonization that's forced on real bodies. We don't acknowledge or examine the human, treaty, and land rights violations that are happening before our eyes. We shut our eyes to how Natives are forced to live out past and present day violations.

6. You have been accused of appropriating indigenous identity in
your work. How would you answer such objections?

My own indigenous knowledges have been crucial to my work. I have
used certain Mexican indigenous cultural figures and terms to formulate concepts such as the Coyolxauhqui imperative, the new tribalism,
nahualismo, spiritual activism, and various other procesos de la conciencia. In this respect sí, re-escribo algunos aspectos de la mitología
náhuatl. For me to bring up these cultural figures and terms is more
of a remembrance, an uncovering, and an exploration of my own indigenous heritage. I do it with a keen awareness that we're living in
Indian land. I do it knowing that Native people in this country suffer
from environmental racism, incarceration, alcoholism, the foster care
system, no health care. I'd like to think that I do it for my own growth
and healing, that I do it to promote social transformation. I try to do
my remembrance (recordamiento) reflectively, I try to stick to my own
indigenous antepasados and not "borrow" from North American Indian
traditions.

According to Chicana scholar Josefina Saldaña Portillo in "Who's
the Indian in Aztlán? Re-Writing Mestizaje, Indianism and Chicanismo
from the Lacandón,"[2] by focusing on Aztec female deities and incorporating them into contemporary mestiza consciousness I exclude and
erase contemporary indigenous subjectivity and practices on both sides
of the border. I appreciate her critique, but my sense is that she's mis-
read or has not read enough of my work.

I think it's important to consider the uses that appropriations serve.
The process of marginalizing others has roots in colonialism. I hate that
a lot of us Chicanas/os have Eurocentric assumptions about indigenous
traditions. We do to Indian cultures what museums do—impose western
attitudes, categories, and terms by decontextualizing objects and symbols, by isolating them, disconnecting them from their cultural meanings or intentions, and then reclassifying them within western terms
and contexts. In my own work I've experienced both a colonization and
a decolonization by first being marginalized and by then being elevated
into the "mainstream." But it's an elevation that reproduces the dynamics of colonialism since that mainstream continues to control, to give or
withhold what's labeled art or theory. I'm included in the canon, in the
Norton, the Heath, and other readers, as a token. I am cited by "whites"
mostly for my work in Borderlands and This Bridge Called My Back, but often

it's a mere referencing and not a deep exploration. I'm glad that others have borrowed and expanded on my ideas.

Some things are worth "borrowing." We are all on a spiritual journey and yearn for a Polaris star to guide us in a search for a spiritual "home." We're all looking for spiritual knowledge, for inner knowledge, the alchemist's quest for the philosopher's stone. If we don't have an inner spirituality, we try to re-root ourselves in other people's spiritual rituals and practices. The goal of spirituality is to transform one's life. In order to achieve this goal we "borrow" Native American spirituality and apply it to our situations. But we often misuse what we've borrowed by using it out of context. Chicana/os are not critical enough about how we borrow from lo indio. Some Indian Americans think all Chicanas/os plunder native culture as mercilessly as whites. Who does the appropriating and for what purpose is a point to consider. Russell Means, former AIM (American Indian Movement) leader, calls those who rip off Indian traditions "culture vultures."[3] If you appropriate indigenous knowledge, shamanic or whatever, because it's marketable and will make you tons of money and give you fame, why bother with the consequences of your "borrowing"? We need to scrutinize the purpose and accountability for one's "borrowings."

7. Do you see any difference between Chicanas and Chicanos recovering and claiming an Indian identity and detribalized urban mixed bloods who do the same?

Yes, I do see a difference. But "detribalized urban mixed bloods" according to whom? Indians, "whites"? There are strong pan-Indian, intertribal urban communities throughout the country. These communities come together to help each other, to remember, to honor, to re-connect. In the case of Chicanos, being "Mexican" is not a tribe. So in a sense Chicanos and Mexicans are "detribalized." We don't have tribal affiliations but neither do we have to carry ID cards establishing tribal affiliation. Indians suffer from a much more intense colonization, one that is even more insidious because it is covered up, and white and colored Americans remain ignorant of it. Natives are really invisible; they are not even put on the map unless the U.S. government wants to rip them off. And mixed-bloods are even more invisible. Chicanos, people of color, and "whites" choose to ignore the struggles of Native people even when it's right in our caras (faces). I hate that all of us harbor este desconocimiento. It's a willful ignorance. Though both "detribalized urban mixed bloods" and Chicanas/os are recovering and reclaiming, this society is killing off urban mixed bloods through cultural genocide, by not allowing them equal opportunities for better jobs, schooling, and health care. Or as Chrystos (Menominee) puts it, "the slop syphilization cooks up" is killing Indians ("Vanish Is a Toilet Bowl Cleaner" in *this bridge we call home*).

8. The focus of this special issue is Indigenous Intersections: American Indian and Chicana/o Literatures. Although some people might see this as redundant, what are the intersections that you see between these literatures?

Alliances—literary, spiritual, and otherwise—have been created and sustained by many writers who are identified as Chicana or Native American. Raza and American Indians share many cultural, creative, historical, political, economic, and spiritual concerns. Both groups are mestizos, although most Native people would reject this terminology. Both lead hybrid lives. Our historical lives have intersected in numerous places. We have many issues in common; we fight against similar oppressions. Both struggle against subordination, racism, etc. Both struggle against internal colonialism. Temas and questions important to American Indians and Chicana/os are political/historical memory, indigenous connections, health issues such as diabetes, the restoration of traditional foods and diet (before the advent of fast foods), and environmental racism. Raza feminism and mainstream feminism must include among their issues the erasure of the cultural practices of Native people, land rights, sovereignty, and self-determination. Less obvious areas to work together on are dealing with cumulative loss and trauma, generations suffering from post traumatic stress syndrome.

Dialogue and collaborations between Native Americans and Chicanas/os is necessary. We need to dialogue about identity, community, culture, language, activism, representation, and continuance. We need to do collaborative work that reveals how connected our past histories and present situations are. We need to explore how our legacies of colonization and displacement have given us a traumatic history, give outlet to our grieving for what we have lost, find ways of healing our damaged psyches and the effects on individuals by trauma inflicted on the group. Edén Torres talks about this in her book *Chicana Without Apology: The New*

*Chicana Cultural* Studies (Routledge, 2003). We need to amicably and respectfully talk about these mutual concerns. Yes, I know that collaborative political movements are difficult to carry out when two groups of people are in conflict and in desconocimiento. Such work is being done by nepantleras. We just need more written and published accounts by the very people who are doing this kind of trabajo.

9. How do you see the relationship of your writing to spirit, to the spirit of the land, to the spirit of the ancestors, to your own spirit?

When I stand before the abyss and am unable to leap; when my inspiration has deserted me and I hit a wall, feel wiped out, gutted; when el cenote, the source of my guiding voices, seems to have dried up; when I want the seas to part, rain to fall but nothing moves—when all of these happen, pierdo las ganas (I lose the will, desire, hunger, drive). Depression results. Depression is a loss of spirit. I get depressed when my creative efforts don't generate enough force and energy to make a difference in my life and in the lives of others. I have to surrender to the forces, the spirits, and let go. I have to allow el cenote, the subterranean psychic norias or reserves containing our depth consciousness and ancestral knowledges, to well up in the poem, story, painting, dance, etc. El cenote contains knowledge that comes from the generations of ancestors that live within us and permeate every cell in our bodies.

Each piece of writing I do creates or uncovers its own spirit, a spirit that manifests itself through words and images. Imagination takes fragments, slices of life and experiences that seem unrelated, then seeks their hidden connections and merges them into a whole. I have to trust this process. I have to serve the forces/spirits interacting through me that govern the work. I have to allow the spirits to surface. Nepantla, el lugar entremedios, is the space between body and psyche where image and story-making takes place, where spirits surface. When I sit and images come to me, I am in my body but I'm also in another place, the space between worlds (nepantla). Images connect the various worlds I inhabit or that inhabit me.

Nature is my source of sustenance and support. It offers images—I usually start each piece with a visual or other sensory image. Invisible energies whisper to me, visions from the subtle realms within me and from nature appear. I follow where the whisperings and images lead. I take their energies and transmit them to the reader. An exchange of energy is what the process of creation is all about. Art is an exchange of energy and conocimientos (knowledge and insights). Writing, nature, and images give me a deeper connection to the sources of life, enable me to connect to certain energies. Every essay, fiction, poem I write is grounded in the land, the environment, the body, and therefore in the past/ancestors. Every piece enacts recovery.

10. How do you see the work you are doing as healing work, as work of recovery and recuperation?

The path of the artist, the creative impulse, what I call the **Coyolxauhqui imperative** is basically an attempt to heal the wounds. It's a search for inner completeness. Suffering is one of the motivating forces of the creative impulse. Adversity calls forth your best energies and most creative solutions. Creativity sets off an alchemical process that transforms adversity and difficulties into works of art. All of life's adventures go into the cauldron, la hoya, where all fragments, inconsistencies, contradictions are stirred and cooked to a new integration. They undergo transformation.

For me esta hoya is the **body**. I have to inhabit the body, discover its sensitivity and intelligence. When all your antenna quiver and your body becomes a lightning rod, a radio receiver, a seismograph detecting and recording ground movement, when your body responds, every part of you moves in synchronicity. All responses to the world take place within our bodies. Our bodies are tuning forks receiving impressions, which in turn activate other responses. An artist has to stay focused on the point of intersection (nepantla) between inner and outer worlds through her senses. Listening to an inner order, the voice of real intuition, allows it to come through the artist's body and into the body of the work. The work will pass on this energy to the reader or viewer and feed her or his soul. The artist transmits and transforms inner energies and forces, energies and forces that may come from another realm, another order of intelligence. These forces use la artista to transmit their intelligence, transmit ideas, values that awaken higher states of consciousness. Once conocimiento (awareness) is reached, you have to act in the light of your knowledge. I call this spiritual activism.

All of my work, including fiction and poetry, are healing trabajos. If you look at my central themes, metaphors, and symbols, such as nepantla, the Coyolxauhqui imperative, the Coatlicue state, the serpent, El

Mundo Zurdo, nos/otras, the path of conocimiento you'll see that they all deal with the process of healing. You'll find all these themes in "now let us shift . . . the path of conocimiento . . . inner work, public acts" in *this bridge we call home: radical visions for transformation* (Routledge, 2002.)

11. How do you see your work in relationship to autonomy and creativity? How does this relationship interweave with indigenous notions of individual visioning on behalf of the community?

I don't write in a vacuum. I have helpers, guides from both the outer realm like my writing comadres and invisible ones from the inner world. I write in-community, even when I sit alone in my room. Whatever I do I have to put my trust in a deeper order, an unknowable trapo (fabric) of divine and creative plan. I must trust in unseen helping guides, must surrender to the mysterious forces that guide me. I rely on the part of myself that has this ability to connect with these forces, to the imaginal world. I call this daimon "la naguala." I rely on others who access esta facultad.

Las nepantleras, modern-day chamanas, use visioning and the imaginal on behalf of the self and the community. Nepantleras deal with the collective shadows of their respective groups. They engage in spiritual activism. We need the work of las nepantleras to bridge the abyss between Native people and Chicana/os. Nepantleras are the supreme border crossers. They act as intermediaries between cultures and their various versions of reality. Las nepantleras, like the ancient chamanas, move between the worlds. They can work from multiple locations, can circumvent polarizing binaries. They try not to get locked into one perspective or perception of things. They can see through our cultural conditioning and through our respective cultures' toxic ways of life. They try to overturn the destructive perceptions of the world that we've been taught by our various cultures. They change the stories about who we are and about our behavior. They point to the stick we beat ourselves with so we realize what we're doing and may choose to throw away the stick. They possess the gift of vision. Nepantleras think in terms of the planet, not just their own racial group, the U.S., or Norte América. They serve as agents of awakening, inspire and challenge others to deeper awareness, greater conocimiento; they serve as reminders of each other's search for wholeness of being.

Nepantleras recognize that the heart of the continent is indigenous, that the heart of the planet is Indian. I know that el árbol de la vida of all people has indigenous roots. But I also know that the past cannot be captured, but it must be remembered. Yet there is a cultural and linguistic revitalization movement going on with strong intertribal exchanges and negotiations. Planetarily, indigenous movements have multiplied, and a new tribalism is emerging. Even though it may be the hardest thing we'll ever do, we have to come together, work with each other, learn about each other, listen to each other, value each other. We stand before the abyss between our worlds, psyching ourselves to leap. We have to use every means to transform ourselves and our society. I watch Coyolxauhqui the moon, I see her rise. And I wait for the sky to rear up.

NOTE: Questions 1, 2, 3, 7, and 8 were formulated by Domino, questions 9, 10, and 11 by Inés, and questions 4, 5, and 6 by Gloria.

## Notes

1. "Professional Aztecs and Popular Culture," *New Perspectives Quarterly* (winter 1991).

2. *The Latin American Subaltern Reader*, ed. Ileana Rodríguez (Durham, N.C.: Duke University Press, 2001), 416.

3. Quoted in Ward Churchill, "A Little Matter of Genocide," in *From A Native Son: Selected Essays on Indigenism, 1985–1995* (Boston: South End Press, 1996), 321.

This previously unpublished poem, last revised in September 2003, illustrates Anzaldúa's later revisionist mythmaking as well as her contemplative self-reflection and further developments in her theories of el cenote and nepantla. Note the ways Anzaldúa identifies herself and her art with both La Llorona and Coyolxauhqui. (For more on these figures, see the glossary.)

## Llorona Coyolxauhqui

### 1. Hija de la Llorona

Soy hija de la mujer que transnocha
I am the daughter of La Llorona
and I am La Llorona herself,
I am the monster's child and monstrous.
Abandoned by my mother culture
for being queer, orphaned,
I left behind las tierras arenosas
and now find myselves in a dark wood
between home and the world
I feel alienated, feel as though I'm outside and apart from the
      world, homeless, lost
I've lost the sense of being alive,
I have become a ghost,
set apart from other beings.
The dream is the "horse" that carries me the shaman
to the other world. The beat of hoofs is the drum
its sound catches my concentration I sink into trance,
and I'm flying

On my shoulder rides a horse's head
my teeth are fangs,
I am the horse with fangs
My mother calls her lost and exiled child
a call to the vocation of artist
La Llorona wailing, beckoning, encouraging the artist to rail
      against injustices. She calls me to act.

### 2. Nepantla

I'm in a holding pen
waiting while something, someone in me

behind me or from on the sidelines out of sight
deliberates,
thinks things out
until finally it decides what to do
and then I get a glimpse of its machinations
imaginations
A journey of encounters, change
The place of passage from one to the other
Tears in the weavings of reality

## 3. Coyolxauhqui

I am daughter that almost killed her mother
Coatlicue of the 400 sons
I am the sole daughter.
My mother brought dishonor to our family
got herself banged up and a bastard grew in her belly.
I gathered my 400 brothers and ranted until they agreed
to help me kill our monstrous mother

I led the assault
and just as we were upon her
the bastard erupted from her belly
and chopped off my head.
He threw my body down the temple
I broke into pieces against the stone steps
One of the 400 brothers betrayed us
told the fetus, Huitzilopochtli,
Córtala a pedazos. Una mente alterada. Piezas.
Desmembrada.

El sacrificio called on by the act of writing or making art,
    Coyolxauhqui, exile displacement, dismemberment. The wish
    to kill the mother. Coyolxauhqui tried to kill Coatlicue when
    Coatlicue was pregnant with Huitzilopochtli.

## 4. Las nagualas

the change, el cambio. The metamorphosis, morph, morphing.
    Changing into something or someone else.

5. Compostura

> putting the fragments together,
> putting Coyolxauhqui back together,
> but in a new way, en una nueva compostura
> con conocimientos y facultades nuevas.

6. El cenote / The Dreampool

I taste a forgotten knowledge triggered by an odor or some trivial incident and suddenly out pours ancestral information stored beyond the files of personal memory, stored as iconic imagery somewhere in that deep dreampool, the collective unconscious. I look at the image, try to decipher its meaning.

Presentiment, a feeling which haunts. World of uncanny signs. A secret language shared with the spirits of trees, sea, wind, and animals. The supernatural presence in things. The shock of waking to other realities—same world, new eyes. A language that speaks of what is other.

> POEM: Las lenguas de memoria
>
> La lluvia no fue del todo mala
> Las tormentas han llenado los ríos y mi casa
> Causaron inundaciones este invierno
> El suministro de agua será suficiente para siempre.
> Es prohibido el desperdicio de agua.
> Cuando llueve mucho me pongo a reír.
> Está llena la presa

Both La Llorona and Coyolxauhqui call me to writing.

All my life I've experienced the tension of living in either of two places: in my body and in the dream worlds I've concocted to escape from the real world. Escaped to inner territories.

I was afraid to let my feelings loose in the world. I began to hold things in—anger, sadness, frustration, fear, guilt. I began to hold in my most closely guarded stories. I hid from myself. I left my body—disassociated. I did not want to inhabit my body. I became a visitor in my own skin. My body's memory—that's what Coyolxauhqui symbolizes for me.

During the fall semester in 2003, I taught a graduate course focused on Anzaldúa's writings. My students were shocked to discover the extent of Anzaldúa's struggle with diabetes, and they had many questions about the ways her health intersected with her self-identity and her work. This e-mail exchange and partially drafted essay grew out of these questions. Although Anzaldúa's words in this selection are not as polished as those in most of her published work, I include them here because they give us important insights into her view of disability issues; moreover, they offer a unique opportunity to learn more about how Anzaldúa saw the relationship between herself, her theories, and her readers.

## Disability & Identity

*An E-mail Exchange & a Few Additional Thoughts*

Date: Mon, 13 Oct 2003 21:06:09 -0400
To: Gloria Anzaldúa
From: AnaLouise Keating
Subject: you & disability studies

hello again, comadre,

Today in my Anzaldúa seminar students discussed your work in the context of disability studies. We read an essay on disability studies, your "now let us shift," & your "La Prieta"; the class has already read a lot of your other writings. I told them to come to class prepared to discuss the following:
  1) In what ways, if any, might Anzaldúa contribute to
     disability studies?
  2) In what ways, if any, might disability studies as a theoretical
     lens offer additional perspectives on Anzaldúa's writings?
Interestingly, the main theme that developed concerned ethics, along these lines: "Well, if Anzaldúa doesn't identify herself as disabled, what right do we have (a) to read her in the context of disability studies and/or (b) to call her 'disabled?'" A close second theme: "*Does* Anzaldúa identify as disabled? why or why not? If it's that she's moving away from social-identity categories, does she still identify as 'queer,' 'chicana,' etc.?" And a third theme: "Does she disavow a disabled identity? Is she distanced from her 'disability' . . . is it a disability?"

It was a very interesting discussion. I was surprised that, unanimously, they were so concerned w/ the first theme I mention. One student is specifically looking at the intersections between disability studies & your work; she wanted me to ask you if you mind that she does so (i.e., reads you within a disability discourse); would you be offended if she ever referred to you as "disabled?" (I'm not sure that she actually plans to do so.)

Below is the exact phrasing from my student con las preguntas about tú y D.S.:

> Thank you for agreeing to ask Anzaldúa about whether or not, in her opinion, she has disabilities and/or would claim "disabled" as an identity (as she has claimed "woman," "Chicana," "lesbian," and "feminist").

She also has 2 more questions, but don't answer if you don't want to, don't have time, etc.:

> Do you believe (a) "that persons with disabilities are among those prone to develop la facultad" & (b) if so, are people with disabilities among those apt to become nepantleras in [your] opinion? In "La Prieta" you included "straight people who are insane" among those whose situation favored the gaining of la facultad, but you didn't mention la facultad when saying that the physically challenged might be at home in El Mundo Zurdo (218). In my opinion (and experience) those of us who survive are apt to display la facultad and may, because of who we are, choose to function as nepantleras.

Please don't feel obligated to answer!
abrazos,
AL

Date: Wed, 15 Oct 2003 03:46:34 -0800
Subject: Re: you & disability studies
From: Gloria Anzaldua
To: AnaLouise Keating

Hello comadre & estudiantes of the Anzaldúa seminar. Your discussion sounds muy muy interesante. I'm dealing with some of your points in my essay SIC (spiritual identity crisis) so I welcome the opportunity to answer your questions.

First of all I'm glad you're reading me in the context of disability studies—I'm happy to be read in any of the disciplinary studies. Though I don't identity myself as disabled or as a diabetic (preferring to say that I have disabilities & that I struggle with diabetes), you are free & have the right to identify me however you want. I believe in free dialogue & abhor academic censorship of any kind, especially that which seeks to "protect" me or "my" image.

I don't identify as disabled or as a diabetic for several reasons: 1) "disabled" would reduce me to an even more partial identity than chicana, feminist, queer, & any other genetic/cultural slices-of-the-pie terms do. & 2) Diabetic would make me a victim. But neither do I deny or reject the fact that I am disabled in some manner or that I suffer from diabetes & its complications. No, I don't feel distanced from my "disability." I feel an in-my-face, up-front-and-personal relationship with diabetes & its disabling complications. I can't escape it. I am concerned with my eyesight when I read, write, watch TV, or go to the movies. I have to pay attention to my blood sugar levels when I eat & exercise, when I stay up all night, when I socialize, & when I travel to do speaking engagements. The state of my feet is foremost in my thoughts at all times. When I forget some of these my body reminds me, sometimes painfully.

To the student looking at the intersections between disability studies & my work, no I don't mind that you read me within a disability discourse. In fact I welcome it. Nor do I mind that you may refer to me as disabled. To answer your questions: I do believe that persons with disabilities are among those prone to develop la facultad. So it follows that people with disabilities are more apt to become nepantleras. I didn't mention la facultad when saying that the physically challenged might be at home in El Mundo Zurdo in *This Bridge Called My Back* because I hadn't uncovered/discovered/created/named these concepts yet. I didn't come up with the concepts of la facultad & nepantla until I wrote *Borderlands* & nepantleras after that. Today I'm still letting the concepts of la facultad y las nepantleras unravel themselves, especially in the "Geography of Selves" essay. Yes, I do feel those of us with disabilities who survive are apt to display la facultad and may choose to function as nepantleras. Any of you estudiantes, please feel free to unravel these concepts (or any other of "my" concepts)—once they go out into the world they cease to "belong" to me.

As for "lesbian" I prefer the word "queer" or "patlache"—lesbian is an identity label that others give me, especially editors of anthologies that reprint my work. Didn't I talk about this in *Interviews/Entrevistas*?

I hope you are enjoying the seminar.

contigo, gloria

Date: Mon, 05 Jan 2004 20:35:46 -0500
To: Gloria Anzaldúa
From: AnaLouise Keating
Subject: New Year Resolutions & a Question

My student Carrie (one of the students from the writing seminar last semester who this semester is writing her professional paper on your work & its potential usefulness for disability studies) had the following question which she was wondering if you would answer. In October, you graciously replied to her question about your relationship to disabilities. In part, you wrote that you don't identify as "disabled" or as diabetic for several reasons, and you stated: " 'disabled' would reduce me to an even more partial identity than chicana, feminist, queer, & any other genetic/cultural slices-of-the-pie terms do.. ... "

Carrie asked me what I thought you meant by this statement & wrote "As I see it, there are at least two possible interpretations of her remark: (1) She's not taking on *any* new slices-of-the-pie terms, and 'disabled' is such a term or (2) 'disabled' is a more limiting partial identity than 'chicana, feminist, queer,' etc., and she's specifically unwilling to apply *it* to herself."

I told her that I didn't know whether you meant either of these things, but that if you did see the label as more reductive perhaps it's b/c it seems to apply solely to the body? In the context of your entire comment (which I'll send to you), I don't think you were at all implying that "disabled" was somehow a lesser label. (Nor does Carrie; I think she's genuinely curious & is having some difficulty knowing how to respectfully position you in terms of disability studies. BTW: Carrie is a sensitive reader/thinker & I believe will get her professional paper published.)

Please don't feel forced to answer this question!
abrazos,
AL

[In early 2004, Gloria was working to convert the above e-mail exchange, as well as her response, into an essay. The following is a draft of a reply Anzaldúa wrote on January 16, 2004, but never sent.–Ed.]

querida comadre,

I've been thinking about my not identifying as "disabled." The disabled category is a particular form of "Otherness;" all such western notions of "Otherness" are exclusive and hierarchical, and tend to homogenize, deface, and compress a large number of people under one particular form of "Otherness," allowing issues of class, cultural diversity, ethnicity, and gender to be ignored. Grouping people with different experiences of oppression and privilege results in the loss of identity, power, and agency. "Disability politics" heralds the emergence of a new group with its own visions of knowledge, politics, and so on.

Like racial identity, a structure that dominant groups use to produce forms of inequality that exclude other groups from access to education, jobs, and other resources, something similar happens to the marginalized "disabled" groups. When marginalized groups fall back on defending identity as a strategy of resistance, when we cling to our identity as "disabled," "immigrant," or whatever and use identity as a basis for political mobilization, we inadvertently enforce our subordination. Our identification is based on an oppositional distinction from another group, the "normal." The social transformations we produce are not free from the identity/disability-based divisions/inequalities that we oppose. We are polarized between dominant, "normal" groups who deny material inequalities based on identity/disability and those of us who support an oppositional form of identity politics. Both remain stuck in the limits of their identity groupings. We get locked in a position of reclaiming power from the sources that produced a sense of powerlessness in the first place. We get locked into the binary abled/disabled, us/them. The "disability" movement, like other identity-based movements, may be effective for short-term political gains, but will it attain long-term visions of social justice?

I'd like to create a different sense of self (la nepantlera) that does not rest on external forms of identification (of family, race, gender, sexuality, class, and nationality), or attachments to power, privilege, and control, or romanticized self-images. But can we talk about ourselves in ways that do not rest on some notion of identity when identity is the means by which we (both individuals and groups) attempt to create a sense of security and belonging in the midst of a fast-paced, ever-changing world?

We mourn (here is where La Llorona comes in) the loss of the "healthy," abled, integrated self, a self we may never have possessed. I can never go back to the way things were before I lost my "health" or home or whatever.

In this, the final essay published during her lifetime, Anzaldúa revisits the events of 9/11 and their aftermath in U.S. foreign policy. Like several other pieces in this collection, "Let us be the healing" was written for a specific project: a cross-border exploration of 9/11: *One Wound for Another/Una herida por otra: Testimonios de latin@s in the U.S. through Cyberspace (11 septiembre 2001–11 marzo 2002)*, edited by Clara Lomas and Claire Joysmith. Although Anzaldúa wanted to withdraw the essay so that she could continue revising it, the editors and her friends persuaded her to publish it. Blending fierce anger with sustained optimism, Anzaldúa maintains her faith in the transformative power of art. She also uses this opportunity to further elaborate on her theories of nepantla, conocimiento, and spiritual activism.

# Let us be the healing of the wound
*The Coyolxauhqui imperative—la sombra y el sueño*

The day the towers fell, me sentí como Coyolxauhqui, la luna.[1] Algo me agarró y me sacudió, frightening la sombra (soul) out of my body. I fell in pieces into that pitch-black brooding place. Each violent image of the towers collapsing, transmitted live all over the world then repeated a thousand times on TV, sucked the breath out of me, each image etched on my mind's eye. Wounded, I fell into shock, cold and clammy. The moment fragmented me, dissociating me from myself. Arresting every vital organ within me, it would not release me.

Bodies on fire, bodies falling through the sky, bodies pummeled and crushed by stone and steel, los cuerpos trapped and suffocating became our bodies. As we watched we too fell, todos caímos. What occurred on September 11, 2001 to the people in the four hijacked airplanes, the twin World Trade Center towers of New York City, and the pentagon happened to us, too. I couldn't detach from the victims and survivors and their pain. This wounding opened like a gash and widened until a deep chasm separated me from those around me.

In the weeks following este tremendo arrebato, susto trussed me in its numbing sheath. Suspended in limbo in that in-between space, nepantla, I wandered through my days on autopilot, feeling disconnected from the events of my life. My house whispered and moaned. Within its walls the wind howled. Like La Llorona lost and alone, I was arrested in susto, helplessness, falling, sinking. Swamped with sadness, I mourned all the dead, counted our losses, reflected on the part our country played in the tragedy and how I was personally responsible. It was difficult to acknowledge, much less express, the depth of my feelings—instead me lo tragué.

Now months later, I'm still trying to move through my depression and into another state of mind. I'm still trying to escape my shadow beasts (desconocimientos): numbness, anger, and disillusionment. Besides dealing with my own personal shadow, I must contend with the collective shadow in the psyches of my culture and nation—we always inherit the past problems of family, community, and nation. I stare up at the moon, Coyolxauhqui, and its light in the darkness. I seek a healing image, one that re-connects me to others. I seek the positive shadow that I've also inherited.

With the imperative to "speak" esta herida abierta (this open wound) before it drowns out all voices, the feelings I'd buried begin unfurling. Vulnerable once more, I'm clawed by the talons of grief. I take my sorrow for a walk along the bay near my home in Santa Cruz. With the surf pounding in my ears and the wind's forlorn howl, it feels like even the sea is grieving. I struggle to "talk" from the wound's gash, make sense of the deaths and destruction, and pull the pieces of my life back together. I yearn to pass on to the next generation the spiritual activism I've inherited from my cultures. If I object to my government's act of war I cannot remain silent. To do so is to be complicitous. But sadly we are all accomplices.

My job as an artist is to bear witness to what haunts us, to step back and attempt to see the pattern in these events (personal and societal), and how we can repair el daño (the damage) by using the imagination and its visions. I believe in the transformative power and medicine of art. As I see it, this country's real battle is with its shadow—its racism, propensity for violence, rapacity for consuming, neglect of its responsibility to global communities and the environment, and unjust treatment of dissenters and the disenfranchised, especially people of color. As an artist I feel compelled to expose this shadow side which the mainstream media and government denies. In order to understand our complicity and responsibility we must look at the shadow.

Our government's hasty handling of the terrorist attacks of 9/11 profoundly disturbs me. We are a nation in trauma, yes. I know that in sudden shocking, stressful situations a person or a nation's habitual response (usually a variant of anger, fear, helplessness, and depression) overrides all others. When others wound us we want to hurt them back. Like the terrorist we hunger for retribution, though for different reasons. In the beginning we're provoked into wanting to strike back with deadly force, but later reason and compassion usually prevail.

However, reason and compassion did not prevail with our president, his right wing allies in the media, and over half of the nation. In the guise of protecting our shores[2] Bush sought to shore up his image and our national identity. He didn't seek a deeper understanding of the situation; he didn't seek justice through international law. Instead, he engaged the terrorists in a pissing contest. Hiding behind the rhetoric of "good versus evil," us versus them, he daily doled out a racialized language attributing all good to us and complete evil to the terrorists, thus forging a persuasive reactionary nationalistic argument. If we didn't support the "war" to defend civilization, the war against terrorism, we were siding with the terrorists. This ruse threw dust in our eyes, preventing us from looking too closely at our foreign policies. We turned a blank eye (desconocimiento) to those we killed in other countries[3] and had buried in our own basement. I ponder what price this country will pay for the secret narrative of Bush and the other predators in power whose agenda allows them to act against the well-being of people in this nation and other countries and against the health of the planet.[4] *Abre los ojos, North America, open your eyes, look at your shadow, and listen to your soul.*

On October 7, 2001 my country beat the drums of war; with military might we fell into barbarism. Championing the show of power and the use of fear and force to control, we became the terrorists. We attacked Afghanistan, a nation that had not attacked us—the nineteen terrorists belong to the transnational Al-Qaeda terrorist network, most from Saudi Arabia. The world's lone super power swiftly shed the blood of civilians as well as that of the Taliban whose atrocities against women and ethnic minorities had been ignored by the U.S. until 9/11. Despite Afghani women's resistance against the Taliban, we had veiled our eyes to the role we played in their oppression. As Sunera Thobani (a Canadian immigrant who writes on violence against women and criticizes American foreign policy and the war against Afghanistan) put it: "Afghani women became almost the poster child for women's oppression in the Third World,"[5] a fact we also ignored.

Except for Congresswoman Barbara Lee (representing Berkeley/Oakland), I have no respect for our government leaders. On September 14 she voted against the bill giving Bush carte blanche to deploy the military against those that our government perceived as responsible for the attacks. Out of a congressional body of 421 members hers was the only dissenting vote. A real "hero" who throws into light Bush's false bravado, her courage made her a target of hate groups and could have cost her political career. In her address she urged that we step back a moment, think through and understand the implications of our actions, use restraint, and not rush to judgment, a counterattack, or open-ended war.[6]

By bombing "the enemy" we sentence to slow death by starvation 7.5 million Afghan refugees (thirty-five times the number that died in Hiroshima and Nagasaki combined[7]) who rely on food and medical aid to survive; relief efforts are blocked by the bombings. By dismissing them as "collateral damage,"[8] we regard their deaths as less valuable than those who died on 9/11. Our hasty retaliatory war against a small, impoverished nation, whose Taliban regime the U.S. formerly funded,[9] shocked the world's conscience.[10] The U.S. lost the world's sympathy; many now view us not only as imperialist neo-colonizers but also as terrorists.[11] Many look at Bush/the U.S. as a modern Hitler, only the genocidal tally may triple Hitler's. Saying evil was done to us, our government claims the moral high ground and the role of victim. But we are now, and have been for decades, the bullies of the planet.

Many accuse the U.S. of using the military to advance economic and political interests around the world and point to a history of colonialism, imperialism, and support of right-wing dictatorships at the expense of freedom and democracy. The U.S. manipulated the overthrow of independent nations in Latin America, Asia, and Africa[12] in order to establish puppet dictators giving them military aid to fund corporate businesses and sweatshops. According to Sunera Thobani, in Chile the CIA-backed coup against the elected Allende government resulted in the deaths of over 30,000 people. The U.S.-backed regime in El Salvador used death squads to kill 75,000 people. The U.S.-sponsored terrorist contra war in Nicaragua led to the deaths of over 30,000 people. As a result of the UN imposed sanctions (enforced by U.S. power), the initial 1990 bombings in Iraq resulted in 200,000 dead. UNICEF estimates that over one million Iraqis have died, and that 5,000 more have died every month in the last ten years. 150,000 were killed and 50,000 disappeared in Guatemala after the 1954 CIA-sponsored coup. Over two million were killed in Vietnam. Authoritarian regimes that have been backed by the U.S. include Saudi Arabia, Egypt, the apartheid regime in South Africa, Suharto's dictatorship in Indonesia, Marcos in the Philippines, and Israel's various occupations of Palestinian territories.

Osama bin Laden alludes to our support of Israel and our indifference towards the plight of the Palestinians as the reason for his terrorist attacks on the U.S. Others blame the U.S. for the worldwide abuse of globalization (destruction of traditional ways of living and exploitation of the poor by the wealthy). Whatever the reason, nothing can justify an act of terrorism whether it's committed by religious fundamentalists, private militia, or prettied up as a war of "just" retribution by our government.

We're the victims here, the war-for-profit mongers proclaimed, pushing a nation-sponsored war against terrorism by invoking the names of the dead in New York City. By justifying the war they hope to veil re-establishing control in the Middle East[13] and exploiting its natural gas and oil reserves.[14] They drove us into the "perceived" enemy's trap of exchanging one wound for another, of justifying the killing of women, children.[15] To boost his cowboy self-image, Bush comes riding in on his white horse, a gunslinger at high noon, bragging that he'll bring in Osama bin Laden "dead or alive" and save the world for us.

In a 180-degree-about-face, Bush assumes a feministic guise and intimates he'll emancipate the Afghan women from their backward and uncivilized third world culture. Oh yeah, sure he'll save these women behind veils whom our policy silenced, reduced to meeting in secret to learn and teach, diminished to begging in the streets. With his war toys he'll ejaculate bombs into their bodies, disremembering that the U.S. supported Pakistan's empowering of the Taliban which in turn silenced and veiled its women. He ignores our own culture's attempt to silence and gag women and men of color. CNN and most of the U.S. media disseminate Bush's savior perspective and the government's propaganda, which originates from the boardrooms of Texas oil companies and other corporations that thrive on a war economy, imperialism, and globalization. We remain un- and mis-informed about the military's role in enforcing policies benefiting U.S. corporations while costing the lives of millions around the world.

All U.S. media (except for alternative)[16] censor news of the massive opposition to the war in every country, including the U.S.[17] Bush and his administration accuse those who protest the war of being unpatriotic, an accusation tantamount to treason. You're siding with the terrorists, they tell us when we demand a peaceful resolution or protest the theft of our human rights in the name of fighting terrorism. No dissent is tolerated, especially if it comes from feminists, progressives, people of color, immigrants, and Arab and Islamic Americans. According to Sojourner's October 2001 editorial, Bush's Justice Department and the new Office of Homeland Security could turn into a witch-hunting squad targeting peace and human rights activists, documented and undocumented immigrants, and those seeking alternatives to Bush's war agenda. His efforts to eliminate civil liberties such as legal and due processes put many of us in danger of

terrorist attacks from our own government. Attacks on activist organizations violate the first amendment that gives us the right to advocate for
change and guarantees free speech. Illegal search and seizures violate the
fourth amendment, and being forced to answer the FBI's or INS' questions violates the fifth amendment, which guarantees the right to remain
silent. When people are jailed without being charged and are indefinitely
detained, the land becomes a police state invasive with security checks and
surveillance.

Racialized language leads to racial profiling, which leads to targeting
dark-skinned, Middle-Eastern-looking and other people of color ear-
marked as potential terrorists. So that white Americans can keep their
illusions of safety and entitlement unmarred, our government sets up oppressive measures such as racial profiling which make people of color feel
disposable, perpetually unsafe, and torn apart like Coyolxauhqui. Bush's
attempts to make the country "safe" from terrorism endanger some of
our residents. Under martial law we would lose most of our rights.[18] In
a TV appearance Barbara Bush, bearing limited knowledge of what goes
on in this country, exhibited her singular and myopic reality by stating
that after 9/11 Americans were no longer safe. She's oblivious to the fact
that for women of color, home and homeland have not been safe places—
our bodies are constantly targeted, trespassed, and violated. Poor white
women and young Black and Latino men have never been safe in this country—a country that internally colonizes people of color, enforces domes-
tication of women through violence, and continues the slow genocide of
Native Americans.

By ignoring the ramifications of his headlong actions, Bush and his yes-
men dishonored the 2,792 dead and the 300 firefighters and police who
died saving lives. They betrayed the people who died in the hijacked jets
and the towers; they sold out the children, families, and friends of the victims. They broke faith with the Ground Zero rescue workers who hunted
through the burning rubble looking for the remains of the dead. They delivered into the hands of the "assumed" enemy the young men and women
in our military who will become casualties of war.[19] They abandoned the
574,000 workers who have lost their jobs since 9/11[20] when they give IBM
a $1.4 billion tax rebate and large sums to other corporations[21] but refuse
to give unemployment insurance to those laid off because of the post-9/11
economic changes. Bamboozled, many of the Ground Zero rescue workers
as well as the newly unemployed believe that Bush honors them. Unlike
progressives and radicals, these "Bush-rescued" people turn their faces

away from our collective shadow and pretend not to see how internally torn apart this country is. But I suspect that the masses have a growing suspicion that Bush is not acting in the best interests of this nation or of the world.

Bush and half of U.S. Americans fell into fear and hate. The instinct toward violence has become so normalized in this country that many succumbed to reacting inhumanly instead of responding compassionately. It's unfortunate that we get our national identity and narrative from this majority who refuse to recognize that conflict is not resolved through war. They refuse el conocimiento (spiritual knowledge) that we're connected by invisible fibers to everyone on the planet and that each person's actions impact the rest of the world. Putting gas in our cars connects us to the Middle East. Take a shower squandering water and someone on the planet goes thirsty; waste food and someone starves to death. Though we comprise approximately 4.5% of the people on the planet[22] we consume 82% of its resources.[23] And fear, ignorance, greed, over-consumption of resources, and a voracious appetite for power is what this war is about. Our rapacious demands have made plunderers of us all. We allow predators like Bush to take control of our nation and kill off the dream (el sueño) of what our culture could be—a model of democracy. Similarly, western neo-colonialism sucks the resources (life force) of third world countries.

Casting a long shadow before me, I keep walking along the sea trying to figure out what good, if any, can come from death and destruction. For one thing death and destruction do shock us out of our familiar daily rounds and force us to confront our desconocimientos, our sombras—the unacceptable attributes and unconscious forces that a person must wrestle with to achieve integration. They expose our innermost fears, forcing us to interrogate our souls. As I continue andando (walking), other people's shadows glide over mine, reminding me of our collective shadow beasts. I see Bush and his cohorts not as the cultural heroes they profess to be but as the darkest aspects of our collective psyche, the parts of our culture that act without corazón y sin razón (without compassion or intelligence) and do so with impunity. Their unconscionable, destructive aspects represent the predators we must brave, whose fangs we must pull out. We're responsible for the failure of our collective imagination which gave us such poor choices that we were forced to put Bush in office (the legitimacy of Bush being elected president was silenced after 9/11 in the name of patriotism and "standing by" our man). It's up to us either to prune his powers or to kick him out of office.

I'm aware that all of us harbor a Bush-type raptor within our psyches. I know that Bush and his gang are not totally evil nor one-dimensional, though their motives are suspect. I think he acted as though he was exhibiting restraint by waiting for the Taliban to turn bin Laden over to the U.S. before declaring "war." But here I suspect he was pandering to his ego, acting tough in order to hide his fear of being weak. Surely he can't be so tapado (mentally clogged) that he can't see beyond black and white into the gray areas and other versions of reality? Right now it's hard for me to be charitable. Our nation is a powerful horse and he is riding it badly.

A momentous event such as that of 9/11 es un arrebatamiento con la fuerza de una hacha. Castañeda's don Juan would call such times the day the world stopped. The "world" doesn't so much stop as it cracks. What cracked is our perception of the world, how we relate to it, how we engage with it. Afterwards we view reality differently—we see through its rendijas (holes) to the illusion of consensual reality. The world as we know it "ends." We experience a radical shift in perception, otra forma de ver.

Este choque shifts us to nepantla, a psychological, liminal space between the way things had been and an unknown future. Nepantla is the space in-between, the locus and sign of transition. In nepantla we realize that realities clash, authority figures of the various groups demand contradictory commitments, and we and others have failed living up to idealized goals. We're caught in remolinos (vortexes), each with different, often contradictory, forms of cognition, perspectives, worldviews, belief systems—all occupying the transitional nepantla space. Torn between ways, we seek to find some sort of harmony amidst the remolinos of multiple and conflictive worldviews; we must learn to integrate all these perspectives. Transitions are a form of crisis, an emotionally significant event or a radical change in status. During crisis the existential isolation all people experience is exacerbated. Unruly emotions and conflicts break out. In nepantla we hang out between shifts, trying to make rational sense of this crisis, seeking solace, support, appeasement, or some kind of intimate connection. En este lugar we fall into chaos, fear of the unknown, and are forced to take up the task of self-redefinition. In nepantla we undergo the anguish of changing our perspectives and crossing a series of cruz calles, junctures, and thresholds, some leading to a different way of relating to people and surroundings and others to the creation of a new world. Nepantleras[24] such as artistas/activistas help us mediate these transitions, help us make the crossings, and guide us through the transformation process—a process I call conocimiento.[25]

The ending of one way of being and the beginning of another brings to mind the prophecies of ancient indigenous cultures, which predict that the materialistic present cycle is coming to an end and a more spiritual cycle is commencing. In terms of evolutionary stages, the world is presently between el quinto sol y el sexto. According to Mayan knowledge, the sixth world starts December 2012. It is this nuevo mundo, this new order, we need to create with the choices we make, the acts we perform, and the futures we dream.

Chaotic disruptions, violence, and death catapult us into the Coyolxauhqui state of dissociation and fragmentation that characterizes our times. Our collective shadow—made up of the destructive aspects, psychic wounds, and splits in our own culture—is aroused and we are forced to confront it. In trying to make sense of what's happening, some of us come into deep awareness (conocimiento) of political and spiritual situations and the unconscious mechanisms that abet hate, intolerance, and discord. This searching, inquiring, and healing consciousness is conocimiento.

Conocimiento urges us to respond not just with the traditional practice of spirituality (contemplation, meditation, and private rituals) or with the technologies of political activism (protests, demonstrations, and speakouts), but with the amalgam of the two—spiritual activism, which we've also inherited along with la sombra. Conocimiento pushes us into engaging the spirit in confronting our social sickness with new tools and practices whose goal is to effect a shift. Spirit-in-the-world becomes conscious, and we become conscious of spirit in the world. The healing of our wounds results in transformation, and transformation results in the healing of our wounds.

In the days after September 11 many of us heard a different kind of call to action, a psychospiritual/political call. Americans in great numbers gathered together in public spaces to pray. We set up peace organizations, vigils, marches, and interfaith prayer meetings. We gave speeches, donated blood, frequented Middle Eastern restaurants, sent email, signed email petitions, connected to activist organizations through the Internet, and made art. For me this call to respond is symbolized by La Llorona whose cry initiates my will.

As we thrash about in our inner and external struggling grounds trying to get our bearings, we totter between two paths. The path of desconocimiento leads human consciousness into ignorance, fear, and hatred. It succumbs to righteous judgement and withdraws into separation and domination, pushing most of us into retaliatory acts of further rampage which beget more violence. This easier path uses force and violence to socially construct our nation. Conocimiento, the more difficult path, leads to awakening, insights, understandings, realizations, and courage, and the motivation to engage in concrete ways that have the potential to bring us into compassionate interactions. Self-righteousness creates the abyss; conocimiento builds bridges across it. En estos tiempos de La Llorona we must use creativity to jolt us into awareness of our spiritual/political problems and other major global tragedies so we can repair el daño. The Coyolxauhqui imperative is to heal and achieve integration. When fragmentations occur you fall apart and feel as though you've been expelled from paradise. Coyolxauhqui is my symbol for the necessary process of dismemberment and fragmentation, of seeing that self or the situations you're embroiled in differently. It is also my symbol for reconstruction and reframing, one that allows for putting the pieces together in a new way. The Coyolxauqui imperative is an ongoing process of making and unmaking. There is never any resolution, just the process of healing.

I think of the humbleness, compassion, and generosity that the people of our nation are capable of, donating millions of dollars to the victims' families, driving across the country to help at Ground Zero. I see how devastating events can help us overcome our desconocimientos which dehumanize other people and deny their sufferings, prompting us to realize our common humanity. As we see beyond what divides us to what connects us, we're compelled to reach out beyond our walls of distrust, extend our hands to others, and share information and resources. The survival of the human species depends on each one of us connecting to our vecinos (neighbors) whether they live across the street, across national borders, or across oceans. A calamity of the magnitude of 9/11 can compel us to think not in terms of "my" country or "your" nation but "our" planet.

What we do now counts even more than the frightening event, close call, shock, violation, or loss that made cracks in our worlds. En estos tiempos of loss, fear, and confusion the human race must delve into its cenotes (wells) of collective wisdom, both ancient and modern. Though only a small percent of the world's six billion people have achieved a high level of awareness, the collective consciousness of these people has the power to counterbalance the negativity of the rest of humanity.[26] Ultimately each of us has the potential to change the sentience of the world.

In addition to community-building we can transform our world by imagining it differently, dreaming it passionately via all our senses, and willing it into creation. As we think inspiring, positive, life-generating thoughts and embody these thoughts in every act we perform, we can gradually change the mood of our days, the habits of years, and the beliefs of a lifetime. Changing the thoughts and ideas (the "stories") we live by and their limiting beliefs (including the national narrative of supreme entitlement) will enable us to extend our hand to others con el corazón con razón en la mano. Individually and collectively we can begin to share strategies on peaceful co-existence y despararmar (spread) conocimientos. Each of us can make a difference. By bringing psychological understanding and using spiritual approaches in political activism we can stop the destruction of our moral, compassionate humanity. Empowered, we'll be motivated to organize, achieve justice, and begin to heal the world.

As I walk along the ocean seeking a medicine, watching the waves rise and fall, my mind opens to the crimson line on the horizon between water and sky. I seek a way to bring all my feelings and thoughts together to create un testimonio that's harmonious, cohesive, and healing. Only by speaking of these events and by creating do I become visible to myself and come to terms with what happens. Though it is hard to think and act positively en estos tiempos de Coyolxauhqui, it is exactly these times of dislocation/separation that bear the promise of wholeness. We must bear witness to what our bodies remember, what el corazón con razón experiences, and share these with others though we be branded unpatriotic and un-American. These healing narratives serve not just self-nurturing "therapy," but actually change reality. We revise reality by altering our consensual agreements about what is real, about what is just and fair. We can transshape reality by changing our perspectives and perceptions. By choosing a different future we bring it into being.

I listen to waves impact the shore, waves originating from beyond the far edge of the sea, perhaps caused by a storm in a distant corner of the earth or the ice melting in the arctic. What we do has a ripple effect on all people and the planet's natural environment. We are accountable for all the wars, all the disasters caused by humans—none of us are blameless. We ourselves have brought this great turmoil upon ourselves. We are all wounded, but we can connect through the wound that's alienated us from others. When the wound forms a cicatriz, the scar can become a bridge linking people who have been split apart. What happened may not have been in our individual control, but how we react to it and what we do about it is. Let's use art and imagination to discover how we feel and think and help us respond to the world. It is in nepantla that we write and make art, bearing witness to the attempt to achieve resolution and balance where there may be none in real life. In nepantla we try to gain a foothold on los remolinos and quagmires, we try to put a psycho-spiritual-political frame on our lives' journeys.

Levántate, rise up in testimony. Let's begin by admitting that as a nation we're killing the dream of this country (a true democracy) by making war and depriving many of life and basic human rights. Let's acknowledge the harm we've done, the need to be accountable. Let's stop giving energy to only one side of our instinctual nature—negative consciousness. When we own our shadow we allow the breath of healing to enter our lives. Let's look at these events as catalysts that allow us to reframe global disasters, prompt us into re-mapping our priorities, figuring out exactly what we believe in, what our lives mean, and what our purpose is as individuals, as a nation, and as world citizens. Let's call on our inner resources to help us in times of rising and falling, peace and war, compassion and violence. Let's have compassion for all those who suffer from violence. Let's use internal and external conflicts and wounds to enter the soul.

Like the moon rising over the scintillating blue waters, let's be resilient, let's persevere and prevail with grace. Like Coyolxauhqui, let's put our dismembered psyches and patrias (homelands) together in new constructions. It is precisely during these in-between times that we must create the dream (el sueño) of the sixth world. May we allow the interweaving of all the minds and hearts and life forces to create the collective dream of the world and teach us how to live out ese sueño. May we allow spirit to sustain and guide us from the path of dissolution. May we do work that matters. Vale la pena, it's worth the pain.

Down on the beach, drummers serenade Yemayá, ocean mother. I'd like to think they are beating the drums of peace, calling our souls back into our bodies. We are the song that sings us. It begins with "Let us fight no more but heal the wounds of nations. Let us be the healing of the wound." I watch the gray pelicans rise up, up. As day swallows itself la luna rises, rises, guiding me home—she is my third eye. Her light is my medicine.

Contigo en la lucha,
Gloria E. Anzaldúa
February 2002

Notes

1. Gracias a mis writing comadres Carmen Morones, AnaLouise Keating, Kit Quan, Yolanda Venegas, and Irene Lara for commenting on this essay, and Andrew Baum for digging up population statistics.

2. After the first hijacked plane the U.S. closed the Mexican border then the Canadian to reinforce national identity, giving the anti-immigration advocates ammunition. "There are proposals to hire 20,000 more Border Patrol agents and 10,000 military troops for the border. What's ironic is that the terrorists that blew up the buildings entered the country legally with passports and visas, through the Canadian border, not the Mexican border" says Roberto Martínez, American Friends Service Committee, U.S. Mexico Border Program in San Diego, CA. Color-Lines, December 2001, 4.

3. See footnote 10.

4. Not only did the U.S. pull out of the UN World Conference Against Racism in Durgan, South Africa, but President Bush withdrew the U.S. (the world's largest emitter of $CO_2$) from the negotiations of the Kyoto Protocol, made up of 178 nations which met to address critical environmental problems, confront global climate change, reduce emissions of $CO_2$, and set world-wide standards. Bush's energy proposals continue to subsidize fossil fuel industries. Nationwide newspaper editorials have denounced the arrogance of his administration which is in denial about the damage we're doing to the environment and is not willing to share responsibility in finding solutions. Jane H. Meigs, "Sailing Towards A Sustainable Shore," Symposium: The Journal of the Millbrook Symposium (winter 2002). Visit www .newdream.org, an environmental activist website.

5. Sunera Thobani, "You Cannot Slaughter People into Submission," Sojourner, November 2001.

6. Sojourner, October 2001, 5.

7. The bombs killed over 100,000 people (according to others the total is 200,000), most of them civilians. Kathryn Sikkink, "A Human Rights Approach to Sept. 11," Social Science Research Council / After Sept. 11. The website http://www .ssrc.org/sept11/ has short essays written by social scientists specifically in response to 9/11.

8. According to the mainstream media many were facing potential starvation before. The U.S. employed rhetoric of concern for civilians. Commenting on an earlier draft of this piece, AnaLouise [Keating] wrote, "While it's possible that they really do view civilians simply as collateral damage, they took unprecedented care (as compared to previous U.S. violence) to appear to try not to harm them."

9. The U.S. gave $43 million to the Taliban.

10. Not every one has this view. According to Luis Rubio, the general director of the Center for Research for Development (CIDAC) in Mexico City, "What separates the United States from all previous major powers in history is that it is the least territorial and the most idealistic of them all. Americans see themselves as a benign power and are often embarrassed by the use of power, and much more so of force;

hardly the behavior that was the trademark of the Greek, Roman, British or Soviet empires in their times. In stark contrast with those hegemons, Americans like to be loved as they project their power. There's no question Americans have an uphill selling job to do." Luis Rubio, "Terrorism and Freedom: An Outside View," Social Science Research Council/After Sept. 11. Website: http://www.ssrc.org/sept11/.

11. The mainstream media does not document this view.

12. Sunera Thobani, "War Frenzy" in an original e-message from Yael Ben-zvi, sent Sunday, October 21, 2001, 2:10 AM. I thank Michelle Zamora for forwarding it to me.

13. Neil Smith, "Global Executioner: Scales of Terror," Social Science Research Council/After Sept. 11. Website: http://www.ssrc.org/sept11/.

14. President Bush and Vice-President Dick Cheney have backgrounds in the oil business. According to Independent.co.uk in the news article "New U.S. Envoy to Kabul Lobbied for Taliban Oil Rights" by Kim Sengupta and Andrew Gumbel (Jan. 10, 2002), central Asia has almost 40% of the world's gas reserves. The natural reserves in Afghanistan are the world's second largest after the Persian Gulf. http://news.independent.co.uk.

15. Women and children are the majority of those killed and wounded in armed conflicts worldwide and 80% of them are refugees.

16. Like ZNET.com. The Nation, though not alternative media, has interesting articles (www.thenation.com). See also Farai Chideya's website: www.popandpolitics .com.

17. It also refuses to show images of the victims of the bombing in Afghanistan.

18. To get information on your constitutional rights check out the National Lawyer's Guild website (www.nlg.org) and the American Civil Liberties Union website (www.aclu.org).

19. Poverty in the U.S. forces those with no job prospects into the army, which is now 60% people of color.

20. Solidarity, January–February 2002. According to the UAW Region Five Report, the drop in travel hit hard hotels, travel agencies, airlines, and restaurants. The number of workers forced to work part-time (because that's all they could get) rose by 274,000 to 4.5 million. Joblessness also hit minorities and teens harder than other groups. "Job Losses Related to Attacks Continue to Rise," UAW Region Five Report, December 2001, 22.

21. House Republicans shoved through a bill that contained over 25 billion dollars in rebates to corporations for taxes they had paid all the way back to 1986. This bill rewards GOP campaign contributors, 55 percent going to the wealthiest one percent of taxpayers. "Jumpstarting the Economy," AUW Solidarity, January–February 2002.

22. The U.S. is the third most populous country in the world. It has 275 million of the 6 billion world population.

23. For a short video that puts things in perspective in terms of world population and who the privileged are see http://www.luccaco.com/terra/terra.htm.

24. *Nepantleras* is my term for mediators of in-between spaces.

25. For more on nepantla, conocimiento, desconocimiento, and spiritual activism see my essay, "now let us shift . . . the path of conocimiento . . . inner work, public acts" in *this bridge we call home: radical visions for transformation*, edited by Gloria E. Anzaldúa and AnaLouise Keating.

26. According to the *Power of Peace Newsletter*, January, 11, 2002 (peacebreath .com), 1/10th of one percent (.1%) unified by a single cause can change the consciousness of the world. This statistic has been recorded by prophets and sages of times past, and recently by the research of David R. Hawkins. In his book, *Power vs. Force*, he synthesizes years of research by assigning vibrational energy values to different attributes. Fear is measured at 200; love at 500; peace at 600. He has shown that one person at level 500 (love) can counterbalance 750,000 people of a lower vibration. One person at level 700 can raise the consciousness of 70 million people.

# Appendix 1. Glossary

These brief glosses on some of Anzaldúa's most important terms and topics do not do justice to the theories themselves. Check the index to locate her discussions of these topics.

**autohistoria**   Anzaldúa coined this term, as well as the term *autohistoria-teoría*, to describe women-of-color interventions into and transformations of traditional western autobiographical forms. Deeply infused with the search for personal and cultural meaning, or what Anzaldúa describes in her post-*Borderlands* writings as "putting Coyolxauhqui together," both autohistoria and autohistoria-teoría are informed by reflective self-awareness employed in the service of social-justice work. Autohistoria focuses on the personal life story but, as the autohistorian tells her own life story, she simultaneously tells the life stories of others.

**autohistoria-teoría**   Theory developed by Anzaldúa to describe a relational form of autobiographical writing that includes both life story and self-reflection on this storytelling process. Writers of autohistoria-teoría blend their cultural and personal biographies with memoir, history, storytelling, myth, and/or other forms of theorizing. By so doing, they create interwoven individual and collective identities. Personal experiences—revised and in other ways redrawn—become a lens with which to reread and rewrite existing cultural stories. Through this lens, Anzaldúa and other autohistoria-teorístas expose the limitations in the existing paradigms and create new stories of healing, self-growth, cultural critique, and individual/collective transformation. Anzaldúa described *Borderlands/La Frontera* as an example of one form autohistoria-teoría can take.

**borderlands**   When Anzaldúa writes this term with a lower-case *b*, it refers to the region on both sides of the Texas-Mexico border.

**Borderlands**   For Anzaldúa, *Borderlands*, with a capital B, represents a concept that draws from yet goes beyond the geopolitical Texas/Mexico borderlands to encompass psychic, sexual, and spiritual Borderlands as well. These B/borderlands—in both their geographical and metaphoric meanings—represent intensely painful yet also potentially transformational spaces where opposites converge, conflict, and transform.

**La Chingada**   Literally translated to English as "the fucked one," this term is often associated with Malinche, the indigenous woman given to Hernán Cortés upon his arrival on the continent and, as such, the symbolic mother of the Mexican people.

**Coatlicue**   According to Aztec mythology, Coatlicue (Kwat-LEE-kway), whose name means "Serpent Skirts," is the earth goddess of life and death and mother of the gods. As Anzaldúa explains in *Borderlands*'s fourth chapter, Coatlicue has a horrific appearance, with a skirt of serpents and a necklace of human skulls. According to some versions of the story, after being impregnated by a ball of feathers, Coatlicue was killed by her daughter Coyolxauhqui and her other children.

**Coatlicue state**   An important element in Anzaldúa's epistemology; she coined this term to represent the resistance to new knowledge and other psychic states triggered by intense inner struggle which can entail the juxtaposition and the transmutation of contrary forces as well as paralysis and depression. Anzaldúa associates the Coatlicue state with a variety of situations, including creativity and her own writing blocks. These psychic conflicts are analogous to those she experiences as a Chicana; she explains that the opposing Mexican, Indian, and Anglo worldviews she has internalized lead to self-division, cultural confusion, and shame.

**conocimiento**   A Spanish word for "knowledge" or "consciousness," Anzaldúa uses this term to represent a key component of her post-*Borderlands* epistemology. With conocimiento, she elaborates on the potentially transformative elements of her better-known *Borderlands* theories of mestiza consciousness and la facultad. Like mestiza consciousness, conocimiento represents a nonbinary, connectionist mode of thinking; like la facultad, conocimiento often unfolds within oppressive contexts and entails a deepening of perception. Conocimiento underscores and develops the imaginal, spiritual-activist, and radically inclusionary possibilities implicit in these earlier previous theories.

**conocimientos**   While *conocimiento* refers to the theory in general (see above), *conocimientos* refers to specific insights acquired through the process of conocimiento.

**Coyolxauhqui**   According to Aztec mythology Coyolxauhqui (Ko-yol-sha-UH-kee), also called "la diosa de la luna" (goddess of the moon), was Coatlicue's oldest daughter. After her mother was impregnated by a ball of feathers, Coyolxauhqui encouraged her four hundred brothers and sisters to kill Coatlicue. As they attacked their mother, the fetus, Huitzilopochtli, sprang fully grown and armed from Coatlicue, tore Coyolxauhqui into over a thousand pieces, flung her head into the sky, and killed her siblings.

**Coyolxauhqui imperative**   Drawing from the story of Coyolxauhqui, Anzaldúa developed this concept to describe a self-healing process, an inner compulsion or desire to move from fragmentation to complex wholeness. As she explains in "Speaking across the Divide" (included in this volume), "The path of the artist, the creative impulse, what I call the Coyolxauhqui imperative, is basically an attempt to heal the wounds. It's a search for inner completeness." Anzaldúa often associated this imperative with her desire to write and the writing process itself.

**la facultad**  Anzaldúa's term for an intuitive form of knowledge that includes but goes beyond logical thought and empirical analysis. As she explains in *Borderlands/La Frontera*, it is "the capacity to see in surface phenomena the meaning of deeper realities, to see the deep structure below the surface. It is an instant 'sensing,' a quick perception arrived at without conscious reasoning[;]. . . . an acute awareness mediated by the part of the psyche that does not speak, that communicates in images and symbols which are the faces of feelings." While la facultad is most often developed by those who have been disempowered (or as Anzaldúa puts it, "pushed out of the tribe for being different"), it is latent in everyone.

**Guadalupe**  Also known as "La Virgen de Guadalupe," she appeared to Juan Diego in 1531 with a message. Generally viewed as a more recent version of the indigenous goddess Tonantzin, Guadalupe represents a synthesis of multiple traditions. In *Borderlands / La Frontera* Anzaldúa describes her as "the single most potent religious, political, and cultural image of the Chicano/mexicano."

**Huitzilopochtli**  An Aztec sun god and god of war, Huitzilopochtli (Wee-tsee-lo-POCH-tlee) sprang, fully developed and armed, from his mother, Coatlicue, and dismembered Coyolxauhqui (see above).

**La Llorona**  Sometimes referred to as the "Weeping Woman," La Llorona is a central figure in Mexican, Mexican American, and Chicano/a folklore, as well as an important presence in Anzaldúa's work. There are many different versions of the story, but in most versions La Llorona is the ghost of a beautiful young woman, seduced and abandoned by a man. The woman kills her children (usually by drowning) and then commits suicide. She is destined to wander forever crying for her lost children.

**mestiza consciousness**  One of Anzaldúa's best-known concepts, this "consciousness of the Borderlands" is a holistic, nonbinary way of thinking and acting that includes a transformational tolerance for contradiction and ambivalence. For her most extensive discussion, see *Borderlands / La Frontera*.

**mestizaje**  The Spanish word for "mixture," *mestizaje*, as Anzaldúa generally uses it, refers to transformed combinations.

**El Mundo Surdo**  Anzaldúa's original spelling of El Mundo Zurdo (see below). Although *surdo* is typically spelled with a z and pronounced as a z, Anzaldúa intentionally altered the spelling in order to honor and reflect the way the word is pronounced in south Texas—with a soft s sound. The shift in spelling from *surdo* to *zurdo* occurred during the copyediting stage of *This Bridge Called My Back*, without Anzaldúa's knowledge. Although Anzaldúa was not pleased with this alteration, eventually she accepted and even adopted the revised spelling. For more on this issue, see her archives, located in the Nettie Lee Benson Latin American Collection at the University of Texas, Austin.

**El Mundo Zurdo**   One of Anzaldúa's earliest, least discussed concepts, El Mundo Zurdo (The Lefthand World) has various ethical, epistemological, and aesthetic definitions. Most generally, El Mundo Zurdo represents relational difference. Applied to alliances, it indicates communities based on commonalities, visionary locations where people from diverse backgrounds with diverse needs and concerns coexist and work together to bring about revolutionary change. In the late 1970s, Anzaldúa initiated a reading series and writing workshops called "El Mundo Surdo." These readings and workshops, while grounded in women-of-color perspectives, were diverse and open to progressive people of any identity. See figure 1 and Anzaldúa's early poem "The coming of el mundo surdo."

**nagual**   The Náhuatl word for shapeshifter.

**nagualismo**   shamanism.

**nepantla**   Náhuatl word meaning "in-between space." Anzaldúa used this term to develop her post-*Borderlands* theory of process, liminality, and potential change that builds on her theories of the Borderlands and the Coatlicue state. For Anzaldúa, nepantla represents temporal, spatial, psychic, and/or intellectual point(s) of crisis. Nepantla occurs during the many transitional stages of life and describes both identity-related issues and epistemological concerns.

**nepantleras**   A term coined by Anzaldúa to describe a unique type of mediator, one who "facilitate[s] passages between worlds" ("(Un)natural bridges"). Nepantleras live within and among multiple worlds and, often through painful negotiations, develop what Anzaldúa describes as a "perspective from the cracks"; they use these transformed perspectives to invent holistic, relational theories and tactics enabling them to reconceive or in other ways transform the various worlds in which they exist.

**new mestiza**   Anzaldúa's theory of the "new mestiza" represents an innovative expansion of previous biologically based definitions of mestizaje. For Anzaldúa, new mestizas are people who inhabit multiple worlds because of their gender, sexuality, color, class, bodies, personality, spiritual beliefs, and/or other life experiences. This theory offers a new concept of personhood that synergistically combines apparently contradictory Euro-American and indigenous traditions. Anzaldúa further develops her theory of the new mestiza into an epistemology and ethics she calls "mestiza consciousness" (see above).

**new tribalism**   Anzaldúa develops this theory to describe an affinity-based approach to alliance making and identify formation. This post-*Borderlands* theory offers provocative alternatives to both assimilation and separatism.

**nos/otras**   A theory of intersubjectivity Anzaldúa developed in her post-*Borderlands* writings. Nosotras, the Spanish word for the feminine "we," indicates a type of group identity or consciousness. By partially dividing nosotras into two, Anzaldúa affirms this collective yet also acknowledges the sense of divisiveness so often felt in contemporary life (nos implies us, while otras implies others). Joined together, nos + otras holds the promise of healing: We contain the others, the others contain us. Significantly, nos/otras does not represent sameness; the differences among "us" still exist, but they function dialogically, generating previously unrecognized commonalities and connections. Anzaldúa's theory of nos/otras offers an alternative to binary self/other constellations, a philosophy and praxis enabling us to acknowledge, bridge, and sometimes transform the distances between self and other.

**spiritual activism**   Although Anzaldúa did not coin this term, she used it to describe her visionary, experientially based epistemology and ethics. At the epistemological level, spiritual activism posits a metaphysics of interconnectedness and employs nonbinary modes of thinking. At the ethical level, spiritual activism requires concrete actions designed to intervene in and transform existing social conditions. Spiritual activism is spirituality for social change, spirituality that recognizes the many differences among us yet insists on our commonalities and uses these commonalities as catalysts for transformation.

**Yemayá**   According to Yoruban beliefs, Yemayá is the orisha (spirit force or goddess) associated with the oceans and other waters.

# Appendix 2. Timeline

*Some Highlights from Gloria Evangelina Anzaldúa's Life*

**26 September 1942**   born in Raymondville, Texas, to Urbano and Amelia Anzaldúa.

**1948**   Father buys house in Hargill, Texas.

**1950**   Family rents out house and moves to San Manuel Rio Farms.

**1956**   Family moves back to house in Hargill, Texas.

**June 1957**   Father dies.

**1962**   Graduates from Edinburgh High School.

**Fall 1963 to Spring 1964**   Attends Texas Woman's University (Denton). She leaves after a year due to financial difficulties and returns home, where she works for a year in order to earn funds for her education.

**1965 to 1968**   Attends Pan American University, where she majors in English, art, and secondary education. Completes coursework and student teaching for her B.A. in English, with a teaching certificate in secondary education. Puts herself through college by taking on a variety of jobs during the day (library clerk, teacher's aide, packing shed worker, and farmworker picking melons) and attending school at night.

**January 1969 to June 1973**   Works as a teacher, from preschool through high school, for the Pharr, San Juan, Alamo Independent School District (San Juan, Texas). Each summer, she attends the M.A. program in English and education at the University of Texas, Austin. During this period, she reads extensively about indigenous Mexican cultures and becomes involved with the Chicano movement and with a variety of activist organizations, including the Chicano Youth Organization (CYO), Mexican American Youth Organization (MAYO), and AMOS. In **1972** she receives her M.A. in English and education from the University of Texas, Austin.

**May 1973 to September 1974**   Employed by the State of Indiana to serve as liaison between the public school system and migrant farm workers' children, she advises teachers and administrators on curriculum and teaching methods. Takes her first creative writing workshop (with Elaine Hemley). Views this period as the time when she began to write seriously and also to explore the occult.

**September 1974 to September 1977**  Enrolls in the doctoral program in comparative literature at the University of Texas, Austin, where she is introduced to feminism, "gay life," and Chicano studies. Participates in various movements (the Chicano movement, farm workers, antiwar, civil rights, women's rights). Although taking a full load of courses, she focuses much of her time on writing short stories, a novella, and poetry. On **6 November 1974** she is mugged in Austin, and in **September 1977** she determines to devote her life to her writing, leaves Austin, and drives to California.

**October 1977 to May 1981**  After stopping briefly in San Diego, she moves to the San Francisco Bay area. She takes a series of part-time jobs and dedicates the majority of her time to her writing. Joins the Feminist Writers Guild, designs and implements her El Mundo Surdo Reading Series and El Mundo Surdo Writing Workshops, initiates and edits *This Bridge Called My Back: Writings by Radical Women of Color*. From **1979 to 1980** she works as a lecturer in the women's studies program at San Francisco State University, where she teaches feminist journal writing and Third World women's literature.

**1978**  Serves on the Feminist Writer's Guild National Steering Committee.

**February 1979**  Attends workshop led by Merlin Stone. (She later credits her conversations with Stone, at the workshop and afterwards, as the beginning of *This Bridge*.)

**March 1979**  Decides to edit a collection of writings by women of color, tentatively titled *Radical Third World Women's Anthology*.

**April 1979**  Early in the month invites Cherríe Moraga to co-edit the collection; approximately two weeks later, Moraga agrees.

**May 1979**  Memorial Day: falls off cliff. (Anzaldúa mentions this fall in some of her writings.)

**August 1979**  Begins planning her El Mundo Surdo Reading Series, at the invitation of Bob Glück from Small Press Traffic.

**September 1979**  Begins drafting "La Prieta."

**October 1979**  El Mundo Surdo Reading Series begins. Mary Hope Lee, Luisah Teish read on October 17; Cherríe Moraga and Anzaldúa read on October 24.

**November 1979**  Begins drafting "Speaking in Tongues."

**3 March 1980**  Hysterectomy and near-death experience.

**May 1980**  Continues working on *This Bridge* (at this point titled *A Woman to Woman Dialogue: A Radical Third World Women's Anthology*). Interviews Luisah Teish for *This Bridge*.

**Summer 1980**  With Moraga conducts El Mundo Surdo Writing Workshop.

**June 1980**  Tapes interview questions for Barbara and Beverly Smith; Persephone Press calls, offering to publish *This Bridge*.

**Summer and Fall 1980**  Continues working on anthology; types and edits Teish interview and converts it into "O.K. Momma, Who the Hell Am I? An Interview with Luisah Teish." Works with Anita Valerio and others on their contributions for *This Bridge*. Retitles the anthology *Smashing the Myth, This Bridge Called Our Back*, and, finally, *This Bridge Called My Back: Radical Writings by Women of Color*.

**1 October 1980**  Finishes *Bridge* manuscript, makes two copies of the 358-page manuscript, sends it to Persephone Press.

**10 March 1981**  Delivers speech, "Women of Color Speak Out," at the Women's Center, San Francisco State University.

**May 1981**  leaves San Francisco.

**Summer 1981 to Fall 1985**  Moves from San Francisco to the East Coast, where she lives in a variety of locations: from **July 1981 to September 1981** she lives in Cambridge, Massachusetts, house-sitting for friends; from **September 1981 to February 1982** she lives in New Haven, Connecticut; and from **March 1982 to August 1985** she lives in Brooklyn, New York. During these years, she works on a number of writing projects, including her autohistoria, *La Serpiente que se come su cola: Life and Death Rites of a Chicana Lesbian*. She supports herself with small speaking engagements and writing workshops. Each summer, from 1982 through 1986, she teaches creative writing at the Women's Voices Summer Writing Workshop, at Oakes College, University of California, Santa Cruz. From 1984 to 1986 she periodically works as a lecturer in the Adult Degree Program, Vermont College of Norwich University, where she teaches creative writing, literature, and feminist studies.

**1981 to 1985**  Lives on East Coast.

**24 June 1981**  Serves on the panel "What Drives Us Together, What Drives Us Apart: Combating Racism" at the National Women Studies Association third annual conference (Storrs, Conn.). Launches *This Bridge Called My Back* at this conference.

**2 October 1981**  Serves on the panel "Issues Confronting Third World Women Writers and Editors" at the Women in Print conference (Washington, D.C.).

**28 October 1981**  Presents lecture "Words of Power and Revolution," Women's Studies Program Lunchtime Series, Yale University.

**26 September 1981**  Gives speech "Taking Back the Night: A Political Spiritual Ritual" at a Take Back the Night rally (New Haven, Conn.).

**28 October 1981**  Presents lecture, "Speaking in Tongues—Third World Woman Writer," Women's Studies Program Lunchtime Series, Yale University.

**7 November 1981**   Mugged for the second time, almost exactly seven years after the first.

**27–29 November 1981**   Attends workshop "El Mundo Zurdo: Political-Spiritual Vision for the Third World and the Queer" at the Second National Third World Lesbian/Gay Conference and the Second National Coalition of Black Gays, a Unified Rainbow of Strength (Chicago).

**2 January 1982**   Presents lecture "El Retorno/the Return: Another Look at the Chicano Experience," Chicano Studies Lecture Series, University of Texas, Austin.

**5 February 1982**   Presents lecture "Women of Color in the U.S.: Poetry and Experience," University of Maryland (College Park).

**5 February 1982**   Presents lecture "The Writing and Editing Process of *This Bridge Called My Back: Writing by Radical Women of Color*," Women's Studies Visiting Professionals Lecture Series, George Washington University (Washington, D.C.).

**27 March 1982**   Serves on the panel "The Writer and Her Task" at the Chicano/Chicana East Coast Conference, La Reunion '82, Por La Comunidad: the Role of the Chicano Professional, Columbia University.

**22 April 1982**   Presents lecture "Riding the Back of Danger—The Task of the Chicano Queer," Yale University.

**1 May 1982**   Attends the Strength and Solidarity Voice of Women Writing Two-Day Workshop (Buffalo, N.Y.), where she leads a workshop, "Speaking in Tongues: The Third World Women Writer," and presents on a panel, "Becoming Great, The Woman Writer Who's Made It."

**2 May 1982**   Gives speech "Not Letting Our Magic Turtle Go: Cultivating Simplicity and Feeding the Spirit," Native American Anti-Nuclear March to Washington (Buffalo, N.Y.).

**18 June 1982**   Serves on panel "Fusing Politics with Spirituality: Our Only Means of Survival," National Women's Studies Association fourth annual conference, Humboldt State University (Arcata, Calif.).

**Fall 1982**   Receives a MacDowell Artist Colony fellowship.

**Spring 1983**   Looks for new publisher for *This Bridge*.

**February to March 1983**   Leads a creative writing workshop at the Brooklyn College Women's Center.

**6 March 1983**   Presents lecture "Bridging Differences: La Chicana Feminista," New Views of Women Lecture Series, San Diego State University.

**7 April 1983**   Presents a reading and lecture, "Third World Women in Poetry," Women's Center, University of California, San Diego.

**11–12 April 1983**  Attends Common Differences: Third World Women and Feminists Perspectives conferences, University of Illinois, Champaign-Urbana, where she is a moderator and discussant for "Feminism: Cross-Cultural Perspectives"; participates on the roundtable "Chicana, the 80,000 Year Old Immigrant"; and speaks at a panel, "Overcoming the Tradition of Muteness—Women and Language."

**14–16 April 1983**  Conducts workshop "Invisible and Inaudible: The Chicana Lesbian Writer," National Association for Chicano Studies annual conference, Eastern Michigan University (Ypsilanti).

**June 1983**  Teaches in writing workshop at the University of California, Santa Cruz.

**3 September 1983**  Conducts workshop "Dark & Deep Are Our Roots: The Spirituality of Women of Color," Lesbians of Color conference, Santa Monica, Calif.

**Fall 1983**  Signs contract with Kitchen Table Press to publish *This Bridge*.

**16 December 1983**  Conducts workshop "The Politics of Literature," Third World Women's Conference: El Mundo Zurdo—The Vision, Yale University.

**1984**  Becomes contributing editor to *Sinister Wisdom*.

**August 1985 to May 2004**  After careful deliberation, decides to relocate to the West Coast. In August, she moves to the San Francisco Bay Area where she lives in a studio apartment in Oakland. During this time, she works on *Borderlands* and other writing projects. In May 1986 she moves to Santa Cruz, where she will live for the remainder of her life, first renting an apartment on Walti Street and, in 1991, purchasing a house near West Cliff Drive, on Lighthouse Point and about two blocks from the Pacific Ocean. This landscape calls out to her, and figures prominently in her later writings.

**1986**  *This Bridge Called My Back* receives the Before Columbus American Book Award.

**April 1986**  *Borderlands* accepted by Spinsters/Aunt Lute for publication. At this point, the manuscript is a book of poetry, approximately 100 pages in length, and simply titled *Borderlands*. To supplement this poetry, Anzaldúa decides to write a prose introduction, which, she anticipates, will consist of four essays. Her goal is to create a manuscript that is 100 pages of prose and 100 pages of poetry.

**May 1986**  Works as a lecturer in the adult Degree program at the Vermont College of Norwich University.

**22 May 1986**  Moves to Santa Cruz and rents an apartment on Walti Street.

**June 1986**  Conducts Women's Voices summer writing workshop at the University of California, Santa Cruz.

**November 1986**   Changes her manuscript title from *Borderlands* to *Borderlands / La Frontera*.

**1987**   Publishes *Borderlands / La Frontera: The New Mestiza*. Later this year, the *Library Journal* selects *Borderlands* as one of the best thirty-eight books in 1987.

**9 May 1987**   Serves on panel "Homophobia: Fear of Going Home" at the Amor en Aztlan: A Crosscultural Fiesta conference (Santa Cruz).

**9 May 1987**   Gives keynote address "Where Do We Go From Here?" at the Third Annual Empowering Women of Color Conference: Standing at the Crossroads, This Bridge Called My Back, University of California, Berkeley.

**June 1987**   Gives keynote address "The Multicultural Lesbian" at the Lesbian Community Conference: Cabrillo Lesbians Together, Cabrillo College (Capitola, Calif.).

**6–7 June 1987**   Conducts workshop "The Reactionary Offensive against Women," at the Refuse and Resist National Founding Conference in New York City; serves on panel "Borderlands" at the National Women's Studies Association annual conference, Spelman College (Atlanta, Ga.).

**August 1987**   Finishes "En Rapport, In Opposition: Cobrando Cuentas a las Nuestras" for *Sinister Wisdom*. "I regret not having the time to hone it. I never get enough time. The deadlines are upon me before I know it."

**30–31 October 1987**   Serves on panel "Differences within Differences: Issues of Lesbians and Gay People of Color" at the Definitions and Explorations, Lesbian/Gay Studies Conference at Yale University.

**14–15 November 1987**   Delivers speech "Writers As Social Activists" at the Lesbian Political Action Conference, Mission High School (San Francisco, Calif.).

**December 1987**   Presents paper "The Internalized Oppression of Women of Color Lesbians" at the Homosexuality, Which Homosexuality? Lesbian and Gay International Conference in Amsterdam.

**1988**   Applies to doctoral program in history of consciousness at University of California, Santa Cruz, but, much to her dismay, is not accepted into the program; instead, she is accepted into the doctoral program in literature, also at UCSC.

**8 April 1988**   Conducts workshop "Three Chicanas Reading and Talking about Their Writing: Sandra Cisneros, Denise Chavez, and Gloria Anzaldúa Encuentro de Escritoras" at the Chicanas Conference at Stanford University (Palo Alto, Calif.).

**April to June 1988**   Appointed distinguished visiting professor in women's studies at the University of California, Santa Cruz, where she teaches the course Women of Color in the U.S.–Third World Feminism Theory and Literature, and a "historias" creative writing seminar.

**June 1988**  Presents "Remembering and Subverting in Historias by Women of Color," at the third International Book Fair, Montreal. (For a brief description of this presentation, see Lee Maracle's "This is Personal: Re-Visiting Gloria Anzaldúa from within the Borderlands.") Later this month she serves as plenary speaker at the annual National Women's Studies Association conference in Minneapolis. Anzaldúa later revises this talk, titled "Lesbian Alliances," and publishes it as "Bridge, Drawbridge, Sandbar or Island: Lesbians-of-Color Hacienda Alianzas" (reproduced in this volume).

**9 October 1988**  Presents lecture "Politics and Race" in the Politics and Race: Election-Year Reflections on Life in the United States lecture series, Smith College (Northhampton, Mass.).

**6–8 April 1989**  Conducts workshop "Bridge, Drawbridge, Island or Sandbar: Alliances Among Women" at the Women in America Legacies of Race and Ethnicity conference, Georgetown University (Washington, D.C.).

**16 October 1989**  Presents lecture "Speaking in Cultures" in the Building a Multicultural Society Lecture Series, University of California, Santa Barbara.

**17 October 1989**  Loma Prieta Earthquake strikes the San Francisco Bay area. This earthquake figures prominently in "now let us shift" and some of Anzaldúa's other writings.

**1990**  Publishes *Making Face, Making Soul / Haciendo Caras* and continues working on a number of projects including, but not limited to: a collection of short stories, *Entremuros, Entreguerras*; "Ghost Trap" and other *Prieta* stories; her children's stories; her theory of autohistorias; and the prospectus for her UCSC dissertation, tentatively titled "Lloronas, Woman Who Wails."

**3 March 1990**  Delivers keynote address "Autohistorias, Women of Color Inventing their Voices" for Women's History Month at Stanford University.

**16 March 1990**  Presents lecture "Making Borders / Crossing Borders" in the Women's History Month Reading Series at Sacramento University.

**21 March 1990**  Lectures at the University of Colorado at Boulder.

**22–25 March 1990**  Attends the Associated Writers' Program annual conference and book fair, where she gives a talk, "Anecdotal Rigor: Feminist Forms."

**4 May 1990**  Delivers a reading at "Cinco de mayo" California Ethnic Women Writers Series at San Jose State University.

**May 20–23 1990**  Appointed regent's lecturer at the University of California, San Diego.

**21 June 1990**  Presents lecture "Disturbing Identities: Shape-Shifting Mestiza and Postmodern Llorona" at the Literary Criticism Conference, Crossing Borders, Georgetown University (Washington, D.C.).

**22 June 1990**  Organizes and presents a panel, "Haciendo caras / Making Faces: Identity Issues in Ethnicity, Alliances and Literary Production," at the National Women's Studies Association (NWSA) conference in Akron, Ohio. During this conference, many of the women-of-color attendees and their allies walk out, protesting the organization's racism. While Anzaldúa felt equally betrayed by NWSA and empathized with the protestors' decision, she chooses to remain, becoming what she later described as a nepantlera—a term she coins to define a unique type of visionary cultural worker. Anzaldúa discusses the "blow-up" that occurred at this NWSA conference in her essay, "now let us shift."

**September to October 1990**  Appointed writer-in-residence in nonfiction at The Loft (Minneapolis).

**1991**  Receives a National Endowment for the Arts Award in Fiction (her sixth time applying) and uses part of the award to make a down payment on a house in Santa Cruz. This house and the surrounding landscape play a large role in her later writings. She also receives the Southern California Women for Understanding Lesbian Rights Award in this year.

**January to February 1991**  Appointed artist-in-residence in Chicano studies at Pomona College. On 6 February gives a talk "On the Process of Writing Borderlands / La Frontera" to Dorrinne Kondo's class; five years later, she revises the transcript for publication.

**6 March 1991**  Presents lecture "Post-Colonial Stress: Intellectual Bashing of the Cultural Other" at Colby College (Waterville, Maine).

**3 October 1991**  Presents lecture "Five Hundred Years of Resistance: Mestiza not Hispanic, Conocimiento not 'Unity," at the Latinos Unidos Quebrando Barreras Conference, University of Michigan, Ann Arbor.

**10 October 1991**  Presents lecture "Carta a Colón—Resistant Subjects Shout Basta! Challenges of Multiracial Identities and Alliances," at the Alternative Responses to the Columbus Quincentennial, University of Wisconsin, Madison.

**23 November 1991**  Featured speaker at the National Council of Teachers of English and Conference on College Composition and Communication Luncheon (Seattle).

**1992**  Receives Sappho Award of Distinction and is diagnosed with Type I diabetes. Also during this year she has many speaking engagements, only some of which are listed below. In following years, she cuts back on her "gigs" in order to safeguard her health.

**January 1992**  Gives an informal talk and a formal lecture at the Colorado College Symposium: Ethnicity and Identity at Colorado College (Colorado Springs). Her lecture is titled "Mestisaje and the New Tribalism—Identities Subject to Shiftings."

**19 March 1992**  Presents lecture "Writers Reading and Talking about Writing" at the Conference on College Composition and Communication (CCCC), Cincinnati.

**20 March 1992**  Presents lecture "Border Writing and the Production of Knowledge, Theorizing Mestiza Style" in the Women and Creativity Speaker Series, University of Cincinnati.

**21 March 1992**  Conducts workshop "Multiple Contexts, Communities and Possibilities: Writers, Writing Teachers and Researchers Embracing Difference" at the Conference on College Composition and Communication (CCCC) in Cincinnati.

**23 March 1992**  Presents lecture "Border Writing: The Politics of Multiculturalism" at Miami University (Oxford, Ohio).

**24 March 1992**  Presents lecture "Carta Colón: Surpassing the Tongue" at Hampshire College (Amherst, Mass.).

**12–15 April 1992**  Attends symposium, "Feminist Meztizas: Shape-Shifting Identities," eleventh annual Gender Studies Symposium at Lewis and Clark College (Portland, Ore.).

**4 May 1992**  Participates in roundtable "Imágenes de la Frontera," Festival Internacional de la Raza, Centro Cultural Tijuana (CECUT).

**9–17 June 1992**  Conducts seminar La Identidad Estadounidense, La Facultad de Filosofía y Letras y El Centro de Investigaciones Sobre Estados Unidos de América, at the Universidad Nacional Autónoma de México (UNAM) in Mexico City.

**2 July 1992**  Participates in a reading, Poets for Racial and Economic Justice, sponsored by the Santa Cruz/Monterey Local and National Writers Union.

**September 1992**  Delivers speech at Take Back the Night Rally for Rape Awareness and Assistance (Denver).

**22 September 1992**  Serves on panel "Is There a Common Culture in the Americas?" at The Novel in the Americas conference, University of Colorado, Boulder.

**23 September 1992**  Presents lecture "A Tapestry of Faces: Shape Shifting Identity" at Metropolitan State College (Denver, Colo.).

**24 September 1992**  Delivers keynote address "The Stories of Multiculturalism,"

Many Voices—Many Choices Conference on Multiculturalism, University of Northern Colorado (Greeley).

**1993**  *Friends from the Other Side/Amigos del Otro Lado* published.

**12 May 1994**  Delivers keynote address "Reading & Writing the Other: Invoking Cultural & Critical Authority" at University of Washington.

**1995**  *Prietita and the Ghost Woman / Prietita y La Llorona* published.

**6 October 1995**  Presents lecture "Aliens: Dynamic Construction of U.S. Chicana/Latina Experience" at the University of Milwaukee.

**Fall 1995**  Collaborates with a performance artist and three visual artists in a U.S.-Mexico project sponsored by the Latino Arts Center in San José and the Villa Montalvo Artist Residency.

**1996**  Awarded residency at the Norcroft Writer's Retreat. In April, she states, "Much of the writing I'm doing now focuses on theories of composition and art which address writers, visual and other artists and on processes of creativity and memory, censorship and political climate, authority and community and theory vs. creative arts."

**1997**  Begins work on *Interviews/Entrevistas*.

**June to July 1997**  Resident at Hedgebrook, a writer's colony for women ("six weeks of sheer pleasure. . . . Tall order I've set myself: revise & rewrite 24 short stories and work on an essay (memoir) "How I work" for Marla Morris & Mary Aswell Doll. . . . The other enormous task I've set for myself is to challenge the roots of commonly held beliefs, values and assumptions and encourage transformation. I think that fiction is a subtle, even sneaky, way to do this. I'm relying on the subtext of each story to carry this mechanism. In addition I plan to key in 90 pages of handwritten material—this will be one of the ways of entering into the stories and the essay. I'd like to live up to Hedgebrook's permaculture philosophy: growth happens by letting go rather than imposing or controlling."

**Fall 1997**  Resident at Djerassi Resident Artist's Program, where she works on her fiction and "S.I.C." ("Spiritual Identity Crisis").

**19–21 October 1997**  Presents lecture at Simmons College.

**26–28 November 1997**  Attends the Pachanga Conference, Princeton University.

**1999**  Begins work on *this bridge we call home: radical visions for transformation*.

**22–24 February 1999**  Presents lecture "The Cracks between the Worlds and Bridges to Span Them" at Tufts University.

**8–10 March 1999**  Delivers keynote address "Exploring Cultural Legacies: Using

Myths to Construct Stories of Modern Realities" and class lectures at Eastern New Mexico University (Portales).

**3 June 1999**   Presents lecture "Queers of Color" at the University of California, Santa Cruz.

**28–30 October 1999**   Presents lecture "Nos/otros: 'Us' vs. 'Them,' (Des)Conocimientos y Compromisos" at the University of Illinois, Urbana-Champaign.

**2000**   *Interviews/Entrevistas* published.

**17 September 2000**   Presents lecture "Conocimiento in Dialogue" at Stanford University.

**Spring 2001**   Visiting professorship at Florida Atlantic University (Boca Raton).

**2002**   *this bridge we call home: radical visions for transformation* published. Begins work on *bearing witness*, continues work on *Prieta* and other projects.

**February 2002**   Attends conference at University of California, Berkeley, for third reprint of *This Bridge Called My Back*.

**November 2002**   Conducts reading and workshop at the Esperanza Peace and Justice Center (San Antonio, Tex.).

**2003**   Determines to finish her doctorate and returns to her UCSC dissertation, shifts direction.

**12 May 2003**   Delivers Sonoma State University Heritage Month lecture.

**May 2004**   Joins the spirits and ancestors (death due to diabetes-related complications).

# Bibliography

Published Writings by Gloria Evangelina Anzaldúa

## Books

Borderlands / La Frontera: The New Mestiza. San Francisco: Aunt Lute, 1987.

Friends from the Other Side/Amigos del Otro Lado. Illustrated by Consuela Méndez. San Francisco: Children's Book Press, 1993.

Interviews/Entrevistas. Edited by AnaLouise Keating. New York: Routledge, 2000.

Prietita and the Ghost Woman / Prietita y La Llorona. Illustrated by Maya Christina Gonzalez. San Francisco: Children's Book Press, 1995.

## Edited Books

Making Face, Making Soul / Haciendo Caras: Creative and Critical Perspectives by Women of Color. San Francisco: Aunt Lute Foundation, 1990.

This Bridge Called My Back: Writings By Radical Women of Color. 1981. Expanded and revised third edition. Berkeley, Calif.: Third Woman Press, 2002. (Co-edited with Cherríe M. Moraga)

this bridge we call home: radical visions for transformation. New York: Routledge, 2002. (Co-edited with AnaLouise Keating)

## Essays

"Border Arte: Nepantla, El Lugar de la Frontera." La Frontera / The Border: Art about the Mexico/United States Border Experience. Museum of Contemporary Art, San Diego, 1993. 107–203.

"Bridge, Drawbridge, Sandbar or Island: Lesbians-of-Color Hacienda Alianzas." Bridges of Power: Women's Multicultural Alliances, edited by Lisa Albrecht and Rose M. Brewer. Philadelphia: New Society, 1990. 216–31.

"counsels from the firing . . . past, present, future." Foreword to This Bridge Called My Back: Writings by Radical Women of Color. In Moraga and Anzaldúa, eds. This Bridge Called My Back. xxxiv–xxxix.

"Email Interview." Studies in American Indian Literature 15 (Fall 2003): 7–22.

"En Rapport, In Opposition: Cobrando cuentas a las nuestras." Sinister Wisdom 33 (1987): 11–17.

Foreword to Encyclopedia of Queer Myth, Symbol and Spirit, edited by Randy Conner, David Sparks, and Moira Sparks. New York: Cassell, 1996.

"La Prieta." In Moraga and Anzaldúa, eds. *This Bridge Called My Back*, 198–209.

"Let us be the healing of the wound: The Coyolxauhqui imperative—la sombra y el sueño." *One Wound for Another / Una Herida por Otra: Testimonios de Latin@s in the U.S. through Cyberspace (11 septiembre 2001–11 marzo 2002)*, edited by Clara Lomas and Claire Joysmith. Mexico City: Centro de Investigaciones Sobre América del Norte (CISAN), at the Universidad Nacional Autónoma de México (UNAM), 2003. 92–103.

"Metaphors in the Tradition of the Shaman." *Conversant Essays: Contemporary Poets on Poetry*, edited by James McCorkle. Detroit: Wayne State University Press, 1990. 99–100.

"now let us shift. . . . the path of conocimiento . . . inner work, public acts." In Anzaldúa and Keating, eds., *this bridge we call home*, 540–78.

"Putting Coyolxauhqui Together, A Creative Process." *How We Work*, edited by Marla Morris, Mary Aswell Doll, William F. Pinar. New York: Peter Lange, 1999. 242–61.

"Speaking in Tongues: A Letter to Third World Women Writers." In Moraga and Anzaldúa, eds. *This Bridge Called My Back*, 165–74.

"To(o) Queer the Writer—*Loca, escritora y chicana*." *Inversions: Writing by Dykes, Queers, and Lesbians*, edited by Betsy Warland. Vancouver: Press Gang, 1991. 249–64.

"(Un)natural bridges, (Un)safe spaces." In Anzaldúa and Keating, eds., *this bridge we call home*, 1–5.


Fiction/Autohistorias

"El paisano is a bird of good omen." *Conditions* 8 (1982): 28–47.

"Ghost Trap." *New Chicana/Chicano Writing* 1, edited by Charles Tatum. Tucson: University of Arizona Press, 1992. 40–42.

"La historia de una marimacha." *Third Woman* 4 (1989): 64–68.

"Life Line." *Lesbian Love Stories*, volume 1, edited by Irene Zahava. Freedom, Calif.: Crossing Press, 1989. 1–3.

"Ms. Right, My True Love, My Soul Mate." *Lesbian Love Stories*, volume 2, edited by Irene Zahava. Freedom, Calif.: Crossing Press, 1991. 184–88.

"People Should Not Die in June in South Texas." *My Story's On: Ordinary Women, Extraordinary Lives*, edited by Paula Ross. Berkeley, Calif.: Common Differences Press, 1985. 280–287.

"Puddles." *New Chicana/Chicano Writing* 1, edited by Charles Tatum. Tucson: University of Arizona Press, 1992. 43–45.

"She Ate Horses." *Lesbian Philosophies and Cultures*, edited by Jeffner Allen. Albany: State University of New York Press, 1990. 371–88.

"Swallowing Fireflies / Tragando Luciérnagas." *Telling Moments: Autobiographical Lesbian Short Stories*, edited by Lynda Hall. Madison: University of Wisconsin Press, 2003. 3–12.

Writings about Gloria E. Anzaldúa

Aanerud, Rebecca. "Thinking Again: *This Bridge Called My Back* and the Challenge to Whiteness." In Anzaldúa and Keating, eds., *this bridge we call home*. 69–77.

Adams, Kate. "Northamerican Silences: History, Identity, and Witness in the Poetry of Gloria Anzaldúa, Cherríe Moraga, and Leslie Marmon Silko." *Listening to Silences: New Essays in Feminist Criticism*, edited by Elaine Hedges and Shirley Fisher Fishkin. New York: Oxford University Press, 1994. 130–45.

Aigner-Varoz, Erika. "Metaphors of a Mestiza Consciousness: Anzaldúa's *Borderlands / La Frontera*." MELUS: *The Journal of the Society for the Study of the Multi-Ethnic Literature of the United States* 25 (2000): 47–64.

Alarcón, Norma. "Anzaldúa's Frontera: Inscribing Gynetics." *Displacement, Diaspora, and Geographies of Identity*, edited by Smadar Lavie and Ted Swedenburg. Durham, N.C.: Duke University Press, 1996. 41–53.

———. "The Theoretical Subject(s) of *This Bridge Called My Back* and Anglo-American Feminism." In Anzaldúa, ed., *Making Face, Making Soul / Haciendo Caras*, 356–69.

Alcoff, Linda. "The Unassimilated Theorist." PMLA 121, no.1 (2006): 255–65.

Aldama, Arturo J. "Toward a Hermeneutics of Decolonization: Reading Radical Subjectivities in *Borderlands / La Frontera: The New Mestiza* by Gloria Anzaldúa." *Disrupting Savagism: Intersecting Chicana/o, Mexican Immigrant, and Native American Struggles for Self-Representation*. Durham, N.C.: Duke University Press, 2001. 95–128.

Alvarez, María Antonia. "Chicana Deconstruction of Cultural and Linguistic Borders." *Interactions: Aegean Journal of English and American Studies / Ege Ingiliz ve Amerikan Incelemeleri Dergisi* 14, no.1 (2005): 49–59.

Andersen, Corrinne. "Beyond Border Thinking: Gloria Anzaldúa's *Borderlands / La Frontera* and the Mexican-American Diaspora." *Detroit Monographs in Musicology* 40 (2004): 117–24.

Andrist, Debra D. "La Semiótica de la chicana: La escritora de Gloria Anzaldúa." *Mujer y literature mexicana y chicana: Culturas en contacto II*, edited by Aralia López González, Amelia Malagamba, and Elena Urrutia. Tijuana: Colegio de México, Colegio de la Frontera Norte, 1990. 243–47.

Arteaga, Alfred. "Heterosexual Reproduction." *theory@buffalo* (Fall 1996): 61–85.

Barnard, Ian. "Gloria Anzaldúa's Queer Mestisaje." MELUS: *The Journal of the Society for the Study of the Multi-Ethnic Literature of the United States* 22 (1997): 35–53.

Berila, Beth. "Reading National Identities: The Radical Disruptions of *Borderlands / La Frontera*." In Keating, ed., *EntreMundos/AmongWorlds*, 121–28.

———. "Unsettling Calls for National Unity: The Pedagogy of Experimental Multiethnic Literatures." MELUS: *The Journal of the Society for the Study of the Multi-Ethnic Literature of the United States* 30, no. 2 (2005): 31–47.

Bernal, Dolores Delgado. "Learning and Living Pedagogies of the Home: The

Mestiza Consciousness of Chicana Students." *Qualitative Studies in Education* 14 (2001): 623–39.

Bickford, Susan. "In the Presence of Others: Arendt and Anzaldúa on the Paradox of Public Appearance." *Feminist Interpretations of Hannah Arendt.* University Park: Pennsylvania State University Press, 1995. 313–35.

Blanchard, Mary Loving. "Reclaiming Pleasure: Reading the Body in "People Should Not Die in June in South Texas." In Keating, ed., *EntreMundos/AmongWorlds,* 29–40.

Blom, Gerdien. "Divine Individuals, Cultural Identities: Post-Identitarian Representations and Two Chicana/o Texts." *Thamyris: Mythmaking from Past to Present* 4 (1997): 295–324.

Bobel, Chris, et al. "This Bridge We Are Building: 'Inner Work, Public Acts.'" *Human Architecture: Journal of the Sociology of Self-knowledge* 4 (2006): 333–38.

Bost, Suzanne. "From Race/Sex/Etc. to Glucose, Feeding Tube, and Mourning: The Shifting Matter of Chicana Feminism." *Material Feminisms,* edited by Stacy Alaimo and Susan Heckman. Bloomington: Indiana University Press, 2008. 340–72.

———. "Gloria Anzaldúa's Mestiza Pain: Mexican Sacrifice, Chicana Embodiment, and Feminist Politics." *Aztlán* 30, no. 2 (Fall 2005): 5–31.

Bowery, Anne-Marie. "Voices from Within: Gloria Anzaldúa, bell hooks, and Roberta Bondi." *The Gift of Story: Narrating Hope in a Postmodern World,* edited by Emily Griesinger and Marc Eaton. Waco, Texas: Baylor University Press, 2006. 51–68.

Branche, Jerome. "Anzaldúa: El ser y la nación." *Entorno* 34 (1995): 39–44.

Browdy de Hernández, Jennifer. "Mothering the Self: Writing the Lesbian Sublime in Audre Lorde's *Zami* and Gloria Anzaldúa's *Borderlands / La Frontera.*" In Stanley, ed., *Other Sisterhoods,* 244–62.

———. "On Home ground: Politics, Location, and the Construction of Identity in Four American Women's Autobiographies." *MELUS: The Journal of the Society for the Study of the Multi-Ethnic Literature of the United States* 22, no. 4 (1997): 21–38.

———. "The Plural Self: The Politicization and Form in Three American Ethnic Autobiographies." *Memory and Cultural Politics: New Approaches to American Ethnic Literatures,* edited by Amritjit Singh and Joseph J. Skerret. Boston: Northeastern University Press, 1996. 41–59.

Bundy, Mark. "'Know Me Unbroken': Peeling Back the Silenced Rind of the Queer Mouth through the Works of Gloria Anzaldúa." In Keating, ed., *EntreMundos/AmongWorlds,* 139–46.

Calderón, Héctor. "Literatura fronteriza tejana: El compromiso con la historia en Américo Paredes, Rolando Hinojosa, y Gloria Anzaldúa." *Mester* 22–23, nos.1–2(1993): 41–61.

———. "Texas Border Literature: Cultural Transformation and Historical Reflection in the Works of Américo Paredes, Rolando Hinojosa and Gloria

Anzaldúa." *Dispositio: Revista Americana de Estudios Comparados y Culturales* 16, no. 41 (1991): 13–27.

Candelaria, Cordelia. "Una vela por Gloria / A Candle for Gloria." *Frontiers* 25, no. 3 (2004): 1–3.

Capetillo-Ponce, Jorge. "Exploring Gloria Anzaldúa's Methodology in *Borderlands / La Frontera—The New Mestiza*." *Human Architecture: Journal of the Sociology of Self-knowledge* 4 (2006): 87–94.

Caputi, Jane. "Shifting the Shapes of Things to Come: The Presence of the Future in Gloria Anzaldúa." In Keating, ed., *EntreMundos/AmongWorlds*, 185–93.

Carrasco, David. "The Religious Vision of Gloria Anzaldúa: *Borderlands / La Frontera* as a Shamanic Space." *Mexican American Religions: Spirituality, Activism, and Culture*, edited by Gastón Espinosa. Durham, N.C.: Duke University Press, 2008. 223–41.

Castillo, Debra A. "Anzaldúa and Transnational American Studies." PMLA 121, no. 1 (2006): 260–65.

Concannon, Kevin. "The Contemporary Space of the Border: Gloria Anzaldúa's *Borderlands* and William Gibson's *Neuromancer*." *Textual Practice* 12 (1998): 429–42.

Corbin, Michelle. "Facing Our Dragons: Spiritual Activism, Psychedelic Mysticism, and the Pursuit of Opposition." *Human Architecture: Journal of the Sociology of Self-knowledge* 4 (2006): 239–47.

Cota-Cárdenas, Margarita. "The Faith of Activists: Barrios, Cities, and the Chicana Feminist Response." *Frontiers* 14, no. 2 (1994): 241–59.

Cruz, Cindy. "Toward an Epistemology of the Brown Body." *Qualitative Studies in Education* 14 (2001): 657–69.

Davis-Undiano, Robert Con. "Mestizos Critique the New World: Vasconcelos, Anzaldúa, and Anaya." LIT: *Literature, Interpretation, Theory* 11 (2000): 117–42.

Disch, Estelle. "Nurturing the Nepantlera Within: Working in the Borderlands of Four Prejudices." *Human Architecture: Journal of the Sociology of Self-knowledge* 4 (2006): 123–30.

Donadey, Anne. "Overlapping and Interlocking Frames for Humanities Literary Studies: Assia Djebar, Tsitsi Dangarembga, Gloria Anzaldúa." *College Literature* 34, no. 4 (2007): 22–42.

el Moncef, Salah. "Übermenschen, Mestizas, Nomads: The Ontology of Becoming and the Scene of Transnational Citizenship in Anzaldúa and Nietzsche." *Angelaki: Journal of the Theoretical Humanities* 8, no. 3 (2003): 41–57.

Embry, Marcus. "Cholo Angels in Guadalajara: The Politics and Poetics of Anzaldúa's *Borderlands / La Frontera*." *Women and Performance: A Journal of Feminist Theory* 8 (1996): 87–108.

Enslen, Joshua Alma. "Feminist Prophecy: A Hypothetical Look into Gloria Anzaldúa's 'La Conciencia de la Mestiza: Towards a New Consciousness' and Sara Ruddick's 'Maternal Thinking.'" LL Journal 1 (2006): 53–61.

Espinosa-Aguilar, Amanda. "Radical Rhetoric: Anger, Activism, and Change." In Keating, ed., *EntreMundos/AmongWorlds*, 227–32.

Espinoza, Dionne. "Women of Color and Identity Politics: Translating Theory, Haciendo Teoría." In Stanley, ed., *Other Sisterhoods*, 44–62.

Esquibel, Catriona Rueda. "Shameless Histories: Chicana Lesbian Fictions Talking Race / Talking Sex." *Tortilleras: Hispanic and U. S. Latina Lesbian Expression*, edited by Lourdes Torres. Philadelphia: Temple University Press, 2003. 258–79.

Fast, Robin Riley. "Borderland Voices in Contemporary Native American Poetry." *Contemporary Literature* 36, no. 3 (1995): 508–37.

Fishkin, Shelley Fisher. "The Borderlands of Culture: Writing by W. E. B. Du Bois, James Agee, Tillie Olsen, and Gloria Anzaldúa." *Literary Journalism in the Twentieth Century*, edited by Norman Sims. New York: Oxford University Press, 1990. 133–82.

Ford, Katherine. "Spaces Inside Out: Gloria Anzaldúa's *Borderlands / La Frontera*." *Leading Ladies: Mujeres en la literatura hispana y en las artes*, edited by Yvonne Fuentes and Margaret R. Parker. Baton Rouge: Louisiana State University Press, 2006. 83–92.

Fowlkes, Diane. "Moving from Feminist Identity Politics to Coalition Politics through a Feminist Materialist Standpoint of Intersubjectivity in Gloria Anzaldúa's *Borderlands / La Frontera: The New Mestiza*." *Hypatia* 12 (1997): 105–24.

Franklin, Cynthia G. "Another 1981." *Writing Women's Communities: The Politics and Poetics of Contemporary Multi-Genre Anthologies*. Madison: University of Wisconsin Press, 1997. 31–55.

Freedman, Diane P. "Living on the Borderland: The Poetic Prose of Gloria Anzaldúa and Susan Griffin." *Women and Language* 12, no.1 (1989): 1–4.

Gagnier, Regenia. "Review Essay: Feminist Autobiography in the 1980's." *Feminist Studies* 17 (1991): 135–39.

Garber, Linda. "'Caught in the Crossfire Between Camps': Gloria Anzaldúa." *Identity Poetics: Race, Class, and the Lesbian-Feminist Roots of Queer Theory*." New York, Columbia University Press, 2001. 147–75.

———. "Spirit, Culture, Sex: Elements of the Creative Process in Gloria Anzaldúa's Creative Process." In Keating, ed., *EntreMundos/AmongWorlds*, 213–26.

García-Serrano, María Victoria. "Gloria Anzaldúa y la politica de la identitidad." *Revista Canadiense de Estudios Hispánicos* 19, no. 3 (1995): 479–94.

Gaspar de Alba, Alicia. "Crop Circles in the Cornfield: Remembering Gloria E. Anzaldúa (1942–2004)." *American Quarterly* 56, no. 3 (2004): iv-vii.

Gentile, Brigidina. "Gloria Anzaldúa y la travesía transgresiva de las fronteras de la escritura." *Latino Studies* 2 (2004): 322–27.

Gil-Gómez, Ellen M. "Performing 'La Mestiza': Lesbians of Color Negotiating Identities." *Journal of Lesbian Studies* 4, no. 2 (2000): 21–38.

Gómez Hernández, Adriana. "Gloria Anzaldúa: Enfrentando el desafío." *Cuadernos Americanos* 59 (1996): 57–63.

González, Deena J. "Chicana Identity Matters." *Aztlán* 22, no. 2 (1997): 123–39.

González-López, Gloria. "Epistemologies of the Wound: Anzaldúan Theories and Sociological Research on Incest in Mexican Society." *Human Architecture: Journal of the Sociology of Self-knowledge* 4 (2006): 17–24.

Gounari, Panayota. "How to Tame a Wild Tongue: Language Rights in the United States." *Human Architecture: Journal of the Sociology of Self-knowledge* 4 (2006): 71–77.

Grewal, Inderpal. "Autobiographic Subjects and Diasporic Locations: *Meatless Days* and *Borderlands*." *Scattered Hegemonies: Postmodernity and Transnational Feminist Practices*, edited by Inderpal Grewal and Caren Kaplan. Minneapolis: University of Minnesota Press, 1994. 231–54.

Hall, Lynda. "Writing Selves Home at the Crossroads: Anzaldúa and Chrystos (Re)Configure Lesbian Bodies." *Ariel* 30 (1999): 99–117.

Hames-García, Michael. "How to Tell a Mestizo from an Enchirito®: Colonialism and National Culture in the Borderlands." *Diacritics* 30, no. 4 (2002): 102–22.

Hedley, Jane. "Nepantilist Poetics: Narrative and Cultural Identity in the Mixed-Language Writings of Irena Klepfisz and Gloria Anzaldúa." *Narrative* 4 (1996): 36–54.

Hernández-Ávila, Inés. "Tierra Tremenda: The Earth's Agony and Ecstasy in the Work of Gloria Anzaldúa." In Keating, ed., *EntreMundos/AmongWorlds*, 234–40.

Herrera-Sobek, María. "Gloria Anzaldúa: Place, Race, Language, and Sexuality in the Magic Valley." PMLA 121, no. 1 (2006): 266–71.

Hill, Simona J. "Teaching la Conciencia de la Mestiza in the Midst of White Privilege." In Keating, ed., *EntreMundos/AmongWorlds*, 129–38.

Ingenschay, Dieter. "Pepsicoatl, Nation of Aztlán und New World Border: Problematisierung, Hybridisierung und Überwindung der mexicanidad im Lichte der Kultur der chicans." *Grenzen der Macht-Macht der Grenzen: Lateinamerika im globalen Kontext*, edited by Ottmar Ette et al. Frankfurt: Vervuert, 2005. 77–101.

Jacobs, Glen. "Finding the Center: Constructing the Subaltern Master Narrative." *Human Architecture: Journal of the Sociology of Self-knowledge* 4 (2006): 79–86.

Jagose, Annamarie. "Slash and Suture: The Border's Figuration of Colonialism, Phallocentrism, and Homophobia in *Borderlands / La Frontera*." *Lesbian Utopics*. New York: Routledge, 1994. 137–58.

Karrer, Wolfgang. "Gender and the Sense of Place in the Writings of Gloria Anzaldúa and Rolando Hinojosa." *Gender, Self, and Society: Proceedings of the Fourth International Conference on the Hispanic Cultures of the United States*, edited by Renatevon Bardeleben. Frankfurt: Peter Lang, 1993. 237–45.

Kaup, Monika. "Crossing Borders: An Aesthetic Practice in Writings by Gloria Anzaldúa." *Cultural Difference and the Literary Text: Pluralism and the Limits of Authenticity in North American Literatures*. Iowa City: University of Iowa Press, 1996. 100–111.

Keating, AnaLouise. "Back to the Mother? Feminist Mythmaking with a Difference." *Feminist Interpretations of Mary Daly*, edited by Marilyn Frye and Sarah Lucia Hoagland. Albany: State University of New York Press, 2000. 294–331.

———. "Charting Pathways, Marking Thresholds . . . A Warning, An Introduction." In Anzaldúa and Keating, eds., *this bridge we call home*, 6–20.

———. "(De)Centering the Margins? Identity Politics and Tactical (Re)Naming." In Stanley, ed., *Other Sisterhoods*, 23–43.

———, ed. *EntreMundos/AmongWorlds: New Perspectives on Gloria Anzaldúa*. New York: Palgrave, 2005.

———. "From Borderlands and New Mestizas to Nepantlas and Nepantleras: Anzaldúan Theories for Social Change." *Human Architecture: Journal of the Sociology of Self-knowledge* 4 (2006): 5–16.

———. "I'm a citizen of the universe": Gloria Anzaldúa's Spiritual Activism as Catalyst for Social Change." *Feminist Studies* 34 (2008): 53–69.

———. "Myth Smashers, Myth Makers: (Re)Visionary Techniques in the Works of Paula Gunn Allen, Gloria Anzaldúa, and Audre Lorde." *Journal of Homosexuality* 26 (1993): 73–88.

———. "Reading 'Through the Eyes of the Other': Self, Identity, and the Other in the Works of Paula Gunn Allen, Gloria Anzaldúa, and Audre Lorde." *Readerly/Writerly Texts: Essays on Literature, Literary/Textual Criticism, and Pedagogy* 1 (1993): 139–65.

———. "Risking the Personal: An Introduction." *Interviews/Entrevistas*, by Gloria E. Anzaldúa, edited by Keating. New York: Routledge, 2000. 1–15.

———. "Shifting Perspectives: Spiritual Activism, Social Transformation, and the Politics of Spirit." In Keating, ed., *EntreMundos/AmongWorlds*, 241–54.

———. "Shifting Worlds, una entrada." In Keating, ed., *EntreMundos/AmongWorlds*, 1–12.

———. *Women Reading Women Writing: Self-Invention in Paula Gunn Allen, Gloria Anzaldúa and Audre Lorde*. Philadelphia: Temple University Press, 1996.

———. "'Working towards wholeness': Gloria Anzaldúa's Struggles to Live with Diabetes and Chronic Illness." *Speaking from the Body: Latinas on Health and Culture*, edited by Angie Chabram-Dernersesian and Adela de la Torres. Tucson: University of Arizona Press, 2008. 133–43.

———. "Writing, Politics, and las Lesberadas: Platicando con Gloria Anzaldúa." *Frontiers* 14 (1993): 105–29.

Koshy, Kavitha. "Nepantlera-Activism in the Transnational Moment: In Dialogue with Gloria Anzaldúa's Theorizing of Nepantla." *Human Architecture: Journal of the Sociology of Self-knowledge* 4 (2006): 147–62.

Kynclová, Tereza. "Constructing Mestiza Consciousness: Gloria Anzaldúa's Literary Techniques in *Borderlands / La Frontera—The New Mestiza*." *Human Architecture: Journal of the Sociology of Self-knowledge* 4 (2006): 43–76.

Lara, Irene. "Bruja Positionalities: Towards a Chicano/Latina Spiritual Activism." *Mujeres Activistas en Letras y Cambio Social* 4 (2005): 10–45.

———. "Daughter of Coatlicue: An Interview with Gloria Anzaldúa." In Keating, ed., *EntreMundos/AmongWorlds*, 41–55.

Leland, Dorothy. "La formación de la identidad en *Borderlands / La Frontera*, de Gloria Anzaldúa." *La seducción de la escritura: Los discursos de la cultura hoy.* Edited and with an introduction by Rosaura Hernández Monroy and Manuel F. Medina. Mexico City, Mexico, 1997. 170–75.

Levine, Amala. "Champion of the Spirit: Anzaldúa's Critique of Rationalist Epistemology." In Keating, ed., *EntreMundos/AmongWorlds*, 171–84.

Levy-Navarro, Elena. "'So Much Meat': Gloria Anzaldúa, the Mind/Body Split, and Exerting Control over My Fat Body." In Keating, ed., *EntreMundos/AmongWorlds*, 163–69.

Lioi, Anthony. "The Best-Loved Bones: Spirit and History in Anzaldúa's 'Entering into the Serpent.'" *Feminist Studies* 34 (2008): 73–98.

López, Tiffany Ana, with Phillip Serrato. "A New Mestiza Primer: Borderlands Philosophy in the Children's Books of Gloria Anzaldúa." *Such News of the Land: U.S. Women Nature Writers*, edited by Thomas S. Edwards and Elizabeth A DeWolfe. Hanover, N.H.: University Press of New England, 2001. 204–16.

Lugones, María. "From within Germinative Stasis: Creating Active Subjectivity, Resistant Agency." In Keating, ed., *EntreMundos/AmongWorlds*, 85–100.

———. "On *Borderlands / La Frontera*: An Interpretive Essay." *Hypatia* 7, no. 4 (1992): 31–38.

———. "On Complex Communication." *Hypatia* 21, no. 3 (1996): 75–85.

Maracle, Lee. "This is Personal: Re-Visiting Gloria Anzaldúa from within the Borderlands." In Keating, ed., *EntreMundos/AmongWorlds*, 207–12.

Martínez, Jacqueline M. "La Conciencia De La Mestiza: Intra- and Intersubjective Transformations of Racist and Homophobic Culture." *Phenomenology of Chicana Experience and Identity*. Lanham, Md.: Rowman and Littlefield, 2000. 81–101.

Martínez, Theresa A. "The Double-Consciousness of DuBois and the 'Mestiza Consciousness' of Anzaldúa." *Race, Gender, and Class* 9 (2002): 198–212.

———. "Making Oppositional Culture, Making Standpoint: A Journey into Gloria Anzaldúa's Borderlands." *Sociological Spectrum* 25, no. 5 (2005): 539–70.

Martinot, Steve. "Social Justice Movements as Border Thinking: An Anzaldúan Meditation." *Human Architecture: Journal of the Sociology of Self-knowledge* 4 (2006): 163–76.

McMaster, Carrie. "Negotiating Paradoxical Spaces: Women, Disabilities, and the Experience of Nepantla." In Keating, ed., *EntreMundos/AmongWorlds*. 101–06.

Méndez, Zulma Y. "Gloria y yo: Writing silence and the search for the fronteriza voice." In Keating, ed., *EntreMundos/AmongWorlds*, 15–16.

Mignolo, Walter. "Linguistic Maps, Literary Geographies, and Cultural Landscapes: Languages, Languaging and TransNationalism." *Modern Language Quarterly* 76, no. 2 (1996): 181–96.

McRuer, Robert. *The Queer Renaissance: Contemporary American Literature and the Reinvention of Lesbian and Gay Identities*. New York: New York University Press, 1997.

Murphy, Patrick. "Grandmother Borderland: Placing Identity and Ethnicity." *Isle: Interdisciplinary Studies in Literature and Environment* 1 (1993): 35–41.

Neely, Carol Thomas. "WOMEN/UTOPIA/FETISH: Disavowal and Satisfied Desire in Margaret Cavendish's *New Blazing World* and Gloria Anzaldúa's *Borderlands / La Frontera*." *Heterotopia: Postmodern Utopia and the Body Politic*. Ann Arbor: University of Michigan Press, 1994. 58–95.

Neile, Caren S. "The 1,000-Piece Nights of Gloria Anzaldúa: Autohistoria-teoría at Florida Atlantic University." In Keating, ed., *EntreMundos/AmongWorlds*, 17–27.

Nelson, Linda. "After Reading *Borderlands / La Frontera* by Gloria Anzaldúa." *Trivia: A Journal of Ideas* 14 (Spring 1989): 90–101.

Norton, Jody. "Transchildren, Changelings, and Fairies: Living the Dream and Surviving the Nightmare in Contemporary America." In Anzaldúa and Keating, eds., *this bridge we call home*, 145–54.

Ortega, Mariana. "Apertures of In-Betweeness, of Selves in the Middle." In Keating, ed., *EntreMundos/AmongWorlds*, 77–84.

Palczewski, Catherine Helen. "Bodies, Borders, and Letters: Gloria Anzaldúa's 'Speaking in Tongues: A Letter to 3rd World Women Writers.'" *Southern Communication Journal* 62, no.1 (1996): 1–16.

Pérez, Domino Renée. "Words, Worlds in Our Heads: Reclaiming La Llorona's Aztecan Antecedents in Gloria Anzaldúa's 'My Black Angelos.'" *Studies in American Indian Literatures* 15 (2003): 51–63.

Pérez, Laura E. "Spirit Glyphs: Reimagining Art and Artist in the Work of Chicana Tlamatinime." *MFS: Modern Fiction Studies* 44, no.1 (1998): 36–76.

Perry, Yaakov, "The Homecoming Queen: The Reconstruction of Home in Queer Life-Narratives." *A-B:-Auto-Biography-Studies* 15 (2000): 193–222.

Peterson, Carla L. "Borderlands in the Classroom: Meeting Point of Two or More Cultures." *American Quarterly* 45, no. 2 (1993): 295–301.

Pope, Barbara. "Texts of Difference and Ways of Knowing: On Teaching Patricia Hill Collins, Gloria Anzaldúa, and Trinh Minh-ha." *Transformations* 11 (2001): 73–79.

Premo, Cassie. "Mutual Recognition and the Borders within the Self in the Writing of Cherríe Moraga and Gloria Anzaldúa." *Critical Studies on the Feminist Subject*, edited by Giovanna Corvi. Trento: Universita degli Studi de Trento, 1997. 229–43.

Raiskin, Judith. "Inverts and Hybrids: Lesbian Rewritings of Sexual and Racial Identities." *The Lesbian Postmodern*, edited by Laura Doan. New York: Columbia University Press, 1994. 156–72.

Ramírez, Arturo. "El feminismo y la Frontera: Gloria Anzaldúa." *A Ricardo Gullón: Sus discipulos*, edited by Adelaida López de Martínez. Erie, Pa.: Asociación de Licenciados y Doctores Españoles en Estados Unidos, 1995. 3–9.

Ramlow, Todd R. "Bodies in the Borderlands: Gloria Anzaldúa's and David Wojnarowicz's Mobility Machines." *MELUS: The Journal of the Society for the Study of the Multi-Ethnic Literature of the United States* 31, no. 3 (2006): 169–87.

Ramsdell, Lea. "Language and Identity Politics: The Linguistic Autobiographies of Latinos in the United States." *Journal of Modern Literature* 28, no.1 (2004): 166–76.

Reti, Irene. "House of Nepantla." In Keating, ed., *EntreMundos/AmongWorlds*, 57–59.

Reuman, Ann E. "'Wild Tongues Can't Be Tamed': Gloria Anzaldúa's (R)evolution of Voice." *Violence, Silence, and Anger: Women's Writing as Transgression*, edited by Deidre Lashgani. Charlottesville: University of Virginia Press, 1995. 305–19.

Ricard, Serge. "La Fiancée de Frankenstein aux pays des Aztèques: La nouvelle métisse selon Gloria Anzaldúa." *Accra* 20 (1995): 143–55.

Rochel, J. A. Perles. "Revisiting the Borderlands: A Critical Reading of Gloria Anzaldúa's *Borderlands / La Frontera: Towards a New Mestiza*." *Evolving Origins, Transplanting Cultures: Literary Legacies of the New Americans*, edited by Antonia Domínguez Miguela. Huelva: Universidad de Huelva, 2002. 229–35.

Rotger, Ma-Antónia Oliver. "'Sangre Fértil' / Fertile Blood: Migratory Crossings, War and Healing in Gloria Anzaldúa's *Borderlands / La Frontera*." *Dressing Up for War: Transformations of Gender and Genre in the Discourse and Literature of War*, edited by Aránzazu Usandizaga and Andrew Monnickendam. Amsterdam: Rodopi, 2001. 189–211.

Saldívar, José David. "Border Thinking, Minoritized Studies, and Realist Interpellations: The Coloniality of Power from Gloria Anzaldúa to Arundhati Roy." *Identity Politics Reconsidered*, edited by Linda Martín Alcoff et al. New York: Palgrave MacMillan, 2006. 152–70.

———. "Unsettling Race, Coloniality, and Caste: Anzaldúa's *Borderlands / La Frontera*, Martínez's *Parrot in the Oven*, and Roy's *God of Small Things*." *Cultural Studies* 21, nos. 2–3 (2007): 339–67.

Saldívar-Hull, Sonia. *Feminism on the Border: Chicana Gender Politics and Literature*. Berkeley: University of California Press, 2000.

———. "Feminism on the Border: From Gender Politics to Geopolitics." *Criticism in the Borderlands: Studies in Chicano Literature, Culture, and Ideology*, edited by Héctor Calderón and José David Saldívar. Durham, N.C.: Duke University Press, 1991. 203–30.

———. "Introduction to the Second Edition." In Anzaldúa, *Borderlands / La Frontera: The New Mestiza*, 1–15.

Sandoval, Gabriela. "On Skin as Borderlands: Using Gloria Anzaldúa's New Mestiza to Understand Self-Injury among Latinas." *Human Architecture: Journal of the Sociology of Self-knowledge* 4 (2006): 217–24.

Schotten, C. Heike. "Revolutionary Futures: Nietzsche, Anzaldúa, and Playful 'World'-Travel." *Human Architecture: Journal of the Sociology of Self-knowledge* 4 (2006): 303–19.

Short, Kayann. "Coming to the Table: The Differential Politics of *This Bridge Called My Back*." *Genders* 20 (1994): 3–44.

Smith, Sidonie. "Autobiographical Manifestoes." *Subjectivity, Identity, and the*

*Body: Women's Autobiographical Practices in the Twentieth Century.* Bloomington: Indiana University Press, 1993. 153–82.

Stanley, Sandra Kumamoto, ed. *Other Sisterhoods: Literary Theory and U.S. Women of Color.* Urbana: University of Illinois Press, 1998.

Steele, Cassie Premo. "Leading from 'You' and 'I' to 'We': Contemporary American Women's Poetry of Witness." *Leadership Journal: Women in Leadership Sharing the Vision* 2 (1998): 67–80.

———. *We Heal From Memory: Sexton, Lorde, Anzaldúa, and the Poetry of Witness.* New York: Palgrave, 2000.

Suyemoto, Karen L. "Processes of Emergence and Connection: Interrelations of Past, Present, and Future in Journeying into Conocimiento." *Human Architecture: Journal of the Sociology of Self-knowledge* 4 (2006): 339–45.

Tamdgidi, Mohammad H. "Anzaldúa's Sociological Imagination: Comparative Applied Insights into Utopystic and Quantal Sociology." *Human Architecture: Journal of the Sociology of Self-knowledge* 4 (2006): 265–85.

Torres, Lourdes. "The Construction of Self in U.S. Latina Autobiographies." *Third World Women and the Politics of Feminism*, edited by Chandra Talpade Mohanty, Ann Russo, and Lourdes Torres. Bloomington: Indiana University Press, 1991. 271–87.

Torres, Mónica. "Doing Mestizaje: When Epistemology Becomes Ethics." In Keating, ed., *EntreMundos/AmongWorlds*, 195–203.

Vásquez, Edith M. "La Gloriosa Travesura de la Musa Que Cruza / The Misbehaving Glory(a) of the Border-Crossing Muse: Transgression in Anzaldúa's Children's Stories." In Keating, ed., *EntreMundos/AmongWorlds*, 63–75.

Velasco, Juan. "La construcción de la mexicanidad en la narrative chicana contemporanea: La estética de la/s Frontera/s." *Aztlán* 21, nos.1–2 (1992): 105–24.

Watts, Brenda. "Aztlán as a Palimpsest: From Chicano Nationalism toward Transnational Feminism in Anzaldúa's *Borderlands*. *Latino Studies* 2 (2004): 304–21.

Wiederhold, Eve. "What Do You Learn from What You See? Gloria Anzaldúa and Double Vision in the Teaching of Writing." In Keating, ed., *EntreMundos/AmongWorlds*, 109–20.

Wright, Melissa. "Maquiladora Mestizas and a Feminist Border Politics: Revisiting Anzaldúa." *Hypatia* 13 (1998): 114–31.

Yarbro-Bejarano, Yvonne. "Gloria Anzaldúa's *Borderlands / La Frontera*: Cultural Studies, 'Difference,' and the Non-Unitary Subject." *Cultural Critique* 28 (Fall 1994): 5–28.

———. "The Lesbian Body in Chicana Cultural Production." *Entiendes? Queer Readings, Hispanic Writings*, edited by Emilie L. Bergmann and Paul Julian Smith. Durham, N.C.: Duke University Press, 1995. 181–97.

Zaccaria, Paola. "Translating Borders, Performing Trans-nationalism." *Human Architecture: Journal of the Sociology of Self-knowledge* 4 (2006): 57–70.

Zaytoun, Kelli. "New Pathways towards Understanding Self-in-Relation: Anzaldúan (Re)Visions for Developmental Psychology." In Keating, ed., *EntreMundos/AmongWorlds*, 147–59.

———. "Theorizing at the Borders: Considering Social Location in Rethinking Self and Psychological Development." *NWSA Journal* 18, no. 2 (2006): 52–72.

Zimmerman, Bonnie. *The Safe Sea of Women: Lesbian Fiction, 1969–1989*. Boston: Beacon Press, 1990.

Zita, Jacquelyn N. "Anzaldúan Body." *Body Talk: Philosophical Reflections on Sex and Gender*. New York: Columbia University Press, 1998. 165–83.

# Index

academy, 128, 194, 213–14, 245, 285;
elitism in, 203; Trojan mula in, 203,
205, 207–8; universities and, 24, 34,
127; as white, 188
accountability, 313–14; of whites, 130
activism, 125, 247, 290; agency and,
144. *See also* spiritual activism
activists, 141, 143–44
adaptability, 138
adjectives, 164, 182
aesthetics: of Anzaldúa, 24–25; of
decolonization, 277–78; nonwest-
ern, 137, 179; shaman, 8, 121–24,
176, 232
affirmative action, 203
Africa, 210
African Americans: stereotypes of, 28,
112, 151. *See also* women of colors
agency, 125, 244, 311; activism and, 144
Albrecht, Lisa, 155
alchemy, 92, 235
Alcoset, Vicki, 172, 174
aliens, 87–88
Allen, Jeffner, 163
Allen, Paula Gunn, 287
alliances, 127; across differences, 144,
146–55; building, 2–3, 126. *See also*
Mundo Zurdo, El; new tribalism;
women of colors
alliance work, 143–44, 212; ground
rules for, 149
altars, 183; altar-making, 229
"America," 206; other, 239
American Studies, 204, 239–41
Andrews, Lynn, 131–32, 193
androgynes, 37
androids, 88
anger, 72, 127, 129–30, 157, 198; alliance work and, 145; of Anzaldúa,
303–4; of women of colors, 113, 116

anglos. *See* "whiteness"
animals, 94
anti-Semitism, 155
anxiety, 241
Anzaldúa, Gloria: adolescence of, 70;
aesthetics of, 10, 24–25, 97; anger
of, 187–88; awards won by, 13 n. 9,
239, 328–30, 332, 334; childhood of,
2, 5–6, 27, 39–43, 78–79, 84, 103–5,
282; at college, 80–81, 91; creative
process of, 1; death of, 12, 43–44,
199; development of ideas by, 10–11,
15, 36; diabetes and, 13 n. 14, 332;
education of, 106, 208, 240, 325–26,
330; family of, 38, 76, 84, 93, 142,
325; graduate school experience
of, 82–83; health of, 4, 13 n. 14, 14
n. 18; holistic politics of, 2; house of,
242; hysterectomy of, 5, 38, 43–44,
49, 103, 326; inclusionary phases of,
15 n. 28, 36–37; journals of, 3, 31,
51, 70, 74, 217, 236; menstruation
and, 5, 38, 39, 78, 199; mugging
of, 38, 44, 229, 326, 328; multiple
identities of, 185, 211; near-death
experiences of, 38, 229, 326; out-
of-body experiences of, 43–44, 87;
as outsider, 90; as public speaker,
75, 144, 211; readers of, 172–73; on
reading, 193, 229, 235–36; reason for
writing, 240–41; relationship to the
academy, 239; relation to the indigenous, 283, 285, 288–89; scholarship
on, 189, 288–89; self-definition and,
3, 6, 46–47, 95, 164, 188, 216, 299–
300; on sensitivity, 76–78, 192–93;
speaking engagements ("gigs") of,
327–29, 334–35; spiritual awakening
of, 75–80; teaching experience of,
14 n. 17, 20, 81–82, 129–30, 187–88,

The independent scholar and creative writer GLORIA E. ANZALDÚA (1942–2004) was an internationally acclaimed cultural theorist. A versatile author, Anzaldúa published poetry, theoretical essays, short stories, autobiographical narratives, interviews, children's books, and multigenre edited collections. As an editor of three multicultural anthologies (including the groundbreaking *This Bridge Called My Back: Writings by Radical Women of Color*), Anzaldúa played a major role in developing an inclusionary, multicultural feminist movement; and as the author of *Borderlands/La Frontera: The New Mestiza*, she played an equally vital role in shaping contemporary Chicano/a and lesbian/queer identities. Anzaldúa's writings have been included in over one hundred anthologies, and her work has greatly impacted numerous academic disciplines, including (but not limited to) American studies, Chicano/a studies, composition studies, cultural studies, ethnic studies, feminism and feminist theory, literary studies, queer theory, and women's studies. Anzaldúa and her works won numerous awards, including an award from the National Endowment of the Arts, the Before Columbus Foundation American Book Award, the Lamda Lesbian Small Book Press Award, the Susan Koppelman Award, the Smithsonian Notable Book Award, and the Américas Honor Award. *Borderlands/La Frontera* was selected as one of the One Hundred Best Books of the Century by both *Hungry Mind Review* and the *Utne Reader*. Anzaldúa was born in the Rio Grande Valley of south Texas in 1942, the eldest child of Urbano and Amalia Anzaldúa. She received her BA from Pan American University, her MA from the University of Texas, Austin, and her PhD (awarded posthumously) from the University of California, Santa Cruz.

ANALOUISE KEATING, a professor of women's studies at Texas Woman's University, is the author of *Women Reading, Women Writing: Self-Invention in Paula Gunn Allen, Gloria Anzaldúa, and Audre Lorde* and *Teaching Transformation: Transcultural Classroom Dialogues*; co-editor of *Perspectives: Gender Studies* and *this bridge we call home: radical visions for transformation*; and editor of Anzaldúa's *Interviews/Entrevistas* and *EntreMundos/AmongWorlds: New Perspectives on Gloria Anzaldúa*. For over a decade, first in her role as editor of *Interviews/Entrevistas* and later as co-editor with Anzaldúa of *this bridge we call home* and *Bearing Witness, Reading Lives: Imagination, Creativity, and Cultural Change*, Keating worked closely with Anzaldúa and her writings. She is now a trustee of the Gloria E. Anzaldúa Literary Trust.

Library of Congress Cataloging-in-Publication Data

Anzaldúa, Gloria.

The Gloria Anzaldúa reader / Gloria E. Anzaldúa ; AnaLouise Keating, editor.

p. cm. — (Latin America otherwise)

Includes bibliographical references and index.

ISBN 978-0-8223-4555-8 (cloth : alk. paper)

ISBN 978-0-8223-4564-0 (pbk. : alk. paper)

1. Authors, American—20th century.  2. Mexican American women authors—
20th century.  3. Mexican American lesbians.  4. Mexican Americans in
literature.  5. Lesbians in literature.  I. Keating, AnaLouise, 1961–  II. Title.
III. Series: Latin America otherwise.

PS3551.N95A6  2009

818'.5409—dc22      2009029299